0021837

COLLIN COUNTY COMMUNITY

5867

D0930511

DATE DUE

JAN 0 2 1991	
NOV 0 8 1991	
JAN 2 7 1992	
RLL 9-14-92	
MAR. 4 1993	
ILL 9-22-95	
NOV 2 7 1995	
DEC 2 0 1995	
MAY 0 8 1996	
AUG 2 5 1997	

Learning Resources Center
Collin County Community College District
SPRING CREEK CAMPUS
Plano, Texas 75074

BF
723
M54
K87
1987

Kurtines, William
M.

Moral development
through social
interaction

$34.95

© THE BAKER & TAYLOR CO.

MORAL DEVELOPMENT
THROUGH
SOCIAL INTERACTION

MORAL DEVELOPMENT THROUGH SOCIAL INTERACTION

WILLIAM M. KURTINES
JACOB L. GEWIRTZ
Florida International University

A WILEY-INTERSCIENCE PUBLICATION

JOHN WILEY & SONS

New York · Chichester · Brisbane · Toronto · Singapore

Copyright © 1987 by John Wiley & Sons, Inc.

All rights reserved. Published simultaneously in Canada.

Reproduction or translation of any part of this work
beyond that permitted by Section 107 or 108 of the
1976 United States Copyright Act without the permission
of the copyright owner is unlawful. Requests for
permission or further information should be addressed to
the Permissions Department, John Wiley & Sons, Inc.

This publication is designed to provide accurate and
authoritative information in regard to the subject
matter covered. It is sold with the understanding that
the publisher is not engaged in rendering legal, accounting,
or other professional service. If legal advice or other
expert assistance is required, the services of a competent
professional person should be sought. *From a Declaration
of Principles jointly adopted by a Committee of the
American Bar Association and a Committee of Publishers.*

Library of Congress Cataloging in Publication Data:

Kurtines, William M.
    Moral development through social interaction.

    "A Wiley-Interscience publication."
    Bibliography: p.
    1. Moral development—Social aspects. 2. Social
    interaction in children.   I. Gewirtz,
    Jacob L., 1924–   . II. Title.

BF723.M54K87 1987   155.2'5   87-10448
ISBN 0-471-62567-1

Printed in the United States of America

10 9 8 7 6 5 4 3 2 1

Preface

Theory and research on moral development are undergoing dramatic transformation. Traditional theoretical perspectives have been changing and new perspectives have begun to emerge. The change has nowhere been more dramatic than in the area of social process as it affects moral behavior and development. Research on the effects of social interaction on social and moral development has flourished recently and has begun to emerge as a distinct, substantial area of scholarly and research interest. The collection of works in this volume results from and contributes to the growing recognition of the role of social interaction in social and moral development.

Despite the emergence of a literature on the contributions of social interaction to moral development, there currently exists no single source of information on recent developments in the field. This volume bridges this gap by bringing together in one place a representative set of writings of prominent scholars and researchers currently active in the area. The basic theme of the volume is the effects of social interaction processes on social and moral development. The work of the contributors details many of the issues that have emerged to define the growing literature in this area. The chapters highlight the richness and diversity of theoretical and research perspectives as well as innovative developments that have been taking place in the field. Because the chapters that follow represent newly emerging perspectives, they do not lend themselves to organization along traditional theoretical lines. Consequently, the sections of the book are organized around the types of perspectives that have begun to emerge in the field. Although the five perspectives represented in the book are not exhaustive, they do reflect central themes that have helped to define the recent literature.

Part 1 of the book examines moral development from the perspective of developmental processes. Chapter 1 by Damon and Colby outlines a developmental process model to account for moral change. Chapter 2 by Eisenberg examines the ways in which social interactions and social context influence self-attribution and moral development.

Part 2 represents a developmental–constructivist perspective. Chapter 3 by Selman and Yeates examines childhood social regulation of intimacy and autonomy from a developmental–constructionist perspective. Chapter 4 by

Kohlberg and Higgins presents an overview of recent work on integrating Piagetian constructionist as operationalized by Kohlberg's moral stages and neo-Durkheimian symbolic interactionism.

Part 3 examines moral development from a social constructivist perspective. Chapter 5 by Youniss reviews evidence for a social constructivist approach to the study of moral development. Chapter 6 by Kurtines describes a psychosocial approach to moral development that focuses on the role of constructive social–evolutionary processes.

Part 4 presents an interpretive–hermeneutic perspective. Chapter 7 by Shweder and Much outlines a scheme of concepts to account for the construction of meaning in discourse, with special attention to the way a picture of the moral order is indexed and tacitly conveyed through speech. Chapter 8 by Packer examines the psychological study of social interaction from an interpretive–hermeneutic perspective.

Part 5 presents several social process perspectives on moral development. Chapter 9 by Berndt reviews experimental work on processes and theories related to discussion among friends and considers the implications of this body of data for the role of peer relationships in moral development. Chapter 10 by Gibbs addresses the role of social processes in antisocial conduct, arguing for analyses of both affective and cognitive processes in moral development. Finally, Chapter 11 by Berkowitz, Oser, and Althof examines the process of sociomoral discourse itself and presents a preliminary stage model for the development of sociomoral discourse.

This volume would not have been possible without the cooperation and assistance of a number of people and institutions. Invaluable support was received at various stages in its preparation from the College of Arts and Sciences and the Department of Psychology at Florida International University, as well as by the Bi-University Child Development Institute of the University of Miami and Florida International University. We also wish to thank the editorial staff of John Wiley & Sons and others whose contributions at various stages of the project were instrumental in its successful completion.

After this volume was in production, we received the tragic news that Professor Lawrence Kohlberg, a contributor to this volume, had died. Professor Kohlberg's philosophical and psychological contributions to the theory of social and moral development, his basic and applied research, and his good-natured encouragement, as teacher and as colleague of theorists and researchers, have given the field of moral development much of its tone and promise. Professor Kohlberg has been a giant presence in the field. It is in sadness at his passing and in appreciation of his great contributions that we dedicate this volume to the memory of Larry Kohlberg, brilliant philosopher and developmental psychologist, extraordinary conceptual catalyst, and exceptional human being.

WILLIAM M. KURTINES
JACOB L. GEWIRTZ

Miami, Florida
July 1987

Contents

Contributors

WOLFGANG ALTHOF is research associate in education at the Pedagogical Institute of the University of Fribourg, Switzerland. His major research interests are sociomoral discussion, religious development, and sociomoral education.

MARVIN W. BERKOWITZ is associate professor of psychology at Marquette University. He received his doctorate in psychology from Wayne State University. His major research interests are sociomoral discussion, moral reasoning development, and sociomoral education. He has edited *Peer Conflict and Psychological Growth*, and, with Fritz Oser, *Moral Education: Theory and Application*.

THOMAS J. BERNDT is associate professor of psychological sciences at Purdue University. He received his doctorate from the Institute of Child Development at the University of Minnesota. He was on the faculty of Yale University and the University of Oklahoma before assuming his current position at Purdue. Dr. Berndt's primary research interest is in peer relationships, or friendships, during middle childhood and adolescence.

ANNE COLBY is director of the Henry A. Murray Research Center of Radcliffe College. She received her doctorate in psychology from Columbia University. Dr. Colby is the author, with Lawrence Kohlberg and others, of *The Measurement of Moral Judgment*, and "A Longitudinal Study of Moral Judgment."

WILLIAM DAMON is professor of psychology at Clark University. He received his doctorate in developmental psychology from the University of California, Berkeley. Dr. Damon has published a number of books, including *The Social World of the Child* and *Moral Development: New Directions in Theory and Research*.

NANCY EISENBERG is professor of psychology in the Department of Psychology at Arizona State University. She received her doctorate in developmental psychology from the University of California at Berkeley. Her primary interests are in moral development, especially the development of empathy, altruism, and prosocial behavior. She is author of *The Roots of Caring, Sharing, and Helping* (with Paul Mussen) and *Altruistic Emotion, Cognition, and Behavior*, and editor of *The Development of Prosocial Behavior*.

JACOB L. GEWIRTZ is professor of psychology at Florida International University and professor of pediatrics at the University of Miami Medical School. He received his doctorate in developmental and experimental psychology from the University of Iowa. Dr. Gewirtz's theoretical and research contributions have been on the topics of social learning and development including attachment acquisition and loss, imitation/identification, parent–child interaction and directions of influence, and the behavioral effects of shifts in maintaining environments. He edited (with W. Kurtines) *Morality, Moral Behavior and Moral Development*.

JOHN C. GIBBS is associate professor of psychology at the Ohio State University. He received his doctorate in social psychology from Harvard University. His work in sociomoral development has concerned assessment methods, theory, and interventions with conduct-disordered adolescents. Dr. Gibbs is the author of *Social Intelligence: Measuring the Development of Sociomoral Reflection*.

ANN HIGGINS is lecturer in education and research associate at Harvard University. She received her doctorate in developmental psychology from the Pennsylvania State University. Dr. Higgins's interests are in the areas of moral assessment and the educational implications of moral development theory and research. Dr. Higgins is the author of *Moral Education: Justice and Community*.

LAWRENCE KOHLBERG is late professor of education and social psychology and director of the Center for Moral Education and Development at Harvard University. He obtained his doctorate in psychology from the University of Chicago in 1958, where he embarked upon his longitudinal study of moral reasoning of the then preadolescent and adolescent boys. Dr. Kohlberg is the author of *Essays in Moral Development, Vol. 1: The Philosophy of Moral Development*, and *Vol. 2: The Psychology of Moral Development*.

WILLIAM M. KURTINES is professor of psychology at Florida International University. He received his doctorate in psychology from the Johns Hopkins University. Dr. Kurtines's current areas of interest include social, personality, and moral development. He edited (with J. L. Gewirtz) *Morality, Moral Behavior and Moral Development*.

NANCY C. MUCH is research associate in the Department of Behavioral Sciences at the University of Chicago. She received her doctorate in human development from the University of Chicago. Her research interests include discourse and the socialization of cognition, social–cognitive and moral development, and cross-cultural comparison of moral and social belief systems. She was a postdoctoral fellow in cognitive development at Michigan State University.

FRITZ OSER is professor of education and director of the Pedagogy Institute at the University of Fribourg, Switzerland. His major research interests are sociomoral discussion, religious development, and sociomoral education. He is author and editor of a number of books, including *Moralisches Urteil in Gruppen* as well as *Moral Education: Theory and Application.*

MARTIN J. PACKER is research associate at Far West Laboratory for Education Research and Development, having received his doctorate in developmental psychology from the University of California at Berkeley. His interest in hermeneutics began while he was an undergraduate at Peterhouse, Cambridge University, in England. Dr. Packer is the author of *The Structure of Moral Action: A Hermeneutic Study of Moral Conflict.*

ROBERT L. SELMAN is director of the Manville School of the Judge Baker Guidance Center, as well as associate professor of education in the Harvard Graduate School of Education, and of psychology/psychiatry in the Harvard Medical School. His research interests are focused on interpersonal development, with particular interest in how clinical research and clinical contexts can be used to understand the relationship between developmental psychology and psychopathology. He is the author of *The Growth of Interpersonal Understanding.*

RICHARD A. SHWEDER is professor of human development at the University of Chicago. He received his doctorate in social anthropology from Harvard University. His research is in the areas of cross-cultural child development, culture theory, moral development, and social cognition. For the past several years he has conducted research on childhood and adult understandings of social life and family practices in India and the United States. In 1982 he was recipient of the American Association for the Advancement of Science (AAAS) Socio-Psychological Prize for a manuscript entitled "Does the Concept of the Person Vary Cross-Culturally?" He is currently a Guggenheim Foundation fellow and a fellow at the Center for Advanced Study in the Behavioral Sciences. He is co-editor of *Culture Theory* and *Meta-Theory in the Social Sciences.*

KEITH OWEN YEATES is instructor in psychology in the Department of Psychiatry at the Harvard Medical School. He received his doctorate in psychology from the University of North Carolina at Chapel Hill. He recently completed a NIMH postdoctoral fellowship in the Research Training Program in Social and Behavioral Sciences at the Harvard Medical School. Dr. Yeates's research interests include intellectual development among disadvantaged children; social regulation processes among children and the role of social regulation in developmental psychopathology; and the contribution of constructionist perspectives to psychological science.

JAMES YOUNISS is professor of psychology in the Youth Research Center and Department of Psychology at the Catholic University of America, where he received his doctorate. He is author of two recent books that combine the presentation of original data with articulation of a theory of social construction, including *Parents and Peers in Social Development* and *Adolescents' Relations with Mothers, Fathers, and Friends.*

MORAL DEVELOPMENT
THROUGH
SOCIAL INTERACTION

PART 1

Developmental Process Perspectives

CHAPTER 1

Social Influence and Moral Change

WILLIAM DAMON AND ANNE COLBY

The authors gratefully acknowledge support and guidance from the Social Science Research Council's Committee on Giftedness (David Feldman, chair; Lonnie Sherrod, staff) during the planning and initiation phase of the moral exemplar study described in this paper.

This chapter describes a developmental process model for accounting for moral change capable of integrating a diverse array of social and psychological processes. Building on a cognitive–developmental approach and the notion of scaffolding, this chapter proposes a goal theory model with the individual as coarchitect to account for the role of social influence in moral change. The theoretical utility of the model is illustrated by applying it to moral change in children in laboratory experiments and to moral change in late adulthood through life experiences.

Developmental psychology is a discipline dedicated to explanations of change, and one critical distinguishing feature of a developmental theory is its manner of defining processes accounting for change. Developmental theories have risen and fallen in accord with scholars' evaluations of the change processes that they endorse.

Even as particular theories wax and wane, developmental approaches in general have maintained their appeal. Many social scientists recognize that change is at the heart of human behavior and development is the fundamental long-term change. When a hypothesized developmental process loses its credibility, new ones are generated to take its place; or, in some cases, old process models are combined and refitted with new variations that address suspected shortfalls. Over the past three decades there has been a reassessment of change processes in virtually every area of social, affective, and cognitive development. This paper describes one such reassessment in the moral development area.

For several years, in a number of different settings, we have been studying moral change. The first author has documented spontaneous growth in moral conceptions over several years of childhood (Damon, 1977, 1984) and has observed short-term moral changes induced by experimental peer encounters (Damon, 1981; Damon & Killen, 1982). The second author has written about moral judgment changes occurring in boys and men during a 20–year period from childhood into adulthood (Colby, Kohlberg, Gibbs, & Lieberman, 1983). Presently, we are engaged in a project yielding data about how morally exemplary individuals influence their followers.

In the course of our explorations, we have tried out several ideas about processes of developmental change. None has proven wholly adequate for capturing the complexities of the moral changes that we have witnessed. Consequently, we see a need for improved process models of development. Our current research, along with some second thoughts about our past findings, has led us toward models with different features than those that we relied upon in the past.

What are we seeking in a process model for moral development? We are looking for some of the same features that any satisfactory model of development must have. First, the model must account for the contrasts between different age periods that have been widely reported and confirmed in longitudinal and cross-sectional research. Second, the model must account for the short-term changes that can be readily induced by experimental or even by less formal intervention. Third, the model must incorporate processes that are appropriate for explaining the enormous variety of behavioral and cognitive changes displayed in very different cultures.

These are the general features required by any psychological model of developmental change. In addition, a moral development model needs certain features that are not often included in explanations of other areas, perhaps because the need for them is less obvious in those areas. Two special concerns come to mind when dealing with moral change.

First, moral values are more directly connected with the actual social conditions in which they must operate than are many other intellectual or affective functions. Thus morality has an intrinsic social component, and variation in moral values is primarily the product of social–developmental processes. Models of change that deemphasize social influence (e.g., the biological maturation models currently in vogue throughout the field) are necessarily inadequate when it comes to moral growth.

Second, human morality subsumes many behavioral systems that likely derive from a diversity of psychological processes. As perhaps the most prominent example, moral judgment includes both hypothetical thinking about moral problems and actual judgment and behavior in real situations. Taking account of this distinction requires the introduction of a host of motivational and characterological factors that differentially affect these two types of judgment. Further, within both types of judgment, there is another distinction that must be made between moral justification and moral choice. Actual conduct (the moral act itself) is yet another system that must be considered in its own light.

It is not at all clear that in moral development all of these systems change together. In fact, our intuitions about human nature tell us that we cannot predict a change in real–life conduct from a change in theoretical judgment, nor vice versa. It was just this complication that led Richard Peters to call for the study of moral developments, in the plural (Peters, 1971).

All of these general and specific characteristics of moral change have been widely recognized. Any of the available developmental models can be adapted to deal with them. But most models seem stretched beyond their boundaries when confronted with such phenomena, despite the user's agility in theoretical accommodation. The ultimate but as yet unrealized goal is to create a model that incorporates the parameters of moral change gracefully within its own framework, coherently in accord with its conception of development as a whole, and without violation to any of its fundamental assumptions.

For reasons that are explicated more fully elsewhere (Colby & Kohlberg, 1987; Damon, 1979, 1983), we have found structural–developmental models (as in Kohlberg's cognitive–developmental theory) more nearly adequate for our purposes than either social learning theory or psychoanalytic frameworks. First, cognitive–developmental theory is the only one of these perspectives that takes seriously an individuals' moral thinking on its own terms rather than treating it as a reflection of unconscious processes or external influences of which the individual is not aware. Second, cognitive–developmental theory is best suited to describing and predicting the long-term changes that establish contrasting patterns between different age groups. Third, it is the only perspective that includes needed distinctions between judgment, choice, and conduct. Fourth, in cognitive–developmental theory, behavioral variations are viewed as forms of social–contextual adaptation rather than as unhealthy deviations from a norm, as is the case in many psychoanalytic writings. We would argue, therefore, that cognitive–developmental theory provides a better match for our observations and our intuitions concerning moral change than do any of the other prevailing theories of moral psychology.

The cognitive–developmental approach is not itself wholly adequate, however. We noted that one of its advantages is that it draws useful distinctions between components of moral behavior (e.g., between structure and content, reasoning and choice, judgment and conduct) and makes theoretically based predictions about the genesis of each and the relations among them. Unfortunately, these predictions have not proven very powerful. Cognitive developmentalists interested in explaining behavior in real–life contexts have been forced to step outside the usual concern for conceptual knowledge to the unexplored realms of affect, self–interest, context, and moral atmosphere (see Blasi, 1979; Damon, 1983; Rest, 1983).

Beyond this, the cognitive–developmental approach has suffered from another problematic shortcoming of direct concern to our topic today. Although cognitive developmentalists all believe that they are social interactionists at heart, the change processes that they have proposed have not left much room for the workings of social influence. Social factors have been vaguely defined and underemphasized, and as a consequence the process models themselves have failed to be convincing. This has led to the single most enduring complaint against sequential models of development: the shroud of mystery surrounding the mechanisms of transition from one point on the sequence to the next.

Piaget's equilibration theory is probably the clearest example of this problem, since it is the most thoroughly articulated of the cognitive–developmental change models. Piaget sees psychological change coming about through intellectual adaptation to new experience. This adaptation takes place in three phases, which Piaget calls pattern alpha, pattern beta, and pattern gamma. These patterns represent successively improved manners of coping with the perturbations caused by surprising or novel events. As Piaget put it:

> The initial reaction, named "pattern alpha," consists only in an attempt to neutralize or suppress the perturbation by a voluntary ignorance comparable to a kind of repression. The second reaction, or "pattern beta," consists in taking the perturbation into consideration but doing so by seeking a compromise resulting in some displacement both of the perturbing experience and the subject's original system. Finally, the gamma reaction results in a genuine incorporation of the perturbation into the system itself, where it becomes an intrinsic and deducible new variation. (Inhelder, Garcia, & Voneche, 1976, p. ; translated by chapter authors)

This is Piaget's conception of how new information brings about psychological change. But it does not really solve the problem, because we are still left to wonder how a subject who represses information (pattern alpha) ever gets to the point of being perturbed by it (pattern beta). The old riddle remains: How can we recognize the existence of that which we do not know? Or, put more broadly, if human behavior is an organized, coherent, and adaptive system, how can we account for its continual change?

The answer could, of course, come from within the system— biological triggers, for example—but this could hardly explain the many behavioral variations that are socially and culturally related. These force us to look beyond the individual system to what Piaget calls social factors. But if a model is to bring in outside factors, it must do so in a way that plausibly interacts with its own internal features. This is difficult to do within a cognitive–developmental framework, because at the outset (pattern alpha in Piaget) the individual is portrayed as a self–contained system, resisting external inputs. How, then, can social influence invade this barrier?

Whatever the answer, we would prefer a model that avoids formulating social influence as a process of invasion. We believe that human knowledge and behavior are from the start motivated, organized, and communicated through social interaction (see Damon, 1983). This means that the social process is part of the individual's perspective at all times. Our convictions about this have led us to look beyond models like Piaget's, because such models view change as coming about primarily through the individual's reflective abstraction of conflictual confrontations with the outside world. We see the individual as more guided by and less removed from the fruits of social communication.

In the social–psychological literature, as one might expect, there are change models that pay more attention to social influence and its effects. Those most oriented to developmental phenomena (like child rearing and educational sequelae) stem from an attribution theory perspective (Dweck, 1983; Lepper, 1981).

The gist of this approach is a critical distinction between several types of attitude inducement processes. Some of these processes lead to mere compliance while others lead to the genuine internalization of values. The general notion is that tangible reward and punishment promote compliance, whereas persuasion and reasoning promote internalization; this is not a very different line of argument than that put forth by child psychologists who blend learning theory and developmental principles (Baumrind, 1971; Hoffman 1975, 1982). But the question remains as to how persuasion and reasoning can induce children to adopt as their own ideas that come from somebody else. Attribution theory deals with this question by adding a few wrinkles to the social influence process.

In Lepper's account, for example, social influence is seen as permanently effective only if it is guided by the minimal sufficiency principle. According to this principle, the way to change another's behavior for the long term is to apply just enough force or reward to induce the new behavior, but not so much as to make the force or reward the most salient part of the person's new behavioral experience. In other words, the external incentive must be strong enough to effect a change yet weak enough to be forgettable—hence the notion of minimal sufficiency. The point, of course, is that if one forgets the external origin of a behavioral change, one may tend to attribute the change to one's own decisions and beliefs. This will enhance one's conviction in the rightness of the new behavior. It will also produce enduring attitudinal shifts that withstand changing external conditions like the absence of continued coercion or reward.

This model goes further than most others in identifying specific social influence processes affecting development, and it also efficiently accounts for a good deal of experimental evidence. It consequently is gaining credence in many circles beyond social psychology (see, e.g. Damon, 1983; Grusec, 1982; Maccoby & Martin, 1983). But there are some assumptions intrinsic to the model that trouble us. The whole process rides upon one person's accepting another's agenda because the former is tricked into believing that this agenda arose spontaneously from within. This model and others that emphasize the importance of parental persuasion and reasoning assume that social influence is intentionally guided. Furthermore, they assume that internalization is based upon misunderstanding or a failure to recognize deception.

We have a number of objections to these assumptions. First, we believe that social influence generally does not rely on calculated strategies foisted upon unsuspecting recipients. Rather, it comes about through a series of negotiations, cooperative or otherwise, between persons who may or may not be aware that they are influencing one another—and who, as a rule, have given little thought to how influence is strategically accomplished.

Further, deception is impractical in the long run because sooner or later people recognize that they are being manipulated. At this point we would expect a generalized distrust to arise, leading to the cessation of further influence and a wholesale rejection of all previously induced standards. The phenomenon of adolescent rebellion may indicate some such process at work. But it must be remembered that adolescent rebellions usually are partial, temporary, and limited to certain cultural settings. This, therefore, could not provide us with a plausible model for socialization generally.

We also find problematic the assumption that the form and direction of developmental change are externally determined to the degree implied by this model. Such a position trivializes the role of the developing person and is inconsistent with data from studies of both experimentally induced and natural development. Finally, beyond these concerns with the model's plausibility, we object on ethical grounds to a model that attributes development to deceitful manipulation. We would prefer working within a framework that accords more closely with our view of human potential.

There is a change model that is socially oriented in much the same way as the attribution model but avoids some of the latter's disturbing nuances. This is the substitution of goals model advanced by Soviet psychologists, and recently adapted as the scaffolding notion by some of their American followers (Rogoff & Gardner, 1985; Rogoff & Wertsch, 1984; Wertsch, 1979; Wood, 1980). In this model development is brought about through the gradual transformation of goals. Social influence can begin immediately on a behavioral level, in the sense that one party can induce another, through a variety of means, to adopt new actions. But long-term growth is not achieved until the two parties' goals begin to match. This means that the influencer's rationale for the actions must be communicated and accepted. Over an extended period of time, an entire social perspective can be transferred through this route.

This process has been called scaffolding because of the supportive guidance that it requires. It is easiest to illustrate in an example of adult–child influence. The adult leads the child to a pattern of behavior desired by both adult and child, but for different reasons. For example, the adult wishes the toddler to start using a fork for reasons obvious to us adults, and the toddler wishes to use it initially out of a spirit of play. Eventually, through demonstrations, assistance, cajoling, sanctions, and so on, the adult guides the child's original playful response into a competent system of eating neatly. This system comes closely associated with a social perspective on table manners and other related values. As the child assumes more and more of this perspective, the adult instinctively removes the scaffold of support bit by bit.

It is not difficult to see why much of the empirical evidence behind the scaffolding notion derives from modeling experiments. In fact, the notion seems best suited for explaining those instances of social influence in which a skill or belief is directly copied. Some developmentalists who are generally sympathetic to this theoretical approach have worried that it may miss some of the individual's own creative contributions to the adoption of another's goals. Griffin and Cole (1984) have written: "The scaffold metaphor leaves open questions of the child's creativity. If the adult support bears an inverse relation to the child's competence, then there is a strong sense of teleology—children's development is circumscribed by the adults' achieved wisdom " (p. 47).

These authors are also concerned with the model's seeming implication that the adult's guidance occurs mechanically, programmed to match the sequence in which the behavior is modeled. They argue that social influence is a more irregular, almost organic, process. It takes place on many psychological levels at once, and remains closely in tune with the child's own agenda:

> Scaffolding—bolted together tiers of boards upon which humans stand to construct a building—admits far more easily of variation in amount than in kind. Yet the changes in adult support ordinarily reported in scaffolding research point to qualitatively distinct kinds of support. Sometimes the adult directs attention. At other times, the adult holds important information in memory. At still other times, the adult offers simple encouragement. The metaphor becomes more problematic when we focus not on the execution of a specific task but on the changes in the child. A central notion shared by Vygotsky, Dewey, and theorists who use the scaffolding notion is that the discovery of new goals is central to the process of development. To capture the important way in which adult understanding of goals structures the sequence of activities, we would need to add architects and foremen to the building process that scaffolding indexes. Building would have to begin with all the scaffolding in place, and it would have to admit to work starting with the uppermost reaches of the roof as well as the basement. (p.47)

If modified in the manner suggested by Griffin and Cole, a goal theory model may be well suited for capturing moral change. Such a model combines a gradual transformation of goals through processes of social influence with the active engagement of the developing individual (as architect, in Griffin and Cole's terms). Its advantage over a Piagetian framework is that it provides for the incorporation of a new system of motives developed in communication with others, rather than merely for the acquisition of new knowledge. It also assumes that new perspectives are shaped cooperatively (or co-constructed) in the course of many negotiations between persons. This means that all new ideas must owe their shape to some interaction between external guidance and internal belief.

These notions from goal theory, we believe, offer us a more compelling starting point than do the cognitive–developmental assumptions that ideas are formed by individuals "figuring out" the way the world works, and that new ideas simply build upon revisions of old ones in the light of individuals' observations of reality. In the remainder of this chapter, we shall try out these notions on some moral changes that we have observed in our own research and in some second–hand biographical material. The purpose of this exercise is not to test our adaptation of goal theory but rather to see whether these notions can bring to the study of moral development some new insights regarding the ways in which social influence brings about moral change. We may stretch these notions a bit beyond their previous usages in order to exploit their full potential in this area.

TWO EXAMPLES OF MORAL CHANGE THROUGH SOCIAL INFLUENCE

We examine two quite different instances of moral change. The first is a change in childhood conceptions of fairness, induced by a laboratory experiment. The second is a change in moral judgment during late adulthood, brought about through a series of real-life observations, experiences, and communications. Both of these changes were accompanied by affiliated behavioral choices.

The Childhood Change

A few years ago, a series of experiments was conducted at Clark (Damon, 1977, 1981; Damon & Killen, 1982). The experiments varied in their specific procedures, but the general idea was to construct in the laboratory a real–life distributive justice situation. The experiments posed children the task of dividing among themselves (and a younger child previously removed) a reward for making bracelets. Children were agemates, either 4, 6, 8, or 10 ten years old, and the reward was 10 candy bars. The experimental situations all had built into them conditions that encouraged children to consider issues like merit, gender, special need, and age in their discussions. In some versions of the experiment, we focused on the children's conduct and actual choices during the group debate. In other versions, we focused on their moral reasoning several weeks before and after the experiment.

TABLE 1.1. Number of Subjects Constructing Equal and Unequal Distributions at Each of Four Age Levels, and at Each of Three Choice Points

Age	Choice Point					
	Before Group Session		At Start of Group Session		At End of Group Session	
	Equal	Not Equal	Equal	Not Equal	Equal	Not Equal
4	7	29	6	30	15	21
6	19	17	22	14	24	12
8	22	14	32	4	36	0
10	28	8	34	2	36	0

For the present purposes, we shall extract two findings from these experiments. The first reveals a change in behavioral choice that was frequently triggered by the experimental encounter, the second a change in the children's reasoning about fairness.

The first finding can be read from Table 1.1 which shows a bidirectional movement toward equal solutions. This movement was associated both with age and with the progress of the group debate. The age trend is simply that older children constructed more equal solutions than did younger children, at all of the three choice points in the debate. In addition, however, *within* each age there was a progressive increase in equal solutions from choice point one to two to three. In other words, at all ages, the longer the children were in the group, the more likely they were to opt for equality. As can be seen from Table 1.1 the two trends towards equality (age and choice point) reinforce each other, so that all 72 of the oldest children chose equality by the end of the group session.

Equality is one of the fundamental elements of justice, but it is not the only, the best, or the most sophisticated way of dealing with a fairness conflict. Many of the older children in this study showed, both before and after the group sessions, that they often preferred other considerations over simple equality: considerations like merit (extra "pay" for extra work or talent), benevolence (inequality in the service of special need or deprivation), and so on. It was only the children in the lower-middle section of this age range—the 6-year-olds—who preferred equality as a general solution to all sorts of problems. The very youngest children, like the older ones, tended more toward unequal than equal solutions, although in their case equality was eschewed in favor of self-preference rather than merit or need.

Why, then, did equality have such appeal for children of all ages in this experimental situation? To answer this we must look beyond the parameters of justice reasoning to the demands of the group. Our situation was one in which agreement was necessary; the children could not get any of the candy bars until they had reached a consensus among themselves about how to split them up. In such a situation, equality is an excellent way to reach agreement. By definition, it is a perfect leveler of differences. In an equal solution, a person's full deservedness may not be recognized; yet no one's claims are to any great degree ignored. This is why it works in a group even where none of the group's members finds it wholly satisfactory.

In this study, the accomplishment of the older children was to anticipate this quickly, often (temporarily) setting aside their other beliefs about fairness in the process. Many of the younger children also came to recognize this, although it took some exposure to the peer debate to get them there. As might be expected, the younger children did not always manage to figure out in the course of one peer debate what the older children could quickly anticipate. Whereas all of the older two groups eventually reached consensus through equal solutions, 8 percent of the 6-year-old groups and 22 percent of the 4-year-old groups never reached any consensus at all, despite unlimited time and the risk of walking away without any candy.

Our main interest, though, was in neither those children who had already learned how to deal quickly and efficiently with such a situation nor those children who clung to old ways without learning how to resolve the situation. Rather, it was in that sizable group of children who changed their approach in the face of pressing group demands. What were the developmental implications of such a change? Did it show learning? Was it a precursor of genuine growth in social competence? If so, growth of what sort? Was it merely learning new group manipulation strategies or did it have something to do with moral change, despite the pragmatic nature of the goals that triggered it?

Here we refer briefly to a second set of findings, from an experiment designed around these particular questions. This was a training study version of the above situation, complete with pretest, two posttests, and two experimental control groups (one of which was a nontreatment group, the other of which went through a similar–sounding situation hypothetically with an adult).

The gist of the finding was: (1) A majority of children placed in the peer debate situation showed some advance in their reasoning about justice by the time of the posttests; (2) the proportion of children who changed in the course of the actual peer encounter was significantly greater than those who changed in either of the two control groups; (3) the nature of the effected change was an increase in percentage of statements above the reasoning mode, rather than a holistic shift in judgment[1] and (4) children who engaged in conflictual interactions with their peers were the least likely to change, whereas groups of children who accepted each others' statements positively were likely to change, particularly when this happened at the lower age levels.

In prior writings, we have had some trouble explaining this pattern of results from a developmental perspective. The trend toward equality as a behavioral choice seemed connected more with situational than with individual factors, particularly since this choice did not always reflect the typical judgmental preferences of the subjects. As for the reasoning changes induced by the group debate, developmental theory would predict conflict more likely to be associated with change than to be inversely related, as we found. The relation between change and children's tendencies reciprocally to accept one another's ideas would seem to fit with an imitation theory of learning. Yet we also know that the changes we observed were not simple repetitions of ideas that the children had heard. Rather, the posttest responses often included notions never explicitly expressed during the group encounter.

What is needed to account for these findings is a theoretical view showing how social influence guides the child's active construction of judgment and choice. A goal theory notion, at least as modified to incorporate the active participation of the subject as coarchitect, is one such theoretical view. But note that even this view must be further modified to deal with peer influences of the sort observed in the present situation. Adult–child tutoring may be metaphorically compared with scaffolding without great distortion, since eventually the adult's perspective does in some sense substitute for the child's. When the influencing party is another child, however, the induced perspective (or even perspectives) may be new to both parties rather than a substitution of one party's for the other's. This requires us to note that in some cases of social guidance new goals may be jointly discovered rather than transmitted. Goal theory would then be modified to include a variety of negotiation procedures, ranging from inducement and eventual substitution of one party's goals for another's to codiscovery of new ideas that may lead to new perspectives and goals.

We believe that this modified version of goal theory is useful in thinking about the results of this experiment. Certainly our situational parameters—the most prominent of which was group pressure—did guide individual children toward particular moral choices. This guidance influenced a particular response to a particular event (equality as a means of reaching consensus now) rather than individual children's general moral orientations. The older children's greater readiness to anticipate and accept such guidance indicates that (1) there is a lesson to be learned in such peer confrontations, and (2) they had learned at least a good part of this lesson during their own past social histories.

In fact, there was more than one lesson for the children in this encounter. One lesson certainly was the usefulness of equal distribution in resolving differences within a group. This was in large part a practical lesson, a procedure for getting out of the situation with a share of the reward. But it also had moral implications. For the very youngest children, it may have introduced the notion of equal treatment to their moral repertoires. For the older ones, it likely triggered a process of moral reflection that produced some judgmental change. In this case the lesson may have been procedural in another sense; that is, given this particular kind of situation, it is better to distribute the rewards equally even though in other situations it is important to bring in other concerns such as equity or merit. It is important to note that, particularly among the older children, the experimental intervention did not lead to a generalized tendency to use an equality solution to distribution problems.

In this experiment we see individual construction fostered, guided, but not quite directed by social influence. For some children, the peer debate experience forced a choice that posed for them a new possibility—equality of treatment. For others, it provided a chance to hear and discuss other alternatives, some of which they would ultimately consider more morally satisfying than equality, though in the end they would choose equality as a way to resolve the current situation. For still others (a large 44 percent minority), the situation provided no grounds for enhancing their moral reasoning in any detectable way. The situation was the same for all children, and certainly had an impact, yet registered differently on the moral consciousness of different individuals. So at least in this peer–type learning experience, the direction of change is only in part socially determined.

The tendency for change to follow from accepting rather than conflictual interactions does suggest that those children more open to guidance were the ones who profited most by it. The scaffold was available, but the child had to be willing to grow within it. As Griffin and Cole say, the building is in some sense there at the start. The group's direction structured the choices of its participants but did not absolutely determine these choices. Similarly, it made possible some eventual shifts in moral perspective, but did not define the exact nature of these shifts. Nor did it produce these shifts in all participants. We see here a process of co–construction, coordinating social guidance with individual initiative. Scaffolding can account for some aspects of the process but must be adapted to the realities of peer as well as adult–child influence by seeing the shape of the scaffold as being negotiated between the person and the social world.

The Late Adulthood Change

During the past year we have begun a preliminary study of morally exemplary individuals. Eventually we hope to conduct a few in–depth case studies of living moral exemplars. Our initial phase is limited to refining our criteria for morally exemplary behavior and identifying individuals who have demonstrated such behavior. To accomplish this, we are conducting interviews with moral philosophers and scholars of diverse theoretical and political persuasions. At this point, our criteria for moral exemplars are as follows:

1. A sustained commitment to definable moral principles
2. A consistent tendency to act in accord with these principles
3. A demonstrated willingness to affirm (rather than deny or misrepresent) one's acts and to express overtly the principles that constitute one's moral rationale for such acts
4. A demonstrated willingness to risk personal well-being for the sake of one's moral principles
5. A capacity for creating and projecting a moral vision, including particularly the ability to generate innovative solutions to moral problems
6. A talent for inspiring others to moral action
7. A dedicated responsiveness to the needs of others

Also in preparation for conducting case studies, we have been reading biographical material on people who would clearly meet our criteria. These biographical data do not always answer the questions that we would like to have answered, and they raise all the usual questions of perspectivism and veridicality in life histories. In our own case study, we shall attempt to confront these problems through systematic social science procedures like the assisted autobiography procedure developed by DeWaele and Harre (1979).

Even when collected for other purposes, biographical data are helpful in providing material for hypotheses and initial speculations. We have repeatedly been struck by the pertinence of such data to our interest in moral change. In our preliminary interviews and reading, we have encountered several instances of moral change that we believe are illuminated by a goal theory model of social influence.

One such instance is the life of Andrei Sakharov, a man who without question has acted as a moral exemplar according to our criteria. According to his own and others' accounts, Sakharov grew into this role through important changes in his moral orientation over a 20-year span of his middle to late adulthood (Sakharov, 1981, 1984; Titus, 1984). We shall examine these changes here through the lens of goal theory.

Until age 36, Sakharov was a pillar of the Soviet establishment. He was considered both a patriot and a brilliant scientist of unique stature: He was the inventor of the Soviet H–bomb and the youngest person ever elected to the Soviet Academy of Sciences. With these achievements, he enjoyed unparalleled comfort and privilege as a Soviet citizen of the highest order.

Beginning in 1957, however, Sakharov became involved in activities that were permanently to alter his role in Soviet society. These activities, which can only be considered extraordinary from a moral point of view, became progressively challenging to the Soviet order over the next three decades. Their progression reveals some features of moral change in one exceptional adult life. The following is a chronology of significant events:

1957: Sakharov becomes concerned about radioactive contamination following from nuclear weapons tests, issues internal memoranda urging caution.

1961–1962: Sakharov personally contacts Krushchev in a vain attempt to halt further nuclear testing. He is rebuffed and told to cease "meddling" in affairs of state.

1964: In a meeting of scientists, Sakharov criticizes the enduring influence of Lysenko (Stalin's science adviser) in academic discourse.

1966: Sakharov goes public with his dissent for the first time. In an open letter to the Soviet congress, he and others warn against the reintroduction of Stalinism. Later that year, he protests a new antislander law used to silence criticism.

1967: Sakharov writes Brezhnev to plead the case of two dissidents who were harshly sentenced under Soviet law.

1968: Sakharov allows a self–published manuscript entitled "Progress, Coexistence, and Intellectual Freedom" to be published in the West. The manuscript argues mildly for detente and contains little criticism of the Soviet system, nor does it contain secret information. In fact, Sakharov refuses (as in the past) to speak with Western news reporters because of his access to military secrets. Nevertheless, Sakharov soon loses his clearance for scientific work, effectively ending his government career. Later this year, his wife dies.

1969: Sakharov broadly expands his circle of friends. He seeks out other intellectuals and dissidents.

1970: With two of his new acquaintances, Sakharov starts the Moscow Committee on Human Rights. This group at first meets to discuss civil rights and to establish links with international organizations. But as word of the group spreads, it attracts countless pleas from persons to whom injustice has been done. In response to these pleas, the group begins functioning as a legal aid society, conducting appeals and advocacy for persecuted people throughout the Soviet Union.

1973: Sakharov breaks his practice of working within the Soviet system and appeals to the United Nations and other outside agencies for help. He requests Westerners to intervene on behalf of Soviet citizens assigned to psychiatric hospitals, and begins granting interviews to Western correspondents. Shortly thereafter, he is officially warned to stop communicating with foreigners.

1974–1980: As Sakharov is increasingly attacked through the official press and other state channels, his criticism of state policies becomes increasingly broad-based and direct. This escalating cycle of repression and activism ends when he is exiled from Moscow to the industrial city of Gorki.

What does this brief sketch of dramatic events reveal about moral change? For one thing, it shows an ever–expanding (to use Piaget's phrase) course of development. Sakharov's moral concerns, and the actions they generated, constantly broadened in scope and implication throughout his adult life. But we believe that this series of events shows something further about the processes inherent in such moral expansion, and that these processes, though played out by Sakharov in a truly extraordinary fashion, have much in common with normal processes of moral change through social influence.

First, it is clear that Sakharov's active engagement in the civil rights cause occurred only after he had established frequent communication with a group deeply concerned about this matter. Prior to this, his moral energies were devoted to issues, like nuclear testing and scientific integrity, that were directly connected with his own experience and expertise. Sakharov was initially drawn into contact with his circle of dissidents because some of his concerns matched theirs. Soon, as his new colleagues shared information and insights with him, he was introduced to a broader set of issues and was asked to extend his activism accordingly.

One of these transitions came after he had finished a successful campaign aimed at freeing a biologist who had defied Stalinist dogma. His collaborators in this campaign then initiated the idea of forming a committee to observe dissident trials generally. Sakharov recalls being told at the time, "One of the problems in getting involved with us is you do something and, bang, we're right on top of you to do something else." This idea was to become descriptive of Sakharov's Committee on Human Rights. It is clear from Sakharov's account that the idea was co–constructed. In fact, the social guidance that led Sakharov to this idea looks very much like a goal substitution process in which collaborative activity induces in the learner a new and broader set of goals.

It is also significant that the collaborators' original intention was simply to study and witness the trials, not to advocate directly on anyone's behalf. Studying, of course, was a course of action quite familiar and comfortable to Sakharov the scientist. Only later, and under the pressure of repeated urgings and compelling observations, did Sakharov himself take direct public action. So again we see the initial match of goals and procedures, followed by the social communication of new procedures, followed by the trying out of the new procedures, followed finally by the adoption of broader goals.

One advantage of using goal theory to explain change in this manner is that it avoids the fruitless cognition–affect split that has plagued other developmental explanations. A goal is an affectively charged motivator, but also is part of an entire intellectual perspective. This is why genuine goal substitution, whether in childhood or adulthood, takes some time to achieve. Goal substitution entails a gradual transformation, though social influence, of one's perspective on one's actions in the social world. As such, it drives development on the cognitive and affective fronts together.

We do not know what makes some individuals receptive to lifelong goal substitution in the moral area while other individuals seem developmentally "shut down" by early adulthood. This is one of our interests in studying moral giftedness. Certainly in the case of Sakharov we see a history of openness to moral change. Although his emerging new values were not quite self–initiated, they did reflect what we might call an active receptiveness to social influence of particular sort.

There are two things that we can say about this active receptiveness. First, the simple fact that it existed signifies a propensity toward growth even late in life. Second, it was not a blanket receptiveness toward just any sort of influence—witness, for example, Sakharov's equally strenuous resistance of Soviet governmental pressures to conform. Rather, Sakharov's active receptiveness was predirected toward a moral influence that he could not yet define but that he was prepared to recognize.

It is therefore important to emphasize that, at each step in his evolving moral engagement with the Soviet dissident community, Sakharov actively chose to move forward rather than to withdraw. Consequently, we must conclude that the direction and shape of Sakharov's moral growth were co–constructed by the continual interplay between him and his chosen community. The social influences in Sakharov's life cannot be understood without knowing what he himself brought to the process.

In this case (as in others), we can see an individual bringing to his social context a cognitive framework for interpreting morality as well as an identity structured around certain values. For Sakharov, the values of truth and justice were so central to his self–identity that he could not allow himself to draw back from the challenges he encountered, regardless of the personal risk they entailed.

If the social influence of Sakharov's colleagues provided him with a kind of positive scaffolding, the Soviet system of sanctions did just the reverse. As he became an "enemy of the people," he lost all reason to sustain a connection with the social order. He gave up hope of working within the system, and, as a consequence, his actions became more radical. He began to think of his mission as one of creating ideals rather than actually effecting changes in an almost immutable system. He said, "There is a need to create ideals, even though one

Learning Resources Center
Collin County Community College District
SPRING CREEK CAMPUS

can't see a route by which to achieve them; because if there are no ideals there can be no hope, and then one is completely in the dark, in a hopeless, blind alley."

The system, through its punitive rigidity, led him to a state of almost complete detachment from it. In its place Sakharov substituted a system of moral values that one can only call universal. In his Nobel prize address (delivered in Stockholm by his second wife, Elena Bonner), Sakharov writes: "Peace, progress, human rights: these three goals are indissolubly linked. It is impossible to achieve one if the other two are ignored." Yet even at these lofty heights of insight, moral development, and with it the search for still more worthy goals, does not come to a halt. Sakharov writes at the end of the address: "We must make good the demands of reason and create a life worthy of ourselves and of the goals we only dimly perceive."

REFERENCES

Baumrind, D. (1971). Current patterns of parental authority. *Developmental Psychology Monographs, 4* (1, Pt. 2).

Blasi, A. (1979). Bridging moral cognition and moral action: A critical review of the literature. *Psychological Bulletin, 88,* 593–637.

Colby, A., Kohlberg, L., Gibbs, J., & Lieberman, M. (1983). A longitudinal study of moral development. *Monographs of the Society for Research in Child Development.* Chicago: University of Chicago Press.

Colby, A., & Kohlberg, L. (1987). *The measurement of moral judgment.* New York: Cambridge University Press.

Damon, W. (1977). *The social world of the child.* San Francisco: Jossey–Bass.

Damon, W. (1979). Why study social–cognitive development? *Human Development, 22,* 206–212.

Damon, W. (1981). The development of justice and self–interest during childhood. In M. Lerner (Ed.), *Justice and social behavior.* New York: Plenum.

Damon, W., & Killen, M. (1982). Peer interaction and the process of change in children's moral reasoning. *Merrill-Palmer Quarterly, 28,* 347–367.

Damon, W. (1983). *Social and personality development.* New York: Norton.

Damon, W. (1984). Self–understanding and moral development in childhood and adolescence. In J. Gewirtz & Kurtines (Eds.), *Morality, moral behavior, and moral development.* New York: Wiley.

DeWaele, J. P., & Harre, R. (1979). Autobiography as a psychological method. In Ginsburg, R. (Ed.), *Emerging methods of research in the social sciences.* New York: Wiley.

Dweck, C. (1983). Achievement motivation. In E. M. Hetherington (Ed.), *Handbook of child psychology: Vol. IV. Socialization, personality, and social development.* New York: Wiley.

Griffin, P., & Cole, M. (1984). Current activity for the future: The Zo–ped. In Rogoff, B., & Wertsch, J. (Eds.), Children's learning in the "zone of proximal development." *New directions for child development (Vol. 23).* San Francisco: Jossey–Bass.

Grusec, J. (1982). Training altruistic dispositions: A cognitive analysis. In E.T. Higgins, D.N. Ruble, & W.W. Hartup (Eds.), *Social cognition and social behavior: Developmental perspectives.* Cambridge, England: Cambridge University Press.

Hoffman, M.L. (1975). Moral internalization, parental power, and the nature of parent–child interaction. *Developmental Psychology, 11,* 228–239.

Hoffman, M.L. (1982). Affective and cognitive processes in moral internalization. In E.T. Higgins, D.N. Ruble, & W.W. Hartup (Eds.), *Social cognition and social behavior: Developmental perspectives.* Cambridge, England: Cambridge University Press.

Inhelder, B., Garcia, R., & Voneche, J. (1976). *Epistemologie genetique et equilibrium.* Geneva: Neuchatel.

Lepper, M.R. (1983). Social control processes, attributions of motivation, and the internalization of social values. In E.T. Higgins, D.N. Ruble, & W.W. Hartup (Eds.), *Social cognition and social behavior: Developmental perspectives.* New York: Cambridge University Press.

Maccoby, E., & Martin, J. (1983). Socialization in the context of the family: Parent–child interaction. In E. M. Hetherington (Ed.), *Handbook of child psychology: Vol. IV. Socialization, personality, and social development.* New York: Wiley.

Peters R. (1971). Moral developments: A pluralistic approach. In T. Mischel (Ed.), *Cognitive development and epistemology.* New York: Academic.

Rogoff, B., & Gardner, W.P. (1985) Adult guidance of cognitive development. In B. Rogoff & J. Lave (Eds.), *Everyday cognition: Its development in social context.* Cambridge, MA: Harvard University Press.

Rogoff, B., & Wertsch, J. (Eds.) (1984) Children's learning in the "zone of proximal development." *New directions for child development (Vol. 23).* San Francisco: Jossey-Bass.

Rest, J. (1983). Morality. In J. Flavell & E. Markman (Eds.), *Handbook of child psychology: Vol. III. Cognitive development.* New York: Wiley.

Sakharov, A.D. (1975). *My country and the world.* New York: Knopf.

Sakharov, A.D. (1978). *Alarm and hope.* New York: Knopf.

Titus, A.G. (1984). *Sakharov: A life.* Los Angeles: Titus Productions.

Vygotsky, L.S. (1978). *Mind in society: The development of higher psychological processes.* Cambridge, MA: Harvard University Press.

Wertsch, J.V. (1979). From social interaction to higher psychological processes: A clarification and application of Vygotsky's theory. *Human Development, 22,* 1–22.

Wood, D. J. (1980). Teaching the young child: Some relationships between social interaction, language, and thought. In D. R. Olson (Ed.), *The social foundations of language and thought.* New York: Norton.

REFERENCE NOTE

1. This is important as an indication of the slow rate of change. It is our belief that real developmental change is slow partly because it involves a change of goals and motives as well as cognition. On the other hand, the experimental change was not trivial. Although in itself the experimental effect was small, previous research (Damon, 1980) had shown that such changes normally lead to major shifts in subsequent years.

CHAPTER 2

Self-Attributions, Social Interaction, and Moral Development

NANCY EISENBERG

Some of the research described in this manuscript was supported by a grant from NICHD (#1 ROI HD17909). Preparation of this manuscript was supported by the grant cited above as well as an NIH Career Development Award (1K04 HD 00717). The author gratefully acknowledges the collaboration of Robert B. Cialdini in two of the studies described in this chapter.

The purpose of this chapter is to examine (1) the ways in which social interactions and the social context influence self-attributions, and (2) the role of self-attributions in moral behavior and development. Our major premise is that the construction of self-attributions concerning moral actions frequently is influenced by the quality of social interactions, and that the formulation of self-attributions affects subsequent moral behavior. Relevant theory is briefly presented, and research concerning the formation of self-attributions and their role in moral behavior is reviewed. Finally, the role of social interaction and self-attributions in a model of prosocial action is discussed.

Although Piaget (1932/1965) in 1932 emphasized the role of social interaction in shaping moral development, until recently investigations of this issue have been limited in scope and number, and have concerned primarily the usefulness of various socialization techniques embedded in interactions. Only in the past few years have researchers really started to attend to the variety of ways in which social interaction influences moral development (e.g., Higgins, Powers, & Kohlberg, 1984; Youniss, 1980), and to pay more attention to the mechanisms by which components of social interaction may affect morality.

The purpose of this chapter is to consider ways in which social interactions and the social context influence self-attributions, and consequently, moral actions and development. Because there is little research directly pertaining to this issue, it will be necessary to draw upon research only indirectly related to it, and to speculate regarding its interpretation. Moreover, although research and theorizing regarding prosocial behavior (voluntary behaviors intended to benefit another) will be emphasized, the conclusions generally are viewed as pertaining to the broader domain of moral development.

In this chapter, the morality of one's actions is defined in terms of the quality of the motive or reasoning behind the action. For example, behaviors that are egoistic in motivation are considered less moral than those that are other-oriented or motivated by adherence to internalized values. Thus our approach reflects some of the assumptions of cognitive–developmental theory (see Kohlberg, 1984) and, to some degree, Bar–Tal's (e.g., Bar–Tal, 1982) adaptation of cognitive–developmental stages of moral reasoning in his research on motives for prosocial behaviors.

Several issues will be addressed. First, the ways in which the structure of children's social interactions can affect the motives they attribute to their own potentially moral actions will be examined. In doing so, research concerning children's self-attributions about interactions with adults versus peers will be used as an example. Next, the effects of one's self-attributions on subsequent behavior will be considered. Finally, the role of social interaction and self-attributions in a general model of prosocial behavior will be discussed. It is suggested that the construction of self-attributions concerning moral actions frequently is influenced by social interactions, and that the formulation of self-attributions affects subsequent moral action. Before turning to these issues, however, social–psychological perspectives on self-attributions will be briefly reviewed.

SELF-ATTRIBUTIONS IN SOCIAL PSYCHOLOGY

The study of self-attributions has been popular among social psychologists for decades. Much of this interest has been generated by Bem's (1972) behavioristic self–perception theory. According to Bem, individuals have little real access to their own internal states; cognitions concerning one's internal states are really just self-attributions based upon the observation of one's own behavior. In Bem's words:

> Individuals come to "know" their own attitudes, emotions and other internal states partially by inferring them from observations of their own overt behavior and/or the circumstances in which this behavior occurs. Thus, to the extent that internal cues are weak, ambiguous, or uninterpretable, the individual is functionally in the same position as an outside observer, an observer who must necessarily rely upon those same external cues to infer the individual's inner states. (1972, p. 2)

Bem also suggested that children learn to describe themselves as a result of interactions with others who label the children's internal states (based upon the reading of external cues).

Bem acknowledged that internal cues can, at times, be used to interpret one's own behavior and internal states. In his view, one of the important distinctions between self–perception and perception of others is that the self has access, albeit limited, to internal stimuli.

> All of us have approximately 3–4 ft. of potential stimuli inside of us which are unavailable to others but which are available to us for self-attributions. The thrust of Skinnerian analysis of self-attributions is not that we can make no discriminations among internal stimuli, but only that we are far more severely limited than we suppose in this regard because the verbal community is limited in how extensively it can train us to make such discriminations. (Bem, 1972, pp. 40–41)

However, as is evidenced by this quote, Bem emphasized the limited nature of this internal access and focused more on inferences derived from observation of one's own behavior and the circumstances surrounding this behavior.

Others have taken a more extreme view than Bem regarding the accessibility of internal states. For example, Nisbett and Wilson (1977) argued that people generally are unaware of the critical stimuli that influence their responding, their own inferential processing, and their own responses to stimuli. In their view, when attempting to explain their own behavior, people usually do not access their memories of the cognitive processes used in connection with the stimulus; rather, they explain their own behavior by reference to a priori causal theories about the relation between stimulus and response. One can assume that these a priori theories are based, in part, on past observation of one's own and others' behaviors.

Numerous writers have criticized the extreme view that people infer their own behavior primarily by observing external cues or by accessing a priori theories regarding behavior (see Eisenberg, in press; Locke & Pennington, 1982;

Shotter, 1981; Smith & Miller, 1978; von Cranach, Kalbermatten, Indermuhle, & Gugler, 1982; White, 1980). They have argued that people frequently are aware of their own reasons for actions, especially when their actions are novel and interesting (Smith & Miller, 1978) or intentional (Morris, 1981), or follow a difficult decision–making process (Eisenberg, 1986). Indeed, even Nisbett and Wilson (1977) acknowledged that certain cognitive contents are accessible to the individual (or are at least more accessible to the self than to observers), including knowledge of one's current sensations and one's own emotions, evaluations, and plans. Nonetheless, despite the fact that the views of Bem and Nisbett and Wilson may be questioned, Bem and other social psychologists have done much to heighten our awareness of the importance of self–observation in the process of making inferences about ourselves.

The notion that people sometimes make attributions about themselves in a manner similar to that used to make inferences about others can be helpful for understanding some of the ways that the structure of social interaction, as well as the actions of others with whom one interacts, shapes the individual's moral reasoning and behavior. According to self–perception theory, people frequently will use information embedded in a social situation to attach meaning to their own behaviors. Thus information relevant to inferences about one's own motives for behaving in a specific manner may be derived, at least in part, from the processing of how others react to one's behavior and from analysis of factors in the social situation that might account for one's actions. In brief, although people's actions frequently may be motivated by a variety of other conscious cognitions and emotional factors, self-attributions derived in part from features of the social setting also may be important to the understanding of behavior, including moral behavior.

THE EFFECTS OF THE STRUCTURE OF SOCIAL INTERACTION ON SELF-ATTRIBUTIONS

The ways in which the structure of the child's social world influences his or her moral self-attributions seldom have been discussed or studied. Nonetheless, some previous theorizing and work related to moral development can be viewed in terms of self-attributional processes.

Piaget (1932/1965), in his early writings concerning moral reasoning, suggested that one of the three factors affecting the development of children's moral reasoning is the advent of cooperative, equalitarian peer interactions that serve to counteract the negative effects of the unilateral relation between parent and child. Piaget was concerned with the child's movement from the morality of constraint (also called heteronomous morality or moral realism) to the morality of cooperation or autonomous morality. In his view, heteronomous morality involves a focus on the external features of an action (such as its consequences) when determining the morality of an action, and more important, the tendency to judge right and wrong based primarily upon authorities' dictates and whether or not a given course of action is punished. Thus morality is viewed as external, as flowing from those in authority. More specifically, in

Piaget's words, moral realism is "the tendency which the child has to regard duty and the value attaching to it as self–subsistent and independent of the mind, as imposing itself regardless of the circumstances in which the individual may find himself" (1932/1965, p. 111). In contrast, autonomous morality is defined as being independent of external pressures, and as being based on principles of cooperation and mutual respect and on the notion of subjective responsibility.

With regard to the role of social interaction in the development of moral judgment, Piaget suggested that the unilateral power relation between parent and child and the child's unilateral respect for the parent actually retard the young child's moral functioning. Due in part to the fact that moral rules and pronouncements emanate from adults, the child's morality early in childhood is externally based. One possible reinterpretation of what Piaget was saying is that children observe their own "moral" behaviors in interaction with adults, perceive them as being externally controlled, and therefore view morality as heteronomous or as originating from outside the self. Although Piaget viewed moral heteronomy as being a consequence of two cognitive factors (the child's egocentrism and cognitive realism) as well as the nature of the parent–child relationship, a self-attributional perspective is not inconsistent with his theorizing.

The second and higher stage of moral functioning, autonomous morality, was viewed by Piaget as deriving from the equalitarian nature of peer interaction, as well as from declines in cognitive egocentrism and cognitive realism. Because of the natural give and take in the interaction of equals, children are viewed as experiencing a sense of participation in formulating morality (e.g., rules), and as developing a sense of mutual respect for others, resulting in a sense of justice. Here again, one could reinterpret Piaget's observations within a self-attribution framework; as children are given the opportunity to contribute actively to decisions regarding their own moral behaviors, they are more likely to attribute their actions to their own values and internal motives. Thus morality should be perceived as coming from within rather than as originating outside of the self.

Although the veracity of Piaget's assumptions regarding the role of peer interaction in moral development has been questioned (e.g., Kohlberg, 1963; Kugelmass & Breznitz, 1967; see Berg & Mussen, 1975), there is some evidence (albeit not strong) to support the notion that peer interaction is associated with higher-level moral judgment (Lickona, 1976). Similarly, the evidence concerning Piaget's assertions about the negative effects of the parent–child relation is mixed (MacRae, 1954; see Berg & Mussen, 1975; Lickona, 1976), although it is fairly clear that punitive parent–child relationships are associated with lower–level moral reasoning and behavior (Hoffman, 1970, 1977). For our purposes, however, what is of interest is not simply the relation of quantity of peer or adult interaction, nor even the quality of adult–child interaction, to children's moral development, but the different self–perceptions that could result as a consequence of the general structure of the two kinds of interaction.

Youniss's Work

In his recent work, Youniss (1980; Youniss & Volpe, 1978) has further explored issues raised by Piaget concerning the role of adult versus peer interaction in social development. Youniss expanded upon Sullivan's (1953) as well as Piaget's (1932/1965) work and proposed that children construct, through their social exchanges with peers and adults, two different understandings of their social world and two sets of rules to guide behavior. Through interactions with persons who control power and know a system that the child has yet to learn (i.e., adults), the child learns conformity, that is, how to act in accordance with others' social expectations. However, with peers, children discover a social system to be created with others, one that is open to modification and gives a sense of mutual understanding. In peer interaction, because there is initially no set structure, no one person is initially superior or inferior, and the system is open to redefinition through a democratic process. Through reciprocal peer interactions, the child learns concern for peers' well–being and a sense of connectedness to peers and develops intimacy and responsivity to others' needs.

Youniss (1980) examined his ideas by means of a series of studies concerning children's conceptions of adult– and peer–oriented instances of kindness and unkindness, and notions of friendship and repair of offenses. The research regarding notions of kindness and unkindness was the most extensive and is also the most relevant for our purposes. Youniss found that children, especially those in early elementary school, generally viewed acts of kindness directed at adults and peers quite differently. For the younger children, kindness toward adults consisted of being obedient or good, whereas unkindness was the reverse. Older children (approximately 12 to 14 years old) viewed kindness not only as obedience and "being good," but also as doing chores or, occasionally, exhibiting concern for an adult in need. For these children, unkindness was defined as misbehaving, talking back, and, occasionally, not helping an adult. In contrast, kindness with regard to peers was conceptualized as involving giving, playing together, sharing, or occasionally (for older children only), understanding, teaching, and giving physical assistance. Unkindness was defined as not sharing or as aggression (especially for younger children), and as failure to assist a needy peer (for older children). Thus Youniss found that children, especially younger children, defined adult and peer social interactions differently. Adult–child interactions were viewed as characterized by child compliance and obedience whereas peer interactions were perceived as having a more equalitarian and prosocial flavor.

In his work, Youniss did not directly examine real–life behavior; all his investigations involved children's verbal accounts or responses to questions. Moreover, he did not directly examine the ways in which social interaction with peers versus adults might affect children's views of their own motives for behavior. In our own work, we were interested in precisely this issue.

Based upon Youniss's findings as well as Piaget's and Sullivan's theorizing, one would expect children to view their own motives for adult-directed and peer-directed acts of kindness (or unkindness) as being somewhat different. Because of the conformity and compliance that are central to adult–child interaction, children frequently should view their acts of kindness directed at adults as being motivated by the desire to be obedient, to conform, or to "be good." In contrast, because of the emphasis on caring and responsivity to others that appears to be more inherent to peer than to adult social interactions, children should view their peer–directed prosocial behaviors as frequently being motivated by concern for the other's need or one's relationship with the other.

Studies of Self–Attributions

To examine whether children's self-attributions differ somewhat with regard to peer- and adult-directed behaviors, we conducted several studies with preschoolers. In the first two, we (Eisenberg, Lundy, Shell, & Roth, 1985; Eisenberg & Roth, 1983) elicited from preschool children reports of their own motives for naturally occurring compliant behaviors. Compliant behaviors were defined as behaviors occurring in response to either a request or a mild command from another. Many of these behaviors were prosocial, that is, involved acts that directly benefited another (helping or sharing); others had no direct prosocial consequences and appeared to be merely acts of compliance or obedience to an authority, dominant other, or nonprosocial norm or rule implicitly or explicitly referenced by the other. Thus the range of behaviors studied was similar to that defined by Youniss's (1980) children as kind (e.g., acts of obedience, politeness, being good, helpfulness, sharing).

In the two studies, children were observed in their preschool classrooms by familiar adults over a period of months. The familiar adult circulated around the classroom and playground in a systematic manner, and questioned the children regarding their motives whenever he or she observed a "compliant" behavior.

The children's expressed motives were coded into the following categories: (1) authority or punishment orientation (references to authorities' or peers' demands and/or punishment); (2) hedonistic orientation (references to expected gain for the self); (3) direct reciprocity (references to benefits or costs directly deriving from reciprocity—or lack of it—from the one with whom the child complied); (4) pragmatic orientation (references to practical, nonmoral reasons); (5) needs–oriented reasoning (references to another's psychological or physical need as a justification for behavior, e.g., "He wanted some clay"); (6) affectional relationship orientation (references to the relationship between the individual and either the requester or the recipient of aid, including one's liking of the other); (7) approval and interpersonal orientation (references to social approval and/or the desire to enhance interpersonal interactions); and (8) stereotyped good–bad orientation (stereotyped reasons such as "It's nice to help"). Each incident was also coded to indicate whether the behavior requested of the child was prosocial (an act that directly benefited another— usually, but not always, the requester) or nonprosocial (compliance with a command or regulation that did not *directly* benefit another). For example, if a child shared a toy with a peer who requested clay, or was asked or told by an adult to share the toy, the compliant act would be scored as prosocial. However, if a child was asked or told to clean up because it was "cleanup time," or if a child was asked or told to clean up a table that he or she had soiled, the act was coded as nonprosocial.

In general, the children's self-attributions for adult-instigated and peer-instigated compliant behaviors differed in a manner consistent with expectations. Children used more authority– and punishment-oriented reasoning to explain compliance with adults' than peers' prosocial and nonprosocial requests or commands. (It should be noted, however, that this was not the major category of reasoning used to explain even adult-instigated behaviors.) In contrast, children justified peer–instigated compliance more often than adult-initiated compliance with references to others' needs or one's relationship with or liking for another person (the latter for prosocial requests only). The patterns of findings were very similar in both experiments, although the results were somewhat stronger in the study involving the larger sample (See Eisenberg et al., 1985, for details regarding the larger study).

Because of the relatively unilateral nature of adult–child relationships, it is possible that children interpret even adults' requests for assistance as commands for conformity or obedience. This may account, in part, for the difference in children's needs-oriented and authority or punishment reasoning with regard to adult- versus peer-instigated behaviors. In a third study, we (Eisenberg, Pasternack, & Lundy, 1984) examined whether preschool children make different attributions about their compliance with adults' requests versus commands for prosocial behavior. Each of 63 children 3 to 5 years old, on two different occasions, was requested to help and directed to help by two different, familiar experimenters. If the child complied with the request, the child was approached by a different experimenter who interviewed the child to ascertain his or her reasons for helping. The children's motives were coded into the aforementioned categories .

Fifty-one children gave codeable responses in both situations. According to 2 (sex) x 2 (order of events) x 2 (age: older than 54 months vs. 54 months or younger) x 2 (condition: command vs. request) multivariate and univariate analyses computed for the frequently used categories of attribution (authority or punishment, pragmatic, needs oriented), none of the multivariate Fs even approached statistical significance.

In brief, the children did not use differential justifications to explain their compliance with adults' requests and commands. The fact that approximately the same number of children eventually complied in the command as in the request condition also is consistent with the view that children did not distinguish between adults' requests or commands. Perhaps our request ("[(child's name], would you please do me a favor and get me a towel?") and command ("[child's name], please go get me a paper towel") did not differ sufficiently in wording or tone to elicit differences in children's attributions. Alternatively, children may recognize that adults' requests frequently are implicit commands. In any case, the results of this study are at least consistent with the view that children perceive adult–instigated requests for prosocial acts. as commands or directives.

To summarize, the results of our research suggest that children make some-what different self-attributions for compliant behaviors (prosocial or otherwise) that are embedded in social interactions with peers than for those that are embedded in social interactions with adults. Self–attributions for peer–in-stigated compliant behaviors were more prosocial and relationship-oriented than were self-attributions for analogous adult–instigated acts whereas self-attributions for adult–instigated acts were more authority and compliance-oriented. Thus it would seem that children should develop somewhat different conceptions regarding adult and peer interaction.

The results of our research are consistent with the results of other studies in indicating that children's self-attributions for moral behaviors are derived in part from their perception of the circumstances in which the behavior is embedded (see Bar-Tal, 1982; Smith, Gelfand, Hartmann, & Partlow, 1979). For example, Smith and colleagues (1979) found that children were more likely to attribute their behavior to external (the desire to get rewards or to avoid fines) rather than internal (the desire to help or concern about another) motives when they had received material consequences (rather than social or no conse-quences) for sharing. In contrast, children who received social consequences or no consequences for their sharing were more likely than those who received material consequences to attribute their generosity to internal causes. More-over, Schlenker, Hallam, and McCown (1983) found that adult actors made somewhat more positive, internally motivated than nonpositive (social approval-oriented, nonprosocial) self-attributions when the consequences of their prosocial actions for another were large rather than small; this was true even though the participants were not provided with information regarding the consequences of their actions until after the action was performed (so a priori motives were not affected by the manipulation of the consequences). Self-attributions did not vary, however, as a consequence of the public visibility of their sharing. Finally, Bar-Tal (1982) has found that children view their own behavior as more internally motivated when it has been elicited without adults' emphasizing of social expectations or promising of rewards than when proso-cial behavior has been induced by means of external pressures or offers of con-crete rewards. Although it is quite possible that the participants in Bar-Tal's studies (as well as some of the other studies) were reporting true a priori motives and not self-attributions based on observation of their own behavior, the limited research is consistent with the view that people do evaluate their own potentially moral behavior based, in part, on the context in which it is embedded.

The significance of the aforementioned findings for an understanding of moral behavior rests upon the assumption that self-attributions affect sub-sequent moral reasoning or behavior. The validity of this assumption will now be examined.

SELF-ATTRIBUTIONS AND MORAL BEHAVIORS

The Effects of Providing Self-Attributions on Subsequent Behavior

In a number of studies, adults have provided children with attributions related to the children's behavior and have found that these attributions affect the children's subsequent behavior. Apparently, children internalize or adopt adults' attributions concerning their behaviors, and then attempt to act in a manner consistent with these attributions. For example, Miller, Brickman, and Bolen (1975) found that fourth graders who were told by their teachers that they were exceptionally tidy became neater thereafter, whereas children who were told that they had an exceptional aptitude for mathematics subsequently performed better on math tests. With regard to behaviors that are morally relevant, Jensen and Moore (1977) demonstrated that children 7 to 12 years old who were told that they were either cooperative or competitive subsequently behaved in ways consistent with the adults' attributions. Similarly, Toner, Moore, and Emmons (1980) found that girls 5½ to 8 years old who were labeled as patient exhibited more self-control on a subsequent measure of delay of gratification than did children not labeled in this manner. Similar labeling effects have been shown with regard to 8-year-olds' resistance to deviation (Dienstbier, Hillman, Lehnhoff, Hillman, & Volkenaar, 1975) and third and fourth graders' self-punishment following deviation (but only if they were told that other children did not deviate so they could not attribute their deviation to something in the enviroment; Perry, Perry, Bussey, English, & Arnold, 1980). Finally, Grusec and her colleagues have found that elementary–school children were more likely to act in a prosocial manner if they previously had been told that an initial act of donating was due to internal, altruistic motives (that they were helpful people and liked to help others) than if their prior donating was attributed to compliance with adults' expectations (Grusec, Kuczynski, Rushton, & Simuitis, 1978) or no attribution was provided (Grusec & Redler, 1980). In this research, the provision of altruistic attributions apparently influenced subsequent private as well as public compliant helping.

In brief, it appears that attributions provided by others in social interactions can affect children's subsequent moral (or potentially moral) behaviors. Thus one also would expect self-attributions to affect subsequent moral behavior. Another line of research that is consistent with this notion is that related to certain compliance techniques. This line of research, which has been conducted primarily with adults, will now be reviewed.

INDUCING COMPLIANCE: THE FOOT-IN-THE-DOOR AND LOW-BALL TECHNIQUES

The role of self-attributions in mediating potentially moral behavior has been implicated, albeit indirectly, in the empirical research concerning certain compliance procedures studied by social psychologists. One of these, labeled the foot-in-the-door procedure (Freedman & Fraser, 1966), is a compliance technique that is viewed as operating via consistency pressures. With this technique, one gains compliance from target persons to a large request by first inducing them to comply with a smaller, related request. It has been argued that compliance with the initial small request causes targets to change their self-images due to self-attributional processes. After targets are induced to comply with a small request (e.g., making a small donation), they see themselves as the kind of people who are favorable toward performing such requests; consequently, they agree to perform larger, related requests to be consistent with this new self-image. Several reviewers (Beaman, Cole, Preston, Klentz, & Steblay, 1982; DeJong, 1979) have found that there is good support for the technique's effectiveness but have noted a surprising lack of direct evidence concerning the role of one's self-image as a mediator of the effect.

A second relevant compliance procedure is the low-ball technique, a technique used widely in sales settings (e.g., Carlson, 1973) has been found to influence compliance in various nonsales contexts such as charity drives (Burger & Petty, 1981; Cialdini, Cacioppo, Bassett, & Miller, 1978). With this technique, compliance with a costly request is enhanced by first gaining targets' agreement to perform a seemingly mild form of the request and only then informing the targets of the requested behavior's costly features. The target person's initial commitment to perform the favor and the desire to behave consistently with this commitment are believed to underlie the effectiveness of the low-ball tactic. Thus, as for the foot-in-the-door procedure, the frequency of desired behaviors purportedly is increased because of changes in the individual's self-image based upon self-attributional processes, and the pressure to be consistent with one's self-image. However, it is important to note that in public situations people also may act in a way consistent with their initial commitment (in low-ball situations) or behavior (foot-in-the-door situations) in order to appear consistent to others. In current social psychological theory, the desire to appear consistent to others is viewed as having a considerable influence over a range of behaviors, for reasons of impression management (i.e., to behave in a socially desirable manner—see Baumeister, 1982; Schlenker, 1980; Tedeschi, 1981).

To summarize, the results of the social psychological compliance research described above are consistent with the view that people who are induced, often in the course of social interaction, to behave positively or to commit to positive behavior are more likely to act in a consistent manner at a subsequent time. Although there has been virtually no research of this sort conducted with children, there are some data from research concerning socialization procedures that are at least consistent with the foot-in-the-door research. For example, children who have been instructed to assist others or who have been given practice in helping subsequently are more helpful than are other children (Grusec et al., 1978; Staub, 1979; see Moore & Eisenberg, 1984). Moreover, children from cultures in which they are routinely assigned prosocial chores or tasks appear to exhibit more prosocial behavior (Whiting & Whiting, 1975) Consistent with social psychological theorizing, Perry and Perry (1983) suggested that children, especially over a period of time, make internal attributions about positive behaviors that initially were externally induced, and that such internal attributions increase the probability of subsequent prosocial responding. Internalization should be especially likely if the social control used to induce compliance initially is minimally sufficient, that is, if the external control is sufficiently subtle (rather than coercive) to prevent the individual from viewing his or her compliance as being due solely to extrinsic controls (Lepper, 1983). Whether or not any external pressures are remembered and influence subsequent behavior may depend upon the saliency of external pressures versus intrinsic factors in the socialization context (Hoffman, 1983).

Developmental Considerations

There is reason to expect compliance procedures to work better with persons 7 to 8 years of age and older than with younger children. In prior work, Grusec and Redler (1980) found that the pairing of requested donating with altruistic attributions was associated with enhanced subsequent donating for 8- and 10-year-olds but not 5-year-olds. They suggested that young children may have difficulty thinking of enduring dispositional traits; thus they should be less inclined than older children both to believe in intra–individual consistency and to attempt to maintain a consistent self–perception or image. This notion is consistent with research indicating that children have difficulty thinking in terms of dispositional factors as stable characteristics until approximately age 8 (Dix & Grusec, 1983; Rholes & Ruble, 1984; Rotenberg, 1982). Moreover, young children should be relatively unlikely to make self-attributions that affect subsequent behavior because (1) children's abilities to make causal attributions improve dramatically at around 7 to 9 years of age (e.g., DiVitto & McArthur, 1978; cf. Ruble & Rholes, 1981; Sedlak & Kurtz, 1981), and (2) young children apparently have difficulty making inferences about their own behaviors (e.g., Nicholls, 1979; Ruble, Parsons, & Ross, 1976). The improvement in the ability to make causal attributions in the middle elementary school years has been found with regard to attributions about moral as well as other types of behavior (see Eisenberg, 1982, 1986).

Based upon the findings with regard to developmental change, it is reasonable to assume that the self-attributions children make with regard to potentially moral behaviors will not influence the quality of their subsequent moral behaviors until the early school years. However, it is quite possible that self-attributions made at a younger age are remembered and influence behavior once children are old enough to understand consistency of personality and experience internal pressures to maintain a consistent internal image. This is an empirical question to be addressed in future research.

Research on Compliant Prosocial Behaviors

In recent research, Robert Cialdini and I have obtained some support for the notion that compliant prosocial behavior can be induced by procedures that appear to involve self-attributional processes. Aspects of this research that are most relevant to the topic of this chapter are now described.

In one study, we examined the effectiveness of the foot-in-the-door procedure and possible mediators of the effect within a socialization context. In this study, children in kindergarten and second and fifth grades were induced to share prize coupons with needy children through procedures that were not excessively coercive (e.g., prompts). Some children induced to share also were provided by the experimenter with prosocial attributions for their prosocial actions; others were not. Yet other children in a control group had no opportunity to engage in this initial prosocial behavior. Approximately 1 or 2 days later, the children were given an opportunity to help hospitalized children, but at a cost to the self (they could either sort paper into piles to make toys for needy children or play with attractive toys). Moreover, a number of weeks later, children in second and fifth grades responded to a pencil-and-paper measure of self-attributions for helping others in four hypothetical situations (adapted from Silbereisen, Boehnke, & Reykowski, 1984). In each scenario, the child himself or herself was described as helping in a specific circumstance; the child then rated several alternative reasons for assisting with regard to how important they would have been to the child. The options included other-oriented and self-oriented reasons (Eisenberg, Cialdini, McCreath, & Shell, in press).

Children who previously had the opportunity to engage in prosocial behavior helped more than did children who did not. Moreover, the strength of this relation increased with age; condition had absolutely no effect on subsequent helping for kindergartners and had a significant effect for fifth graders. In addition, although children in the various conditions did not differ in report of self-attributions, children who helped the hospitalized children were less hedonistic in their subsequent report of self-attributions. Whether children who perceived themselves as less hedonistic assisted more because of their a priori motives and/or prosocial self-concept or whether the degree of helping affected subsequent self-attributions is not clear.

In a second study, we examined the effects of the low-ball procedure on first, third, sixth, seventh, and eight graders' volunteering of recess time to make toys for needy children. Some of the children initially were asked in a circumstance in which it appeared that their help was required immediately, which was during class time (so helping would be relatively low cost). They responded either privately (by writing down their answer) or publicly (by telling the experimenter whether they would help). Then the children were told that any helping would occur at a later time during recess (for the elementary school children) or lunch period (for the junior high students). Other children in a control group were not initially asked to assist when it appeared that helping would not be costly; they were asked only how much recess or lunch time they would give up to engage in the helping task. Finally, a week to several months later, all children in third, sixth, seventh, and eighth grades responded to the same self-attribution measure used in the other study.

Contrary to our expectations, the initial commitment did not affect volunteering to help under more costly conditions. Perhaps we did not allow sufficient time to pass for children to make self-attributions about themselves prior to the second request for assistance. Alternatively, our manipulations may have seemed contrived or may have created reactance. Nonetheless, whether or not the children made an initial commitment under low–cost conditions did affect their self-attributions. Children who made an initial commitment in private (i.e., under conditions in which they should not attribute their volunteering to social pressure or compliance pressures) made more oth-er–oriented self-attributions for their helping behavior than did children who made their initial commitment in public or who did not have the opportunity to make an initial low–cost commitment. Egoistic self-attributions, which were low for all groups, did not differ by condition.

Commitment condition also interacted with sex and age in their effect on positive, other–oriented self-attributions. The experience of making a private commitment was associated with more prosocial self-attributions for girls at all ages (third grade and up); for boys, the effect of making a private commitment was not evident until sixth grade (Cialdini, Eisenberg, Shell, & McCreath, in press).

In summary, in this study, we found initial support for the notion that social interactions that induce the individual to act in desired ways that are likely to be viewed as internally motivated can affect self-attributional processes over a period of time. Although we did not find an immediate effect of the compliance manipulation on behavior, other research is consistent with the view that such an effect can be expected under some conditions. For children, it merely may take a little time for the integration of new self-attributions into their self-image.

Self-Attributions: Their Role in a Model of Prosocial Behavior

In my view, self-attributions play a significant role in any model of moral behavior. Moreover, because the nature of one's social interactions affects moral values, decision making regarding the performance of moral actions, and post hoc evaluations of one's own behavior, models of moral action that include social interactional as well as self-attributional factors must, by necessity, be complex.

In Figure 2.1, a general model for prosocial behavior is presented. More detail regarding the specific factors indicated by each label can be found in Eisenberg (1986). For the purposes of this paper, it may be sufficient to indicate where relevant self-attributional and social interactional variables fit in the model.

Aspects of social interaction that occur in a specific situation in which a decision regarding moral behavior is being made (e.g., the degree of pressure applied by others) are included in the category of *Characteristics of the Situation* (see Fig. 2.1). The structure and quality of this social interaction, once interpreted by the individual, are viewed as influencing the activation of cognitive and personality factors relevant to decision making (e.g., personal values and goals and one's evaluation of the costs and benefits of assisting), the selection of a course of behavior, and emotional reactions in the situation (e.g., the activation of feelings of sympathy or personal distress; see Eisenberg, 1986). Clearly, cues in a situation pertaining to the other's predicament, costs and gains for given courses of action, and situational constraints regarding the available modes of action frequently are considered when making decisions

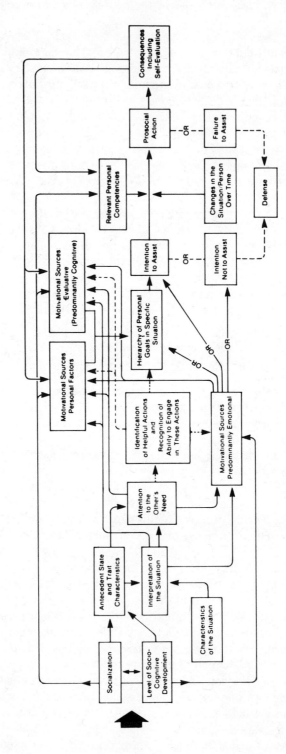

Figure 2.1. A model of prosocial behavior. (Reprinted from Eisenberg, 1986, with permission of Lawrence Erlbaum Associates.)

regarding moral behaviors; moreover, there are individual differences in how identical situational cues are interpreted by different people (cf. Eisenberg, 1986; Staub, 1978).

Although no arrow is shown going directly from *Interpretation of the Situation* (i.e., interpretation of situational factors) to the *Consequences* (including self-attributional processes) that follow the performance of behavior, the way in which situational variables are interpreted and acted upon should affect the nature of one's self–evaluation and self-attributions. For example, one would expect individual differences in the perception of external pressure to help in a given situation indirectly to affect self-attributions, especially if the individual's decision to assist or not assist were based in part on consideration of external demands. Similarly, age differences in the interpretation of situational cues (e.g., as indicating extrinsic motivation as not—Baldwin & Baldwin, 1970; see Eisenberg, 1986) should influence both decision making and self-attributions subsequent to action or inaction.

As was discussed previously, one's choice of behavior should result in consequences that feed back to affect the individual's self-image (included in *Personal Factors*), and perhaps cognitive processing in future situations (included in *Motivational Sources: Evaluative*). For example, the individual who views himself or herself as more altruistic as a consequence of self-attributional processes that occur subsequent to helping may: (1) develop a more altruistic self-image that, because of internal consistency pressures, will enhance the likelihood of future prosocial responding (e.g., Beaman et al., 1982; Grusec, 1983); and (2) view the subjective utility (expected utility—cf. Lynch & Cohen, 1978) of assisting in future situations differently than previously because of increased negative consequences for one's self–esteem if one acts in a manner inconsistent with one's self-image.

Another way in which social interaction indirectly influences both moral behavior and the individual's self-attributions is through prior socializing interactions (see *Socialization* in Fig. 2.1). For example, socializers' provision of altruistic self-attributions, modeling, use of inductive discipline, and so forth are expected to affect personality variables (e.g., values, needs, preferences, self-esteem), cognitive factors (e.g., attributions about the origins of others' needs and evaluation of subjective expected utilities), and, indirectly, both the ways in which various goals are prioritized in a specific decision–making situation and the intent to behave in a moral fashion (see Eisenberg, 1986; Staub, 1978). With regard to the issue of self-attributions, it is important to reiterate that prior interactions with socializers can be expected to have had a formative role in the development of the child's self-image concerning morality via the provision, directly or indirectly, of information relevant to self-attributions (see Eisenberg, 1986; Eisenberg & Cialdini, 1984; Grusec, 1983).

The aforementioned links between (1) self-attributions formulated subsequent to behavior (included in *Consequences*) and self-image (included in *Personal Factors*) and (2) between self-image and future decision making regarding potentially moral behaviors are clearly indicated in Figure 2.1. Much more research is needed to indicate the precise ways in which variables embedded in social interactions of various sorts influence the formulation of self-attributions, and the relative importance of post hoc self-attributions versus conscious cognitive processing during decision making (prior to the execution of behavior) in the formulation of self–evaluations subsequent to action.

Thus far, I have discussed the role of self-attributions in the development and performance of moral behavior, not moral reasoning. It is quite possible, however, that self-attributions stemming from prior behavior can affect individuals' moral judgment. Rholes and Lane (1985) have suggested that dissonance resulting from inconsistencies between one's behavior and moral cognitions (i.e., level of moral judgment) can, through consistency pressures, result in the development of higher levels of moral judgment. In support of this line of thought, Rholes, Bailey, and McMillian (1982) found that adults who delivered a counterattitudinal message prepared by the experimenters tended to change their moral reasoning in ways consistent with the reasoning embedded in the message, provided that (1) they felt they had the choice whether to deliver the message, and (2) the moral reasoning in the message was at a higher level than their initial one. Moreover, consistent with Rholes and colleagues' findings, Haan (1975) and Gilligan and Belenky (1980) found that people who behaved in a manner that they justified with higher-level moral judgment than their normal level of judgment tended to advance more in their overall level of moral judgment than did other persons.

The dissonance that Rholes and Lane (1985) believe is the result of inconsistency between one's behavior and reasoning could be viewed as internal consistency pressures (a type of disequilibrium?) resulting from the discrepancy between a revised self-image (with regard to one's own morality) and one's prior level of moral reasoning. This change in one's self-image as a consequence of moral action is likely to be mediated, at least in part, by self-attributions made as a consequence of evaluating one's own apparently moral action. Thus inducement of action that appears to be moral, often in the course of social interaction, appears to be an effective means of promoting the development of moral reasoning as well as moral behavior.

CONCLUSIONS

In summary, the roles of both social interaction and self-attributional processes in moral action and development have received insufficient attention from psychologists in the past. In this chapter I have tried to delineate some of the ways in which social interaction and self-attributions are interrelated, and the processes by which they might be expected jointly to influence moral action and moral development. Although the discussion is in places speculative, the goal has been to focus more attention on these issues, and to encourage a melding of developmental and social-psychological perspectives in the examination of these and related issues.

REFERENCES

Baldwin, C. P., & Baldwin, A. L. (1970). Children's judgments of kindness. *Child Development, 41,* 29–47.

Bar-Tal, D. (1982). Sequential development of helping behavior: A cognitive-learning approach. *Developmental Review, 2,* 101–124.

Baumeister, R. F. (1982). A self-presentational view of social phenomena. *Psychological Bulletin, 91,* 3–26.

Beaman, A. L., Cole, C. M., Preston, M., Klentz, B., & Steblay, N. M. (1982). Fifteen years of foot-in-the-door research. *Personal & Social Psychology Bulletin, 9,* 181-196.

Bem, D. J. (1972). Self perception theory. In L. Berkowitz (Ed.), *Advances in experimental social psychology* (Vol. 6). New York: Academic.

Berg, N. E., & Mussen, P. (1975). The origins and development of justice. *Journal of Social Issues, 31,* 183–201.

Burger, J. M., & Petty, R. E. (1981). The low-ball compliance technique: Task or person commitment? *Journal of Personality & Social Psychology, 40,* 492–500.

Carlson, M. D. (1973). *How to get your car repaired without getting gipped.* New York: Harrow Books (Harper & Row).

Cialdini, R. B., Cacioppo, J. T., Bassett, R., & Miller, J. A. (1978). The low-ball procedure for producing compliance: Commitment then cost. *Journal of Personality & Social Psychology, 36,* 463–476.

DeJong, W. (1979). An examination of self-perception mediation of the foot-in-the-door effect. *Journal of Personality & Social Psychology, 37,* 2221–2239.

Dienstbier, R. A. (1978). Attribution, socialization, and moral decision-making. In J. H. Harvey, W. Ickes, & R. F. Kidd (Eds.), *New directions in attributional research* (Vol. 2). Hillsdale, NJ: Erlbaum.

Dienstbier, R. A., Hillman, D., Lehnhoff, J., Hillman, J., & Valkener, M. C. (1975). An emotion-attribution approach to moral behavior: Interfacing cognitive and avoidance theories of moral development. *Psychological Review, 82,* 299–315.

DiVitto, B., & McArthur, L. Z. (1978). Developmental differences in the use of distinctiveness, consensus, and consistency information in making causal judgments. *Developmental Psychology, 14,* 474–482.

Dix, T., & Grusec, J. E. (1983). Parental influence techniques: An attributional analysis. *Child Development, 54,* 645–652.

Eisenberg, N. (1982). The development of reasoning regarding prosocial behavior. In N. Eisenberg (Ed.), *The development of prosocial behavior.* New York: Academic.

Eisenberg, N. (1986). *Altruistic cognition, emotion, and behavior.* Hillsdale, NJ: Erlbaum.

Eisenberg, N., & Cialdini, R. B. (1984). The role of consistency pressures in behavior: A developmental perspective. *Academic Psychology Bulletin, 6,* 115–126.

Eisenberg, N., Cialdini, R. B., McCreath, H., & Shell, R. (1987). Consistency based compliance: When and why do children become vulnerable. *Journal of Personality and Social Psychology, 58,* 1174–1181.

Eisenberg, N., Lundy, T., Shell, R., & Roth, K. (1985). Children's justifications for their adult- and peer-directed compliant (prosocial and nonprosocial) behaviors. *Developmental Psychology, 21,* 325–331.

Eisenberg, N., Pasternack, J. F., & Lundy, T. (1984). *Children's justifications for their adult-directed and adult-requested compliance and prosocial behaviors.* Unpublished manuscript, Arizona State University.

Eisenberg, N., & Roth, K. (1983). *Children's attributions about peer- and adult-instigated compliant behavior.* Unpublished research, Arizona State University.

Gilligan, C., & Belenky, M. F. (1980). A naturalistic study of abortion decisions. In R. Selman & R. Yando (Eds.), *Clinical-developmental psychology: New directions in child development, No. 7.* San Francisco: Jossey-Bass.

Grusec, J. E. (1982). The socialization of altruism. In N. Eisenberg (Ed.), *The development of prosocial behavior.* New York: Academic.

Grusec, J. E., Kuczynski, L., Rushton, J. P., & Simutis, Z. M. (1978). Model, direct instruction, and attributions: Effects on altruism. *Developmental Psychology, 14,* 51–57.

Grusec, J. E., & Redler, E. (1980). Attribution, reinforcement, and altruism: A developmental analysis. *Developmental Psychology, 16,* 525–534.

Haan, N. (1975). Hypothetical and actual moral reasoning in a situation of civil disobedience. *Journal of Personality & Social Psychology, 32,* 255–269.

Higgins, A., Power, C., & Kohlberg, L. (1984). The relationship of moral atmosphere to judgments of responsibility. In W. M. Kurtines & J. L. Gewirtz (Eds.), *Morality, moral behavior, and moral development.* New York: Wiley.

Hoffman, M. L. (1970). Moral development. In P. H. Mussen (Ed.), *Carmichael's manual of child psychology* (Vol. 2). New York: Wiley.

Hoffman, M. L. (1977). Moral internalization: Current theory and research. In L. Berkowitz (Ed.), *Advances in experimental social psychology* (Vol. 10). New York: Academic.

Hoffman, M. L. (1983). Affective and cognitive processes in moral internalization. In E. T. Higgins, D. N. Ruble, & W. W. Hartup (Eds.), *Social cognition and social development.* Cambridge, England: Cambridge University Press.

Jensen, A. M., & Moore, S. G. (1977). The effect of attribute statements on cooperativeness and competitiveness in school-age boys. *Child Development, 48,* 305–307.

Kohlberg, L. (1963). Development of moral character and moral ideology. In M. L. Hoffman & L. W. Hoffman (Eds.), *Review of child development research* (Vol. 1). New York: Russell Sage Foundation.

Kohlberg, L. (1984). *Essays on moral development: Vol. II. The psychology of moral development.* San Francisco: Harper & Row.

Kugelmass, S., & Breznitz, S. (1967). The development of intentionality in moral judgment in city and kibbutz adolescents. *Journal of Genetic Psychology, 111,* 103–111.

Lepper, M. R. (1983). Social-control processes and the internalization of social values: An attributional process. In E. T. Higgins, D. N. Ruble, & W. W. Hartup (Eds.), *Social cognition and social development.* Cambridge, England: Cambridge University Press.

Lickona, T. (1976). Research on Piaget's theory on moral development. In T. Lickona (Ed.), *Moral development and behavior: Theory, research, and social issues.* New York: Holt, Rinehart, & Winston.

Locke, D., & Pennington, D. (1982). Reasons and other causes: Their role in attribution processes. *Journal of Personality & Social Psychology 42,* 212–223.

Lynch, J. G., & Cohen, J. L. (1978). The use of subjective expected utility theory as an aid to understanding variables that influence helping behavior. *Journal of Personality & Social Psychology, 36,* 1138–1151.

MacRae, D., Jr. (1954). A test of Piaget's theories of moral development. *Journal of Abnormal Social Psychology, 49,* 14–18.

Miller, R. L., Brickman, P., & Bolen, D. (1975). Attribution versus persuasion as a means for modifying behavior. *Journal of Personality & Social Psychology, 31,* 430–441.

Moore, B. S., & Eisenberg, N. (1984). The development of altruism. In G. Whitehurst (Ed.), *Annals of child development.* Greenwich, CT: JAI.

Morris, P. (1981). The cognitive psychology of self-reports. In C. Antaki (Ed.), *The psychology of ordinary explanations of social behaviour.* London: Academic.

Nicholls J. F. (1979) The development of perception of own attainment and causal attributions for success and failure in reading. *Journal of Educational Psychology, 1,* 94-99.

Nisbett, R. E., & Wilson, T. D. (1977). Telling more than we can know: Verbal reports on mental processes. *Psychological Review, 84,* 231–259.

Perry, D. G., & Perry, L. C. (1983). Social learning, causal attribution, and moral internalization. In J. Bisanz, G. L. Bisanz, & R. Kail (Eds.), *Learning in children: Progress in cognitive development research.* New York: Springer-Verlag.

Perry, D. G., Perry, L. C., Bussey, K., English, D., & Arnold, G. (1980). Processes of attribution and children's self-punishment following misbehavior. *Child Development, 51,* 545–551.

Piaget, J. (1965).*The moral judgment of the child.* New York: Free Press. (Original work published 1932)

Rholes, W. S., Bailey, S., & McMillian, L. (1982). Experiences that motivate moral development: The role of cognitive dissonance. *Journal of Experimental Social Psychology, 18,* 524–526.

Rholes, W. S., & Lane, J. W. (1985). Consistency between cognitions and behavior: Cause and consequence of cognitive moral development. In J. B. Pryor & J. D. Day (Eds.), *The development of social cognition.* New York: Springer-Verlag.

Rholes, W. S., & Ruble, D. N. (1984). Children's understanding of dispositional characteristics of others. *Child Development, 55,* 550–560.

Rotenberg, K. J. (1982). Development of character constancy of self and other. *Child Development, 53,* 505–515.

Ruble, D. N., Parsons, J. E., & Ross, J. (1976). Self-evaluation responses of children in an achievement setting. *Child Development, 47,* 990–997.

Ruble, D. N., & Rholes, W. S. (1981). The development of children's perceptions and attributions about their social world. In J. H. Harvey, W. J. Ickes, & R. F. Kidd (Eds.), *New directions in attributional research* (Vol. 3). Hillsdale, NJ: Erlbaum.

Schlenker, B. R. (1980). *Impression management.* Monterey, CA: Brooks/Cole.

Schlenker, B. R., Hallam, J. R., & McCown, N. E. (1983). Motives and social evaluation: Actor-observer differences in the delineation of motives for a beneficial act. *Journal of Experimental Social Psychology, 19,* 254–273.

Sedlak, A. J., & Kurtz, S. T. (1981). A review of children's use of causal inference principles. *Child Development, 52,* 759–784.

Shotter, J. (1981). Telling and reporting: Prospective and retrospective uses of self-ascriptions. In C. Antaki (Ed.), *The psychology of ordinary explanations of social behavior*. London: Academic.

Silbereisen, R. K., Boehnke, K., & Reykowski, J. (1984, September). *Prosocial motives: A comparison of German and Polish adolescents*. Paper presented at the International Congress of Psychology, Acapulco, Mexico.

Smith, C. L., Gelfand, D. M., Hartmann, D. P., & Partlow, M.P. (1979). Children's causal attributions regarding help-giving. *Child Development, 50,* 203–210.

Smith, E. R., & Miller, F. D. (1978). Limits on perception of cognitive processes: A reply to Nisbett and Wilson. *Psychological Review, 85,* 355–362.

Staub, E. (1978). *Positive social behavior and morality: Vol. 1. Social and personal influences*. New York: Academic.

Staub, E. (1979). *Positive social behavior and morality: Vol. 2. Socialization and development*. New York: Academic.

Sullivan, H. S. (1953). *The interpersonal theory of psychiatry*. New York: Norton.

Tedeschi, J. T. (Ed.). (1981). *Impression management theory and social psychological research*. New York: Academic.

Toner, I. J., Moore, L. P., & Emmons, B. A. (1980). The effect of being labeled on subsequent self-control in children. *Child Development, 51,* 618–621.

von Cranach, M., Kalbermatten, U., Indermuhle, K., & Gugler, B. (1982). *Goal-directed action*. London: Academic.

White, P. (1980). Limitations on verbal reports of internal events: A refutation of Nisbett and White and of Bem. *Psychological Review, 87,* 105–112.

Whiting, B. B., & Whiting, J. W. M. (1975). *Children of six cultures: A psychocultural analysis*. Cambridge, MA: Harvard University Press.

Youniss, J. (1980). *Parents and peers in social development: A Sullivan-Piaget perspective*. Chicago: University of Chicago Press

Youniss, J., & Volpe, J. (1978). A relational analysis of children's friendships. In W. Damon (Ed.), *New directions for child development: Social cognition*. San Francisco: Jossey-Bass.

PART 2

Developmental–Constructivist Perspectives

CHAPTER 3

Childhood Social Regulation of Intimacy and Autonomy: A Developmental-Constructionist Perspective

ROBERT L. SELMAN AND KEITH OWEN YEATES

Pychology is replete with natural divisions: between the helping professions and the academic sciences; between the ideographic focus on case study and the nomothetic focus on robust samples; between the subjective, interpretive, and hermeneutic analyses of mind and meanings and the objective, causal, and positivistic analysis of observable behavior. Developmental psychology, although an approach rather than an object of study, has had rifts of its own, and this chapter is therefore broadly intended to bridge these chasms in the study of social development.

The primary aim of this chapter is to draw on each of these split knowledge bases to suggest how a better integration might occur, with respect to understanding the growth of interpersonal skills during childhood and early adolescence. On the one hand, we will attempt to demonstrate how intensive investigations of the history of specific interpersonal relationships in a therapeutic setting can generate conceptions of important normative developmental themes. On the other hand, we will attempt to illustrate how a developmental research perspective on children's close peer relationships can contribute to facilitating social development in clinical contexts.

In our efforts to accomplish these complementary goals, we make use of observations gleaned from a specific clinical intervention we call pair therapy. This type of therapy brings two children with demonstrated deficits in peer relationships together regularly (usually one hour per week) under the guidance of an adult mediator whose goal is to facilitate the growth of the children's interpersonal skills.

The pair therapy context might be seen as an unusual one in which to seek accurate notions of normative developmental processes in social behavior, both because of the apparent artificiality of having an adult present to mediate peer interactions and because of the restricted sampling of atypical children involved in "pairs." In our opinion, however, these concerns underestimate the role of adults in shaping the natural histories of peer relationships among children and misjudge the rich explanatory value of studying deviations from typical development for understanding normal growth.

Our method of study, then, which we label the empirical case study approach, will be illustrated through a detailed analysis of the transcript of a portion of one pair therapy session. This analysis reflects our emphasis on intensive longitudinal studies of a limited number of dyads as a complement to the more predominant methods of developmental psychology, which emphasize extensive cross-sectional observations of larger numbers of dyads.

Increasingly, we have come to be aware of the limitations of this traditional approach, at least for capturing the general themes that give meaning to children's social interactions and relationships. Traditional observational approaches, couched in a mechanistic paradigm that reflects a positivistic philosophy of science, slice ongoing streams of behavior into arbitrarily small temporal segments and label those segments according to coding schemes that implicitly assume that similar-looking behaviors have similar functions and meaning. Such an approach runs the risk of effectively decontextualizing the behavior, removing it from its natural ground—namely, the ongoing historical relationship within which it occurs—and thereby leaving it open to serious misinterpretation, misinterpretation that is largely untestable.

Our observations, on the other hand, have led us to the hypothesis that the developmental meanings and functions of specific social actions are intimately tied to the history and context of social relationships. In other words, the developmental significance and personal meaning of social actions are socially constructed phenomena, and not purely objective ones. Thus the understanding of important and recurrent themes in the development of children's peer relationships depends on intensive, longitudinal observations of specific, ongoing relationships that are interpreted from both a constructionist and a contextualist perspective.

In particular, we call attention in this chapter to two complementary themes that appear to play a meaningful role in structuring or organizing the history of social relationships: (1) the need for autonomy and agency (self-other differentiation); and (2) the need for intimacy and sharing (self-other integration). We will illustrate how our reflections about these themes are currently guiding our observations of peer interactions and leading to new ideas and questions about social development, which in turn are being applied in a therapeutic setting to facilitate children's interpersonal growth.

THEORETICAL AND METHODOLOGICAL ORIENTATION

Philosophical and Methodological Underpinnings

Since its inception as a scientific discipline, psychology has been guided by a predominantly positivistic and empiricist philosophy of science. Psychological researchers have thought of themselves as moving through a series of steps—hypothesis generation, data collection, and hypothesis testing—toward a closer approximation to or representation of factual truth. From this perspective, facts are facts, waiting only to be discovered; methodology, in turn, is merely a means to this end, so that methodological choices determine only whether the facts are discovered, not the nature of the facts themselves.

In recent years, a new philosophy of science has begun to emerge, one that emphasizes that science involves the competition of various paradigms or worldviews, which themselves are constructed in part as a direct function of their methodologies. From this perspective, there are not simply facts as such, but theories that are constructed from observations and interpretations, which are themselves part and parcel of the particular methods by which they are made. This constructionist perspective on science explicitly acknowledges the contributions that can be made by various paradigms or worldviews. It allows that different metaphors can provide different stories about the world and different methods for constructing those stories. From this view, science becomes not a search for the "truth," but instead a search for better stories about the world— better in terms of comprehensiveness, consistency, coherence, and other related criteria (see Gergen, 1985; Latour & Woolger, 1979; Packer, 1985; Scarr, 1985).

Psychological researchers, by and large, continue to work within a positivistic framework, relying largely on implicit mechanistic and formistic metaphors to guide their efforts. The study of social development in particular reflects these emphases, with a general reliance on coding arbitrarily small pieces of behavior, relating these pieces to one another statistically across large samples, and perhaps comparing the relationships at different ages. The search continues to be for statistically reliable and predictable associations, preferably those that reflect general developmental progressions.

In our own work, we have found that such approaches do not fully capture important themes in social development, themes that appear to give meaning to peer interactions for both participants and observers. Not surprisingly, we believe that the reason for this omission rests in the methods of the predominant approach, which effectively decontextualize children's behavior, omitting the natural context and its attendant explanatory power. We believe that the themes that give meaning to and structure peer interactions are constructed out of the histories of particular relationships as constrained by the developmental levels of their participants, and therefore that only analyses that explicitly acknowledge this constitutive process will be able to identify and refine our understanding of those themes (see Youniss, Chapter 8, Packer, Chapter 5, this volume, for more extensive discussions of this claim).

We have begun to explore the utility of a more contextual metaphor as a guide to investigation. This metaphor allows us to acknowledge that broad-ranging knowledge of the history of a specific relationship is an important definer of meaning in that relationship and to emphasize a more hermeneutic or interpretive approach to the study of interpersonal phenomena. The metaphor and its attendant methods have helped us achieve a richer understanding of significant themes that structure peer interaction, two of which are the focus of this chapter.

Social Regulation as a Topic of Research

Critical opportunities for social and emotional development occur for children of all ages in contexts where they interact with each other under the watchful eye of their elders. As children mature from early and middle childhood into early adolescence, expectations— theirs as well as ours—are that in safe and reasonable contexts they can begin to manage their own social affairs and can more directly regulate their own social behavior. Nevertheless, their elders are usually there—if not close by, then somewhere in the background. And in a healthy, safe, and predictable social environment, what Winnicott (1964) called the facilitating or holding environment, adults serve best when available to mediate conflict among peers, give advice, share wisdom, and generally speaking, enable peers in interaction with one another to grow toward both a sense of autonomy within themselves and a sense of connectedness between themselves. The two classes of social regulation on which we focus are those that give rise to these complementary themes of autonomy and intimacy.

Children and adolescents with interpersonal problems can be thought of as having difficulties in the way they regulate social behavior, both within themselves and in interactions with their peers. Some are overly aggressive and dominant, others far too submissive and withdrawn. In any case, they are unable to manage social actions in ways that are considered developmentally balanced, and consequently require more frequent adult help than expected to structure their interactions.

One form of psychosocial intervention for such children, therefore, would be the introduction of structured adult guidance intended to help them become more adroit at the processes of social regulation typical of the developmental level of children their own age. Serendipitously, such a form of clinical activity also would be a rich context for research. Just as clinical research on pathological processes such as brain damage or aphasia has shed light on normal aspects of neurological or language development, so too can research in the context of treatment of children or youth with interpersonal problems become a means for understanding normative developmental processes of social regulation of behavior.

In our own work, we have attempted to combine exactly these dual clinical and research activities. More specifically, the major focus of our current program of clinical research is on the processes by which two troubled youngsters attempt to regulate their own and each other's behavior socially in a controlled physical and social environment that is established, monitored, and to some extent manipulated by an adult mediator. Two socially maladroit youngsters, who share problems but also interests and abilities, interact with one another regularly under the supportive guidance of this adult. We call this combined therapeutic–research approach pair therapy.

Pair Therapy as a Context for Research

Pair therapy takes place as part of the general clinical treatment provided at the Manville School of the Judge Baker Children's Center in Boston. Students are referred to this day treatment school primarily because they have great difficulties in their social relationships, a particular difficulty being that they do not seem to know how to make or maintain friendships with peers. They tend to be very withdrawn and socially isolated, to be very overtly intrusive and aggressive, or to exhibit both styles of interaction in rapid or unpredictable alternation. Before coming to our school, few if any of these children have had the important early social experience of positive peer relationships, as exemplified in Sullivan's (1953) description of chumship.

From our perspective, therefore, the enterprise of pair therapy has two complementary professional functions—one therapeutic and the other research (Lyman & Selman, 1985; Selman & Demorest, 1984). The therapeutic function is to involve these youngsters in a long term treatment process, sometimes lasting 3 years or more, where they can experience dyadic interactions in a context made safe, secure, and continuous by the presence of an interpersonally oriented adult therapist trained on the one hand to structure activities, encourage decision making, and mediate conflict, and on the other hand to facilitate, or at least enable, mutuality of experiences.[1] The research function of pair therapy, in turn, is to study the processes of intense dyadic interactions among peers, longitudinally, consistently, and in great depth, in a setting that allows for the observation of how a dyadic relationship develops its distinctive history, and of how that history provides a context within which significant and recurrent developmental processes and themes emerge and are used by the children in structuring and regulating their interactions.[2]

Over the 5 years that this joint clinical and research project has functioned 26 pairs have met for 1 or more years, 6 have met for 2 years and 3 have met for 3 years. Sessions of pair therapy have been videotaped regularly, both to improve clinical techniques and to provide a corpus of reviewable material for systematic research analysis. The primary research question that guides our analysis is how best to study developmental aspects of social regulatory processes. This question has a closely related counterpart in a question often asked by clinicians: What does pair therapy do differently than individual or group therapy? We respond to this question not as a challenge to prove pair therapy's comparative efficacy, but instead in terms of the first—as an impetus to study what it is about a long-term dyadic relationship that is uniquely of value to children and adolescents, both those who have interpersonal difficulties and those who do not.

Our hypothesis, based upon extant psychological theories, particularly those of Sullivan (1953), Mead (1934), Piaget (1983), and Werner (1957); recent research (ours and others'); and continuing discussions within our joint clinical research team of our observations, is that an adult-guided therapeutic dyad with its own history of shared activities is an ideal form of interaction for the joint development of the two essential classes of social regulatory processes that have emerged from our analyses as playing recurrent and significant roles in organizing peer interaction, for both normal and socially disturbed children.

The first broad class of dyadic social regulation we have identified functions to establish a developing sense of autonomy in each of the individuals in an interaction. This class includes actions such as the assertion of the self's wants, the development of a repertoire of strategies for the resolution of interpersonal conflict, and the identification of the psychological boundaries between self and other. Particularly important here are the experiences in social interaction that foster the individual's ability to identify affective boundaries. That is, children must develop the capacity to demarcate the locus and cause of those feelings that are generated and experienced by the self rather than making undifferentiated assignment, attribution, or projection of the cause and locus of the self's feelings—often the negative, conflictual, or ambivalent ones—in whole or in part to another person.

The second major class of dyadic social regulation functions in a complementary way. These social regulations bring the self and the significant other into closer alignment with one another. They are based upon the self's needs for types of interpersonal interactions that generate a sense of shared experience with another person perceived as similar or sympathetic to the self. These social regulations lead not to a sense of individual identity or uniqueness or separateness, but to a sense of commonality and relatedness and consensual validation. With respect to the boundaries of affective experience, here the function of social regulation is not to isolate or lock the locus and cause of feelings into one person, but to have the dyad share feelings in a way that brings the partners closer together and makes both self and other significant to one another.

From our perspective, both classes of social regulation are essential to interpersonal growth. In providing brief descriptions of the two classes, however, we run the risk of putting the theoretical cart before the methodological horse. The identification of these classes as significant organizers of peer interaction has occurred only via a program of observational research; moreover, our understanding of the functions of these two classes of social regulation, both independently and in relation to one another, continues to be constructed out of this research. In fact, our particular methods have played no small part in determining this continuing refinement. We cannot continue our exposition regarding organizing themes in social interaction, therefore, without a description of our research methods and preliminary findings.

Contextual Research on the Development of Social Regulation

We call our method an empirical case study approach. Unlike typical "observational" methods, this approach involves the continual extension and refinement of ideas about peer interaction and the identification of themes of social regulation via three interrelated steps: the tentative identification of significant themes of interaction via macroanalyses of the histories of specific dyads; the search for various manifestations of these themes in specific, ongoing interactions via microanalyses of the sessions of those dyads; and the identification of similar and different expressions of those themes via both micro- and macroanalyses of other dyads.

To illustrate the first step in this research approach, let us consider one case very briefly. This is the case of Norman and Andrew, both 9 years old, whose tenure as a pair so far is 1 year. We can describe the year as traversing three phases. During the first phase, lasting about 6 weeks, there appeared to be much social comparison and competition—testing of each other's skills, sizing each other up, and vying for dominance and control—a process involving much interpersonal negotiation. Andrew, with his better athletic ability and greater persistence, appeared to gain ascendancy through battles over such issues as which activity would be chosen, who would go first, and who cheated or not.

In the second phase, the children focused less on concerns about direct power and control and more on each member's asking the other, "What can you do for me?" During this phase, the boys appeared to form an alliance of sorts and, we think, significantly, selected games they could play against the therapist. For instance, they consistently chose a tag game called "cat and rat," wherein the therapist is designated as the cat, and the two boys as the rats. The goal is for each rat to cross from one goal line to the other without being tagged by the cat, who roams the field in between. In this second phase, the twosome played the game at the same time and place but in an individualistic mode, each boy working independently to avoid the cat and reach the opposite safety zone.

After about 8 weeks of playing the game, becoming skilled in its implementation and understanding the range of its strategies, the two boys spontaneously began to play in a more collaborative fashion, working in unison to insure they both evaded the cat: by not crossing the goal line until each was sure the other would also make it across; by shouting warnings to each other whenever one appeared in danger; by saying things such as "I'm sure glad you saved me from getting caught"; or by making symbolic gestures such as handshakes and other nonverbal expressions of togetherness. Perhaps most significant of all, following the defeat of the cat by the rats, both boys made victory signs to each other accompanied by deep and unself-conscious laughter. The shared laughter, the shared feeling of joy and success through collaboration, stand out as powerful illustrations of the type of social regulation that these two boys have had such a difficult time finding and experiencing elsewhere. The emergence of this form of expression marked the transition to the third phase of the year.

In this macroanalysis of the history of this dyad, a three-chapter story emerges that reflects the two boys' history, which they themselves worked into a shared experience. The story suggests several observations about possible themes that help to regulate or organize this experience and to build a more coherent account of their relationship. Two themes, namely the establishment of autonomy and agency and the establishment of intimacy and sharing, are particularly prominent, and they attain ascendancy in a specific order, with autonomy themes preceding intimacy themes. Moreover, intimacy themes emerge only after the establishment of a common ground or home base activity, a shared activity in which both participants understand the rules and are at least minimally competent. Finally, the hallmark of intimacy seems to be a commingling of affect, and we might wonder if this is not the most important—and therapeutic—component in making a dyad such a powerful and magnetic force, not only for these children, but for all people.

Yet these ideas are tentative. A better story might be told after further consideration, one that reflects different themes or refines our understanding of these. It is just such further consideration that constitutes the second step in our research process. We use observations about the processes of social regulation that we glean from histories of specific dyads to focus more detailed analyses of the ongoing interactions that occur in specific sessions involving those dyads.

Consider, for example, the identification of autonomy–agency and intimacy–sharing as significant organizing themes in the interaction of Norman and Andrew. These themes, identified via a macroanalysis of the histories of these two boys and other pairs, have led to closer microanalyses of the specific sessions that constitute those histories. Interestingly, our research program has followed a progression similar to that tentatively identified in the story of Andrew and Norman. That is, we have given most of our consideration to the regulation processes that concern the growth of autonomy and only recently have turned our attention to those perhaps more subtle processes that facilitate the growth of intimacy.

With respect to the regulatory processes that facilitate the growth of autonomy functions, our focus has been on interpersonal negotiation strategies, the ways individuals deal with others in the context of negotiation (Selman,

Level 3

Third Person/Mutual

Strategies that use both self- and
shared reflection to change collaboratively
both self's and other's wishes
in pursuit of mutual goals

Strategies that con- sciously use psycholo- gical influence to change other's mind	Level 2 Self-Reflective– Reciprocal	Strategies that consciously use psychological compliance to value self's wishes only secondarily to other's
Strategies that use willful one-way orders to control other for self's way	Level 1 Differentiated– Subjective	Strategies that use "will-less" submission to wishes of other
Strategies that use unreflective, impul- sive force to get self's goal	Level 0 Undifferentiated– Egocentric	Strategies that use unreflective, impulsive withdrawal or obedience to protect self

Interpersonal Negotiation Strategies in the Other-Transforming Orientation	Social Perspective Coordination Competence	Interpersonal Negotiation Strategies in the Self-Transforming Orientation

Figure 3.1 Developmental model.

1981). We have constructed a developmental model concerned with how individuals coordinate in their conduct their understanding of another's thoughts,
feelings, and motives in conjunction with their own as they attempt to balance
inner and interpersonal disequilibrium. Individual interpersonal negotiation
strategies are defined by four component factors operating in the conduct of the
moment: the construal of the self's and other's perspectives; the primary purpose; the means of affective control; and the action–oriention. The first three
factors (self–other construal, primary purpose, and affective control) work
together to determine a strategy's developmental level, whereas the fourth
factor identifies a strategy's interpersonal style (i.e., self-transforming or other-
transforming orientation). Research has focused on the reliability of methods
for assessing strategies for interpersonal negotiation (Selman, Schorin, Stone, &
Phelps, 1983) and its application to the analyses of the pair therapy process
(Selman & Demorest, 1984).

TABLE 3.1. Some Prototypical Interpersonal Strategies Coded at Developmental Levels 0 to 3 in Each Orientation

Other-Transforming Orientation	Self-Transforming Orientation
	Level 0
A. Forcefully blots out other's expressed wish	A. Takes impulsive flight
B. Unprovoked impulsive grabbing	B. Uses automatic affective withdrawal
C. Absolute repulsion of other	C. Responds with robotlike obedience
	Level 1
A. Uses one-way threats to achieve self's goals	A. Makes weak initiatives with ready withdrawal
B. Makes threats of force	B. Acts victimized
C. Criticizes other's skills as a rationale for self's activity	C. Appeals to source of perceived power from a position of helplessness
	Level 2
A. Uses "friendly" persuasion	A. Asserts self's feelings and thoughts as valuable but secondary
B. Seeks allies for support of self's ideas	B. Follows but offers input into other's lead
C. Goal seeking through impressing others with self's talents, knowledge, etc.	C. Uses self's feelings of inadequacies as a tool for interpersonal negotiation
	Level 3
A. Anticipates and integrates possible feelings of others about self's negotiation	
B. Balances focus on relations with focus on self's concrete goal	

Figure 3.1 gives a visual picture of this model. Strategies for interpersonal negotiation are simultaneously classified at one of four developmental levels (egocentric–impulsive, one-way–unilateral, reciprocal–reflective, or mutual–collaborative) and at one of two interpersonal action orientations (self-transforming or other transforming).[2] Thus to yield to another's wishes by impulsively fleeing the pair therapy room in the face of a potential disagreement would be considered an egocentric–impulsive strategy of a self-transforming type, whereas to suggest the taking of turns but to allow the other person always to go first, while also self-transforming, would be scored at the higher or more differentiated reciprocal–reflective level. Table 3.1 describes some specific strategies classified in each level and orientation. (These sample strategies, incidentally, were identified via the third step in our research process—further micro- and macroanalyses of other dyads, both normative and clinical.)

Our normative research thus far suggests that by preadolescence most children are *able* to utilize strategies that can be classified as reciprocal (level 2), and that by early adolescence most can use, or at least articulate, collaborative (level 3) strategies, at least some of the time (Selman, Beardslee, Schultz, Krupa, & Podorefsky, 1986). However, context appears to play an important part in which level is *implemented*. Even when an individual has the *competence* (i.e., the higher-level strategies in repertoire), there are many other factors that need to be considered in actual *performance* (i.e., the strategy used), not the least of which is the specific relationship within which it occurs.

Much of our initial clinical research has focused on the strategies youngsters in our pairs use to assert power, negotiate decisions, or deal with differences of opinion. We look at how consistently individual children use strategies at a given level or orientation, and how much movement or development to higher levels occurs over the course of the pair therapy sessions.

Other research, concerned with the relative importance of themes of autonomy versus those of intimacy, tends to confirm our notion, as seen with Andrew and Norman, that social regulations in which power and autonomy are negotiated often occupy the center stage during the initial phases of pair therapy, but that, once some balance of power is established in the pair, if the treatment process is going well, these processes become less a dominant "figure" and more an ever present, still powerful but less obvious "ground" upon which social regulations designed to bring the partners closer together become more prominent. Further analyses are being undertaken to determine the ubiquity of this progression.

What, then, of the quality of this second class of regulatory processes, those that emphasize shared experiences? We have spent less time building an account of these processes, and not surprisingly, we intend this chapter to illustrate our growing interest in but uncertainty about them by reporting a detailed microanalysis of a particular pair therapy session. Before proceeding to this analysis, which demonstrates the second step in our research process, we should share the tentative ideas generated via initial macroanalyses of many dyads.

When considering the social regulation of autonomy, even though the negotiation strategies of one person relate to those taken by the other, these actions are still of the individual and are identified and classified as such.[3] In contrast, the phenomenon of shared experience has a different quality. Our observations indicate that it is truly a dyadic phenomenon, not simply because two persons have to interact for it to exist (as is true with negotiation), but because the phenomenon is located in the transaction between partners. This means that shared experience is not only two persons being in the same place at the same time participating in the same events, nor is it one person telling the other person something about the self, nor does it seem to be only a process of imitation, where one peer starts something and the other mimics or picks up on it, although all these aspects may be important. Rather, shared experience appears to be a transactive phenomenon in which each partner makes a contribution to a process that enlarges the experience for both. Because both partners participate, each gains some validation of the self as an experiencer. A critical factor in this process is length of time the pair spends together. Shared experiences are not simply immediate reactions; they are based on a common history that allows each partner to reveal, in a variety of ways, some characteristics of the self to the other, to lower defensive postures, and to be vulnerable.

In studying this phenomenon, one needs to look at both what is shared and how, that is, its content and form; in turn, one also needs to ask what it is that identifies a process that in essence is uniquely constructed by the pair. Based upon a review of our videotapes across pairs, we have identified several types of shared experiences that appear regularly in our corpus of data, shown in

Table 3.2. We have ordered these forms of shared experience in a possible developmental hierarchy that begins with types that are largely unreflective and focused on the physical self, objects, and bodily functions, and moves to those that are more reflective and represent a sharing of inner psychological experiences as well as a concern for persons in relationships. Shared experiences are identified in those instances in which the pair verbally or behaviorally express the *feeling,* even more than the clear *understanding,* that "we are in this together." Although positive forms of shared experience involve cognitive, affective, and behavioral components in varying distributions, the powerful constant across all those forms seems to be the sharing of similar affects. Although these may include a range of feelings, from sadness to anger and indignation, we suspect from many observations, such as those of Andrew and Norman, that the most powerful expression of feeling that provides for cohesive social regulation centers around and takes the form of *laughter.*

These ideas are still tentative, though. We need to refine them, particularly if we are to extend our account to include the relations of the two classes of social regulation to one another. In the following section, therefore, we take up a transcript of a particular pair therapy session, and using its history as a contextual background, proceed to exemplify the type of microanalysis that we believe will help us construct a better account of the processes of shared experiences.

THE SHARED EXPERIENCES OF BRENDA AND DONNA: A MICROANALYSIS OF SESSION 47

An Overview and Initial Questions

As of this writing, the pair described in this section is entering its third year. The two girls have met for over 60 sessions, with all sessions videotaped, most by the same observer. In keeping with the historical emphasis of this presentation, we will first provide a very brief glimpse into each girl's history. Next, we will provide an overview, also relatively brief, of the 2-year history of the pair. Then we focus on the details of one session, number 47, that took place three-quarters through the second year. In this analysis, we will be using both verbatim transcriptions and observers' inferences about affective and motivational aspects of each partner's behavior. The session chosen is by no means a typical or representative one. Compared to many other sessions, it is uncommonly rich in instances of shared experience, even as it is somewhat uncharacteristically lacking in explicit instances of interpersonal negotiation.

In sharing this case with the reader, we ask that the following three questions pertinent to the understanding of developmental processes of social regulation be kept in mind. First, to what degree does the observer attach the same meaning to behavior when the session is viewed as an isolated event as compared to when it is placed in a broader context and lengthier historical setting? Second, what can be said of the relation between autonomy and connectedness processes as gleaned from this session alone as compared to the session in its

TABLE 3.2. Forms of Shared Experience Observed in Pair Therapy Classified by Developmental Level (N-26 pairs, ages 8 to 16)

Level 0:

Shared expression of impulsive and motoric activity. Forms of joint expression of bodily functions or bodily movements shared in time. The activity is often of an unreflective nature, and is poorly self-regulated, so that the experience often becomes contagious, and occasionally an outside force is needed to control the affect expressed by each member of the pair.

Example 1: Jessica (age 12) and Heather (age 11) are playing a board game together. Jessica burps accidentally. Heather laughs, then forces or makes a burp. This leads to a contagious reciprocal process in which the girls enter into a contest to see who can make the loudest burp. Both girls are laughing and giggling to the point of lack of control. Eventually, the process is regulated by an outside force, the therapist, who after a brief period of time asks the girls to end the contest and resume the game.

Example 2: Korey (age 9) and David (age 9) are observed to participate in a form of reciprocal sensorimotor imitation that does not appear to the observer to be conscious or to have a clear-cut leader. If Korey reaches for a drink, David does the same; if David bounces a ball or crosses his leg, Korey does the same.

Level 1:

Shared expression of power, control, or dominance. This form of shared experience is often seen in fantasy play or role-play situations. Critical to this form is the turn-taking component; domination of the play by one party is not considered a shared experience.

Example: Kenny (age 9) and Peter (age 8) enter into a shared fantasy play in which each, in turn, has the "space age" control and power to manipulate the will and behavior of the other. They take turns using imaginary "laser guns" as controller and controlled, but Kenny usually determines when the switch occurs. Thus the experience within the fantasy play is shared, but outside the frame of fantasy, Kenny controls.

Level 2:

Shared expression of reciprocity and cooperation (agreement). The focus of sharing here is on acting together or reflecting together, but each for the sake of his or her individual security or satisfaction (you and me for me rather than we for us). This can take the form of agreed upon competition, collusion against or gossip about a third party, or reciprocal self-reflection but without either making a strong connection between the self's reflections and the other's.

Example 1: Norman (age 8) and Andrew (age 8) act in coordination to play a game to defeat a third party, the therapist. Each in turn comes to the aid of the other, and on winning each emphatically congratulates the other, but each (as he reports it) experiences the interaction as "I won and I helped you too."

Example 2: Donna (age 12) and Alice (age 13) share complaints about how nosy and intrusive each feels a classmate is. They share their dislike of this third party, but neither appears to incorporate what the other is saying or feeling.

Level 3:

Shared expression of collaboration, with mutuality toward each other, either expressed directly or implied. In this form of shared experience, each includes the other party as a part of a mutually experienced "we." The sharing takes the form of reflecting upon similar feelings or gaining a consensual validation through communication. The other party is as significant to the self's concerns as is the self.

Example 1: Donna (age 14) and Brenda (age 14) express to each other their concerns about graduating from one level of the school to the next. They agree that knowing that the other will be there next year will make it a better and more secure experience for both of them.

Example 2: Jessica (age 12) and Heather (age 11) share their sadness that a favorite counselor is going. They discuss why they will miss the counselor, listening to each other's reasons and feelings sympathetically and empathically.

Example 3: Norman (age 9) and Andrew (age 9) act in ways similar to those described in Example 1 at level 2. However, now when they cross the finish line, they laugh together, asserting, "*We* won, *we* beat the cat."

full temporal context? And finally, what function do inferences about affective expression play in understanding processes of social regulation? That is, how is information about affect useful in portraying the means by which one distances the self from the other or brings the self and the other closer together?

In addition to these process-oriented developmental concerns, there are several clinical questions worthy of consideration. One concern is how the present atmosphere of the pair, including the overall safety and security of the environment, allows the pair to reconstruct the past and look to the future. Put in other terms, how does the corrective interpersonal experience of the present situation help each to reconstruct and better understand the past, as well as to cope better with the uncertainties of the future? A second focus of attention from the clinical perspective concerns the function in pair therapy of what we call the home base activity. How does this activity, jointly selected by the pair, become a medium by which the pair regularly practices the processes of social regulation? How does it act as a catalyst to the processes of social development? And finally, we ask a set of questions regarding the function of the adult in the facilitation of the peer relationship as well as the growth of each child. Why does the adult play the natural foil for the peers? What does it mean for the pair to have peer cultural knowledge, as yet unobtained by the adult? Why is a pair member more likely to do certain kinds of social-emotional work for a peer than for the adult?

These combined developmental and clinical concerns, and the multitude of questions they generate, reflect the way in which we approach our data, within the constraints imposed by our current ideas about interpersonal development. Rather than aiming to test specific hypotheses, we are interested in beginning to locate coherent answers to our questions, knowing all the while that in this process still more questions will arise.

A Brief Review of Individual Histories

Brenda is a slender black adolescent who is the youngest child of seven in a large single-parent family. She has a history of severe and chronic skin and asthmatic problems beginning at age 5 months. She was first referred for outpatient psychological services at age 11 for poor behavior and below-average schoolwork. At age 12, she was hospitalized for treatment of depression and suicidal ideation. Soon thereafter, she was referred to our school.

Optimally, Brenda is bubbly, interested, verbal, and meticulous about her appearance. She can be articulate, artistic, and charming. When troubled, however, either she has severe temper outbursts that can require physical restraint, or she withdraws, regressing into thumb sucking or infantile sleeping positions. In addition to these fluctuations between aggressive acting out and depression, and the affective lability they reflect, she presents with features of a histrionic personality. She seeks and draws attention to herself, and portrays herself as a victim of circumstance, particularly at home. She is prone to exaggeration and often overreacts with flamboyant and rather inappropriate behavior.

Brenda's interpersonal relations are marked by her desire and longing for attachments with both adults and peers, despite fear of, and sensitivity in response to, loss and rejection. In individual therapy, Brenda complains of not receiving enough attention from her mother, and of having to compete with her sisters for more. In school, she often becomes quickly enraged at perceived rejections by teachers of whom she is especially fond, and shows little ability to contain these feelings. With classmates, she can be very outgoing, but she clearly likes to be the center of attention, and often relates in a moody and hypersensitive fashion. Consequently, her peer relations also tend to be stormy and unpredictable. Because of her apparent motivation for better peer relations, Brenda was referred for pair therapy by her treatment team during the first month she was enrolled at the Manville School.

Donna, Brenda's pair partner, is an attractive white early adolescent who is the middle of three sisters, also in a single-parent family. Donna was identified quite early as overly dependent, socially isolated, and possibly developmentally delayed. During the third grade, she became school phobic and developed a stiff walk and hunched-over posture. As these behaviors worsened and were joined by signs of severe withdrawal such as not walking and elective mutism, she entered a day treatment program at a local inpatient child psychiatric unit. Donna was referred to the Manville School from this facility, and enrolled a year before Brenda.

Initially, Donna presented as a quiet, sad, withdrawn, and extremely over-compliant child who was rather disengaged. She showed a tremendous need for order and control, managing anxiety by asking about schedules, activities, and rules. She was constricted, lacking in spontaneity, and unresponsive to com-ments or inquiries about her thoughts and feelings.

Interpersonally, Donna was shy and timid. Although just barely able to acknowledge some desire to be special to, or best liked by, teachers, counselors, and peers, she was very ambivalent about attachments, and tended to with-draw in response to anticipated separations. In individual therapy, because of her difficulty using direct verbal interaction, drawings were often used as a medium of communication. Without such an alternative in other contexts, social interaction was quite limited.

By the end of her first year, Donna showed signs of increased comfort in the school setting. She seemed willing to invest energy in new activities, and expressed a strong desire to become more involved with other children. After a year of only individual therapy, her treatment team referred her for pair therapy. They asked that she be placed with another girl of the same age and with similar interests, but one who was not so constricted, passive, and with-drawn. In the fall of the next school year, Brenda arrived, and the two girls were classmates. They were approached about possibly meeting together for pair therapy, and reacted enthusiastically, committing themselves to at least 1 year with each other as pair partners. At the time pair therapy began, both girls were 13 years old.

Pair Therapy for Donna and Brenda: A Review of the First 2 Years

Donna and Brenda were selected as pair partners because they had both similarities and some differences. Both were early adolescent girls with female siblings currently living in single-parent households (each had limited contact with her father). Both girls seemed highly needy of maternal affection and support and had some difficulties in separations from their mothers. Both girls had experienced hospitalizations for their emotional difficulties, and both had done schoolwork that was below their capabilities, due largely to the social and emotional difficulties each experienced. But the girls also demonstrated striking psychological differences in the ways they related to others and dealt with their own negative or frightening feelings. Donna was almost universally withdrawn and constricted (although her mother reported that Donna occasionally got very angry and aggressive toward her), whereas Brenda, when distressed, displayed a kind of stormy rage that made her face look contorted and her body movements rigid and stiff. Brenda liked to be in the limelight whereas Donna found the smallest beam of attention much too bright. This combination of similarity in problems, experiences, and interests and differences in styles of coping (interpersonal orientation) has been found to be an optimal set of factors for matching individuals in pair therapy.

Year 1

From the start, Brenda assumed much of the control of pair therapy. In fact, about halfway through the year, she actually became exasperated during the activity choice period and said, "It's time for Donna to choose." At first Donna seemed somewhat uneasy playing games, apparently due to her lack of experience. At these times Brenda carefully instructed Donna and waived certain rules, saying, "It's only a game." As Donna became more proficient at games and more concerned with winning them, though, as well as more animated and verbal, Brenda started to "miscount," to claim the games were boring, and to show considerable ambivalence toward attending pair therapy sessions.

On subsequent occasions during that year, when Donna voiced any suggestions or requests, Brenda either hesitated to agree or actively ignored her. In addition to controlling the activities during the first year's sessions, Brenda tended to control the mood of the sessions. Sometimes she would enter announcing, "I'm in a funny mood; I want to laugh." Occasionally, however, she would come into sessions feeling dejected, deprecate the activities available, and refuse to be easily cajoled out of her dark moods.

Donna's interactional style during the first year was to defer immediately to Brenda and then to comply passively with Brenda's suggestions. Donna was able to show displeasure in nonverbal ways, by facial grimaces, silent withdrawal, or tone of voice, as she acquiesced to suggestions. She was more able to voice her disagreements or unwillingness with the adult therapist than with Brenda. During the first year, however, Donna also appeared to identify somewhat with Brenda. Brenda dressed in a fashionable and carefully coordinated way, and Donna began to dress in more feminine attire, particularly stylish blouses. Donna also seemed to identify with Brenda's difficulty exerting emotional control. She vicariously experienced some release of her own suppressed anger and frustration by witnessing Brenda's emotional outbursts. And yet Donna was quite unwilling during the first year to discuss or express her emotions, or to ask questions stemming from curiosity or lack of comprehension. Both of these postures were captured in a motto Donna repeated several times over the sessions: When faced with someone or something unpleasant or confusing, Donna would say, "I just bear with it."

Year 2

During the second year, Brenda became an increasingly invested and cooperative pair partner. She adapted better to her partner's more inhibited manner, not especially expecting a vigorous response from Donna, but alternating between taking advantage, pushing greater decisiveness on Donna, and, as Donna became more assertive, moving over psychologically and making some room for Donna on center stage. Brenda clearly still felt very much in control, though. Even during the times she pressed Donna to make all the decisions during the hour, Brenda showed her own satisfaction in this role. During this second year, Brenda also shared more material from her life at home. For example, she clearly enjoyed both Donna's and the therapist's positive response to her enthusiastic retelling of movies or shows.

Brenda did not display temper tantrums in pair therapy the second year but did display, although with decreasing frequency, the stormy rage mentioned earlier. Early in this second year, the anger was precipitated mostly by events outside the pair hour, but in the middle months, it frequently was precipitated by events within the hour, most often losing in a game. Brenda herself was very aware of these rageful feelings and their impact on others. Once, when annoyed by something one of the school kitchen staff had done, she said she would make "my face" and scare the staff person to death.

The primary activity choice (i.e., the home base activity) during the second year was a competitive board game called Sorry. In contrast to the first year, Brenda's responses to the games encompassed a fairly easy adaptation to Donna's increasing assertiveness. Although she made no attempt to hide her displeasure when she fell behind in the game, she no longer let the disappointment and frustration become anger targeted at her game partner, spoiling the game. The shared activity appeared to have acquired a positive value for her that she was not readily willing to sacrifice; also, when Donna won, she did so with such a sweet matter-of-factness that Brenda was left with little choice but to accept her lot with as much grace as she could muster.

Donna's manner also changed subtly over the second year, shifting from communication largely through a shrug of the shoulder or one- or two-word phrase to an articulate paragraph, uttered with genuine affect, or a several minute conversation characterized by mutual give and take. It is notable that these last conversations occurred mostly when the topic was one about which they shared the same feelings. In the absence of this naturally derived support, Donna did not attain such a level of openness. During this second year, Donna more consistently made her wishes clear, at first mainly in stating what she did not want, but later in letting the therapist and her partner know what she did want.

During the many games of Sorry that the girls chose to play during pairs, then, Donna evidenced during the second year a notable tendency to come into her own. At first she made many concessions to Brenda's greater assertiveness.

As she became more confident, she stopped joining in with Brenda and only expressing aggressiveness toward the therapist in the game, and began to play the game in a way guided more fully by her own interest, directing competitive strategies not only at the "benign" therapist but also at the potentially rageful Brenda.

Session 47: An In-Depth Inspection

The session we have selected for in-depth analysis is by no means a typical one. It is unusual in both the amount and the quality of the conversation relative to earlier sessions. It is marked by a relatively greater amount of openness, as well as a good deal of expression of feelings. The sessions subsequent to it were not consistently marked by the same high level of intensity. Our research suggests that such openness is never easy to maintain continually, nor for that matter is it always facilitative of further growth and development.

Viewed in a historical context that includes both 46 previous and 13 subsequent sessions, however, the nature of this session is not particularly surprising; in many ways it was to be expected. For the 10 sessions prior to this one, the two girls had slowly begun to explore each others' lives, and cautiously to reveal to each other some significant features of their own. This exploration developed subsidiary to a serious three-way competition, with the therapist very much included, in playing Sorry. Thus the session examined here was a high water mark in a generally rising stream of quality of interaction over the course of 2 years.

Our method of presentation is to describe four selected "scenes" from the session. Each scene contains instances of what we believe are shared experiences. The scenes are presented verbatim with an accompanying elaboration of the possible intentions and emotions related to participants' verbal and nonverbal behavior. We also present some comments that put the observed interaction into the historical context of the pair.

The transcript of the interaction is set up so that the reader can visually experience the flow of both the verbal and the nonverbal aspects of the session. The verbalizations are transcribed word for word as much as possible; descriptions of the nonverbal and paralinguistic aspects of the session are often based upon inferences and/or interpretations of the videotapes made by the observer(s).

Scene 1

Donna — Description and Interpretation of Nonverbal Behavior	Donna — Verbal Behavior	Therapist	Brenda — Description and Interpretation of Nonverbal Behavior	Brenda — Verbal Behavior
	Who's going first? I'll go first.	Who wants what color?	Brenda appears quiet and moody.	Red
		(Also trying to determine Brenda's mood.) To Brenda: did you stack that deck? To Brenda: How was your weekend?	Brenda is doing well in game.	Doesn't matter to me.
Donna appears tense.			No response.	
		I know. I wouldn't expect it any other way. To Donna: How was your weekend?	Brenda sends Therapist back in game.	Fine. "Sorry" (This refers to the board game.)
	Good. I saw a movie called *Desperately Seeking Susan.* The one with Madonna in it.		Said glumly.	To Donna: It's your move.
	Yeah	*Desperately Seeking Susan?*	Brenda's mood seems to change.	Oh! Was it good?
Donna is leaning her head on her hand so that she is facing therapist *and blocking out Brenda.*	*Yeah we were gonna see Friday the Thirteenth but my sister wouldn't watch it.*			

| Donna | | Therapist | Brenda | |
Description and Interpretation of Nonverbal Behavior	Verbal Behavior		Description and Interpretation of Nonverbal Behavior	Verbal Behavior
	My little sister.	Which sister?		
	No.	Not the one who scratched you? (This is a reference to a scratch Donna had on her neck the week before. She was in a fight with her older sister.) To Brenda: As far as I'm concerned, Donna has two sisters, the one who scratched her and the one who didn't (This refers to a previous discussion.) To Donna: So she wouldn't see it?		
Donna laughs.	No, plus it was rated "R" so we couldn't get in			We got in. Yeah, 'cause like my size, your size—there was a lot of people in there.
Donna sits upright.	What theater did you go to?			Sack 57 (downtown).

Donna looks down at game board and doesn't make eye contact with therapist or Brenda.	I saw 1 and 2. (Porky's). Porky's 1 or Porky's 2? Oh, it was about Madonna—(forgets what movie was about, laughs). Oh, God. Her boyfriend, right, he puts all these ads in, right, like Desperately Seeking Susan. And so she goes around and she goes with men and then she kills them. I don't know, but—she takes pictures and all this stuff—it's really good though.	To Brenda: So you could get in even though it was "R" and you (Donna) couldn't?		I'm going to see Porky's next Thursday. What was the movie about? No, the one with Madonna in it.
			Laughs with Donna.	Oh, oh.
			Now is looking at Donna and listening, becoming more receptive, responsive.	Oh my God!
Donna begins to make eye contact with Brenda after Brenda becomes more responsive and animated about movie.	Then she has a look-alike.	It's really good? It didn't sound so good to me.		Is it my turn?
		She has a look-alike?		You mean that other lady that does it with her? I like her. She's a good actress.

Donna — Description and Interpretation of Nonverbal Behavior	Donna — Verbal Behavior	Therapist	Brenda — Description and Interpretation of Nonverbal Behavior	Brenda — Verbal Behavior
		Who's this character? This main character who does these horrendous things?		
	Madonna.	Who is Madonna?		
	She's a singer.			
Donna exchanges glance with Brenda. Donna uses this a few times during the session to keep a good conversation going or to distract from an uncomfortable moment ("What else?")	Let me think, what else happened? (re: movie)	(5 minutes of playing Sorry.)	Brenda exchanges glance with Donna.	
	Where did it take place? In a cabin?	What did they scream at? I mean, for instance?	Brenda looks at therapist, then at Donna, and decides to answer Donna's question, which she hasn't heard because	There was a lot of good stuff in *Friday the Thirteenth*, though. I mean, people got up and screamed, "Can you believe that!" People got up and screamed in the theatre.

(Look at Donna): Huh?

It took place in the woods.

I know. It started out with Timmy, the main guy who grew up to be ??? He was coming out of a dream, and this crazy man, he's digging at Jason's grave. You know that part where they come rushing on with a knife—he stabbed him here and then he stabbed him here. It was disgusting. Then Jason got up and went to the little boy's face and said, "Timmy." It was pouring rain and then Jason went and stabbed him and then he woke up out of his dream sweating to death. That's how it started off.

therapist and Donna spoke simultaneously.

Very animated.

Did it take place in a cabin or in the woods or something?

Like all of them.

Oh, God.

Laughs.

Listens attentively— makes and maintains eye contact.

Laughs.

65

In the first scene, Donna, Brenda, and the therapist enter the room together. Without speaking, the therapist sets up the game, an action predicated on the decision made at the end of the previous session to continue to play Sorry today. Donna smiles at Brenda shyly and sits down in her usual seat. Taking her seat, a stone-faced Brenda reaches for the cards and begins to shuffle them. In this opening scene, the therapist asks both members of the pair, "Who wants what color?" and, as is typical, Brenda assertively chooses first. As is also typical, Brenda is moody. This inference is based upon past observation of such factors as to whom she directs her eyes and her posture, her tone of voice, and her body language.

What is less typical in the first scene, but becoming comparatively more so, is Donna's (relative) assertiveness. Her statement "Who's going first?" is posed as an open question, not as a request that Brenda make the choice; moreover, when Brenda abdicates the need to have first choice in the matter, Donna asserts her desire to go first. Although this is not a major feat for most early adolescents, for Donna this act of initiation represents an enormous achievement. In the earliest pair sessions, she literally could not make choices. Commonly she would self-consciously say, "I don't care." To say easily "I'll go first" symbolizes an investment of the self; and for Donna, it is taking a chance. While not an interpersonal negotiation per se, this assertive action and others like it in the session (Donna will later interrupt Brenda for the first time in 2 years) have both clinical and theoretical import. Clinically, they suggest that Donna is developing a stronger sense of self. Theoretically, they suggest that she may be ready to use other-transforming strategies in her interactions with Brenda, and that Brenda may be able to accept these strategies as part of their relationship.

Interestingly, although the case for this interaction being a true context for interpersonal negotiation is a weak one, we can still do an armchair analysis of its level. In its give and take and inquiry into Brenda's desires, Donna's behavior smacks of level 2, whereas her earlier compliant, passive responses were usually strictly level 0 or 1.

This interaction, simple enough on the surface, also illustrates at least two of the issues we mentioned earlier. First, the value of the corrective interpersonal experience—with its safety, consistency, and opportunity to generate in practice more positive and effective ways of interacting—is clear. Second, it seems equally clear that an observer's sense of the meaning of the girls' remarks and reactions is immeasurably clearer when they are placed in a broader historical context.

This first scene is also an example of the social regulation of shared experience. As is often the case, it is initiated by a therapist's question to each girl, here "How was your weekend?" Donna goes beyond her usual "fine" or "okay" and reveals that she saw a movie over the weekend. She is particularly responsive to Brenda's inquiry, "What was the movie about?" and responds, "Oh, it was about Madonna." Then a long pause ensues, in which Donna looks down at the game board, avoiding eye contact with either the therapist or Brenda. It appears that she is struggling to organize her thoughts. We should not underestimate how hard it is for Donna to pursue an impulse to express herself, to organize herself to tell a story, even one about a movie. Yet she appears to be highly motivated, because it is Brenda who asks her about the movie. If the adult therapist were to make this request, Donna might not be willing to try so hard, but for Brenda, she uses all her resources to pull herself together to tell the story, perhaps also inspired by the example of Brenda's many animated and "successful" stories in previous sessions.

Here we see, in the effort Donna puts into explaining the movie to Brenda (and we also see it as Brenda begins to pull out of her bad mood in response to Donna), how shared peer cultural knowledge, not possessed by the adult, motivates the girls and helps to establish a further sense of connectedness between them. This occurs several times in this scene (when Brenda chooses to answer Donna's question over the therapist's, when each girl gives a lengthy movie description spurred by her partner's responsiveness), but perhaps most notably when they share incredulity at their therapist's ignorance of Madonna.

The discussion about Madonna provides not only the beginning of a shared experience between the two girls, but in relation to the adult, an exclusive experience. The peers exchange amused, disbelieving glances when the therapist asks, "Who's Madonna?" This clearly puts the girls together and the therapist on the outside. Madonna fills the girls' world but does not even touch the adult's. These incidents also illustrate both how the sharing of positive affect between pair partners builds greater connectedness and how "practice" in positive interactions can grow and build to provide a corrective interpersonal experience. And finally, it is clear that these meanings emerge for us as observers only as we see these examples in a broader context.

At the end of this initial conversation, there is a relatively long break in conversation and the girls reenter the psychological safety of the home base activity, the playing of the game Sorry. After about 5 minutes of playing Sorry, though, Donna, again somewhat uncharacteristically, reinitiates the conversation. She picks up on the theme of movies by saying, somewhat enigmatically, "Let me think, what else happened?" This comment appears to refer to the movie Donna saw and was reporting earlier. However, this comment can also be understood to function as a deflecting move on Donna's part, related to her discomfort with the attention being focused on her the moment before, during the Sorry game. Just before her statement "Let me think, what else happened?" the therapist had declined to make an optional move because "... If I go there, I'll knock Donna, so I won't do that." After glancing at Brenda to see how she was reacting to this, Donna reinitiated the conversation, perhaps in part out of feelings of embarrassment about being "protected."

The "gap" in the conversation, during which all three players returned to intent playing of Sorry, brings us to the importance of the home base activity. For Brenda and Donna over a year was spent in establishing and using a home base activity, here the game of Sorry. During these relatively extended early periods in pair therapy, we have found that some children settle on a home base activity fairly quickly and that some take much longer. In any case, although we stress that this selection is a natural evolution, this activity seems to have to fit certain criteria. First, it must be an activity in which both children can achieve some competence. Second, both children must enjoy it.

Third, they must not quickly tire of it. Once these criteria are met, the simple doing of the habitual activity (for habitual activity is all it really is at this juncture) becomes the focus for the pair. Negotiations of various sorts are played out over time, but as this happens, the activity also begins to take on, or epitomize, the aspects that cause us to call it a home base activity. It becomes safe, predictable, dependable, and known. And finally it becomes a jumping-off place, a foundation, a springboard to higher levels of interaction—potentially conflictual negotiations, sharing that could engender great vulnerability, and greater affective connectedness. And a key feature is that the home base activity, as it embodies the effective pair therapy atmosphere, provides a secure place to which to return after these ventures into chancier territory. Brenda and Donna's forty-seventh session dramatically demonstrates this function, as further scenes will show.

To return to scene 1, although Brenda understands to some degree that Donna intends to continue describing "her" movie, she decides to take her turn to complete the sharing of experience by narrating the movie she saw during the weekend. Perhaps because she is more loquacious and less self-conscious than Donna, Brenda presents a much more extensive narrative. (Only about one fourth of it is reproduced here.) In addition, Donna's reactions suggest that she greatly enjoys listening to her partner's animated discourse and appears to be happy to pass the conversational ball to her. Donna listens quite attentively, asking many more cogent questions than usual. Throughout this interaction, the therapist functions as a facilitator, asking questions both for her own information and to help keep the conversation flowing. Whereas the girls, if left alone, might ask each other factual, objective questions about the movies seen, the therapist is more likely to ask subjective questions about reactions and feelings. For instance, she inquires as to whether the scary movies made it difficult for Donna or Brenda to sleep at night. In response, each girl lends the other mutual support and reassurance, Donna saying, "All you think of is that it's make believe. People make it up," and Brenda quickly following, "Right, it's just make believe. It's all an act," and adding, "but it *was* scary." And then all three participants laugh. This ties the shared experience together in an affective net meaningful to all members of the triad. This, we believe, is another example of the building of a corrective interpersonal experience and of the powerful positive potential of affective sharing.

This incident also illustrates some of the key aspects of the pair therapist's role. Not only is she the safe adult foil against whom the children can act out of their private adolescent world, but also she is a guide, model, and facilitator who has helped to establish the safety and consistency of pair therapy. She also can participate in a shared experience as a trusted adult partner in a positive relationship, an important corrective interpersonal experience for these children.

This shared experience also appears to facilitate thinking back for Donna—using her memory and beginning to reexamine her own past experience. Old movies are a safe place to begin this activity. In a segment of the transcript not recorded here, she actively continues the conversation, asking Brenda, "It was a long time ago, but did you ever see *One Dark Night?*" In the course of her involvement, she is so enthusiastic that for the moment, she forgets about her painful self-consciousness and, for the first time in 2 years, actually cuts Brenda off and continues on to tell her story.

Brenda, although she entered the session in a dark mood, has now, as noted, completely changed her mood and is telling with great enthusiasm and dramatic ability her experience watching *Friday the 13th*. Note how the easy way she talks continues to serve as a role model for Donna. This is one reason we like to match individuals whose orientations toward interpersonal interaction are complementary. Brenda clearly benefits from this complementarity as well. If she, thriving on having center stage, felt she really had to compete with someone for it, she might find it much harder to come out of her powerful and controlling darker moods.

The videotape also reveals how vulnerable Donna still is. Just after our transcript of this scene ends, Donna is trying very hard to follow Brenda's narrative. She loses track of it and asks a question that reveals to Brenda that she has lost it. She seems to be very embarrassed, even ashamed. To repair this breach, the girls retreat once again to the safety of the home base activity. Only later do they build another shared experience, as seen in scene 2.

Scene 2

Donna		Therapist	Brenda	
Description and Interpretation of Nonverbal Behavior	Verbal Behavior		Description and Interpretation of Nonverbal Behavior	Verbal Behavior
		You spend a lot of time watching movies on TV, huh?		
	Not really, Sometimes, 'cause they are usually on late.			Yeah, everything comes on late.
		What time do you go to bed?		
	I go to bed at 7:00 'cause I get up really early, I get up at—so I only get to watch movies on weekends. So I go to bed at 7:00 'cause I have to wake up so early.			
		Why do you have to wake up so early? No, you go to bed because you have to wake up so early.		
	Go to bed?			
		What time does your bus come?		
	'Cause my bus leaves—Needham.			She lives all the way out in Needham.

Same time we get up too. We get up around 5:40, set the alarm.

It comes at 20 past 7:00 I get up at around 5:00

So you have 2½ hours.

Really?

But it takes you over 2 hours to get ready?

Not really. Sometimes though.

Sometimes. I mean, I wouldn't like that, having to go to bed so early and having to get up so early.

I wake my sister up and my other sister too.

The one who scratches you and the one who doesn't?

Yeah.

So you wake up first, wake them up and everybody gets ready and, do you leave first before they do?

Donna laughs a little nervously. Fidgets; she doesn't seem to like to have this kind of attention focused on her (about her sister scratching her).

71

Donna		Therapist	Brenda	
Description and Interpretation of Nonverbal Behavior	Verbal Behavior		Description and Interpretation of Nonverbal Behavior	Verbal Behavior
	No, my older sister leaves first, and then I leave and then my little sister leaves.	To Brenda: And do you leave before all the rest?		I leave last. My mother do. All the girls—you know what I mean.
Donna is looking down. Isn't listening.		To Brenda: So why do you get up so early?		Because, see sometimes, right, since I am the last one that leave, if I don't iron my clothes at night, then I iron them in the morning, right? If I iron them at night, what I do is my sister will wake me up and I help her do her clothes while she's taking her bath or whatever she's doing,

Interrupts therapist
to become part of
conversation.

Oh, you fall asleep?

and then after that,
after both of them
finish what they're
doing, I go in the
bathroom and take my
shower, and then fall
asleep 'til it's time.
I fall asleep until
I have to get up.

Oh that's good.
you get all ready
for school and then
you take a little nap.

Then your bus comes.
What—

What time does
your bus come?

I take it until 7:00.

To Donna: Yours
comes before that?

Yeah.

Exactly 8:00 o'clock
every morning. Exactly
8:00 o'clock every morning

It's a nuisance to
live very far away.

They changed the bus
schedule now. They
changed some of the kids
on Somerville buses.
Talinda is on my
bus. Talinda is on
my bus. Pamela is
on my bus. Ughh!!

73

Donna		Therapist	Brenda	
Description and Interpretation of Nonverbal Behavior	Verbal Behavior		Description and Interpretation of Nonverbal Behavior	Verbal Behavior
		You don't like Pamela?		
Listens attentively.			Imitating how Pamela talks and walks, in a mocking and entertaining way.	She's doofy. She don't know how—I mean, you can act doofy sometimes, but she overdo it, you know? Sometimes—like this morning, she comes back, "Hi Brenda, how you doin'." She came like this. She walk like a penguin!. Like this, "Hi, Bren, how you doin'?" "Fine." Then sometimes she tells some dirty jokes, and she said, "guess what my boyfriend, he gave me some candy." And I said, "No," and she said, "He was stuffing it down my throat." I mean, come on, how stupid!
	She's probably making up a lot of it.			I, know. Like one time in—remember I

told you at the
Jewish camp I went
to?
Camp????
Well, she went there,
right, and this man,
right, and he was white, right,
and he was built,
and he have a nice
complexion and every-
thing, right. His
name was Matt,
And she said that
Matt wanted to marry
her. I mean, she,
overdo it. She kept
saying—she say, "Brenda,
oh guess what, you
won't believe it.
Matt want to marry
me." I said, "Really."
I said, "Really."
I said, "I really
believe that," and
then she said, "I
am not lying, I
am not lying, I
am serious."

Very sarcastic
tone.

Yeah.

Oh, my God.

Donna		Therapist	Brenda	
Description and Interpretation of Nonverbal Behavior	Verbal Behavior		Description and Interpretation of Nonverbal Behavior	Verbal Behavior
	Oh, my God!!			Then she said Matt marry her and they got a divorce. I say, "You overdoing it now." I say, "You over-doing it!" And she say, you know, last year, she paid 50 dollars just to go out with Lance. You know Lance?
			Says something derogatory about Lance, inaudible.	Well, she paid 50 dollars just to go out with him, and he used her for 1 day, just for 1 day.
		When was this?		
Donna has really been into the story about Pamela, very interested, shocked?		Last year. Where did she get 50 dollars?	Enjoying her own story telling.	Last year.
				She stole it from her mother, and her mother caught her. And she sold reefer just to get money just to go out with Lance. 50 dollars.

What's so wonderful about Lance?

That's what I want to know! I said, "What's so great about him?" I said, "He got the looks, but that don't mean he got a nice personality."

I don't know Lance at all. He doesn't have a nice personality?

I don't know. I never went out with him, so I'm not sure. Oh, lordy lordy lordy lordy

Lapse in conversation.

Well, I tell you, you got to watch out for guys like Lance who will take 50 dollars.

What?

He got dukes in his pants, ughhh!!!! He got dukes in his pants!!

What's that?

Laughs.

Doodoo.

Donna throws back her head and really laughs.

Poor Lance. If he knew what was being said about him.

It's true. He do. Some kid say he

Donna		Therapist	Brenda	
Description and Interpretation of Nonverbal Behavior	Verbal Behavior		Description and Interpretation of Nonverbal Behavior	Verbal Behavior
				do it once in a while. He don't hardly do it as much as he used to. Some people say—he has a learning problem because he ????? That's a shame!! Ughhhh! That's disgusting!! That's gooey and all that.
		It doesn't make it sound very pleasant.		
		Let's hope he doesn't sit on it too long, let's hope sometimes he goes and cleans it up.		That's disgusting! He be sittin' on it, eeewwww!!
Donna enjoys the story about Lance and laughs, not nervously but really laughs, especially when Brenda screams.		You know there are some kids who can't control it.		Somebody come up to him and say he got doodoo?????

Is that Bobby who smelled or something?		He stink! He was the one that stink. Bobby come in the classroom, he stink! Oh man!!
		Yes. I mean he stink! Talinda say—as soon as he came over to her, she was sitting down doing her work, and she went like this— "Oh, something stink in here. Oh my God!!"
	Was he in your class?	
	One of the Division kids? (A Division kid is a student attending the school who is hospitalized on a psychosomatic division or ward of Children's Hospital.)	Imitates Talinda looking up, sniffing around.
	You know, you would think a Division kid— someone could send him to get cleaned up	

Donna is referring to a student in her and Brenda's class. Donna ignores this comment by the therapist. Talking about the kids in their class is a topic they are together on, and Donna wants to be a part of it.

Donna throws her head back, laughing.

Donna — Description and Interpretation of Nonverbal Behavior	Donna — Verbal Behavior	Therapist	Brenda — Description and Interpretation of Nonverbal Behavior	Brenda — Verbal Behavior
Donna shakes her head in agreement	Yeah, everytime you laugh in front of her she goes, "Tsk, tsk, you know that isn't nice."	and cleaned off.		Please!! Miss M. just say, "Well, you know you can't help it, it's just people, it's just normal." (Miss M. is the two girls' teacher.)
Joins Brenda in trying to explain how it is to an adult who doesn't understand.			Also trying to explain.	I know, I mean sometimes you know she want to laugh, and she'll laugh like if you keep doing it, it gonna make her laugh. Keep on doing it, you know what I'm saying?
	No.	Well, laugh or no laugh, you still could send the kid up to change and clean up.	Mocking the teacher	But the thing is, she don't want to "hurt his feelings."
	I know.			You know, I mean,

I can understand that.
You can't go up
to a kid and say,
"Could you go upstairs
and get washed up,
please?" I mean—
No, you can't.

No.

Today we were playing
basketball, right, so me
and Bobby had a
basketball and we both
fell and rolled over,
and I went, "Eww! Eww!"
like this, right, and
Dwight say, "Time
out, time out!" and

Brenda laughs.

Oh, yes you can.

You don't say it in
front of the whole
class. You take him
out and you—

Because if you don't
do it, then the kids
are gonna do what
Talinda does.

Donna laughs.

Donna (and Brenda)
ignores therapist's comment.
Donna initiates the
telling of a funny
scene where "you'd go up
to the kid and go
kksshhhh" (spray with a
Lysol can or something).
Donna is now very
loose, having a great
time, cracking up.

Donna		Therapist	Brenda	
Description and Interpretation of Nonverbal Behavior	Verbal Behavior		Description and Interpretation of Nonverbal Behavior	Verbal Behavior
Donna laughs really hard at this story. Enjoys Brenda's antics. The more animated Brenda gets, the more Donna laughs.			Laughs while she is telling the story.	I said, "Oh my God!" It was so funny, I went like this and like it was gonna like it was gonna kill me, and I kept laughing. I had to stop for a little while, I am serious. I was like—oh my God, what is going on?! And I was laughing and Dwight—I had to talk to Dwight 'cause Bobby felt bad, and and everything. And I was going, "Ewww? Time out, time out!" like that. Oh, my God!!
		So Bobby felt bad. I mean, that's why I think it's better to send Bobby up very quietly than let it happen that the other kids are gonna make fun of him.	Gets up and walks around in a circle —the more Donna laughs, the more animated Brenda becomes.	

The second scene of the session involves shared experience via a discussion of the school day and the people who populate it. Once again, the scene begins with an initial question asked by the therapist, a question regarding their nighttime and morning routines, designed to encourage each girl to talk a little more about herself. The therapist plays an interesting role here. She attempts to facilitate a more in-depth examination of morning routines and transitions from home to school, but when each girl seems satisfied with simple reporting and or private reflection, and Brenda moves the conversation to a discussion of transportation and their fellow students, the therapist flexibly shifts her own focus as well, asking questions that enable the girls to expand on this theme, which interests both of them.

Brenda astutely analyzes classmates' strengths and weaknesses. She then discusses the trials and tribulations of being in a school where some students soil during the school day. This section of the scene shifts to a monologue by Brenda, but it is about a topic of great interest to Donna. At first Donna is a very willing and appreciative audience, laughing from deep inside, as Brenda relates her feelings and opinions about the students who soil. This is a public discussion of an experience that is not discussed in its immediate context, the classroom.

Finally, Donna takes her turn in the comic routine, relating the funny fantasy scene, going up to Bobby and spraying him with Lysol. When the therapist remarks to the pair that it is in the best interest of the student who has soiled if the teacher has him or her leave the class, both girls join together in consensual disagreement. Apparently each girl believes that such actions would be too humiliating. Although the therapist persists in stating her point of view, the pair quickly colludes to avoid serious acknowledgment of her perspective. Neither girl really wants to consider it, so they join together in continuing to make fun of the situation. In fact, as mentioned above, Donna, in a very uncharacteristic way, uses humor to express some of her own feelings. She is very loose and uninhibited, which is quite rare for her. And the more Donna laughs, the more Brenda performs. It is a releasing shared experience for them both.

This particular incident is a good example of what Harry Stack Sullivan perceived to be the strengths and weaknesses of consensual validation. On the one hand, each girl's beliefs and attitudes about the situation are confirmed and validated by the other's. Each believes that it would be too humiliating to a student for a teacher to confront or even acknowledge a student's problem with soiling. Even worse would be to direct that student to change his or her clothes during class. But this consensus of two lacks verification; that is, a method by which the validity of the shared belief can be externally tested out rather than internally accepted. The therapist's attempt to educate, founded upon her own years of experience with this type of problem, is disregarded by the girls.

Eventually, the conversation dwindles, and again via therapist intervention, a third scene begins.

Scene 3

Donna — Description and Interpretation of Nonverbal Behavior	Donna — Verbal Behavior	Therapist	Brenda — Description and Interpretation of Nonverbal Behavior	Brenda — Verbal Behavior
		Well, I have learned more about some of the kids in Manville School than I knew before		
		Sure have. What are you doing?	(Implicit: "And we told you.") Brenda is picking something off her soda can.	Sure have.
		Oh, I thought you were scraping on the metal, you'd really do a job on your hands. . . . And before this year you had Miss A., Right?		I'm peeling off the tag that you left on.
	I had her 2 years. She was nice.			
	In Miss M's class you don't learn nothing.	I don't believe that.	Excited.	Oh she was the best!
				I love her.
			Agreeing with Donna.	Oh I know, I swear on my bible! You know how much ???? I have learned this past year?

84

The girls band to-
gether again to educate
the therapist about how
it really is.

What did you learn?

Division—everything. And
you know something? Every-
time we're ready to
review, I forget what
to do.

This year?

I am not lying.
Yes, everything she ever
done or like reading
or something or like
???, you know, like
from before, she reviews
it back to me like
in a couple months
and I forget.

It's so embarrassing
telling people that you
don't even know fractions.

You want to go on
to fractions? Is that
what you want to do?

Right! That's what I'm
saying.

Now Donna is imitating
the teacher's voice.

Yeah, she says, "Oh,
maybe you'll be in
fractions next year."

What are you in now,
decimals? And do you
you know decimals?

I know

Yeah, really good.

Well, why don't you ask?

I did.

Donna   Therapist   Brenda

Donna		Therapist	Brenda	
Description and Interpretation of Nonverbal Behavior	Verbal Behavior		Description and Interpretation of Nonverbal Behavior	Verbal Behavior
	I did. She had this "little talk" with me.			Yeah, I hate when she does that, gives a "little talk," ?????.
Donna and Brenda have both put their cups together with a can in between. Donna uses hers to emphasize a point.	When I go back to public school, right, I will, have to stay back 2 years, because of my work. I'll be in sixth grade, because I was suppose to be in seventh grade this year and next year I'll be in eighth.	But you know once you learn decimals, you can transfer them to fractions really easily. But the thing is you got to really know decimals.	Being supportive of Donna.	Yeah.
		To Donna: Right. When you first came here, had you been in public school and came directly here?		Yup. It's true.

Yeah
I went on over to
this other place and
they didn't have any
schooling, and so I
was there for 2 years.

Same with me.

I see, so you missed
out. I see.

It was like—how
many years? I was
there for 2 years,
then I came over
here for 2 years, this
is my third year.

So when you came
here you had 2 years
to catch up? Okay,
now I understand.

But we had a tutor
there.

When I was in
public school. right—

Did you come from
public school?

Yeah. See I was in
public school but because
of my allergies I used
to get sick so I
quit school almost for
a whole year and I
had to have a tutor.

Did you come
directly—

So you missed a year
or 2.

Donna		Therapist	Brenda	
Description and Interpretation of Nonverbal Behavior	Verbal Behavior		Description and Interpretation of Nonverbal Behavior	Verbal Behavior
	Yeah, I had a tutor too.			The tutor came to my house and gave me work and after that I went back to school and I had a problem with my behavior, and I had a fight with one of my teachers and I actually— she pushed me on the ground and I bit her on the foot. I was really mad.
Donna laughs at "I bit her on the foot." She is resting her chin on the cup so as to be more at a level of eye contact with Brenda.			Everytime Brenda mentions the foot-biting incident, Donna laughs, so she keeps repeating the "I bit her on the foot."	I was really mad. I had to do something to get her back so I bit her on the foot.
Donna laughs again at "I bit her on the foot," this time looking at the therapist, for reaction?				Then I had to see my doctor and get a shot for it and I went back to school, then I came here because

of that—No, I had therapy then, right, and after I bit my teacher on the foot.	
	Brenda laughs.
	Donna laughs.
Oh, you had therapy over it, right? Yeah, I know, it's funny when you look back on it; It wasn't funny then.	Brenda pauses as if to give Donna her cue to laugh, Donna laughs and then Brenda laughs with her.
	Donna laughs.
After I bit my teacher on the foot, right— (pause) they gave me therapy. (ianudible sentence) I never knew nothing about this place. And I was real mad and I was angry at myself so I wanted to go for suicide, right, so they put me up here on a unit, then they sent, me back to public school for 1 more year. Then after that, they told me I was coming to this school.	Brenda talks about her suicidal feelings very matter-of-factly, like a story that has been told a lot.

The previous discussion of the life of the classroom allows the therapist to make an inquiry that switches the focus for this third scene. She gently asks each girl how long she has been enrolled at the Manville School. In the ensuing discussion, Donna reveals, "It's so embarrassing telling people that you don't even know fractions." At first, she suggests that the fault or blame for her difficulty lies with the teacher or school, and Brenda is quick to echo this complaint. However, the therapist uses this as an opening for the gentle exploration of possible other bases for their educational difficulties. She asks Donna a crucial question, to which she already knows the answer (but Donna does not know she knows): "When you first came here, had you been in public school and came directly here?" Spontaneously, Donna says, "Yeah," and Brenda says, "Same with me." However, after a critical pause, Donna makes a very brave and significant qualification: "I went over to this other place and they didn't have any schooling, and so I was there for 2 years." This "other place," as Donna calls it, was a day psychiatric hospital. Brenda, encouraged by this, reveals that she also had been out of school for an extended period of time and begins to tell her story. Once again, the two girls take turns sharing these painful experiences, Donna first, in a slow and tentative way, and then Brenda, in a more humorous mode that provides a kind of transparent cover for the originally painful events.

This scene is a short one, taking only a few minutes, but it is nevertheless quite revealing. Notably, the girls provide each other great support. For instance, each time Brenda tells the story of how she bit her public school teacher on the foot, it elicits from Donna an "it happens" kind of laughter. After the fourth iteration, she tells the most serious part: "I was really mad and I was angry at myself so I wanted to go for suicide." The story is told in a matter-of-fact way, divorced from its original affect, but nevertheless, the story is told; and the past is demystified through its association with a happier and healthier present. A child with a painful, disturbing, and defeating history such as Donna's or Brenda's finds it extremely difficult to discuss it realistically and openly. The cumulative effects of the pair therapy atmosphere, the developing relationship between the girls, and their relationshp with the therapist combine to enable them to confront and share these stressful, and usually hidden, experiences.

Scene 4

Donna — Description and Interpretation of Nonverbal Behavior	Donna — Verbal Behavior	Therapist	Brenda — Description and Interpretation of Nonverbal Behavior	Brenda — Verbal Behavior
	You know, this Wednesday I have to go like for an interview or something—not like an interview, but I have to get some testing done Wednesday, so I won't be coming.		Expressing disappointment.	Oh, my God!
Donna laughs, acknowledging Brenda's disappointment.	Yeah. Like you know, have you ever done testing where you look at these pictures and you say what they are about and things, and so I'm gonna talk to them about public school next year.			Yeah.
			Mocking, imitating Mr. B.	When I first came here to get an interview over the summer with Mr. B.—it was so stupid!! As soon as I came into his office, he just sitting there like that.

91

Donna		Therapist	Brenda	
Description and Interpretation of Nonverbal Behavior	Verbal Behavior		Description and Interpretation of Nonverbal Behavior	Verbal Behavior
Crosses her legs, looks at Brenda with intent eyes, mocking teachers, etc. Donna's second attempt at imitating.	I know. They all do that, you know, they all do this— All of them		Recognizing the posture of the teachers.	Yeah.
				And they look dead in your face. What am I supposed to say? He took me around the school for a while— He asked me if I liked it. I said, "It's all right." Then he took me to the office and he went—
			Imitates Mr. B., gets up and pulls up her pants, sits down and rests her chin in her hand, looks at Donna.	You know, and like that, you know, and I sat down and I said—then he asked me a couple of questions, and he like mmhmmm, mmhmmm . . . .
Dona laughs, enjoys it.		Yeah.		Then you know, he just kept going like that and what else am

92

			I supposed to say? He just looked dead in my face after I finished my sentence, he's like—"So what is your problem?" You know, stuff like that, I'm like, what are you talkin' about?
			I know about upper school next year.
			Jason is down there, Lance is down there.
			Brenda talks directly to Donna throughout this exchange.
		Why?	
	I hope I'm not here next year in upper school.		
	I don't like the upper school.		
	He (Jason?) likes me and I hate him. (If he ever comes near me) I swear I'm gonna punch that boy right in the face.		
		Who are you gonna punch in the face? to Brenda: Who did she say?	
		I'm not worried, I'm just curious who you are gonna punch in the face.	
	Don't worry.		
	Nobody, forget it.		
During this verbal exchange Donna talks directly to Brenda.			
Emphasizing with her can and cups.			
Donna looks at Brenda; there is mutual understanding that neither will tell who she said.			

	Donna	Therapist	Brenda	
Description and Interpretation of Nonverbal Behavior	Verbal Behavior	Verbal Behavior	Description and Interpretation of Nonverbal Behavior	Verbal Behavior
Donna is confortable asserting her opinions.	I don't like him.			
		Oh, all right.		?? is gonna be there.
				Danny is gonna be there. Lance is gonna be there. Tony is gonna leave, praise God almighty he is gonna leave.
		You don't know who is gonna be here and who is not gonna be here.		
		Some kids may not be here; they may be moving.		Yessir, they told me already.
		No way. No way.		(inaudible sentence)— 2 years, 2 years, and 1 ???.
			Strongly asserting her point, that she is right.	Yessir!! That's what Mr. B. told me.
		What, at the upper school?		No, he said if you are here for 2 years, then you go right directly to upper school.

		Oh, you are going to the upper school. So you are going to the upper school next year. But you don't know which upper school kids are gonna be there. That's what I'm saying.	Brenda starts whining, groaning and walking around. Therapist thinks she is imitating someone.	Nobody.
		Who is that?	Indifferent.	
		I thought it was an upper school kid. Anyway—		
			Brenda starts imitating again. Walking around like Abby.	Here's Abby.
Said to Brenda looking at her, sincerely.	I hope you're in my class, though.			
Again. Donna attempts to keep this going.	Who else—who else— Do an imitation of—	(Therapist joins in thinking of someone for Brenda to imitate.) Upper school . . . Upper school . . .		Pamela!! Pamela!!
		I'm gonna have to stop.		
Donna laughs.				

Donna		Therapist	Brenda	
Description and Interpretation of Nonverbal Behavior	Verbal Behavior		Description and Interpretation of Nonverbal Behavior	Verbal Behavior
	She always does that.		Imitating Pamela.	She (Pamela) always comes up to me like, "Hi, Brenda! What you doing now, Brenda!" "Oh, shut up."
Donna laughs at the "Oh, shut up."			The "Oh, shut up" is what Brenda says or would like to say to Pamela.	
		Doug is in the upper school.		Eewww, he's a faggot! Ugh, ugh, ugh—
		Is there anybody who is—		Everybody's mental in that school.
	I wish I didn't have to go (to the upper school). Probably will	Everybody's mental. I I don't think so.		I know.
				I know, no doubt about it.
Getting ready to leave. To therapist:	You want the cans?	I'll see you next Monday. We'll go on with this conversation it's fascinating	Annoyed.	You always want the stupid cans.

The final shared theme is the future. This is as difficult to talk about as the past. Now that they have both revealed their pasts and their fears, Donna reveals indirectly that she is being considered for a return to public school. This is done at some risk, for it may engender feelings of jealousy or loss in Brenda. The words "You know, this Wednesday I have to go like for an interview" in and of themselves are easy to string together. The power of their meaning is only recognized in the context of the entire relationship, including each girl's history and their history together. This is an empirical and theoretical point as well as a therapeutic one. Therapeutically, the adult facilitates such an expression by allowing it to be revealed in a safe and positive environment. This enables the actors to become stronger at saying difficult things when saying them is the best thing to do. No less important is the theoretical and empirical point that if such statements represent interpersonal development, and if they are to be coded as such, then the observers must understand their significance in the full context in which they occur.

Donna is the first to acknowledge her concern about moving from the middle school to the upper school. Brenda seems to share these concerns, expressing them by critically evaluating the students she knows who are there, not only verbally, but through a mocking kind of imitation and mimicry. Together the partners are able to admit their shared fear of the future. And now that each has the consensual validation that the other is also concerned, they can have a discussion of what it is about the upper school that bothers each of them. At this point, the time runs out, but the therapist throws a rope into the future by saying, "We'll go on with this conversation. It's fascinating." This ensures the continuity that may be lacking in other aspects of the girls' lives.

IMPLICATIONS AND CONCLUSIONS

Researchers who use videotapes as a method for the study of social interaction often attempt to share with colleagues, perhaps at a conference or colloquium, the excitement of what they see in these tapes, only to be struck dumb by the gap existing between the delight they take in the order they see in the material and the confusion or chaos reported by those who are viewing the material for the first time. This shock is particularly acute if the players acting out their roles on the tapes are known at a personal level by the researcher, as is the case if they have been observed on some regular and extended basis over the course of time. For under such conditions, not only does the observer know his or her subjects in a different and more meaningful way, but he or she in all probability will have begun to care about them in a different way as well, as persons as well as subjects. As rich as a single videotaped session may be, it is only a slice of a larger and more coherent reality.

In the past, this level of knowing (and caring) has often been viewed with great suspicion by segments of the established social scientific community, who have seen it either as a likely obstruction on the road to the truth about social interaction processes or, worse still, as a downright unscientific way to do business. Our thesis in this paper is that just the opposite may be the case, at least in the developmental study of social interaction and regulation. Indeed, to study developmental processes of social regulation in interpersonal relationships among children may require committing oneself to be an ongoing participant–observer in the process along with one's subjects.

Descriptive developmental models, like those concerning levels and orientations of interpersonal negotiation strategies and forms of shared experience, provide general heuristics for organizing and comparing one's observations of the general regulatory processes used by all children. But the models themselves emerge and have validity only through a historical involvement with each subject, whether "normal" or "disturbed," which provides the context needed to understand in some depth the particular meaning of complex actions—that is, the functional developmental meaning of the diverse behaviors in each case.

Thus rather than interpreting the difficulty in communicating to colleagues what one sees in a videotape as simply a function of different theoretical frames held up to the data, we are suggesting that, even if the same frames are used, observations informed by historical knowledge of the actors' relationships influence the developmental interpretation and meaning of the observations. Thus we want not to do away with more formalistic structural models of the development of social regulation, but instead to emphasize that these models must be complemented by observations of the histories of particular relationships, with their idiosyncratic and contextualized meaning systems.

Earlier, we suggested that a contextual–interpretive reading of a particular session between Donna and Brenda might address a series of questions about the development of processes of social regulation. One such question concerned the interpretation of behaviors in and out of their historical context, especially those behaviors signaling autonomy on the one hand and intimacy on the other. In the session outlined above, we believe some of the most striking instances of development, both for the two individuals and for this relationship, may be missed if the session is interpreted out of historical context. One example is Donna's brief interruptions of Brenda. Such behavior must be interpreted in the context of how both Donna and Brenda appear to feel and function now as compared to the past. Our interpretation is that these apparently unspectacular interruptions reflect both Donna's growing feeling of self-confidence and a developmental shift in the balance of power in the relationship toward reciprocity and collaboration, with each member of the pair engaged in a higher level of turn taking than before.

Another question we raised about the processes of social regulation concerned the role of emotion. With respect to feelings, the session with Donna and Brenda suggests ways in which affect plays a part not only in the development of self-confidence and autonomy, but also in the process of building connections. We are particularly impressed by the function that deep laughter between the pair plays in shaping how the girls deal with serious issues. One poignant example is the laughter shared over Brenda's retelling of the story of how she ended up at the school because she could not control her feelings ("I bit the teacher in the foot"). The example indicates the catalytic function shared laughter may play in helping time to heal old wounds by putting them in a different light.

We also raised questions regarding clinical issues in the context of pair therapy and how they might inform us about the nature of interpersonal development in troubled children. The session between Donna and Brenda provides a number of ideas, we believe, with respect to the roles of the adult therapist and the peers, the function of the home base activity, and the function of the corrective interpersonal experience.

With respect to the role of the therapist, the session demonstrates how the therapist can serve a number of functions: facilitator of conversation, focuser on the affective aspects of interaction, educator, and even foil for the pair's social anxiety. Interestingly, the session also suggests that one of the powerful aspects of this form of treatment may stem from the youngsters' willingness to try harder when asked to reflect upon and report difficult-to-communicate experiences if the request comes from a peer rather than from an inquisitive, albeit well-meaning, adult. This "trying harder" itself, though, may be facilitated by the adult's quiet presence.

But pair therapy is not just talk. It is very much action and activity, even if the activity is not utilized. In this particular session, the home base activity, the game of Sorry, known so well by the pair, was hardly used once the conversation got going. Yet it, like the adult, was there if needed.

And finally, regarding the corrective interpersonal experience, as noted early in this paper, we see an adult and two peers as having particular potential to become a well-equilibrated system, with the adult ready to mediate, facilitate, regulate, and otherwise keep the system functioning, while always being ready to "let go." Such a system allows the peers to explore the past as well as consider the future in the context of a soothing present.

In the end, then, we continue to be excited by the potential that a contextual–hermeneutic philosophical and methodological approach holds for illuminating and providing a richer account of the development of social regulation processes among children. Although such an approach may not generate the objective indices of observable social behavior with which most of us are comfortable, it does afford a more pronounced sense of grappling with the meanings that actually structure reality for peers across the history of particular relationships over the course of ontogenesis. The grip we have on these latter phenomena may be less firm, but perhaps not because of the unusual methodology but instead because of the more thorough account of the nature of interpersonal growth we are trying to provide.

REFERENCES

Gergen, K.J. (1985). The social constructionist movement in modern psychology. *American Psychologist, 40*, 266–275.

Latour, B., & Woolger, S. (1979). *Laboratory life: The social construction of scientific facts*. Beverly Hills: Sage.

Lyman, D.R., & Selman, R.L. (1985). Peer conflict in pair therapy: Clinical and developmental analyses. In M. Berkowitz, (Ed.), *Peer conflict and psychological growth*. San Francisco: Jossey-Bass.

Mead, G.H. (1934). *Mind, self, and society*. Chicago: University of Chicago Press.

Packer, M.J. (1985). Hermeneutic inquiry in the study of human conduct. *American Psychologist, 40*, 1081–1093.

Piaget, J. (1983). Piaget's theory. In W. Kessen (Ed.), *Handbook of child psychology: Vol. 1. History, theory, and methods*. New York: Wiley.

Scarr, S. (1985). Constructing psychology: Making facts and fables for our times. *American Psychologist, 40*, 499–531.

Selman, R.L. (1981). The development of interpersonal competence: The role of understanding in context. *Developmental Review, 1*, 401–422.

Selman, R.L., Beardslee, W., Schultz, L., Krupa, M., & Podorefsky, D. (1986). Assessing adolescent interpersonal negotiation strategies: Toward an integration of structural and functional models. *Developmental Psychology, 22(4)*, 450–459.

Selman, R.L., & Demorest, A. (1984). Observing troubled children's interpersonal negotiation strategies: Implications of and for a developmental model. *Child Development, 55*, 288–304.

Selman, R.L., Schorin, M.Z., Stone, C., & Phelps, E. (1983). A naturalistic study of children's social understanding. *Developmental Psychology, 19*, 82–102.

Sullivan, H.S. (1953). *The interpersonal theory of psychiatry*. New York: Norton.

Werner, H. (1957). The concept of development from a comparative and organismic point of view. In D.B. Harris (Ed.), *The concept of development: An issue in the study of human behavior*. Minneapolis: University of Minnesota Press.

Winnicott, D.W. (1964). *The child the family, and the outside world*. New York: Penguin.

REFERENCE NOTES

1. Validity of the treatment, at least at this point, is based primarily upon progress in the social regulation processes observed within the sessions, and only secondarily upon the generalizability of these social regulation skills to other, less protected contexts. This reflects our belief that what is healthy about the processes developing within an interaction needs to be understood before beginning to explore the ramifications and expectations of their exportation to other places, with other persons, or later in life. That is, the extension of these processes to different contexts, or to relationships with different histories, can only be addressed after those processes themselves are characterized.

2. We use the terms *self-transforming* and *other-transforming* (rather than *submissive* and *assertive*) not as an idiosyncratic and obfuscating jargon, but to stress two points: First, children who tend to be called submissive do indeed take actions in interpersonal contexts, but their actions change the self to accommodate to the perceived needs or wants of the significant other; second, developmentally speaking, the terms *submissive* and *assertive* only capture part of the developmental progression in each orientation. Very early self-transforming strategies are more than submissive; very early other-transforming strategies are more than simply assertive. In pairing two individuals, we find it most effective to match those with complementary orientations. We should note, however, that, regardless of a child's general orientation

across most other relationships, once in the pair context, one child usually takes on the more dominant or other-transforming role while the other acquires the more submissive or self-transforming position. A goal of the treatment is to help children move developmentally to a higher and more balanced level.

3. This is not to say that classification of interpersonal negotiation strategies can occur without reference to the specific context within which they occur. A specific behavior may reflect a different level of strategy development depending on the mutual thoughts, feelings, and intentions of the participants, which must be inferred on the basis of knowledge about the history of the participants and their relationship. Still, the strategies do seem to be emitted by individuals, unlike shared experiences, which seem to be constituted more at a dyadic level.

CHAPTER 4

School Democracy and Social Interaction

LAWRENCE KOHLBERG AND ANN HIGGINS

Since 1974 we have been experimenting and researching the relations between school democracy and the moral development of adolescents. The moral development variables we have looked at have been moral structural stages, our operationalization of Piaget's autonomous as distinct from heteronomous moral types, the strength of sense of community, and actual moral behavior. Currently we are attempting to create democratic alternative programs of about 100 students and five teachers in two Bronx high schools, one of which has drop-out, arrest, school violence, and theft rates as high as any New York City high school, according to department of education statistics.

The moral stages assessment model is familiar to all. The moral type measure, based on Piaget's theory in The Moral Judgment of the Child, scores our moral dilemma responses in a different way. Each of our dilemmas poses a conflict between acting in accordance with strict obedience to rules and adult or institutional authority, and acting in terms of considerations of fairness, human welfare, or benevolence that may be seen as claims of conscience but that are not supported by institutional rules or authority rules. In addition to the subject's being scored as autonomous, the subject's response must also indicate awareness that his or her choice is prescriptive, hierarchical, universal, and grounded on some idea of reversibility role taking and/or mutual respect. The type assessment and its relation to moral actions have been described elsewhere. (Higgins, Power, & Kohlberg, 1984) Preliminary descriptions of the assessments of strength and stage of collective norms and a valuing of community have been presented in works published elsewhere (Higgins, et al., 1984). The norms include both justice norms against stealing, cheating, violence, and community norms of helping and social and ethnic integration. In Kohlberg (1985) we have summarized results indicating that three of the democratic alternative schools, Cambridge and Brookline in Massachusetts and Scarsdale in New York, scored better on all these measures compared to the regular or traditional companion high schools.

The choice of measures has been dictated not only by several theories of moral development but by several theories of school democracy. The measure of collective norms has been influenced heavily by Durkheim's moral theory, which is of course a socialization theory of the learning or internalization of moral content, as well as by our neo-Piagetian theory of the development of moral stage structures. So too, our theory of democratic practice, the Just Community theory, relies heavily on our own revisions of Durkheim's theory of moral education, a revision that makes it democratic rather than resting on the authority of the teacher as a representative or priest of society. This chapter describes our theoretical work on integrating Durkheim's moral theory and our neo-Piagetian theory in the context of the Just Community approach.

There are basically three views of the origins and development of morality. The first is romantic: From Rousseau's *Emile* to Gesell, this view has stressed that moral development is individual and maturationist. The second is culturological: Morality is the learning of cultural moral norms. The third is interactionist: Morality is a construction emerging from moral interaction of certain universal features of moral equilibrium. One view of this is interpersonal: Morality is what comes out of two persons in a relationship, the view of Piaget. A second is my own, Piagetian at core: Morality is constructed through social interaction, but not necessarily in terms of the interpersonal dyad. In this chapter we shall stress the need to integrate the constructivist view with a view of moral culture as central to moral development, a peculiar blend of symbolic interactionism (G. H. Mead (1934), Dewey (1966), and Durkheim (1973)) with Piagetian constructivism. We shall discuss this theoretical integration in the context of our current work using the Just Community approach.

THE JUST COMMUNITY APPROACH IN PRACTICE

Since 1974 we have been experimenting and researching the relations between school democracy and the moral development of adolescents.

As an approach to school democracy, the Just Community approach (Kohlberg, 1985) in practice involves an effort to develop more responsible moral action as well as improving moral reasoning. It holds that responsible moral behavior is a function not only of individual psychological disposition, such as moral judgments of rightness and the moral self (the individual's inclusion of moral norms in his or her self-conception or identity), but also of shared group norms and a sense of community, the moral component of school climate or group character (Higgins, Power, & Kohlberg, 1984). As currently practiced, a group of about 100 students and five teachers composes a community cluster, which has a weekly community meeting to make rules and discipline and plan community activities and policies. At the core of this practice is the idea of participatory democracy—one person—one vote—whether student or teacher in dealing with issues of fairness and community welfare. Issues that are primarily ones of curriculum and administration rather than morality are handled in more traditional authoritarian or bureaucratic ways; our programs or clusters in this way differ from "free" alternative schools popular in the seventies. They are embedded in the larger public high school and in some cases serve to provide leadership for larger high school democratic governance structures. Traditional schools maintain hierarchical relationships between students and teachers and among teachers themselves. They are large formal bureaucratic institutions in which problems are settled by the administration and by teachers.

In contrast, Just Community democratic programs encourage more egalitarian relationships between teachers and students and among students. Problems of the school are settled by open discussion in meetings with students and teachers together. There is explicit attention given to informal sociability and community building. Currently there are Just Community programs in Cambridge and Brookline, Massachusetts, and Scarsdale, New York, and three programs in the Bronx, New York. In creating a Just Community we encourage students to formulate their own perspectives on issues and accept as binding the democratic judgment of the majority of the group. The teachers obviously have special authority by virtue of their position, but they try to operate as formally equal members of a democratic group and exercise authority by virtue of their wisdom and expertise and by means of consent rather than by virtue of their position of authority and by means of coercion. Teachers must walk between excessive advocacy—approaching indoctrination—and excessive permissiveness. To create a Just Community the moral advocacy of the teachers must be strictly bounded by the safeguards of democratic process in order to avoid becoming indoctrinative and the democratic process must be structured, embodied in institutions, in order to avoid becoming rule by the crowd, the strong, or the highly verbal.

The justice side of the Just Community approach is embodied in the democratic process and institutions of the program and in the focus on moral discussions, consideration of fairness, rights, and duties. The community side is an attempt to create a more ideal form of school society in which the pragmatic and associational aspects of schooling (attending classes, teaching and learning, keeping order, forming cliques, etc.) are transformed by a sense of community shared by the members relating toward these issues as not simply school routines that have to be managed, but aspects of communal life that should be shared. Thus community is a call for students and teachers to participate in school in such a way that the rules and the concerns of the program become the personally felt and community-shared responsibilities of all the members. It becomes, along with justice, the main moral content that is advocated within the Just Community approach.

Once each week, the students participate in a small meeting called an advisory group. An advisory group has 10 to 15 students and a teacher/advisor. These small groups explicitly create an informal atmosphere in which the issues of the school as well as personal issues of individual students can be discussed. The close relationships that develop between the teacher/advisor and the advisory group students provide a basis for the students to gain an understanding of the issues and to explore the ways in which they can present their points of view and proposals for the whole group at community meetings. In the advisory group, the quiet students are not intimidated and dialogue is facilitated.

The advisory groups have the task of preparing for the community meeting. These groups prepare the students to discuss the topics on the agenda by having moral discussions on the one or two most important items on the agenda. Each week one of the advisory groups has added responsibility; that is, to prepare the organization of the community meeting and to choose two of its members to chair the community meeting. The chosen students practice being chairpersons by leading the moral discussion of the issues in their own advisory group. This responsibility rotates among the advisory groups.

Since the Just Community program establishes its rules, it must also provide a structure that enables the community to determine fair consequences for those who break the rules. This is one major purpose of the discipline or fairness committee. When individuals fail to maintain the rules, the questions of fair consequences and fair punishment are not theoretical, but involve making decisions about real consequences for one's friends and other community members. Most adolescents are hesitant to accept responsibility for enforcing rules among their personal friends and classmates, even those rules that they believe should be enforced and that they have committed themselves to uphold. In these circumstances they initially become willing and even eager for the adults to administer the appropriate punishment. The conflict for many students begins when they have a choice between ignoring or following up on their knowledge of a rule infraction. Observing a rule infraction or being told about one raises further conflicts for students.

The existence of the discipline or fairness committee in the daily life of the school (it meets once weekly) depersonalizes and demystifies the relation between the processes of rule making and rule enforcement. Discussing and deciding on appropriate sanctions for their peers helps the students on the discipline committee to realize the balance between maintaining loyalty to a friend or peer and fulfilling one's responsibility to the community as a whole.

In each Just Community program the discipline or fairness committee's roles and duties develop over time. Because the committee is acting for the school or program, it becomes clear that the individuals who comprise the committee are fulfilling a school- or program-wide responsibility. In this sense, membership becomes viewed as a duty, not just something to be volunteered for out of interest. This means that most students and staff will serve on this committee for some period during each academic year.

Also, since the discipline or fairness committee represents the community, decisions it makes can be appealed to the whole community for review and reconsideration. The most serious decision, to expel a student from the program, is always appealed to the community meeting after an initial decision has been made in the discipline or fairness committee.

In each Just Community program it has been the case that the duties of the discipline or fairness committee expanded by the second or third year of the school to include hearing cases of interpersonal disputes. In such cases, the committee acts more as a mediation board and as a group of sympathetic listeners who help the people involved to solve their conflicts by taking each other's point of view and coming to a genuine understanding of each other's position (see Table 4.1 for Just Community institutions).

The last institutional component we will mention only briefly. The application of Kohlberg's theory of moral development to education began with classroom discussion of hypothetical moral dilemmas. Curricula in English, social studies, and history have been created that present some of the central ideas and issues as moral dilemmas and use the technique of moral discussion as the means of teaching. Each of the Just Community programs has created at least one class—often combining English and social studies—in which the basic element is the discussion, writing, and identifying of moral dilemmas in literature and in the study of law and government by the students.

TABLE 4.1. The Organizational Structure of a Just Community Program

Institution	Members	Tasks
Agenda committee	8 to 12 students and 2 to 3 teachers	Deciding on issues; putting together the agenda
Advisory group	1 teacher/ advisor and 10 to 15 students	Creating an informal atmosphere for discussing personal problems; having a moral discussion on the 1 or 2 important agenda issues
Community meeting	All students and teachers	Discussing and resolving moral issues; making rules and appealing violations
Discipline committee	6 to 8 students and 2 teachers	Hearing cases of rules violations and interpersonal problems of disrespect; giving sanctions; enhancing interpersonal understanding

Let us illustrate the process of Just Community democracy and some issues and events in the first 2 years of Roosevelt Community School, a program involving primarily black and Hispanic students in a South Bronx high school cited by New York newspapers as having statistics among the worst for New York City schools in terms of violence, theft, drop-out rate, and academic facilities, a school whose principal saw the Just Community program as providing possible answers to these problems. We are in the process of an extensive research evaluation of this program in relation to comparison groups, funded by the W. T. Grant Foundation. The research attempts to document effectiveness of the program not only in improving such school problems but also in conceptualizing longitudinal change in a way that will relate them to the development of moral reasoning, program and school moral climate, and development of responsible moral action.

In a school environment in which classrooms are often locked, instruction is by lecturing, and security and discipline are handled by security officers and deans of discipline, the new-found freedom to discuss and participate in decision making was necessarily at first chaotic, with meetings full of disruptions and inattention to the issues and with only a few students bent on participating in a democratic process. Teachers preaching the need for order and mutual respect in the meetings and the goals of building a community making fair decisions were scarcely heard, let alone understood. Building mutual trust, respect, and a process of dialogue had to emerge in advisory group meetings, "getting to know you" exercises, and a day excursion of the Outward Bound type involving "trust falls" and cooperative team solutions to outdoor challenges. The students readily accepted the teachers' proposal that no drugs or alcohol should be allowed on the trip and proposed that no knives or guns should be allowed, either.

The excursion was a great success, with no violations of these two rules and a good time and a sense of sharing experienced by all.

The next day, however, a teacher told us that she had discovered $20 missing from her purse. She was apprehensive about casting this light of gloom on a happy event and confronting the students with the problem. Let the discipline or fairness committee investigate the facts of the theft, we suggested; her obligation was to confront the community with this violation of trust and of fairness.

The teacher announced the problem at the community meeting and it was agreed that the thief be given the opportunity to return the money anonymously before the next meeting. A few students suggested that if it was not returned the whole community should contribute 25 cents per person to make up the twenty dollars. The money was not returned, and the next week a discussion about collective restitution was held. Many students said that the teacher had helped them and they should help the teacher. Some students said it was not their responsibility; they had not attended the trip. A student asked the teachers whether they would support collective restitution for a student victim of theft, the answer of course being that it was one community in terms of helping.

The majority vote was that the community ask each member for a voluntary contribution but that it not be obligatory. A bag was passed around the room. The result: $10 and some notes meant to be humorous. Several students expressed disappointment, and the bag was passed again. This time $10 more and no humorous notes. The teacher victim said her trust in the community was restored and she would give the $20 to the community activity fund for a later social event.

This of course did not end the discussion of stealing. Teachers asked students how many had been robbed. The majority had. The teacher coordinator, Al, pointed out that in the community meeting students kept on their coats even though the room was hot, and students admitted they were worried about being robbed. The students agreed that even though there was a general school rule against stealing they needed to make their own agreement against stealing and bring a possible violator before the discipline committee. Now students and teachers leave their belongings freely in the community meeting and classroom and no incidents of theft have been reported by students or teachers. Thus teacher support for a community ideal of trust and collective reponsibility helps build norms of justice or individual rights. The community ideal helps even poor and deprived students reach out beyond themselves to help others.

The first spring, 1986, the Harvard research project paid $2 to each student in the control group sample for being interviewed and answering questionnaires. The community cluster had agreed to do these interviews when they volunteered for the program. In a community meeting, students said it was not fair that Harvard should pay the control students but not them. We agreed and said Harvard would pay each student $2 but the community should decide what to do with it. Some students suggested keeping it, some giving it to the cluster community activity fund, some giving it to a charity like leukemia research. Only a few wanted to keep it themselves. Those who most wanted to reach out beyond themselves had to clarify the reasoning. Pedro, a leader said, "If we keep the $2 we give ourselves some extra food and drink. What do we get? Heartburn. If we give it to sick children we help them and we get an award, and our community gets a good reputation and fame." Another student challenged this collective egoism, saying that no one would notice. Pedro answered, "Yes, I guess it must be because it makes you feel good inside to help a sick child."

RCS students reached out that spring to help the larger high school on a number of occasions. On the day before Passover, on which few teachers would be in the school, the principal asked the students to come to the school for the next 2 days as aides to keep order. After kidding, "We're all Jewish," 52 of the 85 students volunteered to come and actually followed through. Reporting on it later, a group from the program said, "We said we'd do it, and we did it. We all worked together."

By this time community meetings were student chaired, and both process norms of order and respect for whomever was speaking were accepted by most students. In the fall of 1986 a concept of obligation to the community was extended to the idea of academic class and community meeting attendance, when one student suggested and the others hotly debated a "no cut rule" motion. This meant any unexcused absences would be taken to the fairness committee, on the grounds that cutting was not the violation of arbitrary school convention, as it is typically seen by students who can readily distinguish between moral and conventional obligation at a fairly early age (Turiel & Smetana, 1984), but as a special norm for this program based on the idea of a certain degree of collective responsibility in a community. The motion passed, but we wait to see how well it will be followed.

Our Initial Piagetian Approach to Moral Education and Its Limits

The practice we have just described, evolving since 1971, has very different theoretical roots than our early practice of moral education as classroom dialogue about hypothetical moral dilemmas initially developed with Blatt (Blatt & Kohlberg, 1975).

Our initial approach to democratic moral education rested largely on our neo-Piagetian structuralism and constructivism. Goals of moral development were conceptualized in terms of the development of moral reasoning vis-a-vis moral stage increase and an increase of autonomy of moral judgment, what we have called type B autonomous as opposed to type A heteronomous moral judgment (Colby & Kohlberg, 1987; Kohlberg, 1984).

The process of moral development was conceptualized in terms of peer dialogue about hypothetical or real dilemmas, with the teacher acting only as a Socratic facilitator of such dialogue. Such dialogue, we believed (and our belief was supported by research—Blatt & Kohlberg, 1975), would lead to stage advance through the influence of cognitive–moral conflict or disequilibrium leading to reconstruction of reasoning to the next stage. Kohlberg (1970) put the approach in opposition to Durkheim's theory of moral education, a theory of morality as a supraindividual societal construction that was culturally relative and internalized through the influence and authority of teachers and others. At that time it seemed both philosophically indoctrinative or rejecting of the child's autonomy and psychologically unsound in appealing only to conformity to authority and the group, rather than to the child's own construction of morality. Certainly in Durkheim's hands, Durkheim's theory led not to a theory of democratic school education but to something readily construed by an educator as a support for what we saw as stage 4 enforcement of institutional rules, order, and goals.

Nevertheless, as we moved into Just Community practice we found our neo-Piagetian theory of classroom peer dialogue an inadequate theoretical base for what we were doing.

Our initial dissatisfaction with classroom dilemma discussion was that of most educators. It dealt with hypothetical solutions to hypothetical (or real) dilemmas. First, it did not deal with real-life problems that had to be decided upon and it did not immediately imply moral action. Second, it did not deal with the school or institutional environment or moral atmosphere outside classroom discussion time. Participatory democracy may at first sight appear to have an adequate theoretical neo-Piagetian foundation of a dialogue among equals in a context of justice as fairness.

LIMITS OF PIAGETIAN THEORY IN PRACTICE AND THE NEED FOR DURKHEIM'S THEORY

In fact, our Just Community practice in the Bronx is far from what neo-Piagetian theory would suggest. As in earlier projects, equal voting was not very motivating to students, nor was a dialogue based on mutual respect easily established. Teachers had to advocate for both the value of taking the time and responsibility to make democratic decisions and a process of dialogue based on mutual respect. Valuing dialogue and mutual respect depends not only upon teacher advocacy, but upon students coming to value a community and membership in it. Feeling a sense of *we*, of collective solidarity, of being a group, was necessary for students to care about fair decision making and moral dialogue. Students began by not trusting either the teachers or each other. When they voluntarily restored the teacher's money, they didn't trust each other to keep their hands out of the donation bag. They had moral sympathies for the teacher, and for children with leukemia, without our Just Community program, but they were morally immobilized by what we call *counter-norms*, peer norms or expectations that violate not only conventional moral norms but the capacity to empathize with each other or take each other's viewpoint. In the larger high school, as students told us, the norm of respect is a counter-norm: "Look at me the wrong way and you're in for a fight." One of us accidentally brushed against a student in the hall and he angrily yelled and continued threatening even after an explanation and apology. As far as the norm of trust, encouraged by the decision for collective restitution, there was the counter-norm of the larger high school: "It's your fault if something is stolen—you were careless and tempting me." This counter-norm was brought into the discussion of collective restitution but didn't carry the day, due partly to teacher advocacy. As the program developed over the year, teachers did less and less advocating and directing. The students took pride and ownership in cooperative and dialogic decision-making and in the capacity of their group to act altruistically or morally.

We do not believe that the students' appropriation of the teachers' advocacy and norms was simply the internalization of adult authority, as a sociologist's theory might suggest. This appropriation of the process of fairness and community was in a sense a Piagetian construction. It was, however, a construction dependent on teacher direction and an appeal to a nascent community. If democracy has roots, as it does, in the adolescent's Piagetian construction of fairness, it also has roots in adult nurturance of community, which requires more than Piaget would give us. Our theory of democratic practice in the Just Community theory, then, relies heavily on our own revisions of Durkheim's theory of moral education, a revision that makes it democratic rather than resting on the authority of the teacher as a representative or priest of society.

In the *Moral Judgment of the Child*, Piaget puts Durkheim's theory of moral education and moral development in global opposition to his own theory and theories of Dewey and other proponents of democratic social education.

For Piaget, the development of moral autonomy and moral maturity emerges from the spontaneous dialogue and cooperation between individuals who are peers having attributes of mutual respect and collective solidarity with one another. We believe, however, (1) that such interaction rests largely on the development of the collectivity of a set of group norms and an atmosphere of group solidarity conducive to dialogue with mutual respect, and (2) that this collective development is one that the teacher must help structure and advocate. In other words, autonomous peer social interaction stimulating moral development is partially dependent on the moral atmosphere of this collectivity. Thus the opposition between Piaget's focus on interindividual dialogue and exchange and Durkheim's emphasis on collective norms and solidarity is for us not opposed but complementary to our theory of democratic social interaction, as we shall try to argue. First we shall review group theory (Durkheim, 1973; Lewin, 1951) and our democratic revision of it.

DURKHEIM'S THEORY

According to Durkheim, the content of moral norms varies from one society to another, but the Kantian formal attitude involves respect for rules, the sense that moral rules are fixed, regular, and categorical and hold regardless of inclination (the feeling of *duty*). The feeling of respect or duty toward rules arises, says Durkheim, because we perceive them as arising not from our own mind but from collective authority. Authority is outside, objective, but is also inside, shared by members of the group.

The second element of morality is *altruism*, an "impersonal or unselfish end" (Durkheim, 1973). Altruism, argues Durkheim, like duty, also comes from a sense of the group.

If our personal interests are not altruistic, neither can the interest of another single individual be. Yet (altruism) must be devotion to another conscious being (not to an abstract idea). Altruism must be (oriented to) something superior (but conscious), the social group. It implies *devotion to, or attachment to the group of which the individual is a member* (p. 56).

Associated with the notion that morality is respect for group authority and attachment to the group is Durkheim's belief that the youth group or school is an intermediary between the child and the society; that is, the school is to represent society to the child.

Intermediaries are necessary [between the child in the family and the society]; the school environment the most desirable. It is more extensive than the family or the group of friends. It results neither from blood nor free choice but from a meeting among subjects of similar age and condition. In that sense, it resembles political society. On the other hand, it is limited enough so that personal relations can crystallize. It is groups of young persons more or less like those of the social system of the school which have enabled the formation of societies larger than the family. Even in simple societies without schools, the elders would assemble the group at a given age and initiate them collectively into the moral and intellectual patrimony of the group (p. 230).

In order to commit ourselves to collective ends, we must have above all a feeling and affection for the collectivity. We have seen that such feelings cannot arise in the family where solidarity is based on blood and intimate relationships since the bonds uniting the citizens of a country have nothing to do with such relationships. The only way to instill the inclination to collective life is to get hold of the child when he leaves his family and enters school and to instill in the child a feeling for collective ends (p. 231).

Durkheim: Group Rule Making and Discipline

Given this notion of moral formation, Durkheim proposes a number of guides to the teacher. The first set involves respect for rules. His concept of discipline implies a great deal of rule-keeping by the teacher as a representative of the group. He suggests the use of punishment, not for deterrence or retribution, but to symbolize the teacher's and class's disapproval of rule violation based on their respect for the rule.

The major things to keep in mind about discipline from Durkheim's viewpoint are:

1. Discipline aids rule maintenance not through hedonistic reinforcement but through reviving respect for the rules and the group that makes them.
2. The discipliner, teacher, or discipline board is seen as a legitimate representative of the group or school, not as an individual, arbitrary personality.

In terms of methods of discipline, says Durkheim: The best punishment is that which (establishes) blame in the most expressive and least . . . . painful way possible. Its purpose is to reaffirm the obligation (to the rule, to reaffirm it) when it is violated both to the culprit and to the other group members whose respect for the rule is demoralized by the offense. The discipline should have some meaning in teaching the positive meaning of the duty violated (p. 56).

The second set of Durkheim's recommendations involves promoting altruism, that is, increasing group cohesion. One of Durkheim's methods for increasing group cohesion involves cooperation, and for him, this may involve a certain degree of reward to the group as a whole. Durkheim discusses interdependency in reward attainment in terms of collective reward and punishment:

A means to awaken the feeling of solidarity is the discreet and deliberate use of collective punishments and rewards. Collective sanctions play a very important part in the life of the classroom. The most powerful means to instill in children the feeling of solidarity are to feel that the value of each is a function of the worth of all.

Durkheim does not generally advocate collective punishment (punishing the group for an individual moral violation). He does advocate collective reward (rewarding the group for a run of general good behavior). He says, "The important thing is for the child to realize he is working for everybody and everybody is working for him. Collective reward (or deprivation of reward) provides a solution to unconfessed violations which are treated as a general sign that the group is not doing well." As an example, under certain conditions our democratic version of Durkheim suggests collective restitution as such. It should be noted that all of Durkheim's recommendations are based on the assumption that there is some group cohesion or sense of community and some recognition of the teacher as a representative of, and advocate for, the group's authority and goals.

Our Democratic Modifications of Durkheim's Theory

As we shall elaborate upon later in response to Piaget's criticisms, we see the core of Durkheim's theory of moral education as resting not on an authoritarian view of the the teacher's role, or expiative punishment, or acceptance of societal authority and laws, but on the idea that moral obligation to norms is based on a group's or community's self-conscious sharing of or adherence to these norms. For Durkheim a sense of moral obligation to a norm rests on a sense of the norm as being shared by a group whose authority the individual accepts and of which he or she feels himself or herself to be a member. As distinct from obligations to rules and norms (the spirit of discipline), Durkheim views an equally important part of morality to be the more spontaneous spirit of altruism, or caring for other members of the community and the community as a whole.

This underlying aim of Durkheimian collectivistic framework, while it superficially may suggest a stage 4 structure of social system maintenance, we believe is compatible with the goals of moral development as defined by stages 5 and 6 in moral judgment as resting on principles of justice or respect for persons—respect including an active benevolence component as well as an unwillingness to violate individual rights. In practice, for instance, in our democratic projects we attempt to ensure that the group democratically discusses and votes on rules and at a deeper level agrees upon norms of equal respect for persons. From this agreement derive concrete rules of respect for property and prohibition of stealing, cheating, and physical and verbal abuse. We also attempt to use democratic moral discussion and voting for the sake of creating norms of altruism or community, norms of trust and mutual aid, that cannot be codified as rules. It is easy to see why, as an extension of Durkheim's own theory, formal democracy should enhance the formation of collective norms of justice and community. Only through democratic discussion and voting can there develop a sense that a collective or shared norm has been created.

In our practical elaboration of democratic community, teachers advocate to students the values of democratic community loosely compatible with Durkheim's theory, solidarity, and its conditions such as trust.

Like Durkheim, we do not equate either the morally right or the welfare of the community with whatever is agreed to by the majority. Minority opposition to the majority rule is not necessarily a violation of the morally right. In our version of democratic community the minority is obligated to try to change the rule through persuasion or civil disobedience, not secretly to violate the rule. Our democratic extension of Durkheim suggests that teachers advocate to students that, if students have shared power and responsibility in making a rule, they have a responsibility to enforce the rule by confronting students who violate it or reporting the violation to a student, teacher, or democratic discipline committee. This is of course a very different responsibility than that of a citizen of a democratic state, who leaves enforcement to the police, or of a student at a bureaucratic high school, who leaves enforcement to teachers and administration. The feasibility of this approach rests partly on the fact that our democratic programs have been voluntary communities, as well as democratic and nonpunitive ones.

So far we have stressed in Durkheim's theory the role of socialization of the content of norms of justice and community, and socialization strengthened by a democracy. As we shall elaborate upon, our broader Just Community theory, with its emphasis on teacher advocacy, on establishing formal institutions of advisory groups, large community meetings, and a student discipline committee, is not directly derivable from constructivistic or Piagetian theory. However, like Durkheim's theory, it does rest on an assumption of moral development as occurring in a community or collectivity that is more than a collection of teacher–student or student–student dyads interacting with mutual respect, the stress of constructivist or Piagetian theory.

LEWIN'S DEMOCRATIC GROUP THEORY

Our own theoretical formulation of democratic community not only extends Durkheim's theory in a more democratic direction but also draws on the social psychological theory of Kurt Lewin, who restated his theory of group dynamics as a psychological or philosophic commitment to democracy. While not explicitly invoking Durkheim, Lewin, like Durkheim, focuses on the creation of group norms as an influence on individual values and the dependence of these on a sense of group solidarity, cohesion, or community.

Lewinian theory includes the following propositions:

1. One (a leader or "expert") can cause change more effectively through group discussion resulting in a group decision than through lecturing to a group or speaking to an individual (Lewin, 1947).
2. A "democratic" leader encouraging parliamentary discussion can produce more change than a directive–authoritarian leader.
3. The sequence of value teaching through group process involves change in the group norm and then acceptance of the group norm outside the group situation.
4. Value change depends upon: (a) the degree of consensus reached on a norm or decision, for example, number agreeing, and (b) the extent to which attitudes on the issue are public in the group; that is, attitudes on the norm or issue are not concealed.
5. Influence toward value change must be noncoercive or voluntary. Festinger's neo-Lewinian theory of cognitive dissonance suggests that, when there is overt behavior change toward conformity to a social force, there will be attitude change toward valuing the conforming act, if "pressure" toward conformity is noncoercive and nonextrinsic. If pressure for conformity is based on high extrinsic threat or reward, there will be external compliance but no genuine attitude change.

According to Lewin (1951) social influence (see item 3 above) will not cause change in an individual's norms if such change is incompatible with the norms of the groups of which the person is a member. In group decisions subject to social influence, the group can change its norms without threatening the individual's membership if he or she changes accordingly. Once a new group norm is set, it is maintained by group pressure to conformity. Decisions made in a group are public commitments to action, so there is a disposition to maintain or follow through on such public commitments.

Group Cohesion

In group dynamics theory, the central characteristic for normative influence by the group on the individual is the cohesiveness of the group. By *cohesiveness* is meant the "groupness" of the group, especially:

1. The attractiveness of the group as a whole to its members (their desire to belong to the group) and the attractiveness (sociometric) of each of the group members to each other member (compared to outside friends, etc.)
2. The sense of "we-ness" or community and common fate of the group members
3. The sense of loyalty or obligation to the group

The following factors have been found to increase group cohesion:

1. Amount of interaction among group members.
2. The attractiveness of other members of the group.
3. The attractiveness of the activities of the group.
4. The power and status possessed by the group qua group relative to those of other groups or authorities.
5. The size of the group (i.e., the larger, over a limit, the less cohesion).
6. The voluntariness of initial membership in the group.
7. The demand that some work or service commitment or contract be made to enter or maintain membership in the group.
8. The existence of the possibility of leaving the group not completely of free will but because of group rejection.
9. The existence of cooperative group goals. A cooperative goal situation is one in which an individual can attain his or her goal only if some or all the other members of the group achieve their goals; for example, if reward to the member (goal attainment) comes only if all members of the group receive like reward (group rewards and punishments) or if there is a group goal or reward to each member. Cooperation can be encouraged by:
    a. Making rewards for goals collective or distributed to the whole group.
    b. Stressing that the purpose of the group is to "help each other better," that the goal can only be reached through helping others in the group.
    c. Encouraging collective goals and activities of all sorts.
10. Democratic leadership (White & Lippitt, 1953).

As compared to authoritarian or laissez-faire leaders, democratic leaders produced group reactions of greater "we feeling" (use of *we* versus *I*, collective action), more sharing of individual property, less aggressive remarks, and more group goal orientation.

DEMOCRATIC COMMUNITY: DEWEY'S THEORY

Before proceeding further let us give a less group centered, less Durkheimian or Lewinian basis to the question of democracy and community in the schools as partially articulated by Dewey, and by liberal educational and political theory. Dewey, like Durkheim, stresses that a school must be a community to mediate the students' learning and membership in the larger democratic community. Dewey defines community as a group with a number of shared tasks or interests, shared interests that require positive cooperation and taking the point of view of the other students. We need to note that school community must deal with conflicts between student–student community and student–teacher community. As an example, student–student community may be reflected in student cooperation in homework and taking tests, a form of community that teachers oppose because teachers have expectations against cheating. Most educators will accept the assumption that schoolwide community is a desirable thing that promotes schoolwide goals of learning, rules of justice, and positive moral or valuing of the school and school experience. Common experience tells us that if students feel themselves part of the same community they will not be unfair to each other by stealing, being violent, disrespectful, or exclusive. We do not need to accept Durkheim's stress on the collective solidarity or group cohesion to explain cooperative aid to one another. Usually small friendship groups or cliques will have this sense of community, and unfairness or lack of care will be shown only to members outside the friendship group or clique, or to teachers and administrators.

The first step in improving the climate or ethos of a school then is "building community," creating opportunities for students to get to know each other and teachers and share personal concerns and interests in an atmosphere of trust and acceptance and an absence of criticism. Schools often attempt to build community through sports, retreats, social events, "getting to know you exercises", and so on. Why should formal democracy be added to this agenda? In the first place, community implies not only spontaneous interpersonal feelings but basic interpersonal norms. These central norms are fairness or respect, trust, and mutual aid. As noted, a real sense of community can hardly be said to exist where trust is violated, individuals are exploited or treated unfairly, and so on. You can have a certain degree of fairness or justice without a strong sense of community, but you can rarely have a strong sense of community without fairness in relations between members of a group. In principle, norms of justice and community may be legislated and enforced by teachers and administrators rather than being made democratically. There are several advantages to making them democratically. Our extension of Durkheim's theory indicates that if a norm is made democratically it will be experienced as endowed with the respect and concern felt by the individual for the entire community or group and not just for the teacher as a person in authority. Second, a rule or norm made democratically is experienced as self-chosen, as "owned" by the self, and thus it is more likely to be internalized. Third, the democratic process of deciding on group norms and goals is a cooperative or community-building process. Spontaneous community building does not resolve conflict between the interests of one person or clique and those of another. Through the democratic process of weighing conflicting rights and claims and deciding what is best for the community as a whole, the community becomes more a community because it becomes a group working toward shared interests and goals.

Social psychology, most picturesquely in Sherrif's robbers cave experiment, demonstrates the effectiveness of superordinate goals for community or group cohesiveness.

So far we have taken democratic community in the school as an end in itself. We have claimed that democratic community creates a fair and more positive and satisfying or self-enhancing ethos or atmosphere, a claim supported by our research findings. Regardless of their long-range educational values, justice and community in schools are ends in themselves. In addition, however, democratic community has an educational value. In its least controversial manifestation this is citizenship education. At the age of 18, an adolescent becomes a voting citizen of the wider political community. To develop the skills and concerns of a citizen means not only reflective voting from the perspective of justice and the public interest but concern and skills of active participation in the democratic or parliamentary process. Such learning and development come through active experience, as educational psychologists from Dewey to Piaget have said.

CONTROVERSIAL ASPECTS OF DEMOCRATIC MORAL COMMUNITY

In the last sections, we expressed noncontroversial reasons for democratic community. Democratic community, however, is a vehicle not only of citizenship education but of moral education. While Dewey agreed that democratic community was a basic form of moral education, he did not, as did Durkheim, accept a clear Kantian distinction between the moral as the obligatory principle-bound or the other-regarding and the exercise of social intelligence and instrumental value choices. Like Durkheim, in our interpretation of democratic community we have stressed a somewhat narrower conception of moral community as the vehicle of moral education than would Dewey. The narrower conception of moral community is most easily conceived in an alternative school or voluntary school setting. In this sense a moral school community is different than the legal and political community into which the student graduates.

This means several things. First, there is an emphasis on establishing the conscious or explicit ideal of community as solidarity as opposed to simply setting up cooperative projects in the school. Second there is a conscious emphasis on moral responsibility or obligation of the individual to a clearly defined community as well as on the obligation of the community to the rights and welfare of the individuals comprising it. Such an emphasis in large part is made possible by and is justifiable in voluntary community. Democratic political and legal society is not a voluntary community; it is a compulsory society of laws and procedures designed to protect the rights and interests of individual citizens when these clash with the rights and interests of others. In the Just Community, the ultimate discipline is expulsion from the community and return to the larger compulsory high school. Because the Just Community is voluntary, it must consciously appeal to the student's desire both to live in a more moral community and to develop himself or herself morally and socially, however this is conceived. Moral community, then, stresses moral as distinct from political and legal obligation to norms and to shared acts of caring for other members of the group and the group as a whole.

A recurrent example described in "The Just Community in Theory and Practice" (Kohlberg, 1985) is collective restitution of a theft where the thief is not identified. In Cambridge and the Bronx this has led to votes of collective restitution, each member of the school contributing a small amount to restore the money to the victim of a theft, votes sometimes making it voluntary, sometimes obligatory. Even a vote for voluntary collective restitution creates an expectation that may violate ideas of individual property rights for "sacrificial" helping in the minds of both teachers and students faced with this issue.

A second example has already been given in our discussion of our extension of Durkheim. As noted, the effort to use the democratic process to engage students in the responsibility of confronting other students who violate the rules is a limitation of the students' freedom usually avoided by leaving that responsibility to paid authorities; that is, teachers, principals, deans. This in turn involves a third example: setting up a student discipline committee that does not use strict rules of evidence and the strict presumption that a student is innocent unless proven guilty but that mediates community conflict. The discipline committee asks the student to admit rule violation on the grounds that he or she will feel better morally, will be a better member of the community, and will be best reinstated as an accepted member of the community in this way. This approach to democratic discipline can be seen as related to a neo-Durkheimian view of moral community. Following Durkheim, a known violation of the norms of a moral community is perceived by its members as weakening the solidarity of the community and respect for its norms. Restoration of the community demands the identification of the rule violator and his or her restitution to the victim and the community for this violation. Though Durkheim is clear on this, our theory of school democracy stresses that discipline is restitutive, not expiative or pain-inflicting, though restitution may demand some sacrifice of material goods or social standing.

Insofar as our theory of discipline is neo-Durkheimian, it is open to other objections by liberal democratic theory that would protect the privacy of a rule-violating student as part of the confidentiality of the relation between the rule violators and the teacher. Neo-Durkheimian theory would assert that violations of rules and ideals of the community must usually be dealt with publicly, rather than be the subject of speculation and rumor. If the rule itself is publicly agreed upon, violations of the rule must be publicly dealt with. This demand, however, is only fair or compatible with the ideal of a moral community if the reaction of the community is nonexpiatory, nonderogatory, and based on compassion and respect for the rule violator. Admission of violations is to be commended as a sign of concern for the community, and the rule violator is to be restored as an equally respected member of the community. In a democratic group, behavior violating a rule or norm that the member has agreed upon poses a discrepancy between avowed judgment and action, a source of cognitive–moral conflict or dissonance. While a Piagetian theory of cognitive conflict would often see this as a source of moral growth, in contrast, various versions of Festinger's cognitive dissonance theory would suggest that such conflicts can be resolved by lowering moral norms to accord with actual deviant behavior, if such behavior is not coerced. Public handling of violation of espoused norms is required for norm violation to be a source of growth. But publicity of a norm violation in a moral community must be based on an attitude of primary respect and care for the rule violator and the responsibility of the community for the welfare of the rule violator. As an example of this attitude, I have cited in "The Just Community in Theory and Practice" (Kohlberg, 1985) the Scarsdale community's decision to help a student named Lisa abide by the rules of attendance rather than expelling her from the school for having violated them and other rules previously.

In conclusion, our characterization of Durkheim's theory often involves fundamental confrontations between individual rights and community norms and solidarity, in both rule making and rule enforcement. Such confrontations if open, elicit dialogues stimulating moral development. When these confrontations are successfully resolved they create a sense of collective solidarity or moral community that is meaningful for adolescent development.

PIAGET'S CRITIQUE OF DURKHEIM'S MORAL EDUCATION

In *The Moral Judgment of the Child* (1948) Piaget makes a number of central criticisms of Durkheim's theory of moral education. He says:

> Durkheim regards all morality as imposed by the group upon the individual and by the adult upon the child. Consequently from the pedagogic point of view, where we would be inclined to find in the "Activity" School, "self-government" and in the autonomy of the child the only education likely to produce a rational morality, Durkheim upholds a system of education based on the traditional model and relies on methods that are fundamentally those of authority (p. 341).

Piaget's critique rests on an ideal-type contrast of two types of social relationships, constraint and cooperation, and a corresponding dichotomy between heteronomous and autonomous morality. For Piaget, of course, relations of cooperation are those between children or persons equal in age, status, and power. A morality of autonomy is based on free dialogue and on the norms of reciprocity and equality that are immanent in social interactions not based on constraint, power, or authority. Piaget draws his empirical examples from the "spontaneous" interaction between children playing and discussing the game of marbles. He is aware, of course, that not all spontaneous agreements between children represent rational or reciprocal morality.

Piaget poses a problem about the agreements spontaneously reached by children. He says:

> It is easy enough to see that mutual consent is sufficient to explain the establishment of the rules of the game, since the child is urged to play both by interest and pleasure. But when we come to actual moral rules (not to lie, not to steal) why is it

that mutual respect does not make the children come to some agreement on the subject of what adults consider to be wrong? Take a band of young ruffians whose collective activity consists in thieving and playing practical jokes on honest folk; is not the mutual consent subsisting between its members comparable psychologically, to the mutual respect that holds between marble players? (p. 97)

Piaget makes two distinctions to avoid confusing these examples. The first is the distinction between mutual respect and mutual consent. He says:

There may be mutual consent in vice, since nothing will prevent the anarchical treacheries of one individual from converging with those of another individual. Whereas the word "respect" implies (at least as regards mutual respect) admiration for a personality precisely insofar as this personality subjects itself to rules. Mutual respect then would seem to be possible only within what the individuals themselves regard as moral (pp. 97–98).

The second distinction Piaget makes is between constituted rules and constitutive rules. He says, "moral rules can generally speaking be divided into constituted rules dependent on mutual consent, and constitutive rules or functional principles which render cooperation and reciprocity possible" (p. 98).

Piaget raises the question, "But how can these constitutive rules be regarded as themselves the outcome of mutual respect since they are necessary to the latter's formation (p. 98)?"

We believe that, rather than relying entirely on spontaneous social interaction to develop an attitude of mutual respect and solidarity (the second of which Piaget relates to mutual respect) and constitutive rules of dialogue and fair exchange, the educator and educational system must take a role in developing these conditions of peer interaction.

We agree with Piaget's questioning of Durkheim's teaching to accept the authority of the teacher, the school group, and the society as the ultimate foundation of morality and moral education. But our approach to democratic community is more structured than Piaget's suggestion that one can rely on spontaneous peer relations to lead to moral development and moral practice. It relies heavily on what Piaget calls the adult "as a collaborator, not a master" (1948, p. 404). In particular, our approach relies on the teacher to aid in establishing the mutual moral respect and the constitutive rules of a fair morality in a much more detailed way than Piaget suggests, as we explain in the next sections.

THE ROLE OF THE TEACHER AS FACILITATOR OF PEER DIALOGUE

Our theory defines the role of the teachers in the peer interaction process in two ways. The first we call process facilitation. Process facilitation methods first developed in hypothetical dilemma discussion groups, are employed in the classroom advisory group in discussions done as a preliminary to the all-school community meetings in which a real moral issue or policy is to be described. The following conditions for moral growth are enhanced when the teacher acts as process facilitator:

1. *Role Taking.* The teacher should encourage students explicitly to consider the feelings and points of view of the other students discussing the dilemma and of the staff, the administration, or community figures. This may extend to actual role playing of reactions in another's place.
2. *Considering Fairness.* The teacher should raise issues of fairness in student or staff discussions of a dilemma or in community meetings.
3. *Treating Decisions as Moral.* (*moral* includes but is more extensive than *fairness*). *Moral* is distinguished from the pragmatic, the legal, or the procedural. The teacher should focus the discussion on the moral issues in the decision.
4. *Exposure to Cognitive–Moral Conflict.* The teacher should highlight or encourage higher-stage reasoning or articulate it himself or herself.

Process facilitation only enhances dialogue and mutual respect that often occur under mutual or more informal conditions or situations. In addition to an attitude of mutual respect, effective dialogue requires role taking; it requires each party to take the perspective of the other. This is what Berkowitz and Gibbs (1983) code as transactive dialogue, which they find correlates with moral stage change in mixed stage partners.

The role of teacher as process facilitator in small groups helps define and support the constitutive rules of dialogue and mutual respect and frames disagreements within moral parameters. In large community meetings, chaired by students, teachers have further roles going beyond process facilitation. These roles of advocacy include:

1. Helping to raise issues and raising issues themselves
2. Helping the chair of the democratic meeting to encourage or ensure participation by all as far as possible
3. Advocating positions on the issue that will develop the group's expectations of justice and community

Where the faculty has a sense that these roles are performed effectively by students, our theory says they should not intervene. We believe that staff advocacy does not represent the introduction of moral constraint but is consistent with the role of the teacher as a member of a democratic moral community. Issues of constraint by either teachers or powerful students should be and are discussed in the community meetings. As a result, teachers as well as students are brought to the discipline committee or community for unfairness or violation of the community norm. Our theory does not make deliberate use of the notion of teacher as exemplar or "role model," an issue raised in a later section, but it does assume that the teacher as advocate and democratic rule maker must not be perceived as a hypocrite by the students.

As an example, the Scarsdale teachers were confronted by students for using alcohol at staff meetings after school. The democratic community rules prohibited use of drugs and alcohol during the school day or at school functions held after school. While there was ambiguity as to whether the informal after-school staff meeting was a school function, the staff decided to abandon the practice to avoid the charge of hypocrisy and, more important, to be consistent with the spirit of the rule, the underlying norm, of sober, active participation in any school-related activity. This is in line with Piaget's (1948) recommendation of the adult's acknowledgment of obligations and mistakes.

> One must place oneself on the child's own level, and give him a feeling of equality by laying stress on one's own obligations and one's own deficiencies. It is quite easy to draw attention to one's own needs, one's own difficulties, even one's own blunders, and to point out their consequences, thus creating an atmosphere of mutual help and understanding. In this way the child will find himself in the presence, not of a system of commands requiring ritualistic and external obedience, but of a system of social relations such that everyone does his best to obey the same obligations, and does so out of mutual respect (pp. 137–138).

We have elsewhere (Kohlberg, 1985) attempted to distinguish the roles of teacher as an advocating member of a democratic community and teacher as "master" or moral authority or indoctrinator. Given this distinction, the Just Community teacher's role as advocate introduces a focus on *products* as well as process of peer dialogues and decision-making. It is also a focus on the content of norms of justice and community as well as on the structure of moral reasoning about the norms. The way in which the advocacy role can facilitate the process of interaction central to structural growth is discussed in the next section.

THE INDIRECT CONDITIONS OF MORAL GROWTH ON MORAL ATMOSPHERE

In the previous section we described four neo-Piagetian ways in which the teacher could be a process facilitator of peer dialogue in a classroom or community meeting in a way that would facilitate moral stage and autonomous moral growth. We call these the direct condition of moral growth. We now want to focus on the ways in which teacher advocacy in the context of democratic community rule making can facilitate cooperation, dialogue, and mutual respect outside the classroom or school meeting. We call these the indirect conditions of moral growth. We maintain that these will foster creation of a good moral atmosphere at the school. They are central to the creation of relations of mutual respect and dialogue stressed by Piaget.

We stressed earlier that Piaget distinguished between the mutual consent and mutual respect of a group of adolescent thieves; and between actual constituted rules and constitutive rules of fairness. Later we will report a controversial example from our democratic school in which the creation of a democratic norm about cheating helped a student to confront a friend who expected her to help her cheat, a possible example of a democratic group norm helping change a friendship of mutual consent to one of mutual respect.

Central to our conception of moral atmosphere are students' perceptions as to whether there are shared expectations or norms held by the self, by the majority of peers, and by the teachers at the school. Most of these norms are ones widely held by teachers and educators in the schools. We divide them into norms of justice, norms of community, and norms of convention. Norms of justice include norms against violence, intimidation and disrespect, norms against cheating, theft, and so on. Norms of community include norms of participation and attendance, norms of helping or aid, and norms of integration (socializing and inclusion across cliques and ethnic groups). Norms of convention include prescriptions regarding conventional behaviors (e.g., dress code, behavior in the halls, etc.). Our assessments by interview or questionnaire focus on the strength of the norm, what we call the phase of collective acceptance and enforcement, and the stage (i.e., developmental level) of the norm. In addition we assess the student's perception of his or her own and the group's intrinsic valuing of community, the solidarity and welfare of the school group for its own sake. We have found that perceived stage of the norm in democratic schools leads or is in longitudinal advance of the individual's stage in reasoning about our classical hypothetical dilemmas. Thus there is reason to believe that building democratic community norms leads to individual advances in both the content and structure of moral reasoning and anecdotally to moral action. In terms of the cases raised by Piaget, however, we want to focus on the ways in which collective moral norms provide conditions of dialogue, mutual respect, and cooperation in informal relations of students outside the classroom and the community meetings. Common sense tells us that perhaps the most critical aspect of adolescents' lives and sense of self is their relations to their peers. In most American high schools, peer groups have no moral responsibilities or commitments. Not only do they not particularly help formal objectives of school learning and rules, but they do not morally support and take responsibility for their own members' welfare. They are often exclusive and competitive; members are dropped or added according to status needs. A clique drops a member if he or she lowers the prestige of the group or deviates from status mores rather than helping them. A clique refuses admission to a student if he or she has "wrong" but morally irrelevant attitudes, is "stupid," or "from the wrong side of the tracks."

This negative perception of high school cliques needs to be balanced by Piaget's, Sullivan's, and Youniss's perceptions of adolescent friendships as representing a major source of overcoming geocentrism and moving toward a concern for the other, for his or her own sake, called love by Sullivan and mutual solidarity and respect by Piaget. The collaborative and cooperative validation of an identity and a consensual view of reality through truthful and open exchange is another aspect of adolescent friendship we will take up in the section on the moral self.

The first emphasis of the Just Community approach is to extend this type of interaction to persons not in restricted cliques or friendship pairs and to develop personal dialogue, mutual respect, and solidarity with members of other cliques and ethnic groups—the norm of integration. The second emphasis of the Just Community approach is to deepen the sense of justice and mutual respect within a friendship group or pair. The first emphasis of the Just Community approach—extension of trust, communication, and positive social interaction to those arbitrarily excluded—may be controversial. However, the second emphasis seems even more so. Let us take a particularly controversial example. In Cambridge, Scarsdale, and the Bronx, democratic school teachers urge a rule against stealing or cheating that is supposed to be partially enforced by confronting the person who violated the rule. This immediately goes against the grain of the loyalty of friends conception existing at several stages of development. As one student in the Bronx said, "That's what a friend is, someone you don't rat on." It is part of what Piaget called honor among thieves. The issue of confronting a friend who is acting unjustly is a very difficult issue that can either enhance or demolish the mutual moral respect that Piaget cites as the core of peer morality. As was demonstrated in the quote on p. 122, Piaget differentiates between mutual consent, based on the convergence of self-interest, and mutual respect, based on attribution of justice and rule following of each partner. In the case of cheating, the appeal to a friend for help on an exam may be seen as an appeal for mutual aid with which we tend to sympathize. On the other hand, it can represent the unfair use of disapproval or threat of termination of friendship if the friend does not engage in a practice that goes against his or her conscience or sense of fairness. In this latter instance, aiding a friend to cheat does not build a relation of mutual respect.

One case in which a confrontation on this issue may have strengthened mutual respect occurred in the Scarsdale alternative school (Kohlberg, 1985). Having noted that students should confront one another about cheating, in a later advisory group a student admitted to cheating. She had made the admission she said, to help a friend who had pressured her to cheat. She said her friend was stronger than she was and she was afraid to say no to her. Encouraged by the advisory group, she talked to her friend and asked her friend to publicly admit cheating, saying that she had already admitted it privately. Her friend did publicly admit it, which did not lead to dire consequences for either; it helped to create a more balanced friendship between the two.

In traditional schools, the teachers are the police, not friends of students. In a democratic school, it is not desirable for friends to be seen as police. It is, however, desirable for friends to have a feeling that at the center of their friendship is a mutual concern about fairness and the sense that their friendship and mutual loyalty exist in some balance within a larger moral community.

In summary, our own view is that Piaget's emphasis on noninterference with the spontaneous process of peer interaction as the center of developmental moral education is somewhat romantic. In the Bronx project, the appeal of democratic community to students is less escape from the authority of teachers than their desire to end theft, intimidation, and isolation in the peer world itself. While the center of our democratic school approach is peer interaction in small groups and community meetings, teacher structuring and teacher advocacy play critical roles in this process. This is not inconsistent with Piaget's critique of the authoritarian role of the teacher in Durkheim's theory, but it is consistent with Durkheim's view of the organized social group in moral development, an aspect neglected by Piaget.

SYMBOLIC INTERCULTURAL THEORY OF THE MORAL SELF

From a moral developmental point of view, why build a moral community in schools? We have given some answers to this question. Additional answers come from the symbolic interactionist theories of the moral self of G. H. Mead (1934), J. M. Baldwin, and Josiah Royce (1982). All stress that the self is constituted through reciprocal interaction and communication with another self, an emphasis consistent with Piaget, but also stress the formation of the self through role membership in a group. All stress that after an initial phase of self-construction through imitation and communicative interaction with particular others in childhood (Baldwin's bipolar self, Mead's play stage) there is the development of a consistent or general self related to a "generalized other" (Mead) or an "ideal self" (Baldwin) that is self-consistent or "has character." This general other is largely constituted by general moral rules or principles. For Baldwin, the ideal self or the moral self is imagitivatively abstracted from the concrete other, prototypically the parent who is imitated, conformed to, and identified with. The ideal self is not simply the self of the parent or the self that conforms to the parent, but is the self I am to become, my conscience. Parallel to this ideal self is a moral law that is above any actual authority, such as parent or teacher, and general to the group. From Baldwin's perspective the notion of the adult or teacher as a role model for morality is a half truth, since the adult must already approximate the ideal self to serve as exemplar.

For Baldwin, the construction of an ideal moral self, or conscience, represents a reciprocal or dialectical interplay between the self and the social others of the child's group. Part of the nature of the moral ideal is that it be valid for all, that it be shareable, or synomic, that it be valid for a community (and ultimately all humanity). While Piaget stresses the reciprocity of pair dyad or small group, Baldwin stresses the need to generalize to all as the foundation of rational conscience. Piaget criticizes Baldwin's contention that the tendency toward universalization will itself create a rational and central moral autonomy, a notion that Baldwin in a sense derives from Kant. But it seems to us that the effort to universalize group rules democratically is a process that helps liberate the adolescent from the concrete expectations of particular parents, teachers, and peers and is a stimulus to moral development and autonomy. From Baldwin's perspective the effort to build a moral community helps to build a moral or ideal self.

Royce (1982), who has a theory similar to Baldwin's, points to the adolescent moral self as focusing on loyalty to a cause, *an ideal* that must be shared with a community. According to Royce, the adolescent in conflict between self-interest and conformity to norm and convention finds a cause that is "outside ourselves" but corresponds to a will "inside ourselves" to serve the cause, and in so doing "dignifies and strengthens the self."

Says Royce:

> Loyalty is social. Since a cause tends to unite many fellow-servants in service, it consequently seems to have to the loyal man a sort of superpersonal quality. It involves the union of the personal and the seeming superindividual about it. It binds many individuals into one service.

Thus Baldwin and Royce accept a version of Durkheim's notion of the "superindividual nature" of the moral community but see it as shaped and shaping personal ideals and an ideal moral self. This is an important corrective to any "conformist" connotations of Durkheim's formulation of the moral group.

Moral community is always an ideal only partially realized in a democratic group. Shared moral ideals, however, have always been recognized as central to adolescent or youth groups, and membership in such moral groups or communities solidifies the moral self. The ideal moral self is not a self of simple conformity to the group as Durkheim's or Lewin's theory might suggest. Rather, the adolescent engages in a dialectic with the group, attempting to shape the group to his or her moral ideals while accepting the norms of group membership that help define the moral self.

Baldwin's theory stresses the ideal moral self and dialectical relation to the social group. Mead's theory stresses the self as a *me*, as defined by role and membership in a group from whose perspective, the perspective of the generalized other, the self gets its definition. This does not simply mean that the self's definition is partially based on the attribution of others in the group; for example, that the self's self-definition as "good" represents reflected attributions by the individuals in the group, teachers or peers, of the self as good. Rather it represents a shared good member of the community role, seen from the point of view of the generalized other with which the self is in dialogue.

CONCLUSION

In this chapter we have stressed that one way of conceptualizing democratic social interaction as contributing to moral development is to see such interaction as interindividual dialogue, reciprocity, and cooperation among peers, the view stressed by Piaget. A second way of conceptualizing democratic social interaction is as the egalitarian building of a moral culture or moral group through the creation of shared moral norms. In our view this moral culture is required not only to create the conditions of interindividual cooperation and dialogue but to build a general moral self, a developmental function of the adolescent years.

REFERENCES

Berkowitz, M. W., & Gibbs, J. C. (1983). Measuring the developmental features of moral discussion. *Merrill-Palmer Quarterly, 29*, 399–410.

Blatt, M., & Kohlberg, L. (1975). The effects of classroom discussion upon children's level of moral judgment. *Journal of Moral Education, 4*, 129–161.

Colby, A. & Kohlberg, L. (1987) *The Measurement of Moral Judgment: Volumes I and II.* Cambridge, England, Cambridge University Press.

Dewey, J. (1966) *Democracy and education.* New York: MacMillan.

Durkheim, E. (1973). *Moral education.* New York: Free Press.

Higgins, A., Power, C., & Kohlberg, L. (1984). The relationship of moral atmosphere to judgments of responsibility. In W. Kurtines & J. L. Gewirtz (Eds.), *Morality, moral behavior and development.* New York: Wiley.

Kohlberg, L. (1970). The moral atmosphere of the school. In N. Overley (Ed.), *The unstudied curriculum: Its impact on children.* Washington, D.C.: Association for Supervision and Curriculum Development.

Kohlberg, L. (1984). *Essays on moral development: Vol. 2. The psychology of moral development.* San Francisco: Harper & Row.

Kohlberg, L. (1985). The Just Community in theory and practice. In M. Berkowitz & F. Oser (Eds.), *Moral education.* Hillsdale, NJ: Erlbaum.

Lewin, K. (1951). *Field theory in social science.* New York: Harper.

Mead, G. H. (1934). *Mind, self and society.* Chicago: University of Chicago Press.

Piaget, J. (1948) *The Moral Judgment of the Child.* Glencoe, Ill.; Free Press.

Royce, J. (1982). *The philosophy of Josiah Royce* (J. Roth, Ed.). Indianapolis: Hackett.

Turiel, E. & Smetana, J. (1984) Social knowledge and action: The Coordination of domains. In W. Kurtines & J.L. Getwirtz (Eds.) *Morality, Moral Behavior and Moral Development,* New York: Wiley.

White, R., & Lippitt, R. (1953). Leader behavior and member reaction in three social climates. In D. Cartwright & A. Zander (Eds.), *Group dynamics; theory and research.* Evanston, IL: Row, Peterson.

PART 3

Social Constructivist Perspectives

CHAPTER 5

Social Construction and Moral Development: Update and Expansion of an Idea

JAMES YOUNISS

For some time, psychological theorists of moral development have emphasized rational reasoning as the means for validating moral judgments. This approach is based on a cognitive model in which the individual is said to construct a moral outlook through the use of self-reflective appraisal of experience. For roughly a decade, a new approach has been evolving to the effect that morality originates in interpersonal interactions and relationships. Data that support this position were initially reviewed in 1981. Additionally, concepts that would follow from a social constructionists orientation were evaluated. The present chapter offers an updated review of evidence, especially that pertaining to adolescents' and adults' commitment to interpersonal relationships. Concepts such as the individual in communicative relations and the primacy of intersubjectivity are also discussed. Finally, the position is located within a sociological orientation that balances strategic, individual functioning with membership in solidary groups.

This chapter is a continuation and update of a previous paper that summarized evidence on behalf of a social constructivist approach to the study of moral development (Youniss, 1981). The basic epistemology behind that paper was taken from Piaget (1932) and consisted of three essential points. First, the individual's moral orientation is being developed through membership in relationships with parents and peers, especially friends. Relationships here mean structured forms that enable and restrict understanding of social and psychological reality. Second, the core processes in this constitution are social interactional and include such things as discussion, negotiation, and consensus seeking. Third, the moral knowledge that is acquired through membership in relationships and participation in interactions must be seen as affective or attitudinal as well as cognitive. Having developed morally through cooperation, persons understand that they are interdependent and interpersonally responsible. These are not add-ons to cognition but are integral by-products of a continuing process of social construction in which the procedures for generating knowledge also engender mutual regard.

Before getting to the work that will be reviewed, one can note that this interpretation of Piaget (1932) is now fairly widely shared. Whereas when the original paper was written there was little consensus about the matter (cf. Damon, 1977; Youniss 1980), in the interim this interpretation has been taken up by several observers (cf. Chapman, 1986; Weinreich-Haste, 1982; Wright, 1982). The fact of agreement is interesting given that for roughly 50 years Piaget's 1932 study was perceived as another paean to the individual child's self-reflective construction of morality. A strong critique of the ideologies of self-direction and logicalness in theories of cognition (cf. Broughton, 1985; Riegel, 1976) may have helped scholars to penetrate the Piagetian text and see that he viewed self-reflection in the context of interpersonal relationships. Simultaneously, the field at large has come to see that social context cannot be ignored in a true interactionist position (Wertsch, 1985).

In the earlier paper, several lines of evidence that had bearing on the thesis were reviewed and discussed. They included: (1) studies of friendship in children, presented as examples of what Piaget (1932) called cooperative relationships; (2) studies of friendship in adults, considered as supporting the continuing importance of cooperation through the life span and as a corrective to excessive individualism; (3) studies in other relationships, for example, among kin and family, that would illustrate how interdependence in social construction inherently engenders solidarity; (4) studies of specific processes that would be the empirical means of socially constructed knowledge; and (5) sociological outlooks that provide a context in which commitment to interpersonal relationship would not be dysfunctional but would benefit the persons involved and be primary to existence.

The present chapter considers evidence that was not previously recognized or available. No attempt is made to be comprehensive. Rather, selections are made that help to exemplify major points. The basic argument is assumed to be well understood: Morality consists of mutual respect that comes out of cooperative relationship. In turn, mutual respect enables cooperation to be practiced. Cooperation functions on two levels. One is cognitive in the standard sense of the use of reason to comprehend experience. In this vein, cooperation refers to joint reasoning in which participants pool ideas, exchange criticisms, work to resolve differences, and otherwise serve as validators for one another. At the second and indisociable level, cooperation functions in the sense of felt commitment. The basic idea here is clearly expressed in Gilligan's (1982) *ethic of caring*. This means that persons in a close relationship cooperate to help and protect each other irrespective of, and sometimes contrary to, the egis of a general, abstract principle. They practice mutual aid because they care about one another. But because caring is founded on cooperation, it itself is principled.

FRIENDSHIP IN CHILDREN

Chapter 9 in this volume, by Berndt, represents a genre of research that has evolved over the past 5 years or so. Prior to 1980, there were few studies of friendship's role in development, but after that date the number increased and the focus turned to new dimensions such as intimacy and conversation. Berndt's reviews here and previously (Berndt, 1982) are important for bringing results to a focus on questions that are pertinent to the present perspective. Conversation is essential to the view that friends co-construct ideas through the verbal exchange of opinions, criticism, and the like. That they do so to seek shared meaning testifies to friendship's cooperative structure. That intimacy results indicates further that what was previously thought to be private and pertain to affect is accomplished in friendship publicly when ideas and feelings are two apparent sides of a single social process.

Two works deserve special mention. One is Gottman's (1983) monograph on direct assessment of children's conversations in the course of becoming friends. Gottman took on-line recordings of conversations from children in natural settings. He applied two kinds of analyses which, for present purposes, can be elided. The first kind of analysis relates to the present perspective as follows. At all ages, friends, defined as children who "hit it off," were found to work toward shared meaning rather than act at cross- or individualistic purposes. This point may be obvious but demands special mention given the typical dismissal of conversation by some cognitive theorists. Gottman's data make eminently clear that friends want to understand as much as they want to be understood. They work toward a meaning that is mutual. This is as true of children in fantasy play as it is of children resolving real conflicts.

The second kind of analysis enables us to see by implication that the cooperation and intimacy found in friendship differentiate it from other relationships. One does not cooperate with strangers or acquaintances to the same extent or for the same reasons. Much less does one open the self by expressing feelings or problems to just anyone. It was suggested earlier that the sense of solidarity, which is so central to morality, is engendered by a special dynamic in friendship (Youniss, 1980). To disclose personal feelings or doubts is something like risk taking in the sense that the other person could take advantage of them. The risk is exacerbated by the possibility that, once private feelings are in the open, they could be spread to third parties. These risks are tempered in friendship by reciprocity so that each person incurs a similar risk and responsibility. When this same dynamic leads to mutual trust, it enables the friends to express themselves openly via a positive feedback cycle. Older children and adolescents have told us, for example, that they disclose doubts or feelings to friends in order to get criticism or to figure things out together—without fear of repercussion (Youniss, 1980; Youniss & Smollar, 1985).

The other work of importance is Selman's (1980) book on social development. In it, he reviews his own studies of children's reflections on friendship. The results are presented by way of stages that are aligned with Selman's well-known scheme for role taking. Although that scheme is not necessarily germane to the current perspective, the stages of friendship are, insofar as they give considerable texture to the development hypothesized by Piaget (1932). One sees in Selman's results a developing interdependence that starts with naive play but becomes embedded in deeper expectations of exclusiveness of mutual regard and caring.

While several other studies could be reviewed, these works by Gottman and Selman have special value. They supply new as well as supporting evidence to the data that were reviewed in the 1981 paper. The conversational findings of Gottman denote in detail the sort of exchanges Piaget (1932) said should occur and in which children studied by Youniss (1980) said they participated. Selman's scheme shows that the steps that lead from naive (constitutive) reciprocity to principled (constituted) reciprocity are, in fact, understood by children as proceeding in that developmental order. It may be important to note here that neither Gottman nor Selman apparently attempted to build upon the 1932 Piagetian framework of social construction; nevertheless the work of each supports and goes beyond it.

FRIENDSHIP BEYOND CHILDHOOD

Three new studies will be described here. The first is our own work on adolescents (Youniss & Smollar, 1985). About 1000 adolescents described aspects of their relationships with close friends. Their descriptions covered conversational topics, types of conflict, feelings about the self, and so forth. This work was undertaken as a follow-up to children's descriptions of interpersonal relationships (Youniss, 1980). In the main, adolescents manifested the principles that older children had identified and showed extensions that one would expect if friendship was to be maintained as a cooperative structure.

With children, we observed that the simple reciprocity of play and sharing gave way to a norm such that reciprocity was an obligation that differentiated friends from nonfriends (cf. Smollar & Youniss, 1983; Youniss, 1980). Subsequently, the exclusiveness of friendship led to what Berndt (1982) and others have called intimacy. Friends begin to share their inner lives and get to know practically everything about each other (see Sullivan, 1953). In our work with adolescents, this step in development is expressed in terms of a dualism. The intimacy of mutual disclosure is practiced for the purpose of gaining clarity through feedback from another person. Subsequently, the friends come to need each other for validation.

Adolescents said that friends were recipients of almost all of their thoughts and feelings; by contrast, parents were exposed selectively to their sons' and daughters' inner worlds. The main form of exposure by friends was mutual and noncoercive. When one friend opened up to another, the other was likely to reciprocate. Moreover, neither friend sought to impose a view on the other. And, third, the purpose of communication was often for *understanding*. Subjects emphasized that individuals frequently needed another person in order to figure out or see clearly what was going on inside themselves. They said that understanding was achieved by "talking out feelings," "talking through problems," "sharing opinions," and "figuring things out together." The reciprocity of disclosure was explicit; adolescents mentioned it spontaneously and agreed that it occurred when we offered it as an option. In the latter respect, friendship was sharply differentiated from relationships with parents, where self-disclosure was low and mutual disclosure was rare.

For what it is worth, the importance of intimacy in friendship remained stable throughout the adolescent period, as there were no major declines from age 12 to age 18. This finding may also answer a question raised about children. In several studies, children have described friendship as a positive relationship in which they are sensitive to others and others support them. While, when asked, children tell us that friends fight and have conflicts, the overall description tends toward the positive side. Thus it is reasonable to ask whether children's depictions are idealistic and might be countered by a more realistic appraisal from adolescents. The answer is that adolescents, too, stress the positive character of this relationship even to the point of asserting that friendship is the one relationship in which they feel most like themselves, that is, "who I really am." This relationship is tolerant of conflict that cannot be avoided if only because adolescents recognize that friends are different personalities and have to have competing interests on occasion.

PARENTS AND FRIENDS

In our work (Youniss & Smollar, 1985) as well as that of others, the structure of friendship was compared with that of relationships with parents. Berndt (1979) has made a valuable contribution in this regard by reporting that adolescents' positive orientation to friends is not necessarily a sign that adolescents have stopped identifying with parents. Berndt's results, from two independent samples of subjects, add to the realization that contemporary adolescents are not ordinarily caught in a disjunctive choice between friends on the one hand and parents on the other. According to these findings, older adolescents, at least, assert that their friends and their parents tend to share values rather than have separate and incompatible value systems.

Berndt's (1979) study forms a valuable bridge to an array of new studies that address the issue of parent–adolescent relationship, its structure, and developmental course. Bell and Bell (1983); Cooper, Grotevant, and Condon (1983); and Powers, Hauser, Schwartz, Noam, and Jacobson (1983) have all studied on-line conversations among an adolescent, a mother, and a father. In these studies, the authors used theory-driven coding schemes to describe key aspects of the communication process. Despite differences in the approaches, these studies share a general result. Adolescents seek and parents seem to grant them independence in expression of ideas. At the same time, however, adolescents remain interested in having their ideas accepted by parents and they listen to their parents' ideas as well. The referent for this result is the implicit hypothesis that maturity consists in achieving independence from the parental relationship in the sense of thinking autonomously for oneself (see Waterman, 1981, for a careful review of this hypothesis).

Given that anchor point, it is significant that, while adolescents become more individual, the parent–adolescent relationship retains the function of validation rather than losing it. On the one side, adolescents seek, listen to, and build on feedback they get on their ideas from their parents. On the other side, parents often reciprocate at least on some matters by soliciting their son's or daughter's opinion and taking it into account. Obviously, parents and adolescents are not peers and the conversations that were studied are laboratory events rather than everyday affairs. Caution is required in interpreting and generalizing from these data. Still the result holds that gains in adolescents' individuality do not eliminate their sense of connectedness to parents.

Grotevant and Cooper (1986) have tied the foregoing work to family systems theory and synthesized the findings through their interpretation of the concept of individuation, or second individuation (Blos, 1967). Adolescents appear to desire that they be seen as individuals and not so much as persons defined primarily by parents, teachers, and others. In this, they try to emphasize their separateness by expressing stances that are their own creations. At the same time, adolescents appear to want to stay connected to their parents in the sense that their parents' approval of the individuals they have become is desired. Moreover, adolescents, despite their desire for individuality, still listen to parents' views and thus remain permeable instead of closed.

Gilbert (1986), a social historian, has provided a valuable service by recapturing the 1950s, when social scientists put forth concepts that stressed the division between youth and adult culture. The former, dominated by peer standards, was feared for its potential to put teenagers at odds with their parents and the traditional value systems that had sustained society. Gilbert traces the origin of this fear to the media, government actions, and particularly creation of a consumer sector that was directed explicitly to youth. It is easy to see how the impression of parent–teen division was fostered. It is less clear how the impression was maintained by social scientists.

From studies by Douvan and Adelson (1966) through those by Kandel and Lesser (1972) through those that have sampled contemporary youth, results have been similar. Adolescents affiliate strongly with peers, in particular, their friends. They are intimate with friends in ways they are not with parents. And they say they learn from friends things that parents cannot teach them. It does not follow, however, that this closeness preempts or displaces identity with parents. Although some theorists assume this to be the case, the data for the past 20 years show otherwise. There are differences in the structure of relationships with friends and relationships with parents. These differences have important implications for development in the sense of what is acquired from which relationship. Nevertheless, for the typical adolescent, closeness to friends is compatible with closeness to parents especially when both are perceived as supportive of the adolescent's growth toward individuality as expressed through interpersonal relationship.

RELATIONSHIP IN ADULTHOOD

There is a fairly extensive literature on voluntary relationship during adulthood. One of the motivations for it is a growing skepticism toward Parsonian functionalism (see Smith, 1980; Wellman, 1979). In Wellman's terms, the issue can be stated as a question of whether contemporary life favors individuals over community and makes community dysfunctional. A strict reading of Parsons on modernity (see Johnson, 1975) would depict the individual as a calculating, achievement-oriented actor who was better adapted to rational society than, let us say, the relationally oriented person.

The reaction to Parsonian modernity is now roughly 20 years in the making. One of the first attacks occurred in the study of *networks*, which was designed to demonstrate that the real business of everyday life was mediated, through face-to-face, personal exchanges (Mullins, 1983; Wellman, 1983). Further demonstrations have consisted of showing that personal familiarity provides advantages by way of favoritism as well as support. The networks have involved both hierarchical relations, such as are found in the spread of ideas among scientists, and symmetric relations, such as are found in positive support among friends, immediate family, and other kin.

A recent study by Fischer (1982) has added considerably to this literature. Focusing on San Francisco and areas within a 200-mile radius, Fischer sampled 1250 adults regarding persons they felt close to and persons with whom they would discuss problems at work, who helped with material chores, who gave counsel about a personal problem, who helped out in an emergency, and so on. Most respondents named specific persons for each function. The three most frequent categories of persons mentioned were close kin (23 percent), friends (23 percent), and other kin (19 percent).

Fischer coded the data on several dimensions, a key dimension being adequacy of social support. He reported the following results. About 65 percent of the respondents showed adequate support in having someone to discuss personal problems with and from whom to seek advice. Over 85 percent had adequate companionship and 75 percent specified others from whom they received practical support by way of having been loaned money or receiving help on household chores. These results held up without statistical distinction for persons across rural, semirural, town, and large city environments.

The other new and important study regarding adult relationships is that of Gilligan (1982). This work is well known to researchers in the moral development area and does not need to be reviewed here. Gilligan's interviews with women indicate that contemporary adults think of themselves and of other persons in terms of relationships that are best described in affective dimensions, as does Fischer's work. For Gilligan, the large conclusion is that there is an ethic of caring that entails concern and obligation whose justification is attachment to the relationship itself. Adult men and women (see Murphy & Gilligan, 1981) do not need to reference action to some abstract principle such as a proposition about human rights to act morally. Rather, actions follow from the fact that persons feel responsible for one another because they have a relationship that is enduring, mutual, and voluntary. And this sense of responsibility is obligatory.

Gilligan's work has generated controversy for some claims such as are made about Kohlberg's (1969) theory or about gender-based differences in moral orientations. Broughton's (1985) commentary on these and other problems seems useful if only for its balance. Among other things, Broughton points to the importance of the form of reasoning that an ethic of caring would engender. Such reasoning differs from what we have come to expect in the model of the formal operatory thinker whose tasks are to be rationally principled as well as logically consistent. It is possible that commitment in relationship takes one in a different direction because the actions that follow are particular in direction, rather than universal, and tolerate exception, instead of supporting a consistent rule. Broughton adds, however, that when data are inspected closely, adults show both kinds of reasoning so that the presence of one does not preempt the expression of the other.

PROCESS

So far the focus has been on relationship and its importance relative to the more typical emphasis on the individual. In the radical epistemology offered by Piaget (1932), relationship is one visible side of interpersonal functioning. It is, however, inextricably bound to the other side, which inheres in what is ordinarily called interaction or social process. For Piaget, process is essential; for example, symmetrical reciprocity is the constituting basis of cooperation because cooperation cannot develop in a context of asymmetry. Likewise, consensus-making discussion is essential for mature morality because it is a norm for settling disputes; persons in conflict turn to it rather than each retreating privately into reflection or stepping out by calling on an external authority.

Three approaches to the study of process will be described briefly because each is represented in the present volume. The first, by Selman and his colleagues (e.g., Selman, Schorin, Stone, & Phelps, 1983), is directed toward the study of children's negotiations in natural settings. The authors observed small groups of children working together on a task for a 3-month period. Conversation, which naturally accompanied the joint task effort, was recorded and then coded into categories that represent steps toward understanding. The codes were then aligned with Selman's well-known developmental, hierarchical scheme.

Minimum processes included such acts as insults or physical force. Higher-level acts involved simple assertions, commands, or threats. Still higher-level acts included offering suggestions, asking for clarification, giving explanations, or specifying feelings. This scheme, obtained empirically from group interaction, was found to correlate with Selman's (1980) scale for reflective understanding. While this finding provides internal validity for the scale, it helps also to illuminate Piaget's original claim that processes that are naively practiced become the constituted rules that subsequently are used to guide social practice consciously. When peers hold to different ideas, cooperation allows them to negotiate toward a new synthesis through open-minded discussion.

Perhaps the point that is most valuable to the present chapter is that children in Selman's situation spontaneously employed several strategies that are clearly in the service of negotiation. One can speculate that these children are not content with merely expressing their own viewpoint. While they want to be heard, they also want to be understood. They use skills that imply that they know about reciprocity; to be heard, they realize that they should listen, and to be understood, they grasp that they should try to understand the other person. This study is one of the few with children older than preschool age that looks directly on consensus building and the specific processes that mediate it. While the plurality of strategies is somewhat forbidding, the breadth of skills that this implies should be a prod to search for the developmental roots that make consensus understanding possible.

A second and important paper is Damon's (1984) review of peer education. Damon described a surprisingly large number of studies in which children have manifested learning (achievement gain) through peer interaction.

Achievement measures range from the familiar Piagetian tasks of operatory development through classic school subject material of spelling and arithmetic. This work supplements Damon's (1977) own findings on peer-generated concepts of distributive justice.

The fact that peer interactions that are relatively free of adult intervention can lead to learning is a critical finding for the Piagetian social epistemology. Piaget argues that, while adult-based learning is indispensable for development, it has major limitations. Some of these limitations are made up for by peers when they enter into cooperative interactions. Not only is there learning of specific content, let us say on mathematics problems, but there is also learning of the very procedures that enable cooperation to be repeated in the future. The array of studies uncovered by Damon is impressive, then, for it is not restricted to one domain of acquisition and shows, because of the variety, that peer learning is a generalized phenomenon.

Here is a summary of Damon's key points: (1) Peers motivate one another to learn by critical feedback that encourages openness to new ideas as well as abandonment of old ideas; (2) normal peer communication fosters acquisition of social skills such as argumentation and negotiation; (3) collaborative thinking can enhance creativity; (4) peer learning may engender development in areas other than those made possible through parent–child interaction; and (5) peer interaction can promote an atmosphere of cooperation that, in turn, is grounds for kindness, fairness, and mutual respect. The last conclusion would seem to reinforce Piaget's proposal that autonomous morality may have humble beginnings in peer play, which ultimately encourages cooperation, which, in turn, is the grounds for mutual respect (Youniss, 1980).

Berkowitz, Oser, and Atthof (Chapter 11, this volume) continue a line of work that is spelled out in Berkowitz and Gibbs (1983). They propose that we know that moral discussion promotes stage development but that we do not know why stage development occurs. Their goal is to identify process elements that mediate it and to this end they put subjects in dyads for *transactive discussion* of moral dilemmas. As with Selman and colleagues (1983), the chief results are presented in terms of codes for actual exchanges.

The kinds of codes they present include simple statements such as requests for clarification as well as complex arguments, to wit, "I can analyze your example to show that it does not pose a challenge to my position." The latter exemplifies what the authors call *operational transacts*. It denotes exchanges in which the persons operate on one another's reasoning to the degree that each confronts the other's reasoning as a critic and as a potential source of validation. In the particular study that Berkowitz and Gibbs report, the degree of operational transacts that occurred in a dyadic discussion predicted in a positive way advancements in moral stage made by members of the dyad.

The specific codes covered by operational transacts bear much in common with categories cited in the original paper by Youniss (1981). Undoubtedly, some of the present codes are more complex and seem to entail argumentation that involves anticipation of the "next steps" in discourse. This is probably due to the use of college student subjects whereas in the previous paper data were drawn mainly from studies of younger subjects. Nevertheless, the themes remain constant in that advantageous discussion consists of interpenetration of reasoning so that each person's starting point is moved along as the other person presents counterreasons or new reasons in turn taking.

SOCIOLOGICAL PERSPECTIVES

It was suggested in the earlier paper that most theories of psychological development seem to presume the Parsonian world of modernity. According to Parsons (e.g., Parsons & Bales, 1955), the personality may be gainfully understood as a functional adaptation to the social systems that impinge on the person from childhood onward. In modern social systems, the press is for achievement (vs. ascription), specialization (vs. diffuse associations), universal (vs. particularistic) relation, affect-neutral (vs. affect-laden) transactions, and ego-satisfying (vs. communally oriented) motives. While no developmental theorist specifies these characteristics as such, they may be read into theories as the implicit features that the mature person possesses when he or she is well adjusted to the environment.

The Parsonian position seemed to offer the correct depiction of American society in the decade following World War II. The nation had witnessed the power of mobilization for war production and it testified to what could be accomplished through rational planning and efficient organization. Further, after the war, there was the palpable experience of upward mobility as men experienced new class standing relative to their fathers through education and employment. Surely, features such as rational calculation and achievement seemed to have replaced tradition and the classic impediments to mobility such as ethnic, racial, or religious membership. It is recalled also that at that time there was a rising belief that government could finally begin to operate according to rational principles that would benefit the many instead of the few. John Kennedy's presidency represented the end of "old boy" political decisions and the dawning of rational policy making (see Lowi, 1969).

But even as this viewpoint was taking root, some sociologists were skeptical and sought an alternative to the Parsonian model. Gouldner (1960) and others pointed out that, although modern social systems—for example, government bureaucracies—were facts, they did not vitiate the importance of face-to-face behavior. For Gouldner, in 1960, Mayor Daley's political machine in Chicago ran with efficiency because of its underpinnings in the mechanism of reciprocity. Still, some political scientists of the day were arguing that machine politics were dead and were about to be replaced by a government that was neutral and made decisions through expertise.

Lowi (1969), Bell (1973), and others have pointed out how misleading the latter viewpoint proved to be. They did not deny the value of competence and expertise but meant to show that politics operated as a matter of human communication between persons or sides that had definite and competing interests. Political decisions were not results of rational, disinterested decisions. Instead they were products of negotiation between interested sides. Moreover, Lowi and Bell were definite in correcting an error found in modernity theory. It was held that rational decision making, in itself, guaranteed moral consequences in the sense that results would be reached that benefited the most persons. In announcing the "end of liberalism," Lowi (1969) gave this point priority. Rationality per se did not produce moral results. In his review of the facts, morality was most clearly achieved when moral concerns were brought into debate and dealt with directly, such as in matters of civil rights.

In the work of Wellman, Fischer, and other sociologists cited earlier (see Smith, 1980), there is a confrontation between the presumption of individualism, which fits modernity, and the possibility that relationship may be the primary and irreducible unit of analysis. Research on networks in part is an attempt to settle the issue. Insofar as relationship entails a communal orientation, it fits within the framework of tradition. In contrast to modernity, care for others, efforts expended for others' welfare, and definition of self in communal terms all say that tradition has not been dissipated. If correct, then the self-directed individual who wends a clever path through impersonal social systems seems to be an exaggeration. For balance, interpersonal negotiation must be given equal consideration. Contemporary life is lived through participation in formal systems but also in engagement with persons. Adequate theories must address this complexity.

HABERMAS AND COMMUNICATIVE RELATIONS

Furth (1983) and Alexander (1985) have taken special note of Habermas's analysis of Parsons and attempt to go beyond Parsons. First, Habermas acknowledges that Parsons has provided a comprehensive description of culture, society, and the personality whereas the rule in social science has been to restrict oneself to some small areas of explanation at the expense of the totality. Second, Habermas recognizes, as have others, that Parsons may have been too precipitous in accepting modernity as fact and tying personality to it via adaptation. In this regard, Habermas (e.g., 1979) proposes a textured reality that includes aspects of modernity but only along with features of tradition that have persisted through history.

The mark of modernity is the framework of objective systems that have formal rules, usually operate in bureaucratic form, and are designed for universalistic application. Functioning in such systems—for example, the economy—persons seem to fit best when they act instrumentally by employing calculated reasoning to gain desired ends. Habermas does not deny this. However, he points out that instrumental functioning does not cover the whole of existence or even the chief parts of it. There are still personal elements in the economic sector such as trust and favoritism. In contrast to the objectivity in systems, Habermas highlights the existence of the intersubjective world. If the former is defined in strategic means–ends routines, the latter consists of something rather different, namely, *shared understanding*.

The general concept of intersubjectivity has had little place in contemporary psychology. When psychology has sought to be scientific, it has usually turned to "hard" bases such as an economic model of self-interest, a physiological theory of needs, or—in recent cognitive approaches—a position on innate rationality. Given this bias, intersubjective understanding may seem like a soft and, at best, a secondary domain. Nevertheless, Habermas considers it primary and places it alongside objective systems in what can be called a *split reality* requiring two modes of operation, not one.

In order to clarify this position, Habermas describes the person, or agent, as a member of communicative relationships. This means, among other things, that he has distinguished this person from the one who functions independently via self-controlled reasoning. In a communicative relation, persons turn to one another to seek understanding. When they then function alone, it is with the assumption that there is a shared foundation and that the person can return to that foundation in moments of uncertainty or of conflict. In the case of disputes, the persons have to return in order to talk out differences and negotiate toward a new understanding. Not to do so implies alienation that can only keep persons apart because discursive consensus seeking was missing or has broken down.

Looked at from a broad perspective, this model of communicative relationships may be valuable in allowing us to address such things as persisting affection for kin, ethnic solidarity, religious belief, or affiliation in voluntary associations. These things share the quality of being noninstrumental in the hard sense. Nevertheless, they have reality in the sense of being evident and central to persons' lives. For example, continued affection for kin is generally found in all studies that look for it. This would seem to require an explanation in a context where ascription no longer counts and one's needs are met by rewards for achievement. Concretely, in the United States since the late nineteenth century, fathers have generally been unable to train their sons for future employment, as the two generations have had differing job opportunities as well as paths to them (e.g., Sennett, 1974). The generations have also frequently faced differing value options that would seem to orient them in different and nonlapping directions (e.g., Braungart, 1980).

Still as Wellman (1983), Fischer (1982), and others have shown, elderly parents, siblings, and other kin remain central in persons' interest and engender feelings of closeness as well as of concern. In the Habermas scheme, these noninstrumental relationships are not atavistic but pinpoint the critical nature of shared understanding. In a pluralistic world, there are multiple meanings. In order to avert alienation or anomie, persons seek shared meaning that not only grounds them but enriches their lives. The mechanism for this is communication that is not merely talk but discussion that is sincerely directed toward consensus understanding.

Alexander's (1985) commentary on this position is addressed to sociologists, whom he sees as needing to extend their view to include intersubjective reality. But as this and the prior paper have emphasized, a generation of sociologists has already moved away from functionalist individualism and toward intersubjectivity. What Habermas provides for them is a new definition of the person that is not fettered by the Parsonian model of an objective system pressing the personality into adaptive shape (Parsons & Bales, 1955). Through the discussion that occurs in a communicative relationship, persons are able to co-construct interpretations of events, objects, and institutions and it is from these interpretations that personalities can be understood.

Furth's (1983) reading of Habermas is especially interesting because he takes what he sees as a sociological stance and puts a psychological and developmental dimension into it. According to Furth, Habermas posits the existence of communicative relationship and, in describing it, gives it formal character and ideal qualities (see also Alexander, 1985). Furth suggests that, were a developmental component made central, one could see that the individual is, from the outset, constituted through relationships in which intersubjective shared meaning is inherent.

Youniss (1984) has followed Furth's argument and suggested that much of what Habermas has put into the ideal speech situation can in fact be found empirically in relationships like friendship. Here the persons voluntarily participate in order to avoid the impasse of equality in reciprocity: "I say this is right; you say that is right." They avoid loggerheads by co-constructing reality through discussion that is transactive in the sense Berkowitz, Oser, and Gibbs have described it. Once co-construction has become a means, it also becomes a necessity because outside it there is a lack of consensual validation.

Finally, it seems to follow that co-construction in communicative relationships has implications beyond knowledge itself. When persons cooperate in the construction of knowledge, they simultaneously construct the rules by which interaction occurs. It is reasonable to assume that these rules entail fairness and meet the needs of both parties. Consequently, it seems logical that continued participation in such relationships has the power to engender mutual respect among the persons. It emanates from the interdependence of co-construction, from the fair procedures that have been used, and from the trust that when uncertainty arises recourse to the relationship is likely to lead to a solution that is mutually fair.

PIAGET AND RELATIONSHIP

The Furth-Youniss commentary on Habermas's position can be readily seen as an extension of Piaget's (1932) epistemology. Piaget argued that knowledge is co-constructed via procedures of debate, discussion, negotiation, compromise, and the like. The proper context for these procedures is the cooperative relationship of peers, or equals, or friends. This form of relationship is for Piaget the source of autonomous morality that is defined in terms of subjugation of the individual to norms of reciprocity and objective discussion; the sincere attempt to express the self clearly while trying to understand the other person.

I need not demonstrate that this definition of autonomy has been systematically overlooked by psychologists who have preferred instead to picture autonomy through the individual's self-reliance on reasoning. One plausible basis for this rejection is that developmental psychologists in general have taken relationship to be central to self-definition for childhood but, thereafter, dropped it in order to picture the more mature individual as independent, self-directed, and grounded in rationality (see Waterman, 1981; Youniss, 1983a). This has especially been the case for relationships with parents that symbolize blind control of authority—the antithesis of reasoning (Youniss & Smollar, 1985).

In recent years, some developmental psychologists have come to see relationship as a constitutive principle of the person (see Damon's review, 1983). The individual is founded through a relationship that is the integrative concept for constituting interactions (Ainsworth, 1969; Sroufe & Fleeson, 1986). The individual does not then simply drop relationship to become a separate entity but remains in relationship albeit in multiple as well as transformed ways. In the case of communicative relationship, cooperative discussion remains central because the individual needs it for self-reference, especially in moments of self-doubt or social conflict.

The classic alternatives have been subjective phenomenology or cognitive rationality. Contemporary developmental theorists have favored the latter because it allows the person to be individualistic but in a nonidiosyncratic way. The presumption is that all right-thinking individuals would reach a common conclusion regarding moral matters as they were guided by logic in their respective self-reflective analyses of experience. Still, something is missing in this formula, and that is why theorists have had to add such things as role taking (Kohlberg, 1969) and empathy (Hoffman, 1980) to make cognition human and moral.

In the position taken in 1981 and here, the acts of cognition are considered to be social and not private. Knowledge is acquired via the exchange of ideas when each person serves as a point of resistance to the other. In a cooperative relationship, resistance is not to be avoided but becomes a resource that helps the person to self-understanding while teaching the person that others are needed for definitional clarity. Not differences of opinion but subjective idiosyncrasy and the illusion of rationality are what need to be escaped.

A thoroughly consistent recognition of relationship would build on the beginnings of, let us say, attachment and friendship, to pursue the person's course through other relationships that have communicative significance. A person constituted in discourse is highly likely not to give it up easily in adolescence or any other later time. Positively speaking, such a person seeks relationship as a natural vehicle for clarifying ideas and enriching them. Regarding the latter, there are limits to what a lone individual can bring to ideas, especially when the time dimension is brought in. However, the relational context allows there to be enhancements that come from the facts of two thinkers who work together as well as the dynamics of their interactions.

Piaget's (1932) point is that cooperative relationship, once discovered, needs no additional force to keep it alive. The persons seek it as an ideal because they gain from it despite the difficulties that cooperation poses. One cannot separate this from the bond of mutual respect that cooperation engenders. Therein lie the roots of morality as this theory sees it. Fifty years later, the task is still open to find the specific procedures of discourse and to spell out the structural characteristics of relationship. We have added here also the task of under-standing the sociological context that yields pluralism and makes consensus building that much more important.

Developmental psychologists have moved ahead on this program in recent years through their studies of relationships, interaction, and communication. There is no need to doubt that this work will not continue in a generative man-ner. What seems to be the larger impediment to advancement, however, is lack of an adequate epistemology that permits knowledge to be socially constructed and then admits to the implications. The first of these entailments is that cogni-tion is social in the making and in the continual doing. The second is that cog-nition is as oriented to explaining reality to others as to explaining reality for oneself. The third is that in wanting to achieve consensus understanding the persons become interdependent. Because relationships persist across time, it can be said that persons become interdependent on particular others for self-definition.

Whether the last point is to refer to affect or caring, the denotation is obvious. A theory that addresses only formal principles of morality and emphasizes universalistic relationships must be found lacking. Piaget (1932) made that argument with reference to Kant, whom he saw as identifying morality with respect for rules because the rules had been derived through logical analysis. Piaget meant to offer a corrective that would synthesize cogni-tion and affect through respect for persons who co-constructed fair rules. To do this, he had to outline a position that gave relationship priority over the indi-vidual and built mutual respect into the very procedures of knowledge acquisi-tion. The speculation here is that the work cited in the present chapter will continue on its own accord and in due time help to fill the outline that Piaget sketched in 1932.

REFERENCES

Ainsworth, M. D. S. (1969). Object relations, dependency, and attachments: A theo-retical review of the infant–mother relationship. *Child Development, 40*, 969–1025.

Alexander, J. C. (1985). Review essay: Habermas's new critical theory: Its promise and problems. *American Journal of Sociology, 91*, 400–424.

Bell, D. (1973). *The coming of post-industrial society.* New York: Basic.

Bell, D. C., & Bell, L. G. Parental validation and support in the development of adoles-cent daughters. In H. D. Grotevant & C. R. Cooper (Eds.), *Adolescent development in the family.* San Francisco: Jossey-Bass.

Berkowitz, M. W., & Gibbs, J. C. (1983). Measuring the development features of moral discussion. *Merrill-Palmer Quarterly, 29*, 399–410.

Berndt, T. J. (1979). Developmental changes in conformity to peers and parents. *Developmental Psychology, 15*, 608–616.

Berndt, T. J. (1982). The features and effects of friendship in early adolescence. *Child Development, 53*, 1447–1460.

Blos, P. (1967). The second individuation process of adolescence. *The Psychoanalytic Study of the Child, 22*, 162–186.

Braungart, R. G. (1980). Youth movements. In J. Adelson (Ed.), *Handbook of adolescent psychology*. New York: Wiley.

Broughton, J. M. (1985). Women's rationality and men's virtues: A critique of gender dualism in Gilligan's theory of moral development. *Social Research, 52*, 597–624.

Chapman, M. (1984). *The structure of exchange: Piaget's sociological theory.* Unpublished manuscript.

Cooper, C. R., Grotevant, H. D., & Condon S. M. (1983). Individuality and connectedness in the family as a context for adolescent identity formation and role-taking skill. In H. D. Grotevant & C. R. Cooper (Eds.), *Adolescent development in the family.* San Francisco: Jossey-Bass.

Damon, W. (1977). *The social world of the child.* San Fransciso: Jossey-Bass.

Damon, W. (1983). *Social and personality development.* New York: Norton.

Damon, W. (1984). Peer education: The untapped potential. *Journal of Applied Developmental Psychology, 5*, 331–343.

Douvan, E., & Adelson, J. (1966). *The adolescent experience.* New York: Wiley.

Fischer, C. S. (1982). *To dwell among friends: Personal networks in town and city.* Chicago: University of Chicago Press.

Furth, H. G. (1983). A developmental perspective on the societal theory of Habermas. *Human Development, 26*, 181–197.

Gilbert, J. (1986). *A Cycle of outrage: reaction to the juvenile delinquent in the 1950s.* New York: Oxford University Press, 1986.

Gilligan, C. (1982). *In a different voice.* Cambridge, MA: Harvard University Press.

Gottman, J. M. (1983). How children become friends. *Monograph of the Society for Research in Child Development, 48*, Serial No. 201.

Gouldner, A. W. (1960). The norm of reciprocity: A preliminary statement. *American Sociological Review, 25*, 161–178.

Grotevant, H. D., & Cooper, C. R. (1986). Individuation in family relationships. *Human Development, 29*, 61–81.

Habermas, J. (1979). *Communication and the evolution of society.* Boston: Beacon.

Hoffman, M. L. (1980). Moral development in adolescence. In J. Adelson (Ed.), *Handbook of adolescent psychology*. New York: Wiley.

Johnson, B. (1975). *Functionalism in modern sociology: Understanding Talcott Parsons.* Morristown, NJ: General Learning Press.

Kandel, D. B., & Lesser, G. S. (1972). *Youth in two worlds: U.S. and Denmark.* San Francisco: Jossey-Bass.

Kohlberg, L. (1969). Stage and sequence: The cognitive–developmental approach to socialization. In D. A. Goslin (Ed.), *Handbook of socialization theory and research.* Chicago: Rand-McNally.

Lowi, T. J. (1969). *The end of liberalism.* New York: Norton.

Mullins, N. C. (1983). Theories and theory groups revisited. In R. Collins (Ed.), *Sociological theory, 1983.* San Francisco: Jossey-Bass.

Murphy, J. M., & Gilligan, C. (1980). Moral development in late adolescence and adulthood: A critique and reconstruction of Kohlberg's theory. *Human Development, 23*, 77–104.

Parsons, T., & Bales, R. F. (1955). *Family socialization and interaction process.* Glencoe, IL: Free Press.

Piaget, J. (1932). *The moral judgment of the child.* London: Kegan Paul.

Powers, S. I.; Hauser, S. T.; Schwartz, J. M.; Noam, G. G.; & Jacobson, A. M. (1983). Adolescent ego development and family interaction. In H. D. Grotevant & C. R. Cooper (Eds.), *Adolescent development in the family.* San Francisco: Jossey-Bass.

Riegel, K. F. (1976). The dialectics of human development. *American Psychologist, 31,* 689–700.

Selman, R. L. (1980). *The growth of interpersonal understanding: Developmental and clinical analyses.* New York: Academic.

Selman, R. L., Schorin, M. Z., Stone, C. R., & Phelps, E. (1983). A naturalistic study of children's social understanding. *Developmental Psychology, 19,* 82–102.

Sennett, R. (1974). *Families against the city.* New York: Vintage.

Smith, C. J. (1980). Social networks as metaphors, models, and methods. *Human Geography, 4,* 500–524.

Smollar, J., & Youniss, J. (1982). Social development through friendship. In K. H. Rubin & H. S. Ross (Eds.), *Peer relationships and social skills in childhood.* New York: Springer-Verlag.

Sroufe, L. A., & Fleeson, J. (in press). Attachment and the construction of relationships. In W. W. Hartup & Z. Rubin (Eds.), *The nature and development of relationships.* Hillsdale, NJ: Erlbaum.

Sullivan, H. S. (1953). *The interpersonal theory of psychiatry.* New York: Norton.

Waterman, A. S. (1981). Individualism and interdependence. *American Psychologist, 36,* 762–773.

Weinreich-Haste, H. (1982). Piaget on morality: A critical perspective. In S. Modgil & C. Modgil (Eds.), *Jean Piaget: Consensus and controversy.* London: Holt, Rinehart, & Winston.

Wellman, B. (1979). The community question: The intimate networks of East Yorkers. *American Journal of Sociology, 184,* 1201–1231.

Wellman, B. (1983). Network analysis: Some basic principles. In R. Collins (Ed.), *Sociological theory, 1983.* San Francisco: Jossey-Bass.

Wertsch, J. V. (1985). *Vygostsky and the social formation of mind.* Cambridge, MA: Harvard University Press.

Wright, D. S. (1982). "The moral judgment of the child" revisited. In D. Locke & H. Weinerich-Haste (Eds.), *Moral judgment and moral action.* London: Wiley.

Youniss, J. (1980). *Parents and peers in social development.* Chicago: University of Chicago Press.

Youniss, J. (1981). Moral development through a theory of social construction. *Merrill-Palmer Quarterly, 27,* 385–403.

Youniss, J. (1983b). Piaget and the self constituted through relations. In W. F. Overton (Ed.), *The relationship between social and cognitive development.* Hillsdale, NJ: Erlbaum.

Youniss, J. (1983a). Beyond ideology to the universals of development. In D. Kuhn & J. A. Meacham (Eds.), *On the development of developmental psychology.* Basel: Karger.

Youniss, J. (1984). Morality, communicative relations, and the development of reciprocity. In W. Edelstein & J. Habermas (Eds.), *Soziale interaktion und soziales verstehen.* Frankfurt: Suhrkamp.

Youniss, J., & Smollar, J. (1985). *Adolescent relations with mothers, fathers, and friends.* Chicago: University of Chicago Press.

CHAPTER 6

Sociomoral Behavior and Development from a Rule-Governed Perspective: Psychosocial Theory as a Nomotic Science

WILLIAM M. KURTINES

The work reported here was conducted at the Laboratory for Research on Psychosocial Development and Behavior, Florida International University. Support for the research was provided by a grant from the FIU Foundation and the College of Arts and Sciences, Florida International University. The author would like to thank the following individuals for their contributions to the work reported here: Mildred Alvarez, Margarita Azmitia, Marvin Berkowitz, Gustavo Carlo, Lois Cooksey, John Gibbs, Esther Grief, Ann Higgins, Robert Hogan, Lawrence Kohlberg, Teri Lanza, Ting Lei, Laura Pace, Richard Shweder, and James Youniss.

The purpose of this chapter is to describe the framework for a program of research that has as its aim the articulation of a conception of psychosocial theory as a nomotic science. Nomotics is the science of human rules and rule systems. One of the basic tasks of psychosocial theory, understood as a nomotic science, has been to develop and refine a theoretical framework and appropriate research methodology for investigating the creative nature of human rule-governed behavior within a constructivist–evolutionary framework. The work reported in this chapter illustrates how the application of a rule-governed perspective yields a number of significant implications for conceptualizing the science of human social and moral behavior and development.

The focus of the work reported here is on the ontogenesis of sociomoral knowledge and understanding. In contrast to traditional psychological theories, which focus on the role of learning and maturational processes in the acquisition and/or development of sociomoral knowledge and understanding, the approach described here views the ontogenesis of sociomoral knowledge and understanding in competent rule users as the outcome of a constructive evolutionary process; that is, as the outcome of the formative process of the subjective construction and intersubjective co-construction of social reality. According to this view, the development of linguistic, cognitive, sociomoral, and communicative competencies defines the interrelated lines of psychosocial development by which the individual becomes a competent member of a social system. Learning and maturational processes are viewed as playing a central role in the development of prerequisite linguistic, cognitive, sociomoral, and communicative competencies, but once these competencies are acquired subsequent ontogenetic change and evolution in sociomoral understanding are viewed as no longer constrained by such processes. Rather, change in sociomoral understanding in competent rule users is viewed as the outcome of the formative process of constructive evolution.

Two domains of nomotic research are delineated: reconstructive and constructive. The goal of reconstructive research is the identification of the universal structures of sociomoral knowledge and understanding. The universal structures of sociomoral knowledge are viewed as the basic building blocks of constructive evolution change. The focus of reconstructive research is thus on the structure of sociomoral knowledge. The goal of constructive research, in contrast, is on the identification of the process by which new or novel forms of sociomoral knowledge emerge. Reconstructive research on the identification and measurement of several basic structural dimensions of sociomoral knowledge will be briefly summarized. In addition, because the approach used here views constructive research as process oriented, a conceptualization of the process of the constructive evolution of sociomoral understanding in competent rule users is outlined. The three working hypotheses that form the core of our constructive research are concerned with: (1) the process by which new or novel sociomoral knowledge emerges; (2) the process by which informational variation in sociomoral knowledge and understanding is disseminated throughout social systems and transmitted across generations; and (3) the process by which selected forms of informational variation are preserved. Research designed to investigate the role of communicative processes in the ontogenetic evolution of sociomoral knowledge and under-

standing will also be described. The aims of this research were to develop a measure for assessing level of communicative functioning during peer interaction involving normative conflict and to test hypotheses with respect to the role of communication in the ontogenetic evolution of sociomoral understanding in competent rule users. Because the approach used here views the evolution of sociomoral knowledge in competent rule users as the outcome of a constructive evolutionary process, a framework for conceptualizing the role of learning and maturational processes in the development of prerequisite psychosocial competencies is described. Research concerning developmental differences in the emergence of sociomoral and communicative competencies is summarized.

Theory and research on sociomoral development are undergoing dramatic transformation. Traditional theoretical perspectives have changed and new perspectives have begun to emerge (Kurtines & Gewirtz, 1984). As this volume indicates, the change has nowhere been more dramatic than in the area of social process and sociomoral behavior and development. Research on the effects of social interaction on social and moral development has flourished in recent years and has begun to emerge as a distinct and substantial area of scholarly and research interests (e.g., Berkowitz, 1985; Berkowitz & Gibbs, 1983; Berndt, 1983; Damon & Killen, 1982; Eisenberg, Lundy, Shell, & Roth, 1985; Haan, 1978; 1985; Higgins, Power, & Kohlberg, 1984; Keller, 1984; Kohlberg, 1984; Kurtines, 1986; Much & Shweder, 1978; Nisan, 1984; Oser, 1984; Packer, 1985; Selman, 1980; Selman & Demorest, 1984; Shweder, Mahapatra, & Miller, in press; Youniss, 1981). The purpose of this chapter is to describe some recent theoretical and empirical work that has been carried out as part of a programatic effort to contribute to the growing recognition of the role of social process in sociomoral behavior and development. The theoretical framework that we have been using in this research has been described in detail elsewhere (Kurtines, Lanza, Carlo, Cooksey, & Pace, 1986). This theoretical heuristic, which is termed *psychosocial role theory*, is intended to provide a theoretically meaningful account of both social and psychological processes.

In developing this theoretical framework we have had to look beyond traditional psychological approaches that focus on maturational and learning processes as related to the individual organism's development. According to this approach, the individual as agent, actor and decision maker does not simply acquire or develop sociomoral knowledge and understanding as a result of the operation of learning or maturational processes. Although learning and maturational processes are viewed as contributing to the development of prerequisite psychosocial competencies, psychosocial role theory also views change and evolution in sociomoral knowledge and understanding in competent rule users as the outcome of the formative process of constructive evolution. That is, psychosocial role theory views the competent rule user as actively participating in the co-construction of an intersubjectively shared network of social and moral rules and rule systems. Psychosocial role theory, consequently, shifts the conceptual focus from maturational and learning processes as related to individual development to the competent rule users' contribution to the intersubjectively *shared* co-construction of sociomoral knowledge and understanding. Thus as we will discuss in more detail later, psychosocial role theory views maturational and learning processes as playing a central role in the development of psychosocial competencies (including sociomoral competencies) necessary for social interaction. However, once the prerequisite competencies are acquired, subsequent evolution of sociomoral knowledge and understanding is viewed as no longer constrained by maturation and learning. Once the necessary competencies are acquired, subsequent change and evolution in sociomoral understanding are viewed as the outcome of constructive evolutionary processes. In this frame, one aim of our empirical work has been the development and refinement of appropriate research methodology for investigating the creative or constructive nature of human social behavior and development.

In this chapter we will consider some of the broader implications of our work for the reconceptualization of the foundations of the scientific study of human behavior. Consequently, psychosocial theory, as it will be described in this chapter, is presented not simply as another theory, but as the application of a new science, the science of human rules and rule systems.

PSYCHOSOCIAL THEORY

The psychosocial role–theoretical approach to social and moral behavior and development described here explicitly adopts a view of the individual as a moral agent whose actions and decisions take place within the context of a socially defined system of rules and roles, thereby providing a conceptual framework broad enough to account for the effects of social as well as psychological processes. Psychosocial role theory is thus a social psychological theory similar in some respects to the social psychological theories proposed earlier by theorists such as Fromm (1947), Lewin (1935), and Sullivan (1953) as well as more modern versions of social psychological theory such as the psychosocial theory of Erikson (1950). Psychosocial role theory differs from these other social psychological theories, however, in its explicit focus on human behavior as rule governed (Kurtines, 1984, 1986). According to this approach, most interesting and important forms of human behavior can be conceptualized as rule-governed behavior. Language and law, science and logic, morality and convention all provide examples of diverse forms of human rule-governed behavior. The notion of human behavior as rule governed is, to borrow a phrase from Stephen Pepper (1972), a *root metaphor*. Using this simple but powerful root metaphor as a starting point, this chapter will attempt to articulate a conception of psychosocial theory as a nomotic science. Nomotics—from the Greek *nomos*, "law, convention"—is the science of human rules and rule systems (Hogan & Henley, 1970).

Central to the conception of psychosocial theory as a nomotic science is the view that the rule-governed nature of human action is fundamentally distinct from the "law-governed" behavior of natural phenomena. Using linguistic behavior as an example, Toulmin (1969) notes:

> In certain crucial respects the rules to which linguistic behavior conforms differ from the laws of the physical sciences. . . . The essential mark of rule-conforming behavior lies in the normative force of relevant rules. An agent who recognizes that he is deviating from a rule acknowledges (at any rate prima facie) a claim on him to correct his behavior. (pp. 86–87)

Rules are thus normative in nature and imply standards against which behavior is evaluated. An individual's violation of a rule, consequently, in no way invalidates that rule. No such situation occurs when dealing with purely law-governed natural phenomena. Toulmin (1969) further points out:

> The motion of the perihelion of the planet Mercury was observed, during the nineteenth century, to be deviating from the precise pattern astronomers had expected on the basis of Newton's dynamical theories. Yet scientists did not treat this deviation as a "failure" or "mistake" on the part of the planet. . . . It would have been laughable for them to talk of Mercury as "recognizing" that it was transgressing the "norm" set by Newtonian law so as to conform more nearly to the norm set by Mercury itself. (pp. 87–88)

This view would thus suggest that human behavior is not subject to a temporally and spatially universal set of laws from which there can be no deviation. Quite the contrary, human behavior conforms to rules that are individually and collectively created, self-imposed, and subject to change. Human beings hence not only conform to rules, but also are free to change or create them in a way that natural laws cannot be created or changed.

Because rules and rule systems are individually and collectively created, self-imposed, and subject to change, social systems are viewed as dynamic rather than static systems, subject to a process of change and evolution. Sociomoral rule systems, as constituent elements of social systems, are similarly viewed as open systems subject to change and evolution. One basic task of psychosocial role theory, conceptualized as a nomotic science, has been to develop and refine a theoretical framework and appropriate research methodology for investigating the creative or constructive nature of human rule-governed behavior within a constructive evolutionary framework. Because the work reported here was conducted as part of an ongoing research program, the framework is viewed as necessarily tentative and preliminary. Though it is tentative, we consider the work to illustrate how the application of such an approach yields some novel and interesting conclusions with respect to the science of human behavior and development.

Reconstructive and Constructive Nomotic Research

In developing our conceptualization of psychosocial theory as a nomotic science we have found it necessary to delineate two basic domains of nomotic research: reconstructive and constructive nomotic research. Each of these domains addresses a distinct but related set of conceptual, empirical, and methodological issues that confront the nomotic sciences. That is, as we will discuss in more detail later, they define two independent but interrelated domains of research, each with a distinct but related set of conceptual, empirical, and methodological issues.

The reconstructive domain of nomotic research involves research that has as its aim the systematic reconstruction of nomotic knowledge (i.e., the competent rule user's implicit knowledge or understanding of rules and rule systems). Nomotic research explicitly recognizes a distinction between a user's implicit understanding of rules and rule systems (competence) and the actual use or application of rules during the process of engaging in sociomoral actions and making sociomoral judgments (performance). This competence–performance distinction recognizes that the competent rule user knows or understands how to achieve, accomplish, perform, or produce a variety of things without explicitly being able to give an account of the concepts, rules, schemata, or criteria on which their performances are based. Nomotic research thus recognizes a distinction between the actor's knowledge or understanding of the rules that underlie performance (i.e., the competence of the rule user) and intervening, external, and contingent limiting factors that contribute to actual performance. In the latter case, the performance of the competent rule user is viewed as interacting with a variety of factors of which the underlying competence of the user is only one.

Reconstructive research has been successfully carried out in the investigation of nomotic knowledge in such areas as theoretical linguistics (Chomsky, 1965), genetic epistemology (Piaget, 1954), and communication theory (Habermas, 1979). Our own reconstructive research in the area of sociomoral knowledge is in many respects similar to the reconstructive research that has been carried out in the areas of language, cognition, and communication. The goal of reconstructive research is to render explicit the universal structures of systems of rules, the mastery of which underlies the competence of a subject to generate meaningful symbolic configurations in each domain (i.e., linguistic, cognitive, communicative, sociomoral). Although reconstructive research is empirical research, its object domain is distinct from that of the natural sciences. The domain of reconstructive nomotic research is symbolically structured reality (McCarthy, 1981). The data used in the formation and testing of reconstructive hypotheses are not presented for direct observation in the natural world but are elicited and tested against the tacit knowledge underlying the actual performances of competent subjects. Although reconstructive hypotheses are tested against actual performances, the ultimate aim of reconstructive research is to reconstruct the *universal* competencies that underlie linguistic, cognitive, communicative, and sociomoral performance species wide, not merely the competencies characteristic of specific individuals or groups in particular sociocultural contexts.

Reconstructive nomotic research focuses on the reconstruction of already existing implicit knowledge, and is thus retrospective in nature. The successes of reconstructive research in such areas as theoretical linguistics, genetic epistemology, and communication theory in identifying species-wide competencies that underlie linguistic, cognitive, and communicative performances attest to the utility of reconstructive research. As noted earlier however, one of the characteristics of human rules and rule systems (as opposed to natural laws) is that they are individually and collectively created, self-imposed, and subject to change and evolution. Such a view serves to restore an element of freedom and creativity to human action and existence. A view of human rules and rule systems as individually and collectively created or constructed out of preexisting nomotic knowledge also raises the question of the process by which new or novel forms of nomotic knowledge evolve, and calls attention to the limits of purely reconstructive research with its emphasis on preexisting structures of nomotic knowledge and competencies. The reconstruction of species-wide competencies cannot, in itself, provide an adequate account of the richness and diversity of forms of human rules and rule systems; it can only provide an account of the preexisting structures that underlie the creation or construction of the variety and richness that is characteristic of naturally occurring human rule systems. Consequently, in this chapter we will argue that nomotic research (i.e., research on human rule systems) must include a constructive domain as well as a reconstructive domain. One of the contributions of psychosocial theory, understood as a nomotic science, has been its focus on the identification of the process by which new or novel variations in forms of nomotic knowledge emerge.

Constructive nomotic research, as distinct from reconstructive research, focuses on the formative process of the construction of new or novel forms of nomotic knowledge and understanding out of preexisting structures and is thus prospective in nature. Consequently, while reconstructive nomotic research as traditionally conceptualized focuses on the *structure* of preexisting nomotic knowledge (i.e., the universal features or structures of nomotic competence), constructive nomotic research focuses on the *process* of the construction or production of new or novel variation in forms of nomotic knowledge and therefore includes performance as well as competence variables. The truth status of reconstructive hypotheses can be empirically tested against a preexisting data base derived from competent rule users. The creation of new or novel forms of nomotic knowledge, on the other hand, is the product of a formative process of construction and co-construction, the outcome of which has yet to be determined. Constructive research is thus more prospective and process oriented than retrospective and structure oriented. The emergence of new or novel nomotic knowledge or understanding, therefore, cannot be approached from a purely reconstructive perspective. Reconstructive research, consequently, provides no direct basis for deriving hypotheses with respect to the constructive evolution of new forms of nomotic knowledge at either the ontogenetic or the sociohistorical level, for such hypotheses would necessarily presuppose that future nomotic knowledge will be similar in form to past nomotic knowledge, a presupposition that is without logical or historical justification. Because we cannot know in advance the nature of future nomotic knowledge, constructive hypotheses focus on the nature of the formative process itself rather than the outcome of the process; that is, the form of new nomotic knowledge. The past can be explained, but the future can be only anticipated (McCarthy, 1981). The social construction of reality is thus a process whose outcome can only be anticipated or projected (as opposed to predicted). Constructivist research thus has as its aim the identification of the process by which new or novel variation in forms of nomotic knowledge emerges and the investigation of the conditions that limit or facilitate preservation or transmission of new forms of nomotic knowledge.

In contrast to reconstructive research, constructive research on nomotic knowledge as such has received relatively little attention. As social scientists we have been traditionally more accustomed to recognizing (and, indeed, participating in) the creation or construction of new forms of knowledge and understanding in the areas of science and technology than in the area of nomotic knowledge and understanding. The social evolutionary history of the species, however, has been one of a continuous process of the creation of new forms of nomotic knowledge and understanding. Thus one aim of psychosocial role theory is the identification of the process by which new or novel variation in sociomoral knowledge evolves at both the individual and the sociohistorical level. Such research requires an investigation of the process by which preexisting competencies interact with performance variables to generate new or novel forms of sociomoral knowledge and understanding.

The next section of this chapter will briefly summarize reconstructive research that we have done on developing a methodology for measuring basic structural dimensions of sociomoral knowledge and a number of the dimensions that we have identified as part of our reconstructive efforts. As with previous reconstructive research, the goal of our work has been to render explicit the universal competencies that underlie the competent subject's performances. These universal competencies are conceptualized as the basic building blocks of sociomoral knowledge and understanding. As noted earlier, however, the identification of the universal structures of sociomoral knowledge and understanding cannot, in itself, provide an account of the richness and diversity of forms of human rule systems. Consequently, the section entitled "The Constructive Evolution of Sociomoral Knowledge and Understanding" will outline a conceptualization of the constructive process by which change and evolution in sociomoral knowledge and understanding occur, provides an account of the emergence of a diversity of forms of sociomoral knowledge and understanding. The next section will briefly summarize some of our research investigating the process of the constructive evolution of sociomoral knowledge and understanding. The final section, "Psychosocial Development," will address the issue of the role of maturational and learning processes in the development of psychosocial competencies.

RESEARCH ON THE RECONSTRUCTION OF BASIC STRUCTURES OF SOCIOMORAL KNOWLEDGE AND UNDERSTANDING

Central to our reconstructive research was the development of a measure of sociomoral knowledge and understanding conceptualized as knowledge and understanding of sociomoral rules and rule systems. From a psychosocial role-theoretical perspective, sociomoral knowledge and understanding at the intra-personal level are viewed as knowledge and understanding of the intersubjec-tively *shared* network or system of rules and norms that govern the relations between individuals within a system. Moreover, sociomoral rules and rule systems are viewed as one component of the individual's nomotic knowledge. Nomotic knowledge is thus knowledge of human rules and rule systems (e.g., linguistic, legal, logical, communicative, conventional, etc., as well as social and moral). At the intrapersonal level, psychosocial role theory takes as its theoretical focus one particular subset of rules, namely, social and moral rules, and one type of nomotic knowledge; namely, sociomoral knowledge and understanding.

The aim of our reconstructive research was to identify empirically in our research population basic dimensions of variation in sociomoral knowledge and understanding at the intrapersonal level. At the intrapersonal (subjective) level, sociomoral knowledge is conceptualized as the competent rule user's knowledge and understanding of sociomoral rules. Sociomoral knowledge, however, is not conceptualized as knowledge of a simple, unorganized collection of specific or discrete rules. On the contrary, the competent rule user's knowledge and understanding of *specific* social and moral rules are hypothesized to be organized around a more basic set of structural dimensions or rule schemata. Variation in sociomoral knowledge (i.e., the competence subject's knowledge and understanding of specific rules and principles) is conceptualized as reflecting more underlying structural dimensions that serve to organize the individual's knowledge and understanding of specific rules. The structural dimensions of sociomoral knowledge thus function as structures or schemata (Bartlett, 1932; Piaget, 1936) that organize and unify the person's sociomoral knowledge and understanding and define the basic dimensions of sociomoral competence. The structural dimensions that make up the core of sociomoral knowledge thus function to provide the underlying dimensions that structure and order the person's social and moral rule repertoire. These structures or schemata are conceptualized as universal structures in the sense of constituting an emergent property of sociomoral rule systems qua rule systems. That is, the structural dimensions are conceptualized as universal features or properties that are unique to sociomoral rule systems and that distinguish them from other types of rule systems. In other words, linguistic, cognitive, sociomoral, and commu-nicative rule systems are all forms of human rule systems. They are, however, not the same rule system. Reconstructive research on sociomoral knowledge is concerned with identifying those properties or features that are unique and universally characteristic of sociomoral rule systems and that distinguish them from other types of rule systems. Our reconstructive research is thus predicated on the assumptions that it is possible to develop research strategies and methods for identifying the structural dimensions along which all sociomoral rule systems vary, and that the development of sociomoral competencies involves the acquisition of knowledge and understanding along these dimensions. In this sense, these dimensions constitute the universal dimensions of competency that underlie moral actions and judgments independent of sociocultural context in the same way that universal structures of language, cognition, and communication underlie linguistic, cognitive, and communicative competence regardless of culture or context. Thus although forms of sociomoral knowledge and understanding (i.e., the specific combinations and permutations of rules that comprise particular sociomoral rule systems) can be expected to vary historically and socioculturally, the structural organization of sociomoral rule systems is hypothesized to vary along the same dimensions. The scale that we developed was designed to measure developmental and individual differences along a number of dimensions that emerged from our empirical work. It should be noted that we consider our work on identifying and measuring these dimensions to be preliminary, and that we view our research methods and findings to be only tentative first steps in the process of the reconstruction of the basic dimensions of sociomoral competence.

Consistent with our social constructionist orientation, we conceptualize the epistemic subject's knowledge and understanding of the basic dimensions and categories of "social" reality as different in significant respects from the knowledge and understanding of the categories or dimensions of "physical" or "natural" reality such as space, time, and causality (cf. Piaget, 1954). Social systems, unlike biological or physical systems, do not have a physical structure. As a consequence, social systems cannot exist independent of the cognitions, beliefs, and expectations (i.e., the intersubjectively shared nomotic understanding) of the individuals who comprise the system. This is not to say that social systems do not have an objective existence. Social systems do have an objective existence, but at a different level of reality from that of physical systems. In Habermas's terms (McCarthy, 1981), society exists as a symbolically prestructured sector of reality toward which we can adopt an objectivating attitude. Nomotic knowledge is thus knowledge of a sector of reality that is open to human construction and co-construction. Nomotic knowledge is knowledge and understanding of an intersubjectively shared network of rules that itself changes and evolves. Thus although the basic dimensions of nomotic knowledge that structure rule systems are universal, the specific forms of sociomoral knowledge generated by these structures vary historically and socioculturally. Consequently, the form of the epistemic subject's knowledge and understanding of specific sociomoral rules is, on the one hand, conceptualized as necessarily conditioned by the intersubjectively shared social–cultural–historical context that constrains such understanding. The epistemic subject is also, on the other hand, conceptualized as co-contributing to the creation of the intersubjectively shared meaning of sociomoral rules and concepts. Nomotic knowledge is not knowledge and understanding of a fixed or invariant set of categories. Rather, nomotic knowledge is knowledge and understanding of a set of rules that are themselves subject to the formative process of constructive evolution and change.

Because human behavior is conceptualized as conforming to rules that are individually and collectively created, self-imposed, and subject to change, sociomoral knowledge and understanding are viewed as forms of cognitive–emotive understanding in that they encompass both the *understanding* and the *respect* for rules that, as Piaget (1932/1985) has observed, constitute the essence of morality. Thus as is not the case with natural laws, conformance with sociomoral rules requires both understanding *and* respect. That is, conformance with sociomoral rules requires not only that individuals understand the rules, but also that they be predisposed to comply with them.

The Sociomoral Competence Scale

The Sociomoral Competence Scale (SCS) was developed and designed to measure developmental and individual differences along several basic dimensions we identified in our reconstructive research. The SCS was conceptualized as a measure of psychosocial competence in the sense of a measure of the competent user's implicit understanding of rules and rule systems. In the next section of this chapter we will address the issue of the developmental emergence of psychosocial competencies. For our reconstructive research the primary focus was on developing a measure of variation in sociomoral knowledge and understanding in competent rule users.

The first stage in the development of the SCS was to explore a number of different methodologies for identifying and measuring dimensions along which sociomoral knowledge varies. During this early phase of the scales development, a pilot study was conducted that involved the development of an initial form of the SCS. Subjects for this study included pilot samples of children, adolescents, and young adult college students. One aim of this phase of the research was to develop a format for the scale that would allow subjects to generate their own dimensions or categories of meaning. That is, consistent with the exploratory nature of our reconstructive research, we attempted to develop a measure that would allow subjects to use self-generated dimensions or categories of understanding. In addition, we attempted to develop a measure that would be appropriate for a wide age range of subjects. The Sociomoral Competence Scale–Production (SCS-P), a production measure, was constructed during this pilot phase. The SCS-P is administered individually in an interview format. The SCS-P consists of three sets of questions and probes. Each set of questions and probes was designed to assess the subject's sociomoral knowledge and understanding in three conceptually distinct but related areas. The first set of questions and probes assesses the subject's understanding of the concept of *justice*; the second assesses the subject's understanding of the concept of *goodness*; and the third assesses the subject's understanding of *morality*. The questions and probes were administered in an open-ended but structured format. The SCS-P was intended to be flexible enough in its administration to allow subjects to generate their own categories of meaning. Subjects were not probed for specific categories, but were allowed to use whatever categories they spontaneously generated in defining the concepts.

The young adult subjects' responses to the questions and probes were used to identify a basic set of dimensions along which sociomoral knowledge varies. The five dimensions we identified as part of our reconstructive research are as follows:

1. *Relativistic–Universalistic.* This dimension was concerned with the nature of moral standards and contrasts a moral orientation that emphasizes universal, absolute, or objective moral standards with a moral orientation that emphasizes the relative nature of moral standards.
2. *Teleological–Deontological.* This dimension is concerned with the basic nature of morality and contrasts a moral orientation that emphasizes the effects, consequences, or outcome of morality with a moral orientation that emphasizes duties, rights, or obligations independent of consequence.
3. *Individualistic–Social.* This dimension is concerned with the locus of morality and contrasts a moral orientation that emphasizes the individualistic basis of morality with a moral orientation that emphasizes the social nature of morality.
4. *Religious–Secular.* This dimension is also concerned with the locus of morality and contrasts a moral orientation that emphasizes the spiritualistic or otherworldly nature of morality with a moral orientation that emphasizes the secular nature of morality.
5. *Intuitive–Rational.* This dimension is concerned with the rationale or conceptual foundations of morality and contrasts a moral orientation that emphasizes the intuitive nature of morality with a moral orientation that emphasizes the rational nature of morality.

A more detailed description of the administration, scoring, and rating criteria for the SCS-P is available in the SCS manual (Kurtines & Lanza, 1983) that was developed as part of the pilot phase.

The SCS-P developed during this phase of the research generated a rich and useful set of data. The subjects' responses indicated a wide range of variability and were useful in identifying a number of basic dimensions such as those just described. However, the SCS-P is individually administered and relatively time-consuming, requiring approximately one hour per administration. Because our subsequent constructive research required the use of multiple administrations to relatively large samples, the main focus of our preliminary constructive research was on the development of a group-administered form of the SCS. Consequently, a second form of the SCS was developed, the Sociomoral Competence Scale–Focal Issues (SCS-FI). The SCS-FI builds on the findings obtained from the SCS-P during the pilot phase, but differs from the SCS-P in three ways. First, it is a group-administered self-report measure. Second, the SCS-FI was designed to assess only two of the dimensions from the SCS-P: Relativism–Universalism and Teleological–Deontological. Third, the scoring of the scale is based on the subject's self-report responses to structured items and can thus be done by computer.

The SCS-FI consists of three sets of items. These sets of items are designed to assess the subject's sociomoral knowledge and understanding in the same three domains as the SCS-P: justice, goodness, and morality. Each of the sets of items is scored for two scales: the Relativism–Universalism (RU) and the Teleological–Deontological (TD) scale. For purposes of the SCS-FI the dimensions are referred to as focal issues. The SCS-FI is thus designed to assess developmental and individual differences in variation in sociomoral knowledge and understanding along two dimensions or focal issues: Relativism–Universalism and Teleological–Deontological.

The items for the SCS-FI were constructed by developing paraphrases derived from the responses of the pilot subjects to the items from the SCS-P. The paraphrases were intended to represent contrasting positions from each dimension (e.g., a relativist versus a universalist position). The SCS-FI asks subjects to suppose two people are talking about what one of the concepts (e.g., justice) means. Each hypothetical person's position is presented and the subject is asked to indicate which person's position comes closest to his or her own and to indicate on a 5-point Likert-type scale how much he or she agrees with each person's position. The items from the SCS-FI were thus intended to assess the subject's relative position on the two focal issues included on the SCS-FI. It should be noted that the items for the SCS-FI were constructed so that the terms were self-explanatory to facilitate their use with children as well as adults. The SCS-FI was successfully pilot-tested on a small sample of fifth grade children in order to assess its suitability for use with children and preadolescents. In addition, the items for the SCS-FI were specifically constructed in order to facilitate their use as discussion stimuli as well as for assessment.

Extensive psychometric analyses were conducted on the SCS-FI. The subjects for our psychometric study consisted of sample (n = 147) of young adult college students. The psychometric analyses that were conducted on the scales included item analyses, internal consistency reliabilities, factor analyses, and gender differences. Overall, the results of this study indicate that the SCS-FI has adequate psychometric properties when used with young adults. First, the two dimensions of the SCS-FI appear to assess relatively independent dimensions as indicated by the factor analysis. Second, both subscales appear to have adequate reliability. Third, the two dimensions appear to be free of the effects of sex differences.

The research we have described thus far has focused on identifying basic dimensions along which sociomoral knowledge and understanding vary at the intrapersonal level; that is, dimensions of variability in the individual's sociomoral knowledge and understanding. As noted earlier, however, a view of rules and rule systems as individually and collectively created or constructed out of preexisting nomotic knowledge also raises the question of the process by which new or novel nomotic knowledge evolves. Traditional psychological theories have focused on change or evolution in the individual's sociomoral knowledge and understanding. Sociomoral knowledge and understanding, however, change and evolve at the social, cultural, and historical level as well as the individual level. Indeed, it has been argued (cf. McCarthy, 1981) that the social evolutionary history of the species, from relatively simple Neolithic societies organized around kinship systems to postindustrial societies with a complex organizational structure of social, moral, legal, political, and economic institutions, has been one of a continuous process of the creation and evolution of new forms of nomotic knowledge and understanding. Social evolution, it has been cogently argued, has replaced biological evolution as the primary adaptive process for the human species (Huxley, 1942; Waddington, 1975). Thus a major focus of our research program has been on developing and refining a conceptual framework and appropriate research methodology for use in constructive research. In developing this conceptual framework, we have had to look beyond those psychological theories that have traditionally focused on development as it occurs at the intrapersonal level. Psychosocial role theory, in contrast to more traditional theories, views the ontogenetic (intrapersonal) evolution of sociomoral knowledge and understanding as necessarily dependent upon and conditioned by the evolution of sociomoral knowledge and understanding at the sociohistorical (interpersonal) level. From this perspective, change and evolution occur not only at the intrapersonal level (i.e., ontogenetic evolution in the individual's subjective knowledge and understanding of sociomoral rules) but also at the interpersonal level (i.e., evolution in intersubjectively shared knowledge and understanding of sociomoral rules). We have, consequently, found it necessary to look beyond the basic processes of maturation and learning that govern change and evolution in the individual organism and to begin to formulate a conception of the formative process of constructive evolution and change at the sociohistorical level as well as the ontogenetic level. In the next section we will outline a tentative framework for conceptualizing the process of constructive evolution in sociomoral knowledge and understanding that we have been using in our constructive research.

THE CONSTRUCTIVE EVOLUTION OF SOCIOMORAL KNOWLEDGE AND UNDERSTANDING

This section describes our conceptualization of the process of the constructive evolution of sociomoral knowledge and understanding. We will describe it in some detail because of the central role that it played in guiding the selection of theoretical constructs as well as research strategies, methods, and hypotheses for our constructive research. In developing our conceptualization we have found it necessary to draw on a wide variety of theoretical and research literatures. We would again point out that the conceptualization outlined in this section is necessarily viewed as tentative and preliminary, but it has proved useful in our work.

The conceptualization of the process of constructive evolution that we propose in this section is viewed as applying to both the ontogenetic and the sociohistorical evolution of sociomoral knowledge and understanding. The *ontogenetic evolution* of sociomoral knowledge involves the emergence at the intrapersonal level of sociomoral knowledge or understanding that is new or novel relative to the individual organism's developmental history. The *sociohistorical evolution* of sociomoral knowledge, on the other hand, involves the emergence at the interpersonal level of sociomoral knowledge that is historically new or novel relative to social systems (i.e., social groups, societies, cultures). The ontogenetic and the sociohistorical evolution of sociomoral knowledge are, however, conceptualized as parallel and interdependent processes rather than independent processes in that both emerge as a result of the intersubjectively shared interactional processes that are at the core of the co-construction of social reality. Social systems, we noted, have an objective existence—they exist as a symbolically prestructured sector of reality toward which we can adopt an objectivating attitude. However, social systems are ultimately the collective co-constructions of the individuals who make up the systems.

Thus for our constructive research we have adopted the view that the course of the constructive evolution of sociomoral knowledge and understanding at the sociohistorical level revolves around the basic problem that confronts all societies, social groups, and social systems—a problem that has been recognized as at the core of morality since classical antiquity —namely, the problem of the good and the just life (i.e., maximizing good while minimizing evil, and distributing goods and evils justly), *and* that this is the same problem that confronts individuals in the course of the ontogenetic evolution of their sociomoral knowledge. Thus in the final analysis the central issue in the construction and co-construction of social and moral knowledge and understanding, ontogenetically *and* historically, is the issue of the meaning of the good and the just life.

The ontogenetic and the sociohistorical evolution of sociomoral knowledge and understanding are, as noted, viewed as interdependent processes that emerge as a result of the intersubjectively shared co-construction of social reality. Social theorists in the constructivist tradition have historically tended to emphasize the creative or constructed nature of social reality (Berger & Luckman, 1967; Goffman, 1959; Mead, 1934). However, relatively little work has been done on specifying the process by which sociohistorical evolution occurs. Because we view ontogenetic and sociohistorical evolution to be interdependent processes, one central aim of our research program has been to identify the process by which the constructive evolution of new forms of sociomoral knowledge takes place at both levels. Traditional psychological theories, we noted earlier, view the evolution of sociomoral knowledge and understanding at the intrapersonal level as governed by either maturational processes, learning processes, or both. Maturational or learning processes, however, cannot provide an account of change and evolution as they occur at the sociohistorical (interpersonal) level. Since relatively little work has been done on investigating the constructive process of social evolution, we have found it useful to draw on a variety of sources outside the psychological literature for theoretical constructs as well as potential research methods, strategies, and hypotheses. Because our work on the constructive evolution of sociomoral knowledge (at both the ontogenetic and the sociohistorical level) parallels in many respects the work that has been done in the area of biological evolution, we have found it particularly useful to draw on the findings of modern Darwinian–molecular theory of evolution in formulating theoretical constructs and working hypotheses.

Modern Darwinian–molecular theory of evolution attempts to integrate evolutionary biology, with its historical roots in Darwinian natural selection, and molecular biology, with its historical roots in Mendelian genetic theory (Monod, 1973). Darwinian–molecular biology seeks to provide an account of the three fundamental processes of life—replication, mutation, and selection. These three processes provide the key to understanding continuity and change in biological species. In our work we have been operating under the assumption that the task of nomotic research is to account for continuity and change in the domain of social evolution, in much the same way that biological evolutionary theory attempts to account for continuity and change in biological species. Thus we have conceptualized the reconstructive and constructive domains of nomotic research to be distinct but related research programs similar to the distinct but related research programs carried out in the field of molecular biology and Darwinian evolutionary theory. The tasks of reconstructive research, as will be discussed below, are in many respects similar to the tasks of molecular biology while the tasks of constructive research are similar to those of Darwinian evolutionary theory.

Research in molecular biology, like the reconstructive nomotic research, has as its aim rendering explicit the basic structures that make possible continuity and change in biological species. In the case of research in molecular biology, however, the basic structures are biochemical rather than nomotic. Several recent advances in molecular biology have contributed to our understanding of how continuity and change occur in the biosphere, and have served as a useful source of hypotheses for our own work. Perhaps the most important accomplishment of recent biology is the determination of the role DNA (deoxyribonucleic acid) plays as the universal building block of evolutionary change. The most significant characteristic of the DNA molecule is its capacity to reproduce its basic structure over an infinite number of replications. In addition to the capacity for reproductive invariance, DNA has the capacity to capture and reproduce random perturbations within its structure over an infinite number of replications (Monod, 1973). With the identification of the double helix as the structure, universal to all life forms, that enables the molecular machinery of replication (DNA) to capture and reproduce random perturbations in its own molecular structure, modern molecular biology has been able to provide an account of both replication and mutation, processes at the core of continuity and change in biological species. The identification of the universal structure of the DNA molecule, however, cannot in itself provide a full account of the emergence of a diversity of forms of life. A full explanation of biological evolution requires an account of the third fundamental life process, natural selection.

In Darwinian–molecular evolutionary theory, the process that provides an account of the selective persistence of some species and the disappearance of others is natural selection. Thus while the *structure* of DNA provides an account of both continuity and change in biological evolution, it is the *process* of natural selection that accounts for the emergence of a diversity of forms of life. The theory of natural selection, when applied to biological evolution, is based on the observation that characteristics within a species are transmitted across generations. To this the theory of natural selection adds the observation that individuals most suited for survival under the specific environmental conditions are also most likely to produce offspring. Thus individuals with the necessary characteristics for survival are most likely to transmit characteristics to succeeding generations, thereby insuring (within species) the selective retention of adaptive characteristics and the selective disappearance of maladaptive characteristics. Moreover, since environmental conditions vary both geographically and historically, the theory of natural selection provides an account of variation and diversity within and between biological species. The theory of natural selection thus provides an account of how the basic structures responsible for continuity and change in biological species interact with the process of natural selection to create new forms of life.

We have discussed recent developments in the field of biology at some length because we view the aims of own work to be similar to work on Darwinian–molecular evolutionary theory. In operationalizing our theoretical heuristic, we have conceptualized the aims of our reconstructive research as similar to those of work in the field of molecular biology in that the aim of the research program is to reconstruct the basic structures of sociomoral knowledge (comparable to DNA) that constitute the building blocks of sociomoral knowledge and understanding. Our constructive research, in contrast, is more similar to work in the field of Darwinian evolutionary theory. The focus of our constructive research is on the process by which change and evolution in forms of sociomoral knowledge occur. More specifically, our aim has been to identify the process (comparable to random perturbations in molecular structure) by which novelty or variety emerges in sociomoral rule systems, the process by which sociomoral knowledge is preserved and transmitted across generations (comparable to genetic transmission), and the process (comparable to natural selection) by which some variations in sociomoral knowledge and understanding survive, persist, and evolve while others fail to evolve. The working hypotheses we have formulated with respect to each of these aims will be discussed in more detail later in the chapter.

Before discussing these hypotheses we should point out that, despite the usefulness of the biological-evolutionary sciences as a source of potential hypotheses concerning the constructive evolution of forms of sociomoral knowledge, we recognize that the analogy between biological evolution and constructive social evolution has its limits. Although social evolution and biological evolution are in many respects similar, there are significant differences between the two processes. For example, unlike the process of biological evolution, the process of social evolution does not appear to be limited by a dependence on the production of random variation. On the contrary, the production or construction of new or novel variation in sociomoral knowledge and understanding (or any other type of nomotic knowledge) arises from a complex, preexisting system of rules that is ontogenetically and historically open to change or modification. Such change, in turn, in feedback loop fashion, contributes to the further production or creation of new forms of knowledge. Constructive social evolution is thus in some respects more similar to a Lamarckian process than to a Darwinian process, in that adaptive responses to environmental changes are viewed as capable of being directly transmitted to future generations. Thus although the process of biological evolution provides a useful source of working hypotheses, we recognize its limits.

The Emergence of New Sociomoral Knowledge or Understanding

The findings of modern evolutionary biology provide the basis for a working hypothesis with respect to the process by which new or novel variation in sociomoral knowledge emerges. The subjective *construction* of new or novel combinations or interpretations of sociomoral rules and the consequent subjective variation in nomotic knowledge are hypothesized to play a role in the constructive evolution of *new* forms of knowledge and understanding that is similar to the role that genetic mutation and consequent genetic variation play in biological evolution. Variation in subjective knowledge and understanding makes available a pool of potentially evolutionarily relevant variety. The existence of variation and variety in nomotic understanding (i.e., understanding of rules and rule systems) makes possible the emergence of new forms of sociomoral knowledge and understanding in the same way that the existence of genetic variation makes possible the emergence of new forms of life.

In attempting to address the issue of the emergence of new or novel forms of sociomoral knowledge and understanding, we have found that we face issues similar to those that confront attempts to account for the emergence of novelty or variety in other complex systems such as language and living systems. Complex systems differ from simple systems in that once a system achieves a critical level of complexity (i.e., passes the complexity barrier) the system takes on new properties (Campbell, 1982). For our purposes, the most important property of complex systems is the capacity to generate novelty or variety by means of rule-related redundancy built into the system. Once the critical level of complexity is achieved (which varies according to the type of system involved), a system acquires the capacity to produce or generate novelty and variety without further increases in complexity. Work in the area of theoretical linguistics, for example, suggests that all natural languages share one significant feature in common: They are equally complex and rich in structure. This appears to be true historically as well as geographically. There appears to be no such thing as a "primitive" language. All natural languages are highly complex. Novelty or change in language does not, consequently, necessarily involve an increase or decrease in complexity. Change involves the evolution of new rules, but not necessarily of more rules. Lakoff (cited in Campbell, 1982) points out:

> Languages have an internal rationale for what is going to change and in what way. As the case system went out in Latin, for example, Latin started to impose a fixed word order, and these changes went inexorably together, because there must be a way of giving information about structure, and if cases no longer do so, then the order of the words in sentences must take over this task. And this is consistent. Even though speakers looking at their language might feel that distinctions are being lost, in every case another way is found of saying the same thing, preserving intelligibility. The conceptual structures of the mind that are responsible for the universal forms of grammar do in fact keep the language running. And those

things do not really change over time. Every language has about the same number of rules. Indeed, we can be reasonably sure that our own language has the same amount of syntax, the same amount of structure, as Proto Indo-European. (quoted in Campbell, 1982, p. 100)

A similar argument has been made concerning the language of genes. The emergence of new forms of life does not require an increase in the complexity of the DNA molecule. Campbell (1982) notes:

Rules are the link between the new biology and the new linguistics. A modest number of rules applied again and again to a limited collection of objects leads to variety, novelty, and surprise. One can describe all of the rules, but not necessarily all of the products of the rules—not the set of all whole numbers, not every sentence in a language, not all organisms which may arise from evolution. (p. 108)

In our research we have adopted the view that sociomoral rule systems, as complex nomotic systems, do not change and evolve in complexity, either ontogenetically or sociohistorically. All sociomoral rule systems are, according to this view, complex systems organized around the basic issue of the meaning of the good and the just life in much the same way that the syntax of all natural languages is organized around the problem of communication. Thus sociohistorical variations in sociomoral rule systems (i.e., morality) are conceptualized as new or novel applications of the same basic structures (i.e., different combinations and permutations of moral rules and principles such as benevolence, utility, justice, fairness, etc.) rather than changes in the complexity of the rule systems. There are, according to this view, no primitive moralities in the same sense that there are no primitive languages. The anthropologist attempting to understand the moral codes and customs of a tribal society is faced with the same type of problem as the linguist attempting to understand the language of the tribe; that is, the problem of how a complex network of specific rules and conventions is generated by a smaller subset of grammatical or sociomoral structures. All morality is thus viewed as equally complex, differing primarily in the way in which rules are applied rather than in the complexity of the rule systems. The emergence of new or novel forms of sociomoral knowledge and understanding involves the construction or production of new or novel combinations, variations, or permutations of rules in response to changes in environmental or historical context for generating solutions to the problem of the meaning of the good and the just life as they are presented, ontogenetically to the individual, and historically to sociocultural systems.

The Transmission of Sociomoral Knowledge and Understanding

The findings of modern biology similarly provided the basis for a working hypothesis about the process by which variation in sociomoral knowledge at the intersubjective level is preserved and transmitted across generations. *Communication* is hypothesized to play a role in the evolution of sociomoral knowledge similar to the role that genetic transmission plays in biological evolution; that is, it constitutes the process by which informational variation is disseminated throughout social systems and transmitted across generations.

In formulating this hypothesis we have drawn on the work of Huxley (1942) and Waddington (1975). Both Huxley and Waddington argue for the view that the mechanism of evolution as well as organisms evolves, and that biological or organic evolution in humans has been supplemented and to a certain extent superseded by cultural and social evolution. The unique feature of the human species, they argue, is that through the process of evolution human beings acquired the capacity for social evolution. Once acquired, the process enabled humans to circumvent the process of organic evolution. Characteristics that lead to successful adaptation, they argue, no longer have to be disseminated throughout the species by the slow, gradual process of genetic transmission. They can be transmitted both within and across generations by social and cultural means. The human species is no longer confined to the slow process of organic evolution. Each generation is capable of accumulating adaptive information and, in a Lamarckian fashion, transmitting it directly to the next generation. In addition, both men argue that the human species is unique in that human beings are aware of the forces that shape their evolution and are therefore in a position to influence those forces. Sociocultural evolution is thus viewed as the most open type of evolution, a process that is open to human construction and co-construction.

Huxley (1942) has proposed an account of the evolution of evolution and the emergence of the capacity for constructive social evolution. There have been, Huxley argues, three distinct stages of evolution. The first phase applies to the evolution of inorganic matter to organic matter, the second to the evolution of biological species, and the third to the evolution of human societies. During the first stage, evolution applied to the process by which *matter* became self-reproducing (i.e., the emergence of the first DNA molecule out of the prebiotic "soup" of complex compounds that had accumulated on the earth's surface 4 billion years ago). Once matter became self-reproducing, the evolution of *biological* forms was governed by the process of natural selection. Natural selection thus operates, according to Huxley, primarily during the second phase of evolution. The third stage of evolution occurred when *societies* became self-reproducing. Social and cultural evolution is not, according to Huxley, a product of the biological process of natural selection. Natural selection only operated to produce the capacity for constructive social evolution.

Building on the notion that social evolution has superseded biological evolution (at least in humans), Waddington (1975) further proposes that socialization is the mechanism that makes social evolution possible.

The human situation is characterized by an enormously important step in the evolution of evolutionary mechanisms. . . . In man, the process of teaching by the older members of the population and learning by the younger ones, have been carried to an incomparably higher pitch than is found in any of the prehuman forms of life. . . . We have here what in effect amounts to a new mode of hereditary transmission. (1975, p. 102)

This development Waddington calls a sociogenetic transmission system, a system of cultural evolution whereby humans, as a species, have the potential to transmit across generations not just new variation in body structure, but conceptual knowledge, beliefs, feelings, aesthetic creations, and so forth. To realize this possibility, it was necessary that humans be biologically structured to transmit and receive nonhereditary information. A sociogenetic transmission system required many evolutionary changes. The development of the capacity for the symbolic use of language for communication was a major prerequisite for a sociogenetic system. The language system plays a role in sociogenetic transmission similar to the role that the DNA biochemical system plays in genetic transmission—one of producing, preserving, and transmitting informational variation. Communication thus provides the foundation for the sociogenetic system. Language constitutes a complex nomotic structure that, like DNA, serves as a carrier for all types of nomotic information. The types of nomotic knowledge or information embedded in its structure include information about not only the syntax of the language itself, but the syntax of all forms of nomotic knowledge. Language is thus the carrier of nomotic knowledge and communication the process by which nomotic knowledge is transmitted. Within sociocultural systems, information is transmitted by means of communication between members of the system. Thus at the interpersonal level communication between members (i.e., information exchange) is the process by which informational variation is transmitted and disseminated throughout social systems and across generations.

The Selective Evolution of Sociomoral Knowledge and Understanding

The findings of evolutionary biology also provide the basis for a working hypothesis about the selective evolution of sociomoral knowledge or understanding. Communication, we noted above, is the process (similar to genetic transmission) by which sociomoral knowledge and understanding are transmitted and disseminated. In this frame, *communicative selection* is hypothesized to play a role in the constructive evolution of sociomoral knowledge similar to the role of natural selection in biological evolution; that is, it accounts for the selective persistence of some forms of sociomoral knowledge and understanding and the disappearance of other forms. New forms of sociomoral knowledge and understanding thus emerge as a consequence of the cumulative effects of communicative selection.

In formulating this hypothesis we have again drawn on the work described above. The process of biological evolution, we noted, has produced in the human species the most open type of evolutionary system—a system of cultural or social evolution that is open to human construction and co-construction. The sociogenetic system, however, like the genetic system, is basically amoral. It is capable of transmitting maladaptive as well as adaptive information. Most genetic mutations, for example, are lethal, and a method for choosing between alternatives is necessary. Natural selection provides the basis for genetic selection. Natural selection, however, cannot provide an account of the selective persistence of forms of sociomoral knowledge and understanding.

Consequently, in formulating our hypothesis with respect to the selective evolution of sociomoral knowledge we have had to look beyond evolutionary biology to work in the area of communication theory.

As noted earlier, within social systems information is transmitted by means of communicative action between members in the system. Communicative action between members (i.e., information exchange) constitutes the process by which information is preserved, disseminated, and transmitted throughout the system and across generations. What is more important, for our purposes, the success or failure of information exchange depends upon the success or failure of communicative actions.

The key to understanding the process by which change or evolution occurs in forms of sociomoral knowledge can thus be found in the process by which communicative actions succeed or fail. As noted earlier, we have hypothesized that the subjective construction or production of new or novel combinations or interpretations of sociomoral rules makes available subjective variation in sociomoral knowledge and understanding that plays a role in the evolution of new knowledge and understanding similar to that of genetic variation in biological evolution. Variation in subjective knowledge and understanding makes available a pool of potentially evolutionarily relevant variety. Not all variation, however, is successfully preserved or disseminated. Because the success or failure of information exchange is dependent upon the success or failure of communicative actions, the process that operates to determine the effectiveness of communicative actions also is hypothesized to operate as the selection mechanism that facilitates or inhibits the constructive evolution of sociomoral knowledge. In our work on identifying the conditions that limit or facilitate the production of new or novel forms of sociomoral knowledge, we have found it useful to draw on Habermas's work in the area of communication theory (McCarthy, 1981). According to Habermas (1979), communication provides the foundation for all human action systems. For Habermas, as for Waddington, ordinary language communication constitutes a type of metainstitution upon which all other social institutions are dependent. Language thus constitutes a complex nomotic structure that, like DNA, serves as a carrier for all types of nomotic information, and communication is the process by which information is exchanged. We will discuss Habermas's communication theory in some detail because of the central role it played in operationalizing our theoretical heuristic for the research studies reported in subsequent sections.

A basic assumption of Habermas's communication theory is that ordinary social interaction rests on a background consensus (a shared mutual understanding) that makes interaction possible. Communication thus not only aims at understanding, it presupposes it. From Habermas's communication-theoretic perspective, the types of actions that occur during interaction can be defined in terms of the understanding that is both a goal and a presupposition of speech. At any point in social interaction there are two basic types of actions that occur: communicative action and goal-oriented (noncommunicative) action. Communicative actions are communicative in that they are actions oriented toward the maintenance or restoration of understanding. Goal-oriented actions are noncommunicative in that they are instrumental actions oriented to the achievement of goals or outcome rather than understanding. Both types of action (communicative and noncommunicative or goal oriented) serve different functions and occur at different points in the interaction process. During normal social interaction, the basic types of actions that occur are ordinary communicative actions (OCA) and goal-oriented actions (GOA). Thus ordinary social interaction involves actions oriented to the achievement of interaction goals (GOA) and the maintenance of shared understanding (OCA). Under certain conditions (to be described later), the consensual basis of interaction may be threatened or break down. When this occurs, either the interaction can break off, or the participants can shift to one of two alternative modes of action: they can either attempt to achieve interaction goals without a consensus or they can attempt to restore consensus. Strategic communicative action (SGA) is oriented to achieving goals without consensus and discursive communicative action (DCA) is oriented to the restoration of a shared understanding and/or the achievement of a new shared understanding or consensus.

Ordinary social interaction is threatened or may break down when the implicit validity claims that make up the background consensus (shared mutual understanding) are threatened or break down. According to Habermas's communication theory, there are four implicit validity claims that the speaker makes on the hearer. These four validity claims are basic to all speech. They represent universal requirements or prerequisites that must be met if the speaker and hearer are to share the type of mutual understanding that is necessary for speech. The implicit validity claims of speech are those of comprehensibility, truthfulness, truth, and rightness. These validity claims, which we shall discuss briefly, are described in more detail in McCarthy (1981).

These validity claims represent four different dimensions along which the shared understanding of consensual speech may break down. First, mutual understanding may break down if the hearer fails to comprehend the speaker's utterance. Consensual speech can be restored if the speaker clarifies the misunderstanding. Second, mutual understanding may break down if the hearer challenges the truth of the speaker's utterances. Challenges of this sort can be rectified by means designed to establish the truth of the speaker's utterances. Third, mutual understanding may break down if the hearer questions the intentions (i.e., the honesty or truthfulness) of the speaker. The speaker's claim to truthfulness rests not on the truth of his or her utterances but on his or her good faith or honest intention. The speaker could, for example, unintentionally (or even with good intention) make a claim that was unknowingly not true. Conversely, the speaker could intentionally make a claim that was knowingly false. In the first case the truth of the speaker's utterance is questioned while in the second case the truthfulness of the speaker is questioned. Consensual speech can be restored if the truthfulness of the speaker can be established. Fourth, mutual understanding breaks down if the hearer challenges the rightness of the speaker's utterance in view of alternative, competing, or conflicting normative validity claims. Consensual speech can be restored if the rightness of the speaker's utterance can be redeemed or a normative consensus reestablished.

Thus according to Habermas's communication theory the shared mutual understanding that forms the basis for consensual speech can break down if one or more of the four validity claims implicit in such a mutual understanding are challenged or threatened. Communicative action in consensual speech is oriented toward maintaining this understanding and resolving challenges to validity claims in each of the four dimensions. Goal-oriented action is thus the content of ordinary social interaction and OCA takes place against a background of shared understanding that makes what in communication theory is termed consensual speech (which includes linguistic, nonlinguistic, and even nonverbal elements) possible. Speech acts that challenge or threaten shared understanding in any of the four dimensions can be thus resolved in the context of consensual speech through ordinary communicative action oriented toward maintaining this shared understanding. If ordinary communicative action fails to maintain understanding in any of the four dimensions, either the communication can break off or the speaker can resort to strategic action such as the use of power, force, deception, manipulation, and so forth in order to achieve interaction goals without shared understanding. Habermas's communication theory, however, does not assign all four dimensions an equal status. In two of the dimensions, truth and rightness, the interaction can move beyond the use of strategic action and shift to a different level of communicative action—discourse.

Discourse involves an examination of the implicit mutual understanding that provides the basis of normal speech in an attempt to establish a new basis for understanding. Discourse represents a break with normal interaction in an attempt to render explicit the normally implicit understanding that is the basis of consensual speech and to subject this understanding to critical or discursive discussion. In discourse the implicit validity claims that the speaker makes themselves become the object of communicative action. Discourse thus involves two interrelated movements: The first is to render explicit the normally implicit understanding that provides the basis of the interaction, and the second is to subject this implicit understanding (now rendered explicit) to a process of critical examination and discursive redemption in order to establish the basis for a new shared understanding. Discourse thus involves discursive communicative action. Habermas's communication theory distinguishes between two different types of discourse, theoretical and practical. Theoretical discourse is concerned with the critical examination and discursive redemption of competing or conflicting truth claims, and practical discourse is concerned with the critical examination and discursive redemption of competing or conflicting rightness claims. When the normative consensus that makes up the background for ordinary communicative action is threatened or disrupted by normative conflict as in the case of conflicting or competing validity claims with respect to norms, standards, values, or principles, then the interaction can either break off or shift to strategic communicative actions or practical discourse.

We have drawn on Habermas's communication theory in formulating our working hypothesis about the selective evolution of forms of sociomoral knowledge and understanding. Because we conceptualize ontogenetic and sociohistorical evolution as interdependent processes, we have adopted the view that both types of evolution are governed by the same process. The existence of subjective variation in sociomoral knowledge or understanding, we noted earlier, makes available an evolutionarily relevant pool of material by insuring the availability of alternative competing normative validity claims. The potential for the emergence of new or novel sociomoral knowledge thus arises at the intrapersonal or ontogenetic level in the form of competing interpretations of sociomoral rules and norms. Communication between members is the process by which informational variation is transmitted and disseminated throughout social systems. Not all forms of informational variation are preserved, however. The successful preservation or dissemination of new forms of knowledge and understanding is hypothesized to be determined by a process of communicative selection. This hypothesis follows from the distinction made earlier between the process by which novelty or variety occurs in complex systems such as language and life forms and the process by which new information is selectively transmitted or disseminated throughout a system. In biological systems, for example, novelty occurs in the form of permutations or mutations in the structure of DNA. The persistence or transmission of novelty in biological forms, on the other hand, is determined by the process of natural selection. The evolution of sociomoral knowledge and understanding is thus hypothesized to be dependent upon the availability of a pool of evolutionarily relevant variation in knowledge and the successful transmission or dissemination of selected variations of this knowledge.

In formulating our hypothesis concerning the role of communication and communicative selection in the evolution of sociomoral knowledge we have drawn on the distinction made earlier between the actor's knowledge or understanding of the rules (i.e., the competence of the rule user) and intervening, external, empirical, and contingent limiting factors that contribute to actual performance. In the latter case, the performance of the competent rule user is viewed as interacting with a variety of factors of which the underlying competence of the user is only one. Within a psychosocial role-theoretical framework, performance is thus viewed as determined by a complex interaction between antecedent maturational and learning variables that determine the individual's competencies *and* intervening social process variables, including communication processes such as the level of communicative action characteristic of the specific situation or episode in which the performance takes place, which contribute to the constructive evolution of sociomoral knowledge and understanding. The potential for new sociomoral knowledge, consequently, is viewed as initially emerging at the intrapersonal level from the preexisting competencies of participants in the interactional or communicative process and subsequently successfully or unsuccessfully preserved as a result of the success or failure of communicative actions.

RESEARCH ON THE CONSTRUCTIVE EVOLUTION OF SOCIOMORAL KNOWLEDGE AND UNDERSTANDING

The conceptualization of the process of the constructive evolution of sociomoral knowledge and understanding described in the previous section provides the background or framework for formulating the research strategies, methods, and hypotheses used in our constructive research. It is in the domain of the constructive evolution of new forms of sociomoral knowledge that psychosocial role theory faces its most difficult challenge. As noted earlier, although reconstructive research has been successfully carried out on identifying linguistic, cognitive, and communicative competencies, relatively little work has been conducted on investigating the constructive process by which new nomotic knowledge and understanding evolve. Therefore, the research methods and procedures that we have developed in the area of constructive research, as in the area of reconstructive research, are viewed as more exploratory than definitive.

As a part of our reconstructive research we developed a measure for identifying and assessing a number of basic dimensions of sociomoral competence. These structural dimensions are conceptualized as existing in the form of rule schemata (i.e., preexisting nomotic knowledge) that in part define the individual's sociomoral knowledge and understanding (i.e., the individual's sociomoral competence). In outlining our conceptualization of the constructive evolution of sociomoral knowledge and understanding we hypothesized that the subjective construction of new knowledge or understanding arises out of this preexisting understanding of sociomoral rules in the form of new or novel interpretations, permutations, or combinations of rules on the part of the competent rule user. The persistence or successful transmission of new forms of sociomoral knowledge, on the other hand, was hypothesized to be dependent upon the successful communication of the new or novel variations in sociomoral knowledge. Variation in sociomoral knowledge was thus viewed as being introduced into the system at the intrapersonal level in the form of competing or conflicting normative validity claims and then subjected to a process of "natural" selection vis-a-vis the success or failure of communicative action. The conditions that facilitate or limit the constructive evolution of new forms of sociomoral knowledge were conceptualized as the same conditions that limit or facilitate communicative action. Our constructive research was designed to investigate empirically the role of communicative processes in the evolution of sociomoral knowledge at the intrapersonal level. More specifically, one of the research hypotheses for our constructive research was that the more closely communicative actions in contexts involving competing or conflicting normative validity claims (i.e., in contexts involving subjective variation in sociomoral knowledge and understanding) approximate the features of discourse (i.e., take place at the level of DCA), the more likely it is that ontogenetic change or evolution in sociomoral knowledge (i.e., change or evolution in the individual's sociomoral knowledge or understanding) will occur. Consequently, one purpose of our constructive research was to develop a procedure for operationalizing level of communicative action as an interpersonal process variable. A second goal was to provide a preliminary test of the hypothesis that higher levels of communicative functioning facilitate ontogenetic change and evolution in sociomoral knowledge (i.e., the emergence of forms of sociomoral knowledge and understanding that are new or novel relative to the individual).

From the perspective of psychosocial role theory, interpersonal interactions are viewed as taking place in contexts involving either normative consensus or normative conflict. Interactions involving normative consensus are characterized by cooperation among participants and presuppose a shared mutual understanding in regard to the validity of respective normative claims of the participants in the interaction. That is, they presuppose a shared mutual sociomoral knowledge and understanding. Interactions involving normative conflict, on the other hand, are characterized by competition among participants and presuppose problematic, competing, or conflicting validity claims.

Interactions involving normative consensus are the most common form of interaction and make up the bulk of ordinary or consensual speech and interaction. Research in the area has traditionally emphasized the role of consensus and cooperation in social and moral development. Piaget (1932/1965), for example, in his classic work on the development of moral understanding in children, argued that the development of a sense of mutual respect and cooperation was an essential element in the evolution of the child's moral understanding. Although consensus and cooperation clearly play a central role in the development of sociomoral understanding, a case can be made that conflict and competition play an equally important role. In fact, because normative consensus presupposes a shared mutual understanding, interactions involving normative consensus are less likely, in our view, to result in the emergence of ontogenetically new knowledge and understanding. Interactions involving normative conflict, on the other hand, because they presuppose problematic, competing, or conflicting validity claims (i.e., the absence of a shared mutual understanding), are more likely to generate new knowledge or understanding. The focus of our constructive research was thus on the ontogenetic emergence of new understanding that arises from normative conflict.

Normative conflict, however, is conceptualized to be only a precondition for new understanding. The existence of normative conflict does not in itself guarantee the emergence of new understanding. For a new understanding to emerge, a second condition must be met: The normative conflict must be creatively or constructively resolved. In order to resolve normative conflict constructively, competing or conflicting validity claims must be rendered explicit, critically examined, and discursively redeemed, and a new shared mutual understanding must be established. It should be noted that a constructive resolution to normative conflict does not simply restore a preexisting shared understanding; rather, it reestablishes a *new* shared mutual understanding. The reestablishment of a shared mutual understanding, because it replaces at least one (and frequently all) prior validity claims, in principle, results in a new understanding on the part of interaction participants.

Thus from a psychosocial role-theoretical perspective the *potential* for the ontogenetic evolution of new sociomoral knowledge and understanding is created by the disequilibrium that results from normative conflict, and new knowledge or understanding emerges from the constructive resolution of conflict and the reestablishment of a new equilibrium. However, unlike theories that focus primarily on the role of intrapsychic or intrapersonal conflict such as cognitive conflict (e.g., Kohlberg, 1976; Piaget, 1932/1965) in the ontogenesis of sociomoral knowledge, psychosocial theory also focuses on interpersonal normative conflict. The processes of consensus–cooperation and conflict–competition that operate in the resolution of interpersonal normative conflict or disequilibrium are thus hypothesized to parallel such processes as assimilation and accommodation that operate in the resolution of intrapersonal conflict or disequilibrium. Ontogenetic change and evolution in sociomoral knowledge can thus be understood at the interpersonal level in the context of the process by which normative conflict occurs and is constructively resolved. Normative conflict occurs in the absence of a shared mutual understanding with respect to norms, moral rules, values, or principles among the participants of an interaction. The creative or constructive resolution of normative conflict results in the reestablishment of a *new* shared mutual normative understanding among the participants.

The creative or constructive resolution of normative conflict is hypothesized to be facilitated by the type of communicative actions that take place during the interaction. Ordinary communicative actions, because they implicitly avoid the issue of normative conflict, are hypothesized to limit the constructive resolution of normative conflict. Strategic communicative actions (i.e., the use of manipulation, intimidation, deception, force, or power), because they represent attempts to impose a unilateral understanding rather than restore a shared mutual understanding, are similarly hypothesized to limit the constructive resolution of normative conflict. Discourse, on the other hand, because it facilitates the establishment of a shared mutual understanding, is hypothesized to enhance the constructive resolution of normative conflict and the emergence of new knowledge and understanding. Discourse, as a form of communicative action, implies a willingness to suspend judgment on competing or conflicting validity claims, including one's own validity claims. It also implies a willingness to examine critically conflicting validity claims and allow the conflicting claims to be resolved by the force of the better argument, which in turn implies the ability to resist resolutions based on power, deception, or manipulation, including the use of such strategic action in support of one's own claims.

The Communicative Functioning Scale

As part of our constructive research we conducted a study that was designed to investigate the role of communication in the constructive evolution of sociomoral understanding. The study had two main goals. The first was to develop an interpersonal process measure designed to assess level of communicative functioning in groups. The second was to provide a test of the hypothesis that higher levels of communicative action facilitate ontogenetic change in sociomoral knowledge and understanding.

The Communicative Functioning Scale (CFS) is a process measure designed to assess level of communicative functioning in groups. The CFS is conceptualized as a generic measure that can be administered to small groups and used to measure the level of communicative action that takes place in the context of group discussion of normative issues. The scoring procedures are described in more detail elsewhere (Kurtines, 1985). Basically, the coding categories were designed for use in classifying the level of communicative actions of participants in interactions involving normative conflict (i.e., conflicting or competing normative validity claims). The levels of communicative action that were used for the ratings were adopted from the communication theory of Habermas described earlier. The coding categories that were developed were thus concerned with three basic levels of communicative action: Ordinary Communicative Action (OCA), Strategic Communicative Action (SGA), and Discursive Communicative Action (DCA). For purposes of the ratings, Discursive Communicative Action (i.e., discourse) was divided into three levels. The coding procedure was thus used to place communicative action into one of five classifications: OCA, SGA, DCA1, DCA2, and DCA3.

The five levels of communicative action that are coded for the CFS can be briefly described as follows:

1. *Ordinary Communicative Action* (OCA). OCA was operationally defined as all nonnormative speech acts that were not strategic (e.g., "What time is it?" "This room is hot." "How long have you been here.") and/or normative speech acts directed toward the speaker's own position or principles ("I think that..."[statement of position]).

2. *Strategic Goal-Oriented Action* (SGA). SGA was operationally defined as nonnormative speech acts that used power, force, intimidation, deception, or manipulation directed toward another person (e.g., "Boy, you sure are dumb!") or a relationship ("If you were my friend you wouldn't say that.") and/or normative speech acts that use power, force, intimidation, deception, or manipulation directed toward the other person's positions or principles (e.g., "That's the stupidest thing I ever heard.").

3. *Discursive Communicative Action, Level 1* (DCA1). DCA1 was operationally defined as nonstrategic normative speech acts that attempt to restore a share mutual understanding by rendering explicit and critically examining positions. The types of normative speech acts associated with this level were actions such as constructively paraphrasing, clarifying, refining, elaborating, and/or critiquing, the *positions* of others represented in the discussion.

4. *Discursive Communicative Action, Level 2* (DCA2). DCA2 was operationally defined as nonstrategic normative speech acts that attempt to restore a shared mutual understanding by rendering explicit and critically examining principles. The types of normative speech acts associated with this level were actions such as constructively paraphrasing, clarifying, refining, elaborating, and/or critiquing the *principles* of others represented in the discussion.

5. *Discursive Communicative Action, Level 3* (DCA3). DCA3 is the highest level of discourse. DCA3 is similar to DCA1 and DCA2 in that it is defined by the absence of SGA, but it differs from DCA1 and DCA2 in that it involves the presence of active attempts to establish a *new* shared mutual understanding. DCA3 was operationally defined as nonstrategic normative speech acts such as integrations and constructions that were

directed toward the integration of *principles* already present in the discussion or the construction of new, mutually acceptable *principles* not previously present in the discussion.

Extensive psychometric analyses were conducted on the CFS. The results of the psychometric analyses indicated that the CFS has adequate psychometric properties, including internal consistency reliability, interrater reliability, and factor validity.

The second aim of our constructive research was to examine the effects of level of communicative functioning on conflict resolution during discussion and on ontogenetic change in sociomoral knowledge understanding as assessed by the two dimensions of the SCS-FI developed as part of our earlier research.

The subjects for this study consisted of young adult college students. An experimental design was used to provide a method for testing the effects of level of communicative functioning on ontogenetic change in sociomoral knowledge and understanding. Participants were pretested on the SCS-FI and then classified into two groups representing different positions on the issues assessed by the SCS-FI. This procedure was designed to experimentally create a context in which disequilibrium (i.e., the absence of a shared understanding with respect to the focal issues assessed by the SCS-FI) existed between participants during the discussion phase of the study. Participants were then randomly assigned to the experimental (discussion) condition and a control (no discussion) condition. The procedure for the experimental phase of the research involved having dyads of participants (with each dyad comprising participants representing different positions on the issue) discuss the issues and attempt to reach an agreement . The participants in the control condition did not discuss the issues. Participants then completed the posttest phase of the study. For the subjects in the experimental (discussion) condition, the posttesting took place from 4 to 8 weeks *after* their participation in the discussion phase of the study.

Extensive analyses were conducted on the data collected as part of this study. The results are presented in detail elsewhere (cf. Kurtines et al., 1986). The results of the analyses provided support for the hypothesis that level of communicative functioning is related to conflict resolution during discussion, but that the results were in the opposite direction from those predicted; that is, the high communicative action group generated less consensus. The results also provide support for the hypothesis that higher levels of communicative functioning were related to ontogenetic change, at least for the teleological-deontological (TD) dimension of the SCS-FI. Thus although subjects in the high level of communicative functioning group achieved significantly less consensus during discussion, there was significantly more ontogenetic change in the high discussion group than in either the low discussion group or the no discussion group for the teleological–deontological dimension. Taken together, these results suggest that communicative processes that more closely approximate discourse result in making the normative nature of conflict more explicit *and* more difficult to resolve during discussion, but that the process of rendering explicit and critically examining normative conflict also increases the probability of subsequent ontogenetic change.

The results of the analyses also suggest that the relationship between interpersonal processes and intrapersonal processes is a complex one. The experimental treatment used in this study, though effective in eliciting discussion of normative issues, was relatively mild. Thus peer discussion involving a mild intervention does not appear to have an equally significant effect on all dimensions of sociomoral knowledge and understanding (as least as reflected in their positions on the issues). The discussion condition, for example, did not appear to have a significant effect on the Relativistic-Universal (RU) dimension of the SCS-FI. The issue of whether moral standards are relative or universal is a relatively clear issue and one on which individuals are more likely to have a clearly defined position one way or the other. An orientation toward consequences versus obligations, in contrast, is less clearly defined. The results of the analyses in this section thus provide support for the view that interpersonal processes such as level of communicative functioning during peer discussion of normative issues *do* contribute to ontogenetic change in sociomoral knowledge and understanding, but that the ontogenetic change that results from relatively brief discussion is less likely to occur for issues on which participants have more clearly defined positions.

PSYCHOSOCIAL DEVELOPMENT

The previous sections described work that we have done on identifying the basic structures of sociomoral knowledge and work on the process by which sociomoral knowledge and understanding evolve. This research, however, utilized young adult populations; that is, competent rule users. The research on the role of communication on the ontogenetic evolution of sociomoral understanding in young adults thus assumed that the subjects in the studies had available the full range of necessary psychosocial competencies (i.e., linguistic, cognitive, sociomoral, and communicative competencies) required for communicative action of the type we have discussed (i.e., DCA) to have an effect on sociomoral understanding. That is, the research assumed not only that subjects had an understanding of the sociomoral issues, but also that they could engage in reflective–hypothetical thinking about and/or critical–discursive discussion of the issues. In this section we will address the issue of the development of the psychosocial competencies necessary for the process of constructive evolutionary change to take place. In addressing this issue, we adopt the view that the particular competencies that are the focus of our research (i.e., sociomoral and communicative competencies) are interdependent and that their development is further dependent upon the development of both linguistic and cognitive competencies. Thus although our primary theoretical interest is in sociomoral and communicative competencies, we adopt the view that psychosocial development involves the emergence of linguistic, cognitive, sociomoral, and communicative competencies that define the interrelated lines of development by which the individual becomes a competent member of a social system. Thus the reproduction of society is viewed as based upon the reproduction of competent members of society, and the necessary competencies include linguistic and cognitive as well as sociomoral and communicative competencies.

The Development of Sociomoral and Communicative Competencies

One conclusion to be drawn from the extensive debate over the role of learning and maturational processes is that there is a large element of validity in both views. Consequently, we view the development of linguistic, cognitive, sociomoral, and communicative competencies as influenced by both maturational processes (i.e., genetically influenced structural changes) and learning processes (the acquisition of competencies through processes such as conditioning, imitation, identification, and modeling). Both maturational and learning processes are viewed as essential to the development of competent members of society. In this section we will describe in more detail the conceptualization of the development of psychosocial competencies.

For our work we have defined psychosocial development in terms of four interrelated lines of development. Table 6.1 presents an overview of the four developmental levels of psychosocial competence that we have adopted for use in our research. The development of psychosocial competencies during levels 2, 3, and 4 is conceptualized as constituting a horizontal decalage within levels. As can be seen from Table 6.1, for example, at level 2 the development of linguistic competency is viewed as a precondition for the development of preoperational thinking. The development of preoperational thinking at this level, in turn, is viewed as a precondition for the development of a basic understanding of sociomoral concepts and an initial sociomoral orientation, in this case a heteronomous orientation. The development of a sociomoral orientation of some type (i.e., a movement beyond the premoral orientation of the sensorimotor stage) is, in turn, viewed as a precondition for engaging in normative communicative actions. The hypothesized levels of psychosocial development described in this section are viewed as providing only an approximate outline of the developmental sequence and the age ranges involved in the acquisition of a full range of psychosocial competencies. These levels are viewed as necessarily tentative and our data only provide for a partial test of the hypothesized levels. The four developmental levels organized in terms of *psychosocial perspective* (i.e., the overriding understanding of social reality that defines the individual's orientation to linguistic, cognitive, sociomoral, and communicative activity) represented by each level are:

Developmental Level 1: Presubjective (ages 0–2). At the presubjective level the infant is linguistically at the preverbal level and in the sensorimotor stage of cognitive development. During this period, the infant is in the process of acquiring basic linguistic and sensorimotor competencies. The sociomoral perspective associated with this level is premoral and the infant's communicative actions tend to be primarily nonnormative goal-oriented actions (GOA) organized around sensorimotor activities.

Developmental Level 2: Egocentric–Subjective (ages 2–7). At this level the child has acquired the basic linguistic competence necessary for verbal interaction. Cognitively, the child is at the preoperational stage. At this level the child is acquiring basic role-taking and role-playing skills and is in the process of moving from egocentric to sociocentric thinking. The sociomoral orientation associated with this level is heteronomous and uncritical. The child acquires a basic understanding of sociomoral rules and concepts, but the rules are viewed as externally imposed. In terms of communicative competence, at this level the child is capable of engaging in ordinary communicative action (OCA) and strategic goal-oriented action (SGA), but has not yet achieved the capacity for discursive communicative action (DCA). The psychosocial perspective associated with this level tends to be *egocentric* (i.e., a

TABLE 6.1. Levels of Psychosocial Development

Psychosocial Levels	Competencies			
	Linguistic	Cognitive	Sociomoral	Communicative
1: (0–2) Presubjective	Preverbal	Sensorimotor	Premoral	Nonnormative GOA
2: (2–7) Egocentric– Subjective	Language →	Preoperational →	Heteronomous (external) →	Normative GOA, SGA
3: (7–12) Sociocentric– Intersubjective		Concrete operations →	Autonomous (internal) →	Normative GOA, SGA, DCA1
4: (12+) Reflective– Critical		Formal operations →	Reflective (hypothetical) →	Normative GOA, SGA, DCA1, DCA2, DCA3

perspective rooted in the ego's or self's understanding) and is typically oriented to *subjective* needs, interests, and expectations, either of the self or of others, but not to shared needs, interests and expectations.

Developmental Level 3: Sociocentric–Intersubjective (ages 7–12). At this level the child's linguistic competence becomes fully developed. Cognitively, the child is at the level of concrete operational thinking and has acquired the capacity for decentered thinking. Along with the capacity for decentered thought, the child has acquired basic role-taking and role-playing skills and the child's thinking tends to be sociocentric. The sociomoral perspective associated with his or her level is autonomous and sociomoral rules are viewed as intersubjectively shared constructions. In terms of communicative competence, at this level the child can engage in OCA and SGA and at later ages some DCA. For example, in interactions in which consensus is threatened the child may recognize the need to render explicit the *shared* understanding that is threatened and even move toward a willingness to suspend judgment on the problematic validity claims. The psychosocial perspective associated with this level tends to be *sociocentric* (i.e., a perspective rooted in shared understanding) and is typically oriented to *intersubjectively* shared needs, interests, expectations, and relationships, now understood as collective co-constructions.

Developmental Level 4: Reflective–Critical (ages 12+). At this level the youth or adult is cognitively at the stage of formal operations. The youth or adult has acquired the capacity for formal, hypothetical thinking that is characteristic of this stage. With the acquisition of hypothetical thinking, the youth or adult acquires the capacity to distance himself or herself from socially constructed roles and conventions as well as norms and values. In terms of role-taking skills, the individual now not only can take the perspective of the potential other in interactions, but also can take the perspective of an objective neutral third person. The sociomoral perspective associated with this level is reflective–hypothetical in that the individual can now adopt a hypothetical perspective vis-a-vis sociomoral rules. In terms of communicative competence, the individual can now render explicit the implicit validity claims that form the basis of consensual speech, suspend recognition of them, treat them hypothetically, and subject them to critical, discursive examination. At this level the individual has the capacity to engage in all three levels of DCA including DCA3, which moves beyond attempts to restore or reestablish a shared mutual understanding to attempts to establish through integration or construction a new shared mutual understanding. The psychosocial perspective associated with this level tends to be *reflective* (a perspective rooted in reflective–hypothetical understanding) and is typically oriented to needs, interests, and expectations (both subjective and intersubjective) now capable of being viewed as hypothetical and open to *critical* examination, negotiation, discursive redemption, and co-construction.

In conceptualizing the development of sociomoral and communicative competencies we have drawn on previous reconstructive research in a variety of areas including theoretical linguistics (Chomsky, 1965), genetic epistemology

(Piaget, 1932, 1965, 1936), and communication theory (Habermas, 1979). To this work, however, we have added our own view of sociomoral rule systems as open systems characterized by a high degree of complexity and structure (Kurtines, 1984, 1986; Kurtines et al., 1986). The emergence of newness or novelty in such systems, as we noted earlier, does not necessarily involve an increase or decrease in complexity. Change involves the evolution of new rules, but not necessarily more rules. Thus all sociomoral rule systems are complex systems organized about the basic issue of the meaning of the good and the just life. Ontogenetic and sociohistorical variation in sociomoral rule systems is conceptualized as new or novel applications of rules rather than changes in the complexity of rule systems. Sociomoral knowledge and understanding are thus conceptualized as knowledge and understanding of a complex system of rules that is open to ontogenetic and sociohistorical change and evolution. As we shall discuss, such a view yields a conceptualization of the process of the ontogenetic evolution of sociomoral knowledge and understanding that differs in significant respects from the theoretical orientations that emphasize maturational or learning processes.

Drawing on the conceptualization of the constructive evolution of sociomoral knowledge and understanding that we outlined in the previous sections, we have adopted the view that the human organism is biologically predisposed to acquire, at a critical point early in its development, a complex set of sociomoral rules, and that, once acquired, this system of rules is as complex as it will ever be. There are, according to this view, no primitive moralities in the same sense that there are no primitive languages. Subsequent development involves the evolution of new or novel applications of this complex set of rules rather than the development of more complex rule systems. Thus in contrast to maturationalist stage theories (cf., e.g., Kohlberg, 1976) that adopt the view that the evolution of sociomoral knowledge throughout the life span proceeds through a predetermined, sequentially invariant series of stages involving qualitative–structural changes, we have adopted the view that once a basic understanding of sociomoral rules is acquired no further ontogenetically predictable qualitative–structural transformations in sociomoral understanding take place. That is, once a basic understanding of sociomoral rules is acquired, the evolution of sociomoral knowledge and understanding is viewed as no longer constrained by a predictable maturational sequence. Thus in contrast to the view that development involves an invariant and sequential movement toward a fixed endpoint defined by a homogeneity of understanding, we have adopted the view of the ontogenesis of sociomoral knowledge in competent rule users as an open-ended process that cannot be defined in terms of a homogeneous fixed endpoint. On the contrary, according to this view, it is the existence of a diversity of subjective variation in sociomoral knowledge and understanding that makes possible the constructive evolution of new forms of sociomoral knowledge and understanding.

In addition, in contrast to behavioral–learning theories (e.g., Burton, 1984; Liebert, 1984) that adopt the view that development involves the direct transmission of preexisting forms of sociomoral knowledge through learning processes such as conditioning, imitation, identification, and modeling, our theory holds that forms of sociomoral knowledge themselves change and evolve and that the constructive evolution of new forms of sociomoral understanding involves the formative process of the subjective construction and the intersubjective co-construction of new or novel applications of sociomoral rules. According to this view, once prerequisite linguistic, cognitive, sociomoral, and communicative competencies are acquired through maturational and learning processes, subsequent constructive evolution of sociomoral understanding is no longer constrained by either maturational processes *or* learning processes (conceptualized as conditioning processes). We have thus adopted the view that the ontogenesis of sociomoral knowledge in competent rule users is not solely or even predominantly defined in terms of either predetermined stages or the direct transmission of preexisting forms of knowledge. Such views implicitly presuppose that future sociomoral knowledge will be similar in critical respects to past sociomoral knowledge (whether conceptualized in terms of predefined stages or preexisting forms of knowledge), a presupposition that is without logical or historical justification. Because it is impossible to predict in advance the nature of future sociomoral knowledge, the theoretical and empirical focus of our work has been on the formative process of the subjective construction and intersubjective co-construction of sociomoral understanding through communication, a process whose outcome cannot be predicted. The social construction of reality is thus a process whose outcome can only be anticipated or projected as opposed to predicted (McCarthy, 1981).

The predisposition to acquire a sociomoral rule system is hypothesized to be similar to the language acquisition device that has been proposed in linguistics (Chomsky, 1965). According to this view, children acquire a basic mastery of the system of sociomoral knowledge of their culture much the same way they acquire a basic mastery of the language of their culture; that is, early in their development during a relatively brief period. Indeed, because we have suggested that language is a carrier of all forms of nomotic knowledge (a metainstitutional embodiment of intersubjectively shared meaning), it follows that the individual's understanding of the basic dimensions of morality is acquired along with the language of his or her culture.

In suggesting the hypothesis that children acquire their basic sociomoral knowledge relatively early in development we have again drawn on the work in the field of evolutionary biology. Waddington (1975), we noted, suggested that the development of a sociogenetic transmission system required many evolutionary changes, including the development of the capacity for the symbolic use of language for communication. However, even more important than the development of language, Waddington argues, was the development that transformed the human into an authority acceptor. Before a sociogenetic system can work, it is necessary that the human child be an authority acceptor—an entertainer of beliefs. To act as a receiver of cultural information, the human child has to be able to accept a whole system of knowledge, beliefs, attitudes, and feelings. Further, the bulk of the transmission is conducted during the child's early years, thus initially requiring uncritical acceptance. Our initial system of knowledge and constellation of beliefs, attitudes and feelings carry with them an implicit or explicit set of moral rules, values, and principles that constitutes our basic sociomoral knowledge and understanding. The human being is, by biological nature, an ethical animal.

> The evolution of man depends on the transmission of ideas and cultural values from one generation to the next. This cultural transmission is the major distinction between man and other animals. The developing human individual becomes an "ethical animal" by the operation of the same processes as those by which he becomes a member of a species with a socio-genetically transmitted system of evolution. (Waddington, 1975, p. 30)

Piaget (1932/1965) has similarly argued that children acquire their basic understanding of sociomoral concepts early in life and that this understanding involves an initially uncritical acceptance of moral rules and standards. In his classic work on moral understanding in young children, Piaget's (1932/1965) data on Swiss children suggested that by the preoperational stage of cognitive development the child has a basic understanding of moral concepts such as justice and responsibility. Piaget further reported that during this stage the child's orientation toward sociomoral rules is defined by what he termed a heteronomous (unilaterally imposed by external authority) view of morality. His data further suggested that this initially uncritical heteronomous orientation toward morality undergoes a transformation during the transition from preoperational to formal operational thinking. During this transition, the child's orientation to sociomoral concepts changes from a view of morality as externally imposed (heteronomous) to a view of morality as internally imposed (autonomous) and subject to the constraints of mutual respect and cooperation. Piaget thus viewed the child as acquiring a basic understanding of sociomoral rules and concepts during the preoperational stage and considered subsequent development to involve a transformation in the child's orientation toward sociomoral rules and concepts. Piaget's data, which provided the basis for our hypothesized levels of sociomoral competencies, further suggested that the transformation from a heteronomous orientation to an autonomous orientation begins at about the age of 7 with the onset of concrete operational thinking and is essentially complete by about the age of 12 with the attainment of capacity for formal thinking. With the attainment of formal operational thinking the individual acquires the capacity to adopt a reflective–hypothetical orientation toward sociomoral rules and concepts. Piaget's data thus suggest that the child acquires a basic understanding of sociomoral concepts relatively early in life during the preoperational stage, and that the child's orientation toward sociomoral concepts undergoes a series of transformations that are linked to cognitive development. Recent research that we conducted (Kurtines & Pimm, 1983; Pimm & Kurtines, 1982) with a standardized version of Piaget's original dilemmas in a 50-year replication using both Swiss and American children yielded data supporting Piaget's view concerning the types of transformations that occur in the child's sociomoral orientation and the age at which the transformations occur.

In this frame, we have adopted the view that children acquire their basic understanding of the complex system of sociomoral rules and concepts that defines the morality of their culture during the preoperational stage. The child's sense of morality is thus viewed as not simpler or more primitive than the adult's. On the contrary, the child is viewed as having an understanding of the same basic sociomoral rules and concepts as the adult. Consistent with the work of Piaget and Waddington, we have also adopted the view that this initial understanding involves an uncritical acceptance of the morality of their culture. The development of subsequent levels of sociomoral competence is viewed as involving ontogenetically predictable transformations in the child's *orientation* toward sociomoral rules and concepts rather than ontogenetically predictable qualitative–structural transformations in sociomoral knowledge and understanding itself. The development of sociomoral competence is thus viewed as involving a transformation from an initially heteronomous orientation to an autonomous orientation during the transition to formal operational thinking and that the acquisition of formal operational thinking enables the child to adopt a reflective–hypothetical orientation toward sociomoral rules and concepts.

The research to be summarized next provided the opportunity for a partial test of our hypotheses about the age at which children acquire a basic understanding of sociomoral rules and concepts and the age at which individual differences in sociomoral understanding begin to emerge. The data, however, only provide a partial test of our hypotheses because of the restriction in the age range of the subject population. The age range of the subjects in the third study (children and preadolescents) was also selected to allow us to test developmental hypotheses with respect to communicative competence as well as sociomoral competence. The age range of the subjects used in this study was thus selected to provide data for preliminary tests for the emergence of individual differences in sociomoral knowledge or understanding *and* the emergence of higher levels of communicative functioning. More specifically, the three grades used in the study (fifth, seventh, and ninth) span the ages from the beginning of concrete operational thinking to the ages of formal operational thinking and encompass developmental level 3 (Table 6.1), the level at which the capacities for reflective–hypothetical sociomoral competence and critical–discursive communicative actions are hypothesized to begin to emerge.

DEVELOPMENTAL DIFFERENCES IN SOCIOMORAL COMPETENCE AND LEVEL OF COMMUNICATIVE FUNCTIONING

Subjects for our developmental research consisted of 145 children and preadolescents in fifth, seventh, and ninth grade. The experimental design and procedures for our developmental research were essentially the same as those in the previous study. All 145 subjects were pretested on the SCS-FI and participants were classified into one of two groups representing different normative positions on the SCS-FI. As in our previous work, the experimental condition was designed to examine the effects of level of communicative functioning during peer discussion on pre-to-posttest changes in sociomoral competence as assessed by the SCS-FI. In addition, because three different age–grade levels were used, the research was also designed to collect data on developmental differences in sociomoral competence and communicative functioning.

Because our measures had been previously only pilot-tested on children and preadolescents, the same psychometric analyses used in the previous research were conducted for the children and preadolescents. The results of these analyses indicate that the SCS-FI and CFS both have adequate psychometric properties when used with children and preadolescents. For the SCS-FI, both dimensions of the SCS-FI also appear to have adequate internal consistency reliability, indicating that subjects were consistent in their responses across items. In addition, as will be discussed in more detail under the developmental differences analyses, all three age–grade levels displayed a full range of item responses with individual subjects at all age–grade levels displaying consistent and different positions on both dimensions. Finally, the factor analysis essentially replicated the factor-analytic results obtained with the young adult college students.

Similar psychometric analyses were conducted on the CFS. The results of the analyses indicate that the CFS has adequate psychometric properties when used with children and preadolescents. The relatively low rate of occurrence of DCA in the preadolescents, however, appears to limit the utility of the coding categories when used with younger children. The results also suggested that the CFS has more limited utility when used with younger populations due to distinct developmental trends in the levels of communicative action obtained for this sample.

In addition to the psychometric analyses, a number of analyses were conducted examining developmental differences in sociomoral competence and communicative functioning. With respect to sociomoral competence, the results of the analyses indicated that there were no significant developmental differences in either mean, ranges or, variance for either of the SCS-FI scales. These results, when combined with the results of the psychometric analyses of the SCS-FI, appear to support the hypothesis that children acquire a basic understanding of sociomoral rules and concepts at a relatively early age and suggest the existence of relatively stable individual differences in how children understand such concepts.

With respect to communicative functioning, the results of the analyses indicate the existence of distinct developmental differences in communicative functioning. Thus although there appear to be no significant differences in sociomoral competence, there were highly significant differences on every index of communicative functioning used in this study. More important, the pattern of differences was consistent with developmental levels hypothesized in Table 6.1. An examination of the results across age–grade indicated that the relative frequency of OCA is inversely related to age, decreasing as subjects get older and relative frequency of strategic and discursive communicative actions increases with age.

Finally, analyses were conducted examining the effects of peer discussion on ontogenetic change in sociomoral understanding. These analyses examined pre- to posttest change in sociomoral competence using residualized change scores.

The analyses indicated that there were no significant differences between groups on change scores for either scale for the fifth grade and the seventh grade subjects. In addition, the analyses indicated there were no significant differences between groups for change scores on the RU scale for the ninth grade subjects. There were, however, marginally significant differences between groups on the TD scale. This finding, it should be noted, essentially parallels the finding with the college students.

The most theoretically significant findings for this set of data were related to developmental differences in sociomoral and communicative competence. Although the data provided for only a partial test of our developmental hypotheses, the results were highly suggestive. As noted earlier, we have adopted the view that children are predisposed to acquire early in development a basic understanding of sociomoral rules and concepts and that once a basic understanding is acquired no further ontogenetically predictable transformations in their basic understanding take place. The young child's *understanding* of sociomoral rules and concepts (e.g., justice, responsibility, consequence, obligation, etc.), we suggested, is not simpler, less complex, or more primitive than the adult's. Rather, the young child is viewed as having an understanding of the same basic rules and concepts as the adult. The child's *orientation* toward sociomoral rules and concepts does, however, undergo an ontogenetically predictable series of transformations (heteronomous, autonomous, reflective–hypothetical) that are linked to the development of prerequisite cognitive competencies. The results obtained in this study provide partial support for this view. Furthermore, the data obtained for this study appear to be difficult to reconcile with traditional psychological approaches that focus on maturational or learning processes.

Maturationalist-type theories, we noted, view the evolution of sociomoral knowledge and understanding itself as undergoing an ontogenetically predictable sequence of directional qualitative–structural transformations. Kohlberg (1976), for example, has proposed that the ontogenetic evolution of sociomoral knowledge proceeds through a fixed sequence of stages that is initially defined by a *teleological* (consequence) and *relativistic* perspective (the preconventional level). This initial level of sociomoral understanding is viewed as evolving through an ontogenetically predictable series of stages toward an endpoint that is predefined in terms of a formalistic *deontological* perspective that views moral obligation as determined by *universal* moral principles (the postconventional level). The results obtained with the SCS-FI in this study, however, are difficult to reconcile with such a view. The finding, for example, that there was a full range of relativistic and universalistic positions represented in the fifth grade sample appears to suggest that by 10 years of age children have an understanding of the issue of relativism and universalism and that there is considerable variability in how children understand this issue. Similarly, the finding that there was a full range of teleological and deontological positions represented in the fifth grade sample appears to suggest that by 10 years of age children have an understanding of the role of consequence and obligation and that there is considerable variability in how children understand this issue. By themselves, these findings are not inconsistent with the hypothesis that sociomoral knowledge and understanding undergo a qualitative–structural transformation after middle childhood from a teleological–relativistic understanding to a more deontological and universalistic understanding. It might be argued, for example, that the child with a teleological understanding of sociomoral concepts at this age will undergo a transformation toward a more deontological understanding at a subsequent developmental level. In fact, one might even argue for the reverse (i.e., that the deontologists will be transformed into teleologists). Similarly, it might be argued that the relativists in the sample will undergo at a subsequent stage in development a transformation to a more universalistic position (or the reverse).

The finding that a full range of teleological and deontological or relativistic and universalistic views was represented in seventh and ninth grade subjects is similarly not inconsistent with the hypothesis that subsequent development will involve a qualitative–structural transformation in one direction or the other. Finally, the finding that a full range of teleological and deontological or relativistic and universalistic views was also represented in the young adult college sample is again by itself not inconsistent with the hypothesis that the evolution of sociomoral understanding undergoes a predictable sequence of development. However, the finding that a full range of positions appears to be represented at *all* age–grade levels and that there were no significant differences with respect to either the ranges, means, or variances for these variables would appear to be difficult to reconcile with the view that the evolution of sociomoral understanding follows a developmentally determined direction. These findings do appear, on the other hand, to be consistent with the view that individuals acquire a basic understanding of sociomoral concepts early in life. That is, the results appear to provide support for the view that children have an understanding of the sociomoral issues assessed by the SCS (e.g., relativism–universalism, teleological–deontological) that does not differ significantly from the adult's understanding and that stable individual differences along these dimensions of sociomoral understanding emerge early in life.

Learning-type theories, on the other hand, view the evolution of sociomoral understanding as the outcome of the process of the direct transmission of forms of sociomoral knowledge and understanding through such processes as conditioning, imitation, identification, and so on (Burton, 1976, 1984; Liebert, 1984). The findings obtained with the SCS-FI in this study are, again, not inconsistent with the hypothesis that children acquire their initial understanding of sociomoral rules and concepts through learning and conditioning processes. As we noted earlier, for a sociogenetic transmission system to work, it is necessary that children acquire a basic understanding of the morality of their culture early in life and that this involves the initially uncritical acceptance of a complex constellation of nomotic knowledge, including sociomoral knowledge and understanding. The findings obtained with the CFS, however, appear to be inconsistent with the view that learning and conditioning are the only or, indeed, even the primary type of processes associated with the subsequent evolution of sociomoral knowledge and understanding in competent rule users. Although the CFS is a performance measure rather than a competence measure, the levels of performance on the measure do provide an estimate of the underlying level of communicative competence of the subjects in the samples. The data from our sample of children and preadolescents indicated that there were developmental differences on every index of communicative functioning used in the research. Moreover, the pattern of differences was consistent with the developmental levels outlined in Table 6.1. There were no occurrences of discursive communicative action (DCA) in the fifth and seventh grade samples. The use of DCA did occur in the ninth grade sample, but at a far less frequent rate than in the sample of young adult college students. These findings, in combination with the results obtained with the SCS-FI, suggest that although the children in the fifth and seventh grade samples had an understanding of the sociomoral issues (i.e., relativism–universalism, teleological–deontological) they lacked the cognitive (reflective–hypothetical) and communicative (critical–discursive) competencies to engage in discursive discussion of the issues. More important, however, although peer discussion did not have an effect on ontogenetic change in sociomoral understanding in the fifth and seventh grade samples, it did have an effect on ontogenetic change in the ninth grade sample. Further, the effect occurred for the teleological–deontological (consequence vs. obligation) issues, which was consistent with the finding of an effect for the same variable for the young adult college students. These results thus provide support for the view that, with the attainment of the prerequisite competencies, critical–discursive interactional communicative processes play an increasingly more significant role in the evolution of sociomoral understanding. Thus although these results are not inconsistent with the view that the direct transmission of forms of sociomoral understanding through learning and conditioning processes continues to play a role once the necessary psychosocial competencies have been acquired, they do provide support for the view that ontogenetic change in competent rule users is also the outcome of a constructive evolutionary process; that is, the formative process of the subjective construction and the intersubjective co-construction of sociomoral rule systems.

The findings from this study also provide indirect support for the hypothesis that the individual's *orientation* toward sociomoral rules and concepts undergoes an ontogenetically predictable sequence of transformations. The capacity for hypothetical thinking that is characteristic of the stage of formal operations was hypothesized to be a developmental precondition for a reflective–hypothetical orientation toward sociomoral rules and concepts. Both formal operational thinking and a reflective–hypothetical orientation toward sociomoral rules and concepts were, in turn, hypothesized to be developmental preconditions for critical–discursive communicative actions. The results obtained with the SCS-FI indicated that subjects at all age levels had an understanding of the issues assessed by the scale (and that stable individual differences existed in the way in which the issues were understood), but that the capacity to engage in critical–discursive discussion of these issues did not begin until the ninth grade (about age 14) with the beginning of formal operational thinking, and that critical–discursive communicative action occurred at a significantly more frequent rate in young adult college students who had achieved formal operational thinking and a reflective–hypothetical sociomoral orientation.

In summary, the absence of developmental differences on the SCS-FI appears to support the view that children acquire an initially uncritical understanding of the same sociomoral rules and concepts as adults relatively early in life vis-a-vis the operation of maturation and learning processes. The presence of significant developmental differences on the CFS appears to provide support for the view that the subsequent development of cognitive and communicative competencies enables the competent rule user to engage in reflective–hypothetical thinking about and/or critical–discursive discussion of these concepts. Finally, the results of the analysis of the effects of peer discussion provide support for the view that the constructive evolution of sociomoral understanding in competent rule users is the outcome of the formative process of subjective construction and intersubjective co-construction.

SUMMARY AND IMPLICATIONS

The purpose of this chapter has been to outline a framework for a program of research that has as its aim the articulation of a conception of psychosocial theory as a nomotic science. Nomotics is the science of human rules and rule systems. A basic thesis of this research program is that human behavior can be conceptualized as rule governed. Throughout, social and moral behavior and development have been looked at as paradigmatic forms of rule-governed behavior. In this context, one of the basic tasks of psychosocial theory has been to develop and refine a theoretical framework for investigating the creative or constructive nature of human rule-governed behavior within a constructive evolutionary framework. In establishing our research program we have identified two relatively distinct but related research domains; that is, research related to the reconstruction of specieswide sociomoral competencies and research related to the construction or creation of new forms of sociomoral knowledge and understanding. In the domain of the reconstruction of sociomoral competencies, our work has resulted in the tentative identification of a number of basic structural dimensions of sociomoral knowledge. Research was summarized describing procedures for operationalizing these dimensions. In the domain of constructive research, we developed a measure of communicative functioning and tested hypotheses with respect to the role of communication in the ontogenetic evolution of sociomoral understanding. Data were also summarized with respect to the development of psychosocial competencies. The rule-governed metaphor thus appears to provide a useful research heuristic. The power of the rule-governed metaphor, however, extends beyond the formulation of research hypotheses. A rule-governed perspective has at least two paradigmatically significant implications for conceptualizing human behavior.

First, a theoretical framework such as the one described here shifts the conceptual focus from the individual in isolation to the individual within a social context. The current literature on social and moral behavior and development is distinguished by a partiality for theoretical models that focus on psychological processes such as maturation and learning. Such models tend to be unable to provide a theoretically integrated account of both psychological processes (e.g., maturation, learning) and social processes (e.g., communication). More important, although the approach described here explicitly recognizes the role of learning and maturation in the development of psychosocial competencies, the theoretical heuristic also shifts the conceptual focus to the constructive evolution of sociomoral knowledge and understanding. From such a perspective, the constructive evolution of sociomoral knowledge and understanding in competent rule users is viewed as the outcome of the formative process of the subjective construction and intersubjective co-construction of new forms of sociomoral knowledge and understanding. Such an approach obviously represents only a first approximation of a conceptually adequate theoretical heuristic; nonetheless, the approach does appear to allow the integration of both social and psychological variables within a constructive evolutionary framework.

Second, a view of human behavior as rule governed explicitly recognizes the creative or constructive nature of human behavior. Such a view shifts the conceptual focus from the law-governed nature of human behavior to the formative process of the subjective construction and co-construction of social reality, thereby restoring an element of freedom and creativity to human behavior. Human beings, we noted, not only conform to rules, but also are free to change and create them in a way that natural laws cannot be created or changed. A view of human behavior as rule governed, therefore, focuses not only on the historical determinants of human behavior but on the constructive processes that facilitate the emergence of new forms of sociomoral knowledge and understanding.

REFERENCES

Bartlett, F. C. (1932). *Remembering* London: Cambridge University Press.
Berger, P. L., & Luckman, T. (1967). *The social construction of reality*. New York: Doubleday (Anchor).
Berkowitz, M. W. (1985). The role of discussion in moral education. In M. W. Berkowitz & F. Ozer (Eds.), *Moral education: Theory and application*. Hillsdale, NJ: Erlbaum.
Berkowitz, M. W., & Gibbs, J. C. (1983). Measuring developmental features of moral discussion. *Merrill-Palmer Quarterly*, 29, 399–410.
Berndt, T. J. (1983). Effects of friendship on prosocial intentions and behavior. *Child Development*, 52, 636–643.
Burton, R. V. (1984). A paradox in theories and research in moral development. In W. Kurtines & J. L. Gewirtz (Eds.), *Morality, moral behavior and moral development*. New York: Wiley.
Campbell, J. (1982). *Grammatical man*. New York: Simon & Schuster.
Chomsky, N. (1965). *Aspects of the theory of syntax*. Cambridge, MA: MIT Press.

Damon, W., & Killen, M. (1982). Peer interaction and the process of change in children's moral reasoning. *Merrill -Palmer Quarterly, 28*, 347–368.

Eisenberg, N., Lundy, T., Shell, R., & Roth, K. (1985). Children's justifications for their adult and peer-directed compliant (prosocial and nonprosocial) behaviors. *Developmental Psychology 21*, 325–331.

Erikson, E. H. (1950). *Childhood and society*, New York: Norton.

Fromm, E. (1947). *Man for himself*. New York: Rinehart.

Goffman, E. (1959). *The presentation of self in everyday life*. New York: Doubleday.

Haan, N. (1978). Two moralities in action contexts. *Journal of Personality & Social Psychology, 36*, 286–305.

Haan, N. (1985) Process of moral development: Cognitive or social disequilibrium? *Developmental Psychology, 21*, 966–1006.

Habermas, J. (1979). *Communication and the evolution of society*. Boston: Beacon.

Higgins, A., Powers, C., & Kohlberg, L. (1984). The relationship of moral atmosphere to judgments of responsibility. In W. Kurtines & J. L. Gewirtz (Eds.), *Morality, moral behavior and moral development*. New York: Wiley.

Hogan, R., & Henley, N. (1970). Nomotics: The science of human rule systems. *Law & Society Review, 15* 135–146.

Huxley, J. (1942). *Evolution: The modern synthesis*. New York: Harper.

Keller, M. (1984). Resolving conflicts in friendship: The development of moral understanding in everyday life. In W. Kurtines & J. L. Gewirtz (Eds.), *Morality, moral behavior, and moral development*. New York: Wiley.

Kohlberg, L. (1976). Moral stage and moralization: The cognitive developmental approach. In T. Lickona (Ed.), *Moral development and behavior: Theory, research, and social issues*. New York: Holt, Rinehart & Winston.

Kohlberg, L. (1984). *Essays in moral development: The psychology of moral development (Vol. 2)*, New York: Harper & Row.

Kurtines, W. (1984). Moral behavior as rule governed behavior: A psychosocial role–theoretical approach to moral behavior and development. In W. Kurtines & J. L. Gewirtz (Eds.), *Morality, moral behavior, and moral development*. New York: Wiley.

Kurtines, W. (1985). *The Communicative Functioning Scale manual*. Unpublished manuscript, Florida International University.

Kurtines, W. (1986). Person and situation effects on moral decision making: A psychosocial role-theoretical approach. *Journal of Personality & Social Psychology, 50*, 784–791.

Kurtines, W., & Gewirtz, J. L. (Eds.). (1984). *Morality, moral behavior, and moral development*. New York: Wiley.

Kurtines, W., & Lanza, T. (1983). *The Sociomoral Competencies Scale manual*. Unpublished manuscript, Florida International University.

Kurtines, W., Lanza, T., Carlo, G., Cooksey, L., & Pace, L. (1986). *Communication and understanding: Interpersonal and intrapersonal processes in the constructive evolution of sociomoral knowledge and understanding*. Unpublished manuscript, Florida International University.

Kurtines, W., & Pimm, J. (1983). The Moral Development Scale: A Piagetian measure of moral development. *Educational & Psychological Measurement, 43*, 89–105.

Lewin, K. (1935). *A dynamic theory of personality*. New York: McGraw-Hill.

Liebert, R. (1984). What develops in moral development? In W. Kurtines & J. L. Gewirtz (Eds.), *Morality, moral behavior, and moral development*. New York: Wiley.

McCarthy, T. (1981). *The critical theory of Jurgen Habermas*. Cambridge, MA: MIT Press.

Mead, G. H. (1934). *Mind, self, and society from the standpoint of a social behaviorist.* Chicago: University of Chicago Press.

Monod, J. (1973). *Chance and necessity.* New York: Knopf.

Much, N. C., & Shweder, R. A. (1978). Speaking of rules: The analysis of culture in breach. In W. Damon (Ed.), *Moral development.* San Francisco: Jossey-Bass.

Nisan, M. (1984). Content and structure in moral judgment: An integrative view. In W. Kurtines & J. L. Gewirtz (Eds.), *Morality, moral behavior, and moral development.* New York: Wiley.

Oser, F. (1984). Cognitive stages of interaction in moral discourse. In W. Kurtines & J. L. Gewirtz (Eds.), *Morality, moral behavior, and moral development.* New York: Wiley.

Packer, M. J. (1985). *The structure of moral action: A hermeneutic study of moral conflict.* Basel: Karger.

Pepper, S. C. (1973). *World hypotheses: A study of evidence.* Berkeley: University of California Press.

Piaget, J. (1936). *The origins of intelligence in children.* New York: International Universities Press.

Piaget, J. (1954). *The construction of reality in the child* (M. Cook, Trans.). New York. Basic.

Piaget, J. (1965). *The moral judgment of the child* (M. Gabain, Trans.). New York: Free Press, (Original work published 1932)

Pimm, J., & Kurtines, W. (1982). Moral development in contemporary American and Swiss children. *Archives de Psychologie, 50,* 225–235.

Selman, R. L. (1980). *The growth of interpersonal understanding: Developmental and clinical studies.* New York: Academic.

Selman, R., & Demorest, A. P. (1984). Observing troubled children's interpersonal negotiation strategies: Implications of and for a developmental model. *Child Development, 55,* 288–305.

Shweder, R., Mahapatra, M., & Miller, J. G. (in press). Culture and moral development. In J. Kagan (Ed.), *The emergence of moral concepts in young children.*

Sullivan, H. (1953). *The interpersonal theory of psychiatry.* New York: Norton.

Toulmin, S. (1969). Concepts and the explanation of human behavior. In T. Mischel (Ed.), *Human action: Conceptual and empirical issues.* New York: Academic.

Waddington, C. H. (1975). *The ethical animal.* Chicago: University of Chicago Press.

Youniss, J. (1981). Moral development through a theory of social construction: An analysis. *Merrill-Palmer Quarterly, 27,* 385–403.

PART 4

Interpretive–Hermeneutic Perspectives

CHAPTER 7

Determinations of Meaning: Discourse and Moral Socialization

RICHARD A. SHWEDER AND NANCY C. MUCH

This chapter was written while Much was a post-doctoral fellow in the Department of Psychology at Michigan State University and Shweder was a John Simon Guggenheim Foundation fellow and fellow at the Center for Advanced Study in the Behavioral Sciences. We are grateful for the financial support provided by the National Institute for Child Health and Human Development and by the Spencer Foundation. An earlier draft of this manuscript was read by several friends and colleagues, and we have benefited much from their critical comments. We wish to thank especially Marvin Berkowitz, Roy G. D'Andrade, Sandy Dixon, Herbert Fingarette, John B. Haviland, Ann Higgins, Lawrence Kohlberg, and Robert I. Levy. Our research in India would not have been possible without the support, encouragement, and counsel of Dr. Manamohan Mahapatra and Professor S.K. Misra.

This chapter is concerned with social communication and its power to represent and transmit moral beliefs. Viewing moral development as a problem in the acquisition of moral knowledge, in the first part of the chapter we propose that moral beliefs have their ontogenetic origins in the messages and meanings implicitly conveyed through talk, conversation, discourse, and customary practice. The basic idea is that children are continually assisted by local guardians of the moral order in constructing their notions of right and wrong, and that the inferences children draw about the moral (its form) and what's moral (its content) are personal reconstructions recreated within a framework of tradition-based modes of apperception and evaluation represented in everyday discourse.

We present a scheme of concepts (communicative array, indexicality, instantiation, background knowledge) to account for the construction of meaning in discourse, with special attention to the way a picture of the moral order is indexed and tacitly conveyed through speech; and we outline a method of discourse analysis based on the expansion or unpacking of what is said to reveal propositions about the moral order that remain unsaid yet are nonetheless effectively communicated through everyday speech. The method of expansion is justified by reference to our theory of how meaning is constructed in discourse; since speakers always mean and convey more than they say, meaning is revealed by making explicit the relationship between the said and the unsaid.

In the second part of the chapter we apply our "theory" of meaning and "method" of expansion to one part of the text of a moral dilemma interview (Kohlberg's Heinz dilemma) conducted with an orthodox Hindu informant in India. Expert coders classify the unexpanded text as an instance of stage 3/4 conventional reasoning. Not until the text is expanded or unpacked to explicate implicit meanings is it possible to recognize the postconventional reasoning of the informant, in which the informant represents the Heinz dilemma as a problem in the irrationality of committing a sin, rather than as a problem of rights, justice, or life versus property. We suggest that codings of unexpanded moral development interview protocols, based exclusively on propositions explicitly stated in an interview, are likely to misrepresent the moral beliefs of informants.

In the third part of the chapter we offer an explanation for moral development researchers' avoidance of the study of everyday moral discourse, and we wonder why most theories of moral socialization and/or moral development have so little to say about social communication and its power to represent and transmit moral beliefs. In trying to make sense of this widespread academic phobia for studying everyday talk we are led to rethink the terms of the rather destructive debate over whether moral judgments (that's wrong; that's bad) are cognitive or noncognitive (emotive) judgments. It is argued that both cognitivists and emotivists have perpetuated an unfortunate conception of what it ought to mean for moral judgments to have reference to natural or objective entities in the world. That unfortunate conception of what it ought to mean to be truly objective misleads emotivists to view moral judgments as entirely subjective, and to dismiss moral discourse or argumentation as pretense, or as a mock or illusory rhetoric disguising its real underlying pragmatic function (e.g., to preserve privilege or power). The same unfortunate conception of genuine objective knowledge misleads cognitivists to search for the objective foundations of moral judgments in an abstract–formal–logical realm far removed from everyday thoughtful talk.

Offering a "softened" view of what it ought to mean to have objective knowledge in the "hard" cognitive–scientific disciplines, we outline a neorationalist approach to moral development. Our neorationalist approach shares the assumption, characteristic of cognitivist approaches to morality, that there exist natural or objective moral entities and that moral understandings are a form of knowledge about some objective moral world. Our neorationalist approach is defined, in addition, by three distinctive assumptions: that genuine objectivity can be, in some measure, subject dependent; that the existence of moral facts and moral knowledge is compatible with the existence of multiple objective moral worlds and alternative forms of postconventional moral reasoning; and that each of those several objective moral worlds is found in, and maintained through, the ordinary conversations of everyday life.

DISCOURSE AND THE FRAMING OF A MORAL UNIVERSE

During the last several years we have been conducting research on moral development in India and the United States (Shweder, 1985; Shweder, Mahapatra, & Miller, in press; Shweder & Miller, 1985). The research in India has been carried out in a Hindu temple town on the east coast of India among various Oriya Brahman subcastes and among various castes referred to as "scheduled" castes by the government of India (scheduled for affirmative action programs), referred to as Harijans ("children of God") by Mahatma Gandhi, and referred to as unclean or "untouchable" by the local Brahmans.

In many ways, although certainly not in all ways, the moral career of an orthodox Hindu Oriya stands in contrast to our own moral career. Consider a short list of typical Oriya Brahman practices. Marriages are arranged. Dating and premarital sexual play are strictly forbidden. Widows may not remarry, and there are restrictions concerning the foods they may eat and the clothes they may wear. Certain relatives—for example, a woman and her husband's elder brother or a man and his wife's elder sister—are not permitted to talk to each other or be in each other's presence. A menstruating woman is not allowed to sleep in the same bed with her husband or enter the kitchen or cook or engage in prayer or groom herself or touch her children. Untouchables are not allowed in the local temples. At night children are kept in the same bed with their parents or grandparents until at least the age of 6 or 7, and it is not uncommon for children to be caned for misconduct. Husband and wife do not eat together, and there is no communal family meal. Adult women are not allowed to leave the house without permission. No one may enter the local temple for 12 days following a birth or death in the family. Eating beef is prohibited.

Each of those practices is experienced by orthodox Hindus as more or less reasonable (i.e., legitimate); and each of those practices experienced as reasonable has associated with it, more or less consciously, a line of argumentation. For example, in defense of their practices, it is argued by Oriya informants that so many people, including ancestral spirits are affected by one's marriage choice that one cannot possibly leave it up to one young person, driven by sex, passion, and infatuation, to make such an important decision. Or it is argued that the body is a temple with a spirit (what we call the self or the observing or transcendental ego) dwelling in it, and it is an obligation of life to preserve the sanctity of temples and keep them clean, unpolluted, and pure. The body of a menstruating woman is impure and is associated with sin. Hence she must be kept at a distance from all holy or sanctified ground, including all temples, the body of her husband, the household kitchen and prayer room, and so on.

Each line of argumentation culminates in, or makes use of, one or more propositions or presuppositions about persons, nature, and society: People have souls and they transmigrate; the body is a temple with a spirit dwelling in it; nature is just (in the long run you reap what you sow) and received inequalities are there for a reason; to be born a woman is an indication of prior sin; ancestral spirits will not accept food from an impure woman or a woman of the wrong caste; customary practices are a guarantee against sin; it is irrational to commit a sin, and so on.

Notably, in Orissa, arguments favoring or defending a practice are often presented in the form of a narrative account. Indeed, for orthodox Hindus a major way to prove a point is to recount a historical or personal narrative, and a central body of evidence about what the causal structure of the world is like consists of "historical" experiences recorded in the Hindu scriptures, especially the Puranas and the Epics (the *Ramayana* and the *Mahabharata*). Orthodox Hindus believe that the experiences of their forefathers recorded in the scriptures are a reasonable guide to the causal structure of reality and thus not unreasonably most expositions about what the world is like or ought to be like begin, "Let me tell you a story."

Let me tell you a story about stealing. Once some sadhus [wandering mendicant holy men] came to a poor man's house. He and his son were the only members of the family. The sadhus wanted this man to be their host for that night. Holy men never ask for credit. They never steal. They have only what they earn from begging alms, which they cook and eat.

The sadhus arrived at the man's house as guests, and as guests they were considered as a God. So whatever belongings the man and his son had they pawned and arranged dinner for the sadhus. Before going to their dinner the sadhus said that ghee (clarified butter) was essential for their dinner. [Ghee is classified in the native theory of foods as a "cool" food. Unlike "hot" foods such as onions, garlic, fish or meat, cool foods do not stimulate the senses or draw the consumer's attention to such bodily or organic process as taste or digestion. Thus cool foods are conducive to the quest of the sadhu, which is, after all, the distillation of the spirit in an attempt to transcend this worldly and momentary material existence.] Both the father and the son pondered again and again where to get the ghee. They were really "in a stew."

They went to the sadhu of a nearby monastery to get some ghee. But the sadhu refused to give them ghee. So they made a hole in the wall and the son entered into the store room of the monastery. It was full of wealth but the son only picked up the ghee pot. While he was halfway through the hole, suddenly the sadhu got up and caught hold of the son's two legs. But outside the father was pulling the son's hands. So a tussle went on for some time. The son told the father to take the pot of ghee and offer it to the sadhu guests. He also told his father to cut off his head and take it away so the sadhu of the monastery would not be able to recognize him. The father did this and threw away his son's head.

The father did such things only because he wanted to help the sadhus. After he offered ghee to his guests the sadhus were satisfied. The next morning the father bid them farewell, and they asked "Where is your son. He is not seen." The father started to cry. The sadhus asked him why he is crying? So he told all the details and facts, and said it was nobody's fault.

The sadhus said, "You have done a mistake. Okay. If you have done it only to satisfy us. If you had no evil intention under it. If you had no temptation for the wealth, and if your son died only for this, then we will pray to god for his life." They asked "where is your son's head?" They wanted to show God the decapitated head. The father took the head of the son to the sadhus. They sprinkled some Tulsi water on the head. So the son returned to life. [Tulsi is a basil plant. The leaf of the plant in water produces a substance believed to have various potent causal powers. Among orthodox Hindus there is a well-known story about how Tulsi became a basil plant. In brief, Tulsi was the loyal, chaste and devoted wife of a demon. Her husband was very successful at terrorizing the Gods. He could not be killed unless he was weakened, and the only way to weaken him was to violate the chastity of his wife; her chastity made him strong. So the Hindu God Vishnu disguised himself as Tulsi's husband and slept with her. The demon was killed. When Tulsi discovered the treachery she cursed Vishnu and told him he would turn into a log or piece of wood. In fact Vishnu is today represented as a log in the Temple of Juggernaut in Orissa. Vishnu, however, blessed Tulsi and made compensation to her by turning her into a holy plant, which he always keeps with him, and which is today worshipped by wives and widows all over India. In the courtyard of every Brahman household is a Tulsi plant.]

That story was narrated to Shweder in the context of a Kohlbergian interview concerning whether Ashok (the local stand-in for Heinz) should steal a drug to save the life of his wife. The full interview text appears in the appendix to this chapter. Later in this chapter we shall discuss the moral argumentation of the informant, who maintained throughout that Ashok should not steal and who told many stories in defense of his point of view.

We have here provided the most minimal explication or expansion of bits and pieces of the text, clarifying references that are obviously opaque to a Western reader (e.g., What is a sadhu?; Why is it important for sadhus to have ghee for dinner? What is Tulsi?). There are, however, many things in the text that are opaque without being obviously so, and there are many unstated propositions that must be made explicit if an uninformed reader is to appreciate the compelling nature of the case that is being advanced by the informant against committing the sin of stealing. At this point in the essay we merely note the characteristic Oriya form of moral argumentation: telling stories related to pre-cedents recorded in the scriptures that reveal truths about the causal structure of reality as a natural–physical–moral order.

So far we have tried to describe, in a relatively superficial and summary fashion, a few of the differences between orthodox Hindu culture and secular American culture. One of the more striking findings of our moral development research in India and America (Shweder, Mahapatra & Miller, in press) is that, by age 5 Oriya children are very Oriya and American children are very Ameri-can. When it comes to judgments about what is right and what is wrong there is virtually a zero-order correlation between the judgments of the 5-year-olds in the two cultures. That is also true of the moral judgments of older children and adults in the two cultures.

Thus while there are some areas of agreement between the 5-year-olds in the two cultures (e.g., that it is wrong to break a promise, destroy a picture drawn by another child, kick a harmless animal), there are just as many areas of dis-agreement. Oriya (but not American) 5-year-olds believe it is wrong to eat beef or address one's father by his first name. American (but not Oriya) 5-year-olds believe it is wrong to cane an errant child or to open a letter addressed to one's 14-year-old son.

Moreover, while the obligations (whatever they are thought to be) associated with each of those issues are conceived by 5-year-olds in both cultures to be natural or objective obligations (i.e., unalterable and, in most cases, universally binding), the Americans, but not the Oriyas, represent those obligations in terms of natural rights and in terms of values associated with liberty, equality, and secular happiness. On the other hand, the Oriya concept of dharma and sin and the concept of the moral authority of custom or tradition are alien to the moral sensibilities of secularized American informants.

Finally, the evidence of Shweder and colleagues (in press) suggests that, within each culture, those moral judgments that are *common* to both cultures (e.g., that it is wrong to engage in arbitrary assault, break promises, destroy property, commit incest) are learned at about the same rate as those moral judgments that are *distinctive* of each culture (e.g., in America, that it is wrong for a husband to beat his wife if she repeatedly leaves the house without per-mission; or, in India, that it is wrong for a widow to remarry or eat fish or meat or wear jewelry). That finding, of a roughly equal rate of acquisition for culture-specific versus universal moral content, leads us to speculate that the universal aspects of a moral code and the culture-specific aspects of a moral code may be learned by means of the *same* process.

Children, 5 years of age and older in orthodox Hindu India and secularized America have orthogonal judgments about what is right and wrong, conceive of obligations in somewhat divergent terms (e.g., it's my right; it's a sin, etc.), and achieve an understanding of the culture-specific aspects of their moral code at the same rate as they achieve an understanding of those aspects of their moral code that are shared with other cultures. Our social communication approach to moral development is an attempt to identify a unitary process of moral socialization that might explain those three facts.

Our basic (and perhaps commonsensical) notion is that children develop the moral ideas they have because local guardians of the moral order (parents, teachers, peers) re-present and convey to children powerful morally relevant interpretations of events. Those interpretations are conveyed, we believe, in the context of routine, yet personally involving, family, school, and social life practices (practices having to do with eating, sleeping, grooming, possessing objects, distributing resources, etc.). They are conveyed, we believe, through the verbal exchanges—commands, threats, sanction statements, accusations, explanations, justifications, and excuses—necessary to maintain routine practices. We assume that morally relevant interpretations of events are gotten across and made salient, as well, by the emotional reactions of others; for example, anger or disappointment or "hurt feelings" over a transgression. Finally, we assume that moral interpretations of events are expressed through and are discernible in the very organization of routine practices (a separate bed for each child, a communal meal, lining up—first come, first served—to get tickets). In sum, it is our view that the emerging moral understandings of the child are the product of continuous participation in social practices (the mundane rituals of everyday life), and that those socially produced and reproduced understandings are the grounding for the child's later attempts reflectively or self-consciously to reconstruct his or her own moral code.

It is an axiom of our social communication approach to moral socialization that local guardians of the moral order persistently and powerfully trace for children the boundaries of a normative reality and assist the children at stepping into the frame.

Language is perhaps the most powerful means of social communication and thus in illustrating our social communication approach we focus on the analysis of discourse. The data corpus available to us (Much, 1983; Much & Shweder, 1978) consists of conversations between children (ages 4 and 5) and adults in situations of accountability (Much & Shweder, 1978) in an American preschool. Our route to understanding those symbolic forms is by way of what Geertz (1973) has called "thick description". While what is said in everyday discourse in preschool settings may seem "thin" and obvious, what is implied, suggested, gotten across, or accomplished by what is said is "thick" and often surprising. Implicit in or presupposed by what is said is a conception of an objective moral universe.

Incident 1: All the Children Are Friends in School
It is "rug time." Children are seated around Mrs. Swift on the rug. Emily sits just to the left of Mrs. Swift and Andrea sits next to Emily. Vicki leaves her seat and approaches them.

1. VICKI: I want to sit next to Emily.
2. MRS. SWIFT: There's no room and you stay where you are. [Vicki would have to place herself between Mrs. Swift and Emily or between Emily and Andrea in order to sit next to Emily.]
3. VICKI: Emily. . . . my friend.

4. MRS. SWIFT: All the children are friends in school.

5. VICKI: Yeah, but some children say they're not my friend.

6. MRS. SWIFT: Well, then you try to make them your friend.

Incident 2: The Value of Friendliness

Mr. Price and some children are sitting in the back playroom. A teacher from another classroom appears at the door with a child from her unit. Alice addresses them.

1. ALICE: What are you doing in our class?

2. TEACHER: Well, we came up the stairs and we didn't know where we were going and here we are.

3. ALICE: Get out of our class.

4. TEACHER: That's unfriendly of you.

5. MR. PRICE: That's not very friendly.

6. MR. PRICE: You should be friendly to visitors.

7. MR. PRICE: Sometimes you go up and visit their classroom.

In both incidents local guardians of the moral order trace for these 4-year-olds the boundaries of a moral universe and assist the children at stepping into the frame. In incident 1 Vicki presses for the privilege of affiliating with Emily on the grounds that Emily falls into a certain category of person, "my friend" (utterance 3). Mrs. Swift, however, will not allow Vicki to treat this category as an exclusive class; she introduces a norm including all classroom members in the category "friend" (4). Mrs. Swift's proposition (4) may appear like a factual proposition, but it is used to deliver a moral message; it describes the way things ought to be, not the way they are. Whether in this instance Vicki understood the normative force of Mrs. Swift's utterance is ambiguous; Vicki's next utterance (5) introduces a contrary fact, which calls into question Mrs. Swift's inference. This suggests that Vicki either interpreted Mrs. Swift's utterance (4) as a factual proposition or understood its normative implication yet tried to evade its normative force by conveniently "misreading" it as a statement of fact.

But notice how carefully Mrs. Swift monitors the uptake of her own messages. Vicki's factual objection is met not by further factual reasoning, but by another statement of a normative proposition (6), which is a prescription for appropriate action. Vicki has objected to Mrs. Swift's reasoning on the grounds that Mrs. Swift's words do not describe the classroom as Vicki knows it. Mrs. Swift, however, proffers a norm making it unambiguous to the children that she expects them, through their actions, to get the world of the classroom to line up with her words. The conversation portrays for these young children a moral world based on free or at least nonexclusive affiliation.

In incident 2 ("get out of our class") the child, Alice, tries to understand the event in terms of rights (what is ours and not yours) (1,3) and the attendant privilege of imposing one's own intentions (3). However, adults in the episode are interested in instructing Alice in the expectations of free and nonexclusive affiliation. They represent for Alice and call her attention to a moral universe in which three evaluative criteria compete with Alice's one-dimensional evaluation of the event in terms of who holds rights. The norm of "friendliness" is introduced and prescribed (4,5,6) along with a category "visitor" (6), which is supposed to classify the outside teacher as a person with whom one is expected to affiliate. A rationale for affiliation is expanded in utterance 7 by reference to the actions of the outside teacher relative to the actions of members of Alice's class, that is, a norm of reciprocity is represented and brought to bear. The message is that rights are not the only or most important consideration bearing upon the event, and that in the moral universe in which we are going to live together rights must be weighed or balanced against other values.

Our brief (although "thickening") commentary on incidents 1 and 2 illustrates our social communication approach to the analysis of moral development. Everyday conversation and social interaction between adults and children are viewed as a relentless process of representation and rationalization making salient certain powerful belief conclusions about the nature of experience. At home and at school young children are (to borrow an apt metaphor from Judith Dunn) continually "bathed" in verbal evaluations and discourse-based representations of a moral universe. The discourse indexes, or points in the direction of, a conception of a moral world that has been worked on over many generations. That collectively evolved conception of a moral universe is a complex network of ideals, supposed facts, maxims, presuppositions, and much more, which not only specifies the kinds of persons and events that exist in that moral world but also places limits on what is going to count as a sensible argument in defense of the rationality, objectivity, and hence legitimacy of that moral world. One goal of our analysis is to make explicit that network of objectifying knowledge.

Yet there is more to it than that. In constantly monitoring and assisting them as they go about describing and evaluating events, American middle class adults not only treat children as novice recipients of knowledge and insights into the objective nature of the moral order. American adults also expect young children to uphold the moral order, to care about upholding the moral order, and to become their own local moral guardians. Through discourse an objective moral universe is not only represented; it also comes to be reproduced.

Incident 3: The Foundation of Rights, or "I Had It First and I'm Using It"

Clifford is seated at a table, using a felt-tip marker to color a wooden dinosaur he has built. Mrs. Swift stands nearby. Sean enters the room and comes to the table.

1. SEAN: Hey Clifford, I need this [indicating the marker].
2. CLIFFORD: Yeah, but I got it first.
3. CLIFFORD: You mean it's yours?
4. SEAN: Yeah.
5. CLIFFORD: Did you take it home? [meaning: bring it from home?]
6. SEAN: No.
7. CLIFFORD: Were you using it before?

8. SEAN: Yeah.
9. MRS. SWIFT: He was using it before he went downstairs.
10. CLIFFORD: Well, I was just using it.
11. MRS. SWIFT: Well, but you should ask.

This conversation reveals not only Clifford's emerging competence (and sophistication) in representing events in terms of who holds rights, but also several features of the way rights are conceived in the moral universe undergoing reconstruction in the mind of the 4-year-old American child.

First, when Sean wishes to claim an article in Clifford's possession Sean objectifies his claim by oblique reference to some purpose or constraint. Sean's utterance "I need this" (1) implies an intention to use the implement for some purpose he holds in mind. Whether such a purpose is actually present "in Sean's mind" is a separate question, which, in this context, is of little importance. Nursery school children have learned the advantage of using "I need" where "I want" could also be used; it works to lend an air of legitimacy to a demand or request. While the usage certainly does not guarantee the success of the claim, it does tell us something about the norms for making a legitimate claim on communal resources. Purposiveness has become a reasonable basis for personal removal of resources from the common pool.

It is noteworthy that Sean extends a justification by reference to purpose to account for a claim to an implement already in the possession of another child. Sean's reasoning represents the standard justification among members of the preschool classrooms for demanding or requesting rights to material resources in another's possession or use. Here Clifford meets the demand–request with an assertion of his own rights to the implement on the basis of a widely recognized principle for establishing temporary personal claim to communal property, namely, priority (2). But Clifford rechecks Sean's meaning (3); Clifford wants to know whether Sean's claim was also supported by established rights. Sean indicates that it was.

A sequence follows (5–8) in which Clifford tries to determine the basis of Sean's rights. Clifford begins by testing the hypothesis that the implement is Sean's private property, that Sean has brought it from home. This would constitute the strongest kind of claim to rights that Sean could have. But, as Sean indicates (6), this is not the case. The next principle Clifford checks is priority (7)—was Sean using the implement even before Clifford was? Sean assents to this condition as the basis of his claim and Mrs. Swift (9) swiftly, and with considerable weight, enters to support his contention.

The argument thus far has been concerned with determining who has established rights over the implement, a not uncommon type of argument in the nursery school. Once the basis of Sean's rights has been established, apparently to Clifford's satisfaction, Clifford not only submits to Sean's claim but accounts for his own actions with a constituting denial (10).

A constituting denial disclaims the blameworthiness of an action by constituting or defining it in such a way that the action as constituted or described does not breach the norm in question; typically a contrast is implied between the action as defined and another possible definition of the action that would make it appear as a breach. That move may be accomplished with the use of "only" or "just" ("I was just using it"; "I was just seeing it") or by substitution with the alternative definition ("You stole my chair!" "No, nobody was in it and I sat in it").

What is noteworthy about Clifford's constituting denial (10) is that he recognizes his potential liability to some blame, although it is unclear whether that recognition is the result of his reasoning or the result of the teacher's intervention, or both. In his constituting denial (10) he defines his action in such a way as to disclaim intent to infringe upon Sean's rights; Clifford seems to be saying that what he did was not really bad because he did not know the marker was already claimed.

In the closing utterance (11) Mrs. Swift, a guardian of the moral order acting on her didactic agenda, seizes an opportunity to teach Clifford a principle: you should ask before using something. This is a fascinating admonition. Does Mrs. Swift really intend that Clifford conduct a systematic inquiry for establishing prior rights every time he wants to use an article of communal property? She certainly does not. What she probably does intend is to make salient for Clifford a general responsibility to anticipate possible rights of others over resources even when prior claims are not immediately evident. How incessantly yet delicately we trace for each other the boundaries of our moral universe, and our responsibilities to it and within it.

SOCIALIZATION AND THE CONSTRUCTION OF MEANING IN DISCOURSE

Our theory about the acquisition of moral beliefs is a theory about how meaning is constructed in discourse. Recent work on the analysis of discourse and conversation has made it axiomatic that ordinary talk means far more than it says and carries information about cultural beliefs and knowledge systems that transcends the grammatical and referential aspects of language (Labov & Fanschel, 1977; Longacre, 1983).

For example, in the utterance (Ervin-Tripp, 1976) "Oh, dear, I wish I were taller" at least three things are happening. The speaker is explicitly stating a proposition regarding an intentional state (wishing to be taller). The speaker is implicitly requesting a service ("Please get the dishes down for me".) The speaker is implicitly communicating something about her relationship to the interlocutor (that he is familiar; that he may be expected to have a solicitous attitude toward the speaker; that he is taller than the speaker). In ordinary conversation what is said is never a complete representation of what is implied or suggested or gotten across by what is said.

One way to state the axiom is that what is said carries *indexical* meaning—it points beyond itself to implications and suggestions whose connection to what was said is inferential. Alternatively stated, the meaning and coherency of any stretch of conversation are dependent upon processes of inference that tie the utterance to features of the context in which it is embedded, and to various unstated background propositions. A corollary of the indexicality axiom: In drawing inferences from what was said to what was unsaid, participants need to be informed, and in fact become informed, about things that were never mentioned.

A second axiom is that the major condition for an inference to occur in the construction of meaning is that the recipient or observer of a communication have sufficient prior knowledge to infer the implication or suggestion that is the meaning of what was said. The basic idea is that prior knowledge (knowledge of categories, propositions, maxims, contexts, intentional states, logical relations, etc.) is the most powerful factor in generating further knowledge (the meaning of what was said).

A corollary of the prior knowledge axiom is a principle of intersubjectivity that states: (1) participants in conversation construct utterances addressing them to listeners who are assumed to have sufficient prior knowledge to understand them; (2) participants monitor the uptake or comprehension of their utterances and watch for indications that they may be wrong in their assumption that the listener has sufficient prior knowledge; and (3) conversation is a self-corrective process in which an equilibrium is sought between what is said and the prior knowledge needed to comprehend it.

That self-corrective process can be thought of as a progressively constrained dialectic that proceeds iteratively in two directions. From one direction prior knowledge consisting of unstated propositions is brought to bear in interpreting what was said; to the extent the interpretation "works" it gives a sense of reality or objectivity to the unstated propositions. This is sometimes referred to as the *instantiation* of beliefs—the utterance is seen as an instance of an unstated general proposition that is already known.

In the other direction what is taken as known is used to draw inferences beyond itself, as part of an effort to make sense of what was said and to search for a propositional content that is not yet known but is implicit in what was said. Again, in forcing participants to draw inferences from what was said to what was unsaid discourse has the power indirectly to inform participants (e.g., children) or observers (e.g., ethnographers) about things that were never explicitly mentioned.

A third axiom of discourse analysis is that the relevant unit of analysis is the entire communicative array linking by means of knowledgeable inference what was said to what was meant. A communicative array is a set of coexisting elements: (1) speech (what is said); (2) context; and (3) background knowledge, in which the three elements bear a mutually constraining relationship to one another. Thus to construct the meaning of discourse in a communicative array, as either a participant in the discourse or an observer of it, involves referring the explicit content of speech (what was said) to two indexed levels, the context and all the relevant prior background knowledge needed to make sense of what was said. Indeed, everyday discourse is abbreviated, condensed, and implicit (indexical) precisely because participants count on each other to count on (and can count on each other to take account of the other counting on) context and a (presumed) shared body of prior knowledge to contribute the knowledge needed to draw a reasonable inference to what was meant, from what was said.

A corollary of the communicative array axiom is that objective determinations of meaning are possible. That is not the same as saying that there are formal, logical, deductive, or structural principles that can be mechanically, automatically, or routinely applied to an utterance to arrive at a determination of what it means; if the meaning of an utterance is indexical there is no formal or structural feature of the utterance per se that determines what it means, yet the utterance may still have a determinate meaning that can be determined objectively.

Thus given sufficient prior knowledge of context, background assumptions, usage and so on, it is possible to distinguish between valid and invalid inferences about what an utterance means, to recognize improper or implausible deductions about what was left unstated, presupposed, or assumed in the communication, and so on. The process of determining the meaning of an utterance in a communicative array is somewhat like solving a hermeneutic jigsaw puzzle, but if you have enough pieces in place it becomes easy to see how the rest should be filled in. An illustration may be helpful to see how the process works.

Incident 4: "That Is Not a Paper Cup"

Alice (age 4 years) is seated at a table. She has a glass full of water. Mrs. Swift (the teacher) approaches and addresses Alice.

1. MRS. SWIFT: That is not a paper cup.

The episode contains two further utterances, but for the moment consider only the initial one. It is noteworthy that while there is no formal, abstract, or logical feature of the utterance that marks it as an "accusation", the context, the discourse, and certain background knowledge make the teacher's utterance readily identifiable as such.

It is also noteworthy that at the time of recording the episode the observer (Much) had not yet learned of the classroom rule that children are supposed to use paper cups and not glasses (except at snack time with the teacher's supervision). However, upon hearing Mrs. Swift's utterance (1) the rule could be immediately inferred or constructed, at least as far as "children are supposed to use paper cups and not glasses." Indeed, it is only because of that rule that the utterance "That is not a paper cup" is the kind of speech act it is at all—an accusation.

In other words, the rule, a context-specific and unmentioned entity, is crucial for the very constitution of the speech act. Yet a listener who did not previously know about the existence of the rule not only is able to understand the speech act (as an accusation) but also is able to infer the rule and become informed of its existence from the very fact of its functional presupposition. A hermeneutic dialectic is at work and it operates rapidly, unconsciously, and effectively.

Here we have the principle that if we have enough pieces of the puzzle we can fill in the missing ones. In the episode we recognize expressions of belief and desire through voice and action cues in context, and those tell us how to interpret or go beyond the surface content of what was said. We are assisted by our general knowledge of cultural belief propositions concerning the relevant differences between glasses and paper cups (the former break and the latter do not) and the anticipated competences of children 3 to 5 years old (who, we believe, might knock things over and get hurt). Even though lacking a formal procedure or generalized coding instruction for identifying accusations as accusations, knowledgeable observers of the communicative array have little difficulty reliably classifying utterance 1 as an accusation. The utterance has a determinate meaning that can be objectively determined.

The episode continues:

2. ALICE: I want to put it down [broken, whimpering voice].
3. MRS. SWIFT (taking the glass away from Alice): No, that's just for snack time when the teacher is at the table.

It is ambiguous from utterance 2 whether Alice had prior knowledge of the rule that constitutes the accusation. The fact that Mrs. Swift initially engaged in an indirect indication of the rule (1) suggests that she thought it was something the child already knew; in other words, Mrs. Swift expected Alice to recognize the rule even though it was only implicit in what was said. Alice's utterance (2), however, is not a definitive confirmation of Mrs. Swift's expectation, as Alice seems to appeal to some intention that she believes mitigates the breach (if I put it down rather than hold it in my hand I won't be breaking any rule).

What is clear is that Alice recognizes Mrs. Swift's speech act and the intention behind it. Alice knows that she is being told that she is doing something wrong. This is confirmed by her plaintive tone and her effort to "repair" the situation. Mrs. Swift, in utterance 3, seems to express doubt that Alice has comprehended fully utterance 1 or that Alice has correctly inferred the rule implicit in that utterance. This can be inferred from the fact that Mrs. Swift responds to Alice by giving the rule further explicit formulation in utterance 3, telling Alice that the glass is just for snack time when the teacher is assisting.

We hope it is clear from this illustration that determining the meaning of a stretch of discourse (as either a participant or an observer) is no formal or mechanical matter, yet it is objectively constrained. It calls for a good deal of prior cultural knowledge, and it is through the process of determining the meaning of a symbolic form that more cultural knowledge is acquired by both the child and the outside observer. Of course in interpreting the meaning of discourse one is always trying to make sense of what was explicitly said, and that is a major constraint on attributions of meaning. But there are other kinds of constraints as well.

One constraint is the way language gets used indexically. Note how Mrs. Swift's utterances, though quite condensed, powerfully summarize the cognitive–normative core of the event and point the child in the direction of understanding it. Although abbreviated, the utterances crystallize and transmit the moral meaning of the event. The utterance "That is not a paper cup" is basically a category contrast, meaning "That is not a paper cup, it is a glass." It refers the meaning of the event to what is assumed to be known about the relevant differences between paper cups and glasses (a potential for harm through breakage), focusing the meaning of the event on the issue of potential harm.

Although the teacher's utterances never explicitly mention the issue of harm, the child seems to understand it, as she shows by her offer to "put it down" (so that she would be less likely to break it?).

The teacher's final utterance gives additional normative content to the event and corrects the child's partial misunderstanding. Glasses in the classroom are used only for snack time and only when a teacher is supervising. The teacher's utterances (1,3) leave a lot unsaid. No one has actually stated that paper cups are different from glasses because glasses break, and glasses are dangerous when broken, or that young children (you, Alice) are insufficiently competent or conscientious to be trusted with the unsupervised use of fragile and potentially harmful materials.

Nor has anyone mentioned the "obvious" moral proposition behind this: that teachers should take responsibility for protecting young children from classroom activities in which they are likely accidentally to injure themselves. All of that propositional content remains unspoken, and all of it is necessary for a true and objective understanding of the episode.

However, what is spoken points to or implicates that material so powerfully that anyone to whom those belief propositions are familiar will connect them with the event—the event will instantiate the beliefs. And if one happened to be an observer (like Much) or participant (like Alice) who did not have prior knowledge of those propositions, he or she would, at the very least, be alerted to search or query for them; in trying to comprehend what was going on it would be obvious that something of importance was missing—that is, one would wonder *why* the teacher wanted Alice to use a paper cup instead of a glass except at snack time.

A second constraint on the interpretation of the meanings implicit in a communicative array has to do with the monitoring of the participants' expressed state of mind. Expressed intentions are important as evidence of the uptake of an utterance. In incident 4, Alice's rather plaintive reply (2) and her offer to put the glass down instead of giving it up suggest a rather partial recognition of the teacher's meaning. Senders of messages about cultural propositions, like Mrs. Swift, tend to be alert to indications of the uptake of their messages, and any expression by the child of only partial recognition generates even more explicit message content.

In other words, guardians of the moral order often respond to what they themselves consider to be evidence that an inference or construction of meaning has not taken place. The child's responses, verbal and nonverbal, to attempted regulation often function as queries or probes for further explication of content. What is not understood gets clarified with supplements to the prior knowledge base, thus revealing indexical meanings and moving the conversation in the direction of an intersubjective equilibrium point where what is said is understood because there is sufficient prior knowledge. Whether one is concerned with the acquisition of moral beliefs by children or the interpretation of moral beliefs by an outside observer, several sources of evidence converge to constrain the extraction of indexical meaning from a communicative array.

UNPACKING THE BABAJI INTERVIEW: HEINZ IN ORISSA

In this section of the chapter our method for expanding implicit meanings is applied to one stretch of questions and answers from a moral development interview (Kohlberg's well-known Heinz dilemma) conducted with an orthodox Hindu in India.

The discourse in moral development interviews is often processed and coded as though what was explicitly said is a complete representation of what was meant or being argued. By expanding or unpacking one part of the text from a single interview, and by identifying its implicit argument structure, we raise some doubts about the ability of current coding and classification procedures accurately to represent the moral reasoning of an interviewee. If discourse is to be the measure of moral understanding and reasoning, then we must be concerned not only with what was said, but also with what was presupposed, implied, suggested, or conveyed by what was said; and we need a theory of how meaning is constructed in discourse to help us go from what was said to what was meant.

The interview, conducted by Shweder in Orissa, India, will be referred to as the Babaji interview. One reason for focusing on this particular interview is that the Babaji, a male adult in his thirties, gives expression to a central concept in the Hindu worldview, the concept of dharma. If we are to understand the Hindu moral order, either in its own terms or in relationship to Kohlberg's stage scheme for moral reasoning, this interview is a good place to start.

The Babaji, as a young child, was betrothed to a goddess to protect him from various misfortunes predicted by an astrologer, and he was raised in a village monastery. After being placed under the protection of the goddess, he did in fact survive childhood, and as a young adult he was returned to the everyday world, where he got married and fathered children. He is not a Brahman, although he is a member of a high-status "clean" caste. His formal education is limited to approximately 5 years of primary school education. He is literate. He understands automobiles, how to drive them, and how to fix them, which helps him earn a living. Shweder, who has known the Babaji for many years, views him as an articulate and highly intelligent participant in the devotional, meditative, and mystical aspects of Hinduism as they apply to the management of one's personal life.

A second reason for focusing on the interview is that our analysis of the expanded text raises several issues, in need of further discussion among moral development researchers, concerning: (1) the proper meaning of postconventional moral reasoning; (2) the comprehensiveness of Kohlberg's stage scheme; and (3) the hazards of interview scoring procedures that operate exclusively on unexpanded texts and code only those explicit utterances that come in propositional form.

Before we present an expansion and analysis of the Babaji interview, a few points should be made explicit about the goals and methods of our text expansion. We proceed on the assumption that the interview text per se (the totality of recorded and transcribed utterances) is only a partial, even fragmentary, representation of its own meaning. In other words, we assume that the interview text points beyond itself to a network of ideas about social and cognitive events, which co-constitute what the interviewee is trying to get across through the utterances inscribed in the interview text.

That assumption was exemplified in incident 4; the meaning of the utterance "That is not a paper cup" could be determined only with reference to its context, plus certain background knowledge instantiated in that scene. The context included, among other things, a teacher approaching a child holding a glass of water and a classroom rule. The background knowledge included, among other things, beliefs about the relevant properties of glass objects, the competencies of young children, the probabilities of harmful consequences, and the responsibilities of teachers. It was not the surface text alone, but all of those things, and more, that constituted the meanings that were gotten across by what was explicitly said ("That is not a paper cup").

If we are to use ordinary language to investigate moral reasoning or moral understanding, it would seem to follow that we must have some way of taking account of the implicit meanings of utterances. One way of doing that involves giving explicit propositional form to the implicit material that co-constitutes the meaning of an utterance. The procedure is illustrated by Labov and Fanschel (1977), who give it the name *expansion*.

The relevant implicit meanings, to be drawn out and stated in propositional form, might have various kinds of referents. Propositions might refer to observations (it is raining), rules (thou shalt not steal), beliefs or assumptions (if a man sins, he will suffer), roles, statuses, or other social identities (wife, holy man, untouchable), and so on. Some propositions might be quite specific to the situational context (a child is holding a glass in a nursery school classroom). Other propositions might have a content of a more general nature that happens to be instantiated by this or that event (young children are apt to have accidents with breakable glass objects). To expand an utterance or stretch of text is to unfold its meaning by bringing its implicit meanings forward in explicit propositional form, as if they had occurred on the same plane as the text itself.

We limit ourselves to two orders of expansion in our analysis of the Babaji interview. In the first-order expansion of the text we expand upon what was stated in the interview by making explicit various assumptions, rules, and beliefs of the interviewee, which lend meaning to what was stated but were presupposed, taken for granted, or otherwise left unstated during the interview.

Then, in the second-order expansion of the text, we try to highlight the "logical" or "rational" organization of the first-order expansion, so that its coherence as a form of reasoning can be seen. As it turns out we have not been able to maintain a neat division between the first-order expansion and the second-order expansion of the text, although we believe the distinction is helpful even if not neat.

What we refer to as the second-order expansion of the text involves drawing out the logical, rational, or inferential relations (*since, therefore, insofar as, although, because, if . . . then*, etc.) that organize into a reasoned argument in support of a particular conclusion the propositional content of the first-order expansion of the interview text. In drawing out some of the inferential relations implicit in the interview text we have been greatly assisted by Longacre's (1983) classification of basic logical relations expressed in natural language discourse.

It will not be possible, in this essay, to give either a complete analysis of any part of the Babaji interview or a partial analysis of the entire interview, nor will it be possible to present our systematic coding of the expanded text using Longacre's (1983) categories. That would require a monograph. What we shall do is carry out a partial and informal expansion of approximately 30 percent of the interview. Then we shall draw some implications of the analysis for Kohlberg's stage scheme and the theory of language presupposed by Kohlberg's *Standard Issue Scoring Manual* (Colby et al., in press). The complete unexpanded interview appears in the appendix to this chapter. The original interview was conducted in Oriya at Shweder's residence in Orissa, India. The Heinz dilemma (Kohlberg's Form A) was modified in trivial ways to eliminate obvious culture-specific or ethnocentric features of the original dilemma (see appendix). In the Oriya version the protagonist is not Heinz, but rather Ashok.

INTERVIEWER: Should Ashok steal the drug?
BABAJI: No. He is feeling desperate because his wife is going to die and that's why he is stealing the drug. But people don't live forever and providing her the drug does not necessarily mean she will live long. How long you live is not in our hands but in God's hands. And there are other ways to get money like selling his landed property or even he can sell himself to someone and can save his wife's life.

First-Order Expansion: Ashok is feeling desperate because his wife is going to die. It is his desperation that impels him to steal the drug. Because he is desperate he overlooks the fact that stealing is wrong, insufficient, and unnecessary. If he were not desperate he would recognize that there is a natural limit to (a given) human life; that providing the wife with the drug will not necessarily prolong her life; that it may be this woman's destiny to die at this time; and that if that is the case the drug will not prolong her life. It is God's intention and not human intervention that ultimately determines matters of human life and death. It follows that providing the drug is neither a sufficient nor a necessary condition for saving the woman's life. From the human point of view the result of providing the drug is unpredictable.

Moreover, other means are available to raise needed money. Ashok could sell his property or, if need be, sell himself into indentured servitude in order to raise the money. Since those alternative means exist and have not been exhausted, stealing is not a necessary condition for obtaining the drug.

Since the drug itself cannot be assumed to be effective in determining the course of events, and since one can assume the existence of alternative means to obtain the drug, there is no justification for stealing the drug.

Second-Order Expansion: The argument attributes the intention to steal to confusion deriving from desperation, in contrast to a well-considered and informed motive. The argument locates the ultimate efficient cause (including necessary and sufficient conditions) for human life and death with divine agency rather than human intervention into events. The understanding is that human destiny is an expression of divine intention, and that human destiny is an actual plan given to an individual by God. The implication that follows from that proposition is that any specific human intervention is neither a necessary nor a sufficient condition in the determination of life and death.

Having set forth that implication in the first part of this piece of reasoning, the Babaji then changes the focus of logical evaluation to a different locus in the causal structure for events. Having first dealt with the question of necessary and sufficient conditions and the ultimate causal course determining matters of life and death, in the latter part of his response he considers causality from the viewpoint of possible human interventions.

The argument takes administering the drug as the proposed intervention, which presupposes, of course, that the drug must be obtained. That goal then becomes the focus of evaluative reasoning in the argument. The argument asserts, in essence, that, even if one were to assume that administering the drug is the best intervention, stealing the drug is not a justifiable means for obtaining it. Rather than stealing the drug, it is argued that there are other ways to raise the money to buy it at the asked price. Assuming, for the sake of argument, that the goal is to obtain the drug, the argument contrasts stealing to obtain the drug with an alternative causal or instrumental sequence (sell one's property or sell oneself), with the additional meaning that the alternatives are to be preferred.

In essence the Babaji's response states that if Ashok steals it is because he has become confused in his desperation and lost sight of reality, and not because stealing the drug is a defensible solution. There are no informed grounds for concluding that one ought to steal the drug, and this is why:

INTERVIEWER: He has no other way out. He has neither money nor anything.

BABAJI: Stealing is bad. He has made a mistake.

INTERVIEWER: But his wife is going to die!

BABAJI: There is no way within Hindu dharma to steal even if a man is going to die.

INTERVIEWER: But doesn't Hindu dharma prescribe that you try to save a person's life?

BABAJI: Yes. And for that you can sacrifice your blood or sell yourself, but you cannot steal.

INTERVIEWER: Why doesn't Hindu dharma permit stealing?

BABAJI: If he steals it is a sin, so what virtue is there in saving a life? Hindu dharma keeps man from sinning.

INTERVIEWER: Why would it be a sin? Isn't there a saying "one must jump into fire for others"?

BABAJI: That is there in our dharma—sacrifice, but not stealing.

First-Order Expansion: The act of stealing is wrongful and not virtuous. It is prohibited by Hindu dharma (religion–duty–obligation–natural law–truth). If a man commits such an act he makes a serious moral and spiritual error, which, because of the nature of cause and effect, will head him further away from virtue and wisdom and in the direction of ignorance and suffering.

The dharma prohibits such acts even at the cost of human life. The purpose of dharma is to instruct man in how to live a virtuous life that will spiritually benefit himself and others; its purpose is to keep individuals from committing grave errors that will lead to spiritual degradation and suffering. If a man steals he commits a grave sin, so that even if he saves a life in doing so the outcome is not virtuous. According to Hindu dharma, it is virtuous to save a person's life. The dharma instructs that one may endure extreme hardship or even sacrifice oneself in order to help others. But even though the dharma condones extremes of personal self-sacrifice in order to help others, it does not condone actions like stealing. As a means to help others stealing is an unvirtuous action that goes contrary to the natural order.

Second-Order Expansion: The Babaji classifies stealing as a sinful and unvirtuous action and asserts that such actions are always wrong. He does not tell us, at this point, why it is always wrong to commit a sin, yet two points seem to be involved. First, the Babaji would seem to hold that those actions classified as sins by dharmic law are wrong independent of circumstance, good intention, or apparent outcome; sins are by nature wrongful actions.

Second, a further expansion of the concept of sin could be proposed, based on general Hindu belief as it is explicitly expressed by the Babaji further on in the interview: Actions classified as sins by dharmic law have certain natural consequences as part of their inherent causality. The Hindu concept of sin, in fact, entails causal implications. In general, actions that are sinful tend to lead persons to situations or conditions that are still more desperate than the one they were trying to get free of in the first place. In those desperate situations a person is likely to become confused and commit even further errors. Sinful actions lead an individual away from virtue and wisdom and into ignorance and suffering.

In essence the Babaji argues that the purpose or end of instruction in dharma is to enable human beings to distinguish virtuous actions from sinful ones, so that they will be able to avoid committing sinful actions. The reason for avoiding sinful actions is that they have destructive consequences, for they lead people into degraded forms of existence where both their suffering and their ignorance are greater and where it becomes still more difficult to distinguish truth from falsity and illusion. In addition, specific instruction with regard to the act of stealing is attributed to the dharma. From that the Babaji derives an obligation: a man should not steal, for if a man steals he commits a great sin.

But there is more to it than that, for the nature of sin entails something further. What is apparently the ultimate conclusion of the argument is expressed in the Babaji's interpretation of dharma concerning the relationship of moral polarities at the means–ends loci of a causal structure. That is, if a sin is committed (e.g., stealing) the action is considered sinful and not virtuous even though it may be for a virtuous purpose (e.g., to save a life).

The argument implies that the moral value of the ends locus does not exert important, or at least decisive, influence on the evaluation of the means locus. Rather, the important moral influence operates in the reverse direction. To save a life is virtuous if and only if it is accomplished by virtuous means. If it is accomplished by sinful means, it becomes a sinful act; seemingly, it becomes a different act altogether.

It seems possible, given what we know about the Hindu worldview as expressed by the Babaji in this and numerous other interviews, that the Babaji's reasoning is based on distinctions concerning God-given constraints on human action that have the force of natural law. As long as a man exerts his efforts in accordance with dharmic law, he can feel that he serves God and dignifies human existence. However, if he commits sinful actions such as stealing, even in the interest of a virtuous purpose, he has overstepped the constraints on human action according to natural law and God's design. His action, therefore, offends God and nature and risks obstructing divine intention or divine order. Nothing truly good can result from such an act because: (1) acts congruent with the will of God (helping others) cannot be achieved with acts that are forbidden by Him (stealing); and (2) sinful actions always have evil as their consequence, if not immediately then in the long run. No lasting good can be achieved through sinful actions. A maxim would seem to follow: Do one's dharma; that above all else!

In the final part of his reply the Babaji comments on the moral implications of the means adopted for attaining an apparently virtuous end. Again the moral values are attributed directly to the laws and teachings of dharma. As he has argued previously, to commit sinful actions in the service of a virtuous purpose is to act in a way that is sinful and not virtuous. The true moral course of action in any situation is quite otherwise. It is to exert maximal and even heroic effort toward virtuous ends, but only through such courses of action as are defined as virtuous, or at least permissible, by divine law. The moral course of action is to be followed regardless of how any fallible individual (mis-) perceives the apparent contingencies or projected outcomes of sinful versus virtuous action.

In understanding the Babaji's reasoning it is important to recognize that he is arguing that a virtuous means of conduct is the *only* conceivable efficacious route to an end. One cannot cheat divine or natural law, for it simply will not work. The functioning of natural moral law is not dependent on one's good will, intentions, or knowledge. If one jumps off a roof one is going to fall to the ground. If one seeks to attain an end by means of unvirtuous actions, the result, in the long run if not in the short run, will simply not be satisfactory. The Babaji ends with a contrast between the virtuous means given by dharma through which one may aid others, and sinful acts such as stealing that are forbidden even though done in the service of a virtuous purpose. The purpose under consideration (saving a life) is assumed to be virtuous as long as it is achieved within the rightful limits of human action.

INTERVIEWER: But if he doesn't provide the medicine for her she will die. Wouldn't it be a sin to let her die?

BABAJI: That's why, according to the capabilities and powers which God has given him, he should try to give her shamanistic instructions and advice. Then she can be cured.

INTERVIEWER: But that particular medicine is the only way out.

BABAJI: There's no reason to necessarily think that that particular drug will save her life.

First-Order Expansion: Yes, it would be wrong for a man not to do what he could to save the life of his wife. But he must act in recognition of the limitations of man's rightful place in the natural order, and he must act within the constraints on virtuous conduct set forth in the dharma. For example, according to the capabilities and powers God has given him, he should try to give his wife shamanistic instructions and advice. It is conceivable that she could be cured that way. But it is our moral duty to pursue right ends by right means, as set by dharma, and it is not human action that truly decides the fate of other persons or the outcome of events. The actual outcome does not rest solely in our hands. Nor can such things be attributed to any one particular material causal factor; there is no reason to think that the drug in question would be necessary or sufficient to save the woman's life. Consequently there is no reason to neglect other courses of action and press only that one.

Second-Order Expansion: Here the Babaji separates two aspects of the causal structure of the original dilemma, two aspects that Kohlberg presupposed to be fused in the context of the dilemma as presented. According to the Babaji, given his understanding of the causal structure of nature, saving the woman's life is not to be equated with providing her with the drug. Providing the drug is neither a necessary nor a sufficient course of action for saving the woman's life, even if it should turn out that in this case human intervention can influence the outcome. By separating aspects of the causal structure that we might fuse, the Babaji creates an additional issue around which a proposed solution is argued.

Indeed for the first time in the interview it becomes clear that the Babaji believes that there is a moral obligation to make an attempt to save the woman's life. Even though it is a person's God-given or natural destiny that is decisive in matters of human life and death, that does not relieve an individual from personal responsibility to act on behalf of another. It would be a sin to simply let her die if there is anything one *can* do to save her life. The Babaji's arguments, in fact, suggest that somewhat heroic measures might be expected. What the Babaji says one can do, however, is in some ways expanded and in other ways restricted relative to the predominant Western worldview. On the one hand, the range of efficacious actions (including ritual and prayer) through which the woman might be cured is greater than what is allowed for in the original dilemma. On the other hand, the domain of possibility is held to be constrained by the limits of the opportunities and capabilities that exist for action in accordance with the laws of dharma. Action that is sinful should be regarded as simply "impossible."

A notable feature of this reasoning is that the Babaji here and elsewhere perceives no conflict between what is effective and what is moral; indeed, the efficacy of action is viewed as proportionate to its moral value, and thus what Kohlberg views as a moral dilemma (preserving life vs. upholding the law) is not a dilemma, given the Babaji's view of the world. Within that view of the world it is as if the contingencies of action were functions of interrelationships in a consistent system of natural order in which physical and social contingencies are but one further manifestation of moral law.

INTERVIEWER: Let's suppose she can only be saved by that drug, or else she will die. Won't he face lots of difficulties if his wife dies?

BABAJI: No.

INTERVIEWER: But his family will break up.

BABAJI: He can marry other women.

INTERVIEWER: But he has no money. How can he remarry?

BABAJI: Do you think he should steal? If he steals he will be sent to jail. Then what's the use of saving her life to keep the family together?

First-Order Expansion: It is false to believe that his family will suffer great hardships if his wife dies, for he can marry another woman to take her place in the family. Even if he were unable to remarry, it would be foolish to steal in order to preserve his family, because if he steals he will end up in jail, which would be as disruptive to his family as the death of his wife. In that case the good of his family would not have been served by saving her life.

Second-Order Expansion: In this argument the Babaji once again demonstrates the uselessness of an act such as stealing. Here the interviewer introduces the question of the possible social and domestic consequences that Ashok and his family would suffer if Ashok's wife were to die.

In reply the Babaji offers a causal argument concerning the uselessness of stealing as a means to avoid such consequences. If Ashok steals his family will suffer hardship on account of that, and no one will be any better off. It would be better simply to remarry or suffer the loss of the spouse. Contingencies are indicated describing what the results would be should Ashok steal. The argument becomes a warning against stealing, in the form of a comparison of the uselessness of stealing with the more preferable implications of other possible courses of conduct, including simply bearing the loss of his wife.

To this point in the interview the overall sense of the argument is that unvirtuous courses of action do not bring about satisfactory results. There is nothing to recommend unvirtuous action, even from a mundane instrumental point of view. Because of the evil consequences it bears at every level, unvirtuous conduct defeats even its own purposes.

Viewed in the broader context of other arguments in the interview this last stretch of discourse is a restatement, this time at the level of immediate social causality, of the belief that from an objective point of view "sin does not pay." At every imaginable level, actions that are sinful fail to bring about the desired result. If there is any way at all to achieve something (and there may not be), sin is never the only way. Intelligent action and virtuous action are the same. No genuine benefit can come to anyone through unvirtuous action; and things will appear to be otherwise only to those ignorant of the true laws of cause and effect.

BABAJI: She has enjoyed the days destined to her. But stealing is bad.

First-Order Expansion: A person comes into the world with a certain destiny, which can be attributed to God's plan or purpose for that person in that particular life. It may be that this woman has enjoyed the days destined for her and it is time for her to go to her next life. If that is the case it is useless to interfere. Her death at this time is the fulfillment of divine intention or natural law. Her death is right and good. But to steal is bad and goes against God's law and natural order. If that is her destiny it is better to let her die than to commit sinful acts in a desperate attempt to save her.

Second-Order Expansion: Here the Babaji is making an argument about the end that is presupposed in the original dilemma. He implies that the rightness of the proposed goal (that the wife's life should be saved) is questionable, at least as an absolute value. In his view it is possible that it may be right or even best that the woman should die because it may be time for her to end this particular life and go on with her journey of the spirit through its various rebirths. In his view allowing her to die may be the action most consistent with a concern for her well-being.

Note, again, that the Babaji does not take this conclusion lightly. He does not assume that, because such things are destined, an individual has no responsibility to intervene in another's illness or imminent death. Quite the contrary, even to the point of great personal sacrifice, one must do all one can to help another. It is rather that the Babaji's view allows for the possibility that the woman is meant to die at this time. That possibility enters as a consideration that has a bearing on reasoned action. But it is not something that can be known directly or assumed to be the case. Therefore, the mere possibility that it is the case does not relieve one of the responsibility to act.

Indeed, it would seem that the way to discern such issues of destiny is to act in whatever way one can within the constraints of dharmic law, and then observe the outcome; the fact that a given end could not be accomplished in that way is evidence that the outcome was destined to be what is was. If one tries aggressively to intervene in events by means of actions that violate dharmic law, then one is trying to force the outcome to one's own will, and one is not respecting the destiny of others nor honoring the intentions of God.

On the other hand, if one neglects the actions that one could take in accordance with dharma, then one is neglecting to take one's rightful or intended place in the outcome of events, for it might also be the case that one had a destined or intended role to play in the event. That view would seem to rest on a notion of coincidence just the opposite of our view of chance or accident. It is assumed that the way that things come together in any particular situation is meaningful and morally instructive, an expression of natural moral law or divine intelligence. Accordingly, what is moral coincides with what is efficacious and what is beneficial or advantageous.

According to that view, conflict between motivational domains (what's right and what's advantageous) is merely apparent, the result of our ignorance of the reality underlying events and the totality of circumstances involved. What is right or wrong in any situation is not a matter of subjective judgment but rather an objective process; but, since one's personal ability to discern what is right or good in a situation is limited, it is an objective process of which one typically has only a partial view. Through instruction in dharma one has been given certain guidelines for acting in situations without overstepping the boundaries of what is humanly knowable. Given the known limitations of mortal judgment there is good reason to respect those guidelines.

BABAJI: Our sacred scriptures tell that sometimes stealing is an act of dharma. If by stealing for you I can save your life, then it is an act of dharma. But one cannot steal for his wife or his offspring or for himself. If he does that it is simply stealing.

INTERVIEWER: If I steal for myself then it is a sin?

BABAJI: Yes.

INTERVIEWER: But in this case I am stealing for my wife, not for me.

BABAJI: But your wife is yours.

First-Order Expansion: Our sacred scriptures tell of cases where stealing is considered a virtuous act condoned by dharma. In order for that to be the case the act would have to be completely unselfish, involving absolutely no personal gain for the person committing the act. For example, if I were to steal to help a stranger who had no personal relationship to me, that might be an act of dharma. This would be particularly true if the act where committed in the service of a holy man or individual who could be regarded as particularly God-like, close to God, or in some significant way equivalent to God. In such cases it is as if one were acting directly in God's service.

But it is not an act of virtue if one steals for selfish motives. A person cannot rightfully steal for himself or his wife or his children. A man's wife and children belong to him. They are complementary to and interdependent with him. So he has a selfish interest in them. If a man steals for himself or those who belong to him it is not a virtuous act; it is ordinary selfish stealing. What distinguishes stealing as an act of dharma from ordinary stealing is the complete absence of any self-serving motive.

Second-Order Expansion: Here the Babaji proposes a certain variety of apparent exceptions to the generalizations he has already advanced about the inherent wrongfulness of stealing. Later in the interview the nature of such apparent exceptions is specified with further precision, particularly when it becomes the topic of the first of six dramatic narratives or stories used by the Babaji to clarify and defend his conception of natural moral law.

The apparent exceptions in question are attributed directly to the scriptural record of historical experience and are not presented as personal opinion or subjective interpretation. The narrative that comes later (the story of the father and son who steal ghee in order to have the right food to serve their sadhu guests) illustrates the customary nature of the type of apparent exception being drawn by the Babaji, and it suggests that it is not an exception at all but rather the kind of case that proves the rule of dharmic consequences for sin, including bad consequences for even selfless stealing.

Basically the Babaji argues that there is a point of view from which stealing could be seen as a virtuous act. This is true even given what has already been said about how such an act would be wrong for the sake of saving the life of one's wife. The Babaji's argument once again focuses on the ends presupposed by the causal structure of the original dilemma. Earlier the Babaji had considered the moral value of ends (stealing the drug in order to make it available to the woman) from the point of view of outcomes: the degree of likely benefit to the recipient of the action and the general harmony of action with the natural moral order. Here the Babaji considers the moral value of the end in relationship to the motives of the actor.

The Babaji proposes that it would be an act of virtue if one were to steal for the benefit of a stranger (or, as we shall soon see, a holy man). That is virtuous because such an act is devoid of mundane self-interest. But to steal for one's wife or one's child is just like stealing for oneself; it is ordinary selfish stealing. One's wife or one's children are part of one's household and their contribution to one's life and their proximity to one's identity are so great that their life and death could not possibly be considered independently of one's own mundane advantage or personal attachment. Because of the purity of its motive, an act done out of compassion with no relation to personal gain or even to personal duty or personal responsibility has an exceptional status (and that is so even if the act is intrinsically a sin and is not to be recommended). Further explication of that position follows in our expansion of the Babaji's first dramatic narrative. The interview continues:

INTERVIEWER: Doesn't Ashok have a duty or obligation to steal the drug?

BABAJI: He may not get the medicine by stealing. He may sell himself. He may sell himself to someone for say 500 rupees for 6 months or 1 year.

INTERVIEWER: Does it make a difference whether or not he loves his wife?

BABAJI: So what if he loves his wife? When a husband dies the wife does not die for him, or vice versa. We have come into this world alone and we will leave it alone. Nobody will accompany us when we leave this world. It may be a son or it may be a wife. No one will go with us.

INTERVIEWER: For whom do you feel one should steal? Let's say it is not his wife but a holy man or a stranger. Would it have been better if he had stolen for them?

Babaji: Stealing is bad. It is not right according to Hindu dharma, but if he stole for himself the degree of sin would be more.

INTERVIEWER: Is it important to do everything one can to save another's life?

BABAJI: Yes. But that does not mean stealing. You can borrow from someone. You can go without eating. You can give your food to others, or you can sell yourself.

INTERVIEWER: Suppose Ashok had come to you, told you his situation and sought your advice whether or not to steal. What would you have told him?

BABAJI: I would have asked him not to steal. We have a practice in the villages. Everyone would have decided to give him the required money from the village common fund, or they would have collected some donation. But he should be advised not to steal.

INTERVIEWER: But shouldn't people do everything they can to save a life?

BABAJI: One should try to save another's life. Because, after all, he is a human being. But you should not do it by virtue of stealing.

To save space we shall not expand this stretch of the interview text, or unpack its implicit argument structure. (It is to be hoped that our expansions of the earlier text have made it easier for the reader to perceive the underlying consistencies and reiterations in this last section of overexpanded text.) Instead we shall conclude this illustrative exercise by examining in some detail the very next moment in the interview where the Babaji adopts a traditional Oriya mode of moral argumentation, summarizing and justifying his conception of natural moral law with the first of six historical narratives.

INTERVIEWER: Is it against the law for Ashok to steal?

BABAJI: Yes. It's against the law.

INTERVIEWER: Are the laws always morally right? Do you feel all laws are right?

BABAJI: Let me tell you a story about stealing. Once some sadhus came to a poor man's house. . . . [Here the Babaji narrates the story about the father and son who stole the ghee pot. The reader should now reread that story.]

Second-Order Expansion: Let me tell you a story about an incident from which you can see for yourself the consequences of committing a sinful action such as stealing, even in one of those apparently exceptional cases involving selfless motives. A primary implication of the story is that although the man stole for righteous motives devoid of self-interest, the action nonetheless bore the dharmic consequences of sin, involving him in further sin and greater suffering.

The story focuses on the host–guest relationship between ordinary men and holy men. In the Hindu worldview the way one treats a guest is a test of one's relationship and attitude to dharmic truth (the divine), and when the guests turn out to be holy men that issue is especially salient.

The Babaji begins by pointing out that holy men, who are certainly more aware of dharmic truth than we are, never steal or ask for credit. They are able to meet all their needs by simply begging, and no one ever hesitates to give them what they need. The implication is that if Ashok had lived a more noble or holy life he would not find himself contemplating theft (this interpretation is borne out later in the interview); throughout his life Ashok must have been swimming against the dharmic current.

In any case the host, an ordinary man, stole only in order to honor the godliness represented in his guests. That is the purest of ends, yet his action resulted in disaster because he foolishly believed that the end could justify any means. His guests asked for ghee, a food suitable for holy men because it is a "cool" food and is one of the products of the holy cow (or holy mother). The man stole the ghee only after exhausting all other means available to him. He had already sacrificed his worldly possessions to provide the meal. He had begged the sadhu at the monastery to give him the ghee. Surely this is an exceptional case, far more compelling than the case of Ashok, who has not exhausted every possible dharmic means and only wants to save his own wife. If stealing is foolish and hence unjustified in this case certainly we must judge it to be foolish in the case of Ashok. Look at what happened to the man and his son and learn from it!

The man sets in motion a chain of cause and effect relations that escalates into disaster. Having determined to steal the ghee he causes his son to commit the act. Because the son was in the storeroom stealing he was apprehended. It did not matter that he passed by all the treasures of the monastery and was not stealing for himself. Things just kept getting worse, because father and son were desperate to deliver the ghee and escape the humiliation of capture, the son's life was sacrificed through decapitation, thus causing the father intense suffering.

The Babaji's point in retelling this incident is to show a chain of events in which purposes intertwine with arising circumstances in such a way that once one is headed in the direction of sin (the "downward path", as it were) circumstances conspire to embroil one in increasingly desperate situations.

The basic idea is that the moral and the physical order are not separate domains, and punishment and reward in this world are not dependent merely on the legal processes of society. Reward and punishment follow automatically, though not always immediately, from the nature of action. To commit sinful actions in order to free oneself from difficult circumstances is only to become further entangled in increasingly desperate circumstances. Not only does sin not pay, but what better way is there to determine which actions are sinful than to learn from the historical record of the suffering of others?

Even the holy men tell the ordinary man that what he has done is wrong; the tragic consequences were the result of his error. Yet his action, while foolish, is exceptional, because his sin had been committed for the sole purpose of serving the sadhus and without any trace of self-serving motive or personal gain on the part of the father or the son. Because of the purity of the motives of the father and the son, the sadhus are willing *through dharmic means* (prayer and ritual upon the severed head of the son) to reverse the natural consequences of the sin and instruct the father and son in the truths of dharma. Where theft had failed, dharmic means (prayer and ritual) worked, even to restore a dead person to life. The message is to avoid sin, even when, unlike Ashok, you have motives that are pure and meritorious.

We shall not in the context of this chapter undertake an expansion or unpacking of all the beliefs and arguments implicated by the interview text. The point of the exercise is to suggest that the analysis of interview materials must be informed by a theory of how meaning is constructed in discourse. If one attempts to understand the moral reasoning and beliefs of a "subject" by merely coding propositions explicitly mentioned in the surface structure of the interview text and matching them against a list of proposition types in a standard coding manual, one has committed oneself to a view of language in which what is said is a complete and isomorphic representation of what is meant. How defensible is that approach to language and the analysis of interview texts?

One practical way to answer that question is to ask: How shall we classify the Babaji's moral reasoning? How would it be stage-classified following Kohlberg's standardized coding procedure in which the surface structure of the interview text, consisting of explicit propositionalized judgments, is matched to criterion statements set out in a coding manual? How would it be classified if we analyze, as well, the expanded text and its implicit argument structure?

Kohlberg (1981) classifies moral reasoning into three developmental levels, each divided into two stages. In brief, in the lowest, "preconventional", level (stages 1 and 2) subjects define the meaning of rightness and wrongness in terms of the subjective feelings and interests of the self. If the self likes it, it is right; if the self does not like it, it is wrong. There are no higher obligations. Egoism and self-interest reign.

In the intermediate, "conventional", level (stages 3 and 4) a consciousness of the collective emerges, and, although subjects continue to define the meaning of rightness and wrongness by reference to subjective feelings, now the collective feelings of others are what matter. The idea of obligation is equated with the authority of the group (the commands of parents, interpersonal expectations concerning proper role behavior, the laws of legislatures). If one's reference group likes it, it is right; if one's reference group does not like it, it is wrong. Conformity and consensus reign.

In the highest, "postconventional", level (stages 5 and 6 in Kohlberg's earlier formulations, stage 5 in more recent formulations; Kohlberg, Levine, & Hewer, 1983) rightness and wrongness are defined by reference to objective universalizable principles that stand above the subjective feelings of either the self or the group. Those principles are justice, natural rights, and a humanistic respect for all persons, and they can be appealed to by a postconventional reasoner to criticize social institutions and personal preferences.

The Babaji interview was analyzed and stage-classified by two expert coders (Lawrence Kohlberg & Ann Higgins) following the procedures detailed in the *Standard Issue Scoring Manual* (Colby et al., in press), whereby one restricts the coding to what is explicitly stated in propositional form in the interview text. Kohlberg (personal communication) made several observations about the interview and the coding process. He noted that "much of the material [in the interview] was unscorable." One reason some of the material was unscorable was that it involved "spontaneous elaborations by the informant in the form of stories or allegories and references to Hindu mythology." Fortunately, however, according to the coders, "there was enough scorable material to match to manual points even though many interesting points could not be fit to the manual."

Not surprisingly, Kohlberg comes up with several perceptive informal observations on the interview. He notes that for orthodox Hindus society seems "to be defined by a mixture of custom and tradition and religious dharma as distinct from legal and political rules and systems." He notes that orthodox Hindus seem "less oriented to individual rights and to interpersonal balancing of feelings through role-taking and more oriented to custom." He notes that the interview material

> fit our manual much less easily than the Turkish and Israeli data on which I have personally worked. When the Turks invoked religious references it was either to straightforward divine command and punishment or to following the norms of being a good Muslim as a defined religious group.

Kohlberg wonders whether the distinction between convention and morality would hold up for orthodox Hindu adults (it does not; see Shweder et al., 1985) and notes that while orthodox Hindus seem to "make much of the distinction between the legal and the religious. . . . the religious encompasses the conventional and the moral for them." Kohlberg classifies the Babaji's orientation to religious dharma as "essentially stage 4 though somewhat unlike American law oriented or American religious-law oriented stage 4. American stage 4's seem to use a more clear social systems perspective when explaining or using their religious codes." Kohlberg and Higgins give the Babaji interview a global stage score of 3/4. Kohlberg remarks that "scoring by the manual fit our clinical intuitions as to stage though our ignorance of the Hindu culture made us somewhat uncertain about our own clinical intuitions." Having found the interview "very interesting" he notes that he is somewhat surprised that it ends up with the score of an "average American adult"— stage 3/4.

Kohlberg and Higgins classify the moral reasoning of the Babaji adhering to the strictures of the *Standard Issue Scoring Manual*; they code only propositions explicitly mentioned in the surface structure of the interview text. As a consequence they ignore the entire narrative content of the interview and are unable to take account of the implicit argument structure in the text. From our point of view they were methodologically doomed to end up with a stage classification that deforms the moral reasoning of the informant, assimilating it to the requirements of an a prior interpretive scheme while leaving us with very little insight into the Babaji's view of the moral order.

Was the Babaji really trying to tell us that obedience to social consensus is a goal in its own right (a stage 3/4 doctrine)? Did he really deny the stage 1/2 doctrine that what is right is closely related to obtaining desired practical consequences for oneself? Did he not give strong expression to the stage 5/6 doctrine that there are nonrelative objective values, including respect for the dignity of human beings, that must be upheld in any society and regardless of majority opinion?

Kohlberg is quite right when he notes that the interview does not easily fit the manual. But perhaps, instead of trying to assimilate the interview to the requirement of the stage scheme and the coding manual, we should try to accommodate the coding procedures and our classification of forms of moral reasoning to the requirements of the interview. It might turn out to be instructive to interpret not only what the Babaji explicitly said in propositional form, but also what was implicit in what he said, regardless of how he said it (dramatic narratives). What does the expanded text and its implicit argument structure tell us about the Babaji's form of moral reasoning?

In the Babaji's version of the orthodox Hindu view of the moral order, moral laws are no less objective than the laws of physics. Moral cause and effect is as real and concrete as material cause and effect, while having at the same time the subtlety of social and psychological cause and effect. The laws of morality are completely independent of personal or group opinion.

There are, however, according to the Babaji's view, certain persons who have greater knowledge about the truths of moral law; and one of the best guides to natural moral law is the historical experiences recorded in the Hindu scriptures. A thoughtful person will also take into account the authority of certain customary practices, many of which, it may be assumed, are relatively good adaptations to the requirement of objective moral law.

In the orthodox Hindu view moral decisions have their own natural causality, and there is a direct interplay between moral causality, material causality, and social causality. Thus the consequence of a sin may be disease or a bad marriage.

Considerations of space lead us to focus, in summary fashion, on only a few salient features of the Babaji's view of the moral order. In Western academic circles we sometimes perceive a conflict between what is the morally right thing to do and what is the expedient or personally beneficial thing to do; and for us moral acts are not thought to be directly linked to material and social consequences. In the Babaji's orthodox Hindu view, with what is moral coincides with what is expeditious for personal well-being. The conflict is only apparent; the perception of conflict results either from ignorance of the laws of moral cause and effect or from limited human understanding of complex circumstances. The Babaji believes it is arrogant to presume that we know which outcome is truly in the best interests of any or all persons involved, for those individual interests extend far beyond this life and are not usually knowable to us as ordinary mortals.

The Babaji believes that certain kinds of actions (e.g., stealing, killing) are inherently sinful and other kinds of actions (e.g., giving alms, sacrificing) inherently virtuous. Those qualities of sin and virtue belong to the actions themselves; intentionality and circumstances are not constitutive or eliminating of sin. The act is sinful even if it is done unknowingly. In that view circumstances "out of one's control" are regarded as one's own fault; they are the manifestations of prior sinful actions.

In that view wrongful action is not a breach against society or other people; it is sin against dharma, an attack on God and the natural order of things. And it is destructive not of society or other people, but to the person's own eternal spirit, the essence of the person that is most Godlike. To sin brings degradation to your truest self; and because it is this self that is connected to all living beings, it is a sin against the whole of existence. The implication of that view of sin is that man should strive to be perfectly Godlike, strive to be so enlightened or omniscient that no act is unintentional, strive to have no motive corrupting of dharmic choices for action, and strive to have no circumstance out of control.

In his arguments the Babaji understands Ashok's point of view, but he is more concerned with Ashok's spiritual well-being than with his worldly or social well-being or even with the prolongation of this particular incarnation of Ashok's wife. The Babaji applies the same rigorous rules to Ashok that he would apply to himself. He achieves a moral and objective point of view by being impartial in exactly that way.

The Babaji also takes the perspective of Ashok's wife, but again this is done from the point of view of her spiritual well-being rather than the point of view of one particular worldly life. His assertion on behalf of Ashok's wife is that she has her own spiritual journey, which has been arranged for her by God, seemingly in a very personal and individual manner. Since a person's spiritual path quite reasonably entails matters concerning when one life situation is to be ended and another begun, the time of one's death can be regarded as part of a beneficent plan. If Ashok clings desperately to the life of his wife it is selfish, not empathic or compassionate; it may even obstruct rather than benefit her spiritual development—like keeping a child from entering school because one would rather have him or her at home.

The Babaji has a clear hierarchy of spiritual and material goals, and he argues that there is a relationship between spiritual and material well-being. He does not at all deny the value of human life; quite the contrary, it is the supreme value of the material world. But it derives its value and sacredness from its relationship to the spirit or soul, of which material life is a manifestation. For that reason material well-being is not privileged over spiritual well-being. Spiritual well-being is fundamental because it is the condition and degree of purity of one's soul that has a decisive influence on the particular state of one's body (male or female; healthy or sickly, etc.) in successive rebirths.

For the Babaji human beings are responsible agents in the extreme for events within the domain of their authority to act, yet that domain has certain limits. He recognizes that his own human position is neither omniscient nor omnipotent within the scheme of moral–physical causality and he does not consider his own intelligence to be the highest or most perfect intelligence acting upon human events. It is for the Babaji a matter of objective fact to acknowledge the limits of his own understanding and efficacy. In the West there is a large residual of causal determinacy that is written off to "chance." In India the universe is thought to be fully determinate, and given that there are serious spiritual consequences associated with any course of action, the boundaries for legitimate action are greatly respected.

That does not mean that human beings are impotent, or even that the limits on human action and accomplishment are narrow by Western standards. The Babaji does not view the human being as powerless or constrained to enact a limited set of obligatory roles or routines. Extraordinary and heroic effort is possible and may accomplish extraordinary ends. Restricting oneself to the accounts and narratives in the interview, one finds possibilities for altruism that achieves its end through almost unthinkable sacrifice, knowledge that can cure the sick and bring the dead back to life through prayer and ritual and other dharmic techniques, repentance by a world conqueror moved by a moment of imparted insight into the divinity of life, and disciplines that lead to prescience into the course of the divine plan. Indeed, the range of possible solutions to human problems is greatly extended compared to what we are accustomed to think of in our own pragmatic terms. While there is a respect for the limits of human knowledge, heroic efforts are possible, and, if those efforts run with, instead of against, the current of dharmic law, extraordinary things may be accomplished. Such efforts make a human being more Godlike; one cannot defeat the mind of God but one can share in it.

One of the remarkable features of the interview is that the Babaji does not represent the dilemma in terms of rights or justice or life versus private property. He represents the dilemma in terms of the cause and effect relations associated with human action and he argues that it is irrational to commit a sin once the laws of cause and effect and the interdeterminacy of moral and material events are properly appreciated.

It seems impossible to deny the informant an interest in abstract universal principles. In fact, abstract universal considerations dominate the interview; for example, dharmic virtue over material life.

Perhaps most significantly the Babaji seems to view the "dilemma" in terms of a causal structure that is not at all coincidental with the causal structure that is presupposed, and thus unwittingly privileged, by those who composed it as a dilemma. The causal structure as understood by the Babaji is as follows:

1. *Agency.* One cannot assume human agency to be the only agency operating in the event. Considerations of divine intention place limits on human authority to act.
2. *Separation of Fused Causes.* It cannot be assumed that administering the medicine will save the woman's life; it will not save her if it is her destined time to die. It cannot be assumed that the medicine is the only way to intervene, or even a superior form of treatment. It cannot be decisively determined that to save her is the responsible and compassionate thing to do. Since such things are not fully open to our view they require sensitive testing by taking rightful action and observing the consequences. If we fail to save her life by taking every morally permissible action, that is evidence that her dying at this time is part of her destiny.
3. *Consequences of Action.* Sinful actions never fulfill their purposes, at least not in the long run. Sinful actions have such disastrous consequences that no thoughtful person would use unvirtuous action as a route out of trouble. Those consequences pertain least of all to legal or societal punishment or to matters of social consensus; rather they pertain to mental, physical and social well-being in this and future lives.

It is a sign of prior sin and negligence that Ashok finds himself in such a desperate situation. A householder who lives a life of dharma and attends to his responsibilities typically has a little money or property or credit or can raise money if he is in need. It is likely that Ashok is already blameworthy, and further acts of moral desperation (like stealing) will not help matters, but will only lead him further along the path of sin and spiritual degradation.

There is a common illusion that what is personally beneficial does not always coincide with what is virtuous. The wise understand that if a result cannot be accomplished by virtuous means then the result is not as beneficial as it may seem to be from the limited viewpoint of ordinary persons.

Presumably the Babaji interview was coded by Kohlberg and Higgins as stage 3/4 (conventional) because the informant does not weigh the value of life against property or speak about rights and justice, but rather refers repeatedly to a norm (dharma) construed *by the coders* as a social norm. There are several problems with classifying the interview as stage 3/4. Indeed Kohlberg's stage scheme seems unable within its own theoretical terms to represent accurately the orthodox Hindu view of the moral order. Here are some of the problems:

1. The Babaji views dharma not as a social norm, but rather as an independently existing and objective reality—somewhat like the laws of physics.
2. The Babaji argues that the moral–physical world is such that wrong actions lead to suffering and spiritual degradation, and thus if one understands the laws of cause and effect, committing a sin is irrational. Again, social consensus has little to do with it.
3. Although his concept of objective obligations has nothing to do with justice and rights, the Babaji adopts a hyperrational perspective on morality. There is no strain of subjectivism or egotism running through the interview, and moral obligation is understood to be entirely independent of individual or group preference or opinion.
4. There is no hedonistic orientation in the interview. There is no motive to avoid pain or maximize personal pleasure in this world. Indeed there is an expressed willingness to undergo painful sacrifice to help others. While there is a strong motive to avoid actions that bring degradation to the spirit or soul and cause suffering in future rebirths, to call that hedonism is to equate hedonism with the principle that spiritual cleansing is the highest possible value.

In expanding the Babaji interview text and identifying its implicit argument structure it seems apparent to us that the interview gives articulate expression to an alternative form of postconventional reasoning that has no place in Kohlberg's stage scheme. In a sense the stage scheme is exploded by its own inability to classify adequately the moral reasoning of the Babaji. One may also begin to wonder how many other moral development interviews coded as stage 3/4 would turn out to be alternative forms of postconventional reasoning, if only we permitted ourselves to move from what is said to what is unsaid, to expand the interview text and identify its implicit argument structure.

NEORATIONALISM AND DIVERGENT RATIONALITIES

In the first section of this chapter we drew attention to the power of everyday conversations to transmit moral beliefs to children. Ordinary conversations, we argued, not only carry in condensed form a vision of the moral order; but it is also through those ordinary conversations in which we describe and evaluate events that the moral order is reproduced. Why, then, we ask in this final section of the chapter has there been among moral development researchers such a studied avoidance of morality-relevant talk, conversation, and discourse?

One might naively have expected moral development researchers to take much theoretical interest in the moral worldview indexed in and through everyday talk. Verbal interview protocols are, after all, a primary source of evidence in moral development research. Yet, somewhat counterintuitively, every well-known school of thought dealing with moral development quickly moves us away from any sustained reflection about the nature of ordinary language use.

Thus psychoanalytic researchers, with an interest in the development of conscience, limit their attention to the child's intrapsychic conflict anxieties and to defensive processes leading to identification with powerful, envied, or feared others, while cognitive structuralists limit their attention to the child's purported efforts to construct for himself or herself the formal features of moral reasoning. Social learning theorists, it is true, do examine social communication, but they have bleached it of all implications or message content except reward and punishment, approval and disapproval; and they have kept narrow their field of vision, focusing on the process of modeling or mimicking significant others. No one has taken seriously the substance, content, or meaning of what children and adults say and do to each other. Few have taken to heart the idea that moral development is, in large measure, a problem in the acquisition of moral *knowledge* through the inferences embedded in social communications.

There has been a long and destructive debate in philosophy and in the social sciences over whether moral judgments (that's right or wrong; that's good or bad) are cognitive or noncognitive (emotive) judgments. In our view one of the main victims of that debate has been research on the moral arguments embedded in ordinary conversations in everyday life.

The moral noncognitivists or so-called emotivists (the designation includes, among others, the social learning theorists and the psychoanalysts) premise their research on the idea that rightness and goodness are not real or natural or objective qualities of things. Since, as the emotivists argue, rightness and goodness do not describe anything objective in the external world, moral judgments cannot appropriately be said to be either true or false, nor are moral judgments capable of justification through argumentation or other rational means.

And since from the point of view of the moral noncognitivists there is nothing really out there to be described with such terms as *right* or *good*, the only thing that is real in moral discussions is their pragmatic use in nondescriptive ways—to express opinions, to command or commend, to dominate and control, to preserve privilege, to resolve intrapsychic conflicts, and so on. Not surprisingly, the moral noncognitivists emphasize the pragmatic use of moral discourse and, for the most part, display little interest in either the semantic content of the moral universe suggested by a moral judgment or the reasons, grounds, warrants, or arguments in support of a moral judgment advanced implicitly or explicitly in moral discourse.

It seems to us that the moral noncognitivist or emotivist viewpoint has been driven by two very special and probably false assumptions about what it is to be a truly cognitive–scientific discipline. The first questionable assumption is the positivist's assumption that any term or concept that plays a part in the production of knowledge must be verifiable either by logical interdefinition or by empirical means. The relevant terms or concepts in the moral arena are terms like *right* or *good*. Since, as the moral noncognitivist's argument goes, moral concepts cannot be verified in that way, it follows that there cannot be genuine moral facts or objective moral knowledge.

The second questionable assumption made by the moral noncognitivist is that real objective knowledge implies convergence in beliefs, and that in any genuine cognitive–scientific discipline disputes go away over time. The moral noncognitivist's conclusion: Since disputes over what is right or wrong (abortion, capital punishment, polygamy, arranged marriage, adolescent circumcision) do not go away over time, moral judgments cannot be a form of objective knowledge.

Ironically the moral cognitivists (a designation that includes Kohlberg and other cognitive structuralists) share with the moral noncognitivists precisely those two assumptions about the nature of genuine objective knowledge. The moral cognitivists, however, actually think they can achieve that kind of objective knowledge in the moral domain. Given that goal it is understandable that the moral cognitivists are not interested in the pragmatic uses of moral discourse or in nonrational processes (imitation, modeling, identification, reward and punishment, indoctrination, genetic inheritance) for reproducing moral judgments in the next generation.

Instead, the moral cognitivists set themselves the task of defending the objectivity and rationality of moral judgments in terms of those very two assumptions about genuine objectivity and rationality mentioned earlier. Thus the moral cognitivists have launched themselves on various projects to establish that moral disputes (all moral disputes? some of them? at least one of them? the disputes we will *define* as moral?) could be resolved by the methods associated with (what they viewed as) genuine science, by inductive inference from indisputable facts or by deductive reasoning from undeniable premises.

The goal as conceived by the moral cognitivist is to build an abstract airtight moral system whose rational appeal will be universally obvious to any *competent thinker* (a slippery notion) whether a Hindu priest, a Chinese Mandarin, an African Bushman, or a Radcliffe undergraduate. In practice the competent thinkers usually turn out to come from a small pool of philosophers, mostly Western, and even they never seem to be able to agree on what is rationally appealing. It is small wonder that the moral cognitivists have taken so little interest in the parochial and context-bound moral discourses of everyday life, where premises are always deniable, terms are rarely explicitly defined, and a complete and consistent account of the entire moral order is never forthcoming.

A second reason for the lack of attention to everyday moral discourse in the child development field may have something to do with the history of high-status research in the psychological sciences. Laboratory experimental research programs on perception, memory, learning, and decision making (the traditional high-prestige topics) have made some progress by relying on a small set of research heuristics or rules of thumb. Heuristic 1: Be indifferent to content; process and structure are primary. Heuristic 2: Language is epiphenomenal; it can be ignored. Heuristic 3: What's really real is inside the skin; the individual is the only relevant locus of analysis. Heuristic 4: Search for universals and/or study automatic processes; if psychology is to be a genuine science it must uncover highly general laws. Heuristic 5: Don't think about anything that can't be measured.

Whatever the explanation for the survival power of those heuristics in the history of American psychology, they are widely diffused, institutionally entrenched, and deeply intuitive for many psychological researchers. Thus it is not surprising that there has been resistance to the study of the semantics of everyday moral discourse. To study meaning is to study content. To study discourse is to study language. To study language is to shift the locus of study beyond the individual to the communicative array, a collective product. It is to credit as much importance to what is local and special as to what is general and universal. And it is to recognize that objective knowledge is possible even in the absence of a formal, general, or standard measuring device.

Our own interest in the socialization of moral beliefs by means of inferences and "arguments" implicit in, and carried by, everyday discourse is not unrelated to our view that it is time to displace the tiresome terms of the traditional dispute between cognitivists and noncognitivists. We also believe it is time to replace some of our research heuristics, especially in the study of moral development.

That displacement is today conceivable thanks to several important insights from the philosophy of science. In effect what has happened is that we are in a position to "soften" (David Wong's apt expression) our view of the real hard-knowledge-producing disciplines. It turns out that convergence may not be not a defining feature of a genuine cognitive–scientific enterprise, and paradigm conflicts do not always go away, even in physics (Hesse, 1972; Pinch, 1977). It turns out that not all respectable concepts or terms can be verified by logic or direct observation; knowledge systems are presuppositional, analogical or metaphoric, and holistic. And theories cannot only not be proved (by now a commonplace piece of received wisdom), but it may turn out they cannot be disproved, either; measurement error and anomaly may not be distinguishable on any formal grounds.

In another context (Shweder, 1986) this neorationalist approach has been identified with the idea of "divergent rationalities" and with the attempt to broaden the notion of rationality to include not just inductive and deductive logic but several other cognitive elements as well: the presuppositions and premises from which a person reasons, the metaphors, analogies, and models used for generating explanations, the categories or classifications used for partitioning objects and events into kinds; and the types of evidence viewed as authoritative—intuition, introspection, external observation, meditation, scriptural evidence, evidence from seers, prophets or elders, and so on.

One effect of all this softening up of the hard sciences is that it is now possible to "harden" our view of the soft sciences and disciplines, and to define a more realistic rationalist agenda for studies of morality and moral development. For example, it is possible to argue that moral concepts and judgments refer to natural or objective entities in the world, as long as it is understood that the existence of moral facts and objective moral knowledge is not incompatible with the existence of irreconcilable moral disputes, and that there can be more than one valid moral universe, just as there can be more than one valid representation of the nature of light.

Earlier we argued that the Babaji presents us with an alternative version of an objective postconventional moral world. Given a neorationalist conception of objective knowledge, there is no longer any necessity to deny that it is rational, or postconventional. The objective moral world is many not one; or as Nelson Goodman (1984) has put it: "One might say that there is only one world but this holds for each of the many worlds"(p. 278).

REFERENCES

Colby, A., Kohlberg, L., Gibbs, J., Candee, D., Hewer, A., Power, C., & Speicher-Dubin, B. (in Press). *Measurement of moral judgment: Standard issue scoring manual.* New York: Cambridge University Press.
Ervin-Tripp, S. (1976). Speech acts and social learning. In K.H. Basso & H. Selby (Eds.), *Meaning in anthropology.* Albuquerque: University of New Mexico Press.
Geertz, C. (1973). *The interpretation of cultures.* New York: Basic.
Goodman, N.(1984). Notes on a well-made world. *Partisan Review, 51,* 276–288.
Hesse, M. (1972). In defense of objectivity. *Proceedings of the British Academy, 58,* 275–292.
Kohlberg, L. (1981). *The philosophy of moral development: Moral stages and the idea of justice* (Vol. 1). San Francisco: Harper & Row.
Kohlberg, L., Levine, C., & Hewer, A. (1983). Moral stages: A current formulation and a response to critics. In J.A. Meacham (Ed.), *Contributions to human development* (Vol. 10). New York: Karger.
Labov, W. & Fanschel, D. (1977). *Therapeutic discourse.* New York: Academic.

Longacre, R. (1983). *The grammar of discourse.* New York: Plenum.

Much, N.C. (1983). *The microanalysis of cognitive socialization.* Unpublished doctoral dissertation, Department of Behavioral Sciences, University of Chicago.

Much, N.C. & Shweder, R.A. (1978). Speaking of Rules. The analysis of culture in breach. In W. Damon (Ed.), *New directions in child development: Vol. 2. Moral development.* San Francisco: Jossey-Bass.

Pinch, T.J. (1977). What does a proof do if it does not prove? A study of the social conditions and metaphysical divisions leading to David Bohm and John von Neumann failing to communicate in quantum physics. In E. Mendelsohn, P. Weingart, & R. Whitley (Eds.), *The social production of scientific knowledge.* Boston: D. Reidel.

Shweder, R.A. (1985). Menstrual pollution, soul loss, and the comparative study of emotions. In A. Kleinman & B. Good (Eds.), *Culture and depression.* Los Angeles: University of California Press.

Shweder, R.A. (1986). Divergent rationalities. In D.W. Fiske & R.A. Shweder (Eds.), *Metatheory in social science: Pluralisms and subjectivities.* Chicago: University of Chicago Press.

Shweder, R.A., Mahapatra, M., & Miller, J.G. (in press). Culture and moral development. J. Kagan & S. Lamb (Eds.), *The emergence of moral concepts in early childhood.* Chicago: University of Chicago Press.

Shweder, R.A., & Miller, J.G. (1985). The social construction of the person: How is it possible? In K. Gergen & K. Davis (Eds.), *The social construction of the person.* New York: Springer-Verlag.

APPENDIX: THE BABAJI INTERVIEW USING KOHLBERG'S INTERVIEWS FORM A (MODIFIED)

A woman suffered from a fatal disease. To cure her, doctors prescribed a medicine. That particular medicine was only available in one medicine shop. The pharmacist demanded ten times the real cost of the medicine. The sick woman's husband, Ashok, could not afford it. He went to everyone he knew to borrow money. But he was able to borrow only half of the price. He asked the pharmacist to give him the medicine at half-price or to give it to him on credit. But the pharmacist said, "No, I will sell it at any price I like. There are many persons who will purchase it." After trying so many legal ways to get the medicine, her desperate husband considered breaking into the shop and stealing the medicine.

Should Ashok steal the drug?
No. He's feeling desperate because his wife is going to die and that's why he is stealing the drug. But people don't live forever and providing her the drug does not necessarily mean she will live long. How long you live is not in our hands but in God's hands. And there are other ways to get money like selling his landed property or even he can sell himself to someone and can save his wife's life.

He has no other way out. He has neither money nor anything.
Stealing is bad. He has made a mistake.

But his wife is going to die?
There is no way within Hindu dharma [religion, duty, obligation, law] to steal even if a man is going to die.

But doesn't Hindu dharma prescribe that you try to save a person's life?
Yes. And for that you can sacrifice your blood or sell yourself, but you cannot steal.

Why doesn't Hinda dharma permit stealing?
If he steals it is a sin—so what virtue is there in saving a life. Hindu dharma keeps man from sinning.

Why would it be a sin? Isn't there a saying, "One must jump into fire for others"?
That is there in our dharma—sacrifice, but not stealing.

But if he doesn't provide the medicine for his wife, she will die. Wouldn't it be a sin to let her die?
That's why, according to the capabilities and powers which God has given him, he should try to give her shamanistic instructions and advice. Then she can be cured.

But, that particular medicine is the only way out.
There's no reason to necessarily think that that particular drug will save her life.

Let's suppose she can only be saved by that drug, or else she will die. Won't he face lots of difficulties if his wife dies?
No.

But his family will break up.
He can marry other women.

But he has no money. How can he remarry?
Do you think he should steal? If he steals, he will be sent to jail. Then what's the use of saving her life to keep the family together. She has enjoyed the days destined for her. But stealing is bad. Our sacred scriptures tell that sometimes stealing is an act of dharma. If by stealing for you I can save your life, then it is an act of dharma. But one cannot steal for his wife or his offspring or for himself. If he does that, it is simply stealing.

If I steal for myself, then it's a sin?
Yes.

But in this case I am stealing for my wife, not for me.
But your wife is yours.

Doesn't Ashok have a duty or obligation to steal the drug?
He may not get the medicine by stealing. He may sell himself. He may sell himself to someone for say 500 rupees for 6 months or 1 year.

Does it make a difference whether or not he loves his wife?
So what if he loves his wife? When the husband dies, the wife does not die for him or vice-versa. We have come into this world alone and we will leave it alone. Nobody will accompany us when we leave this world. It may be a son or it may be a wife. No one will go with us.

For whom do you feel one should steal? Let's say it's not his wife but a holy man or a stranger. Would it have been better if he had stolen for them?
Stealing is bad. It is not right according to Hindu dharma, but if he stole for himself the degree of sin would be more.

Is it important to do everything one can to save another's life?
Yes. But that does not mean stealing. You can borrow from soneone. You can go without eating. You can give your food to others, or you can sell yourself.

Suppose Ashok had come to you, told you his situation and sought your advice whether or not to steal. What would you have told him?
I would have asked him not to steal. We have a practice in the villages. Everyone would have decided to give him the required money from the village common fund, or they would have collected some donation. But he should be advised not to steal.

But shouldn't people do everything they can to save a life?
One should try to save another's life. Because, after all, he is a human being. But you should not do it by virtue of stealing.

Is it against the law for Ashok to steal?
Yes. It's against the law.

Are the laws always morally right? Do you feel all laws are right?
Let me tell you a story about stealing. Once some Sadhus [holy men] came to a poor man's house. He and his son were the only members of the family. The Sadhus wanted this man to be their host for that night. Holy men never ask for credit. They never steal. They have only what they earn from begging alms—which they cook and eat.

The Sadhus [holy men] arrived at the man's house as guests, and they considered a guest as a God. So whatever belongings they had they pawned and arranged dinner for the Sadhus. Before going for their dinner the Sadhus said that ghee [clarified butter] was essential for their dinner [it is "cool" food—one of the foods eaten by holy men]. Both the father and the son pondered again and again where to get the ghee. Really, they were "in a stew." They went to the Sadhu of a nearby monastery to get some ghee. But the Sadhu refused to give them ghee. So they made a hole in the wall and entered into the store room of the monastery. The son entered into the store room. It was full of wealth, but the son only picked up the ghee pot. While he was halfway through the hole, suddenly the Sadhu got up and caught hold of the son's two legs. But outside the father was pulling the son's hands. So a tussle went on for some time. The son told the father to take the pot of ghee and offer it to the Sadhu guests. He also told his father to cut off his head and take it away so that the Sadhu of the monastery would not be able to recognize him. The father did this, and threw away his son's head.

The father did such things only because he wanted to help the Sadhus. After offering ghee to his guests the Sadhus were satisfied. The next morning the father bid them farewell, and they asked, "Where is your son? He is not seen." Then the father started to cry. The Sadhus asked him why he is crying? So he told all the details and facts, and said it was nobody's fault.

The Sadhus said, "You have done a mistake. Okay. If you have done it only to satisfy us. If you had no evil intention under it. If you had not temptation for the wealth, and if your son died only for this, then we will pray to God for his life." They asked, "Where is your son's head?" They wanted to show God the cut head. The father took the head of the son to the Sadhus. They sprinkled some Tulsi water on the head. [The story of Tulsi and how she became a holy tree and leaf is well known by Hindus.] So the son returned to life.

In the story the Sadhus brought the son back to life because he had stolen for others. Likewise Ashok is doing this for his wife, isn't he?
The relationship between a wife and husband and between a man and a holy man are quite different. Suppose a river is flowing. This idea is also from our sacred scriptures. Pieces of wood are all tied together in a bundle and floating down the river. They are tied perfectly. Slowly the tie loosens. After some time individual pieces of wood leave the flow and stop on the bank of the river. They become changed. They could not be together as they were before. This world is like that. The son will go his way. We will go our way. If you think only of the truth. If you obey Hindu dharma then stealing is not allowed. Maybe we are together, five souls [literally "hearts"] are joined and we are sitting here. You will go to your home. I will go to my home. No one has the power to detain anyone. So anyone who has faith in God, he will not try to steal to detain his wife's journey.

Don't people steal in certain circumstances?
Yes, people are stealing, and we cannot know what punishment they get for this. If you understand how you have come into this world you will not steal. Stealing is a great sin.

Which is a greater sin, to kill a man or to steal?
Both are great sins. You must have gone to Dhauli [the battlefield where the King Ashoka slaughtered hundreds of thousands of Oriya Kalinga in battle—the place where in repentance for the slaughter Ashoka converted to Buddhism, later to spread Buddhism to Southeast Asia]. When Ashok conquered Kalinga, a monk came to him and said: "You are defeated." Ashok said: "What? I have already conquered Kalinga, killed thousands of people, and with their blood the water of the river Daya has turned red. What do you mean 'I am defeated'?" The monk said: "You are born as a man. You proclaim that you are a great man." Ashok said: "You please come with me, so you can see how many persons are beheaded, how many dead bodies are lying down there. You see my sword. I have killed many persons with this sword."
The monk said: "It is by killing hundreds of thousands of people that you have failed. If you can give life to any one of these then I will say you are great. Their wives and children, those who depend on them, how they are crying. You are only killing. You have not recognized the atman [soul, divinity] in them. How have you conquered?" So Ashok, the butcher, changed. He threw down his sword and begged forgiveness from the monk.

Isn't the husband killing his wife by not stealing the drug?
No, he is not killing. If something is with me and I do not give it, then it is my fault. The husband must have some homestead land, or some vehicle. If he has nothing then he has at least his self, which he can sell.

No, Ashok has nothing. He is poor.
He can sell himself. We have the tradition of "Havis Chandra"—the king who sold himself to give remuneration that he owed. It is a time when God puts you to a test. At such a time you can sell yourself. Suppose I earn 7 rupees a day. I can borrow 500 rupees on a condition to serve the man for 5 years. Alternatively, when the wife is going to die, he can die in her place. He will die in sorrow anyway.

But had he stolen the drug, he would have saved her.
Definitely it will be a sin. Thinking in terms of dharma he cannot steal. This is a fact. If I steal it's my dharma that's involved. My wife will not be sent to jail. I will be sent. Dharma is like that—I will be at fault. There's a story I want to tell you. During the age of the *Mahabharata* [the Indian epic] Kali [the goddess of destruction] came to earth and Dahadebu tied her up. She was bound. That was during the age of Satyayuga (Truth). A peasant was ploughing the land of a Brahman. Once while he was ploughing he found a golden armlet in the earth. So he went to the Brahman and said: "Here, take this golden armlet since I have found it on your land." The Brahman said to the tiller: "It's yours to take since you ploughed the land." So they quarrelled with each other, each trying to give the golden armlet to the other. When one gives it to the other the latter says, "Why should I commit a sin?" So no one took the armlet.
Both of them went to the king, Yudhisthira. It was the tradition in those days to give such disputed things to the king. The king said: "Our time of rule is over and we are going to the Himalayas. We cannot stay here and there is no use of taking such property with us to the Himalayas." So Yudhisthira told them to ask Sahadeba to judge the dispute. Sahadeba was a man capable of seeing both the past and the future. So do you know what he did? He freed Kali! He let her loose. Immediately the Brahman claimed the armlet. Then the tiller claimed the armlet as he got it while ploughing.

The fighting continued between them. Everything depends on the age [yuga], whether it's the age of Kali (Darkness) or the age of Satya (Truth). This is the age of Kali.

Do you know any laws that are morally wrong?
Family planning. According to dharma it is wrong.

What's wrong with it?
The operation and the sterilization. They are murdering through abortion.

Is the law forbidding dowry morally wrong?
Dowry is not part of our dharma. But it's in practice nowadays. One should give voluntarily.

What about the law permitting untouchables to enter the temple? Is that law morally wrong?
There is a history of touchable and untouchable. It's not a sin if a Hadi [an untouchable caste in Orissa] touches a Brahman or a Karan [a clean caste in Orissa] or visits the temple. But there is a reason behind the idea of untouchable. Suppose you have taken your bath and I have not. Untouchables do not keep their own sanctity. Human being means all are equal. God has created the hierarchy among them so that they will work according to their duty. Untouchables can enter the temple but they should be cleaned. They should perform their daily duties like bathing properly.

If they perform their daily duties properly can they enter then?
Yes. No restriction. Even God has not restricted them. You know what the Goddess Laxmi [goddess of wealth, consort of Vishnu] has said: "From Hadi [sweeper] to Chandala [another untouchable caste] all will touch prasad [a holy food] on their head."

What about the law requiring equal inheritance between son and daughter? Is that law morally wrong?
Both son and daughter are equal; they are born to the same father, and for him everyone is equal. But the thing is that the daughter gets married and becomes part of her husband's family. It is the son who takes care of his parents. They live with him. And it is the son who performs all the death rituals and after the parents' death other rituals for the ancestors as well. That's why we do it: 60% for the son and 40% for the daughter. If both of them were unmarried and the brother did not finance the sister's marriage, then as in the government's law, it ought to be 50/50.

But the law says that even if the son and daughter are married they must share equally. Is that morally correct?
The son has many duties to perform for ceremonies and other occasions. They are costly. If he manages all these duties then the daughter cannot take an equal amount. Thinking in terms of dharma the government law is wrong.

Can you think of any Indian custom or tradition which is morally wrong?
Eating with your younger brother's wife is against our custom. It's not wrong according to dharma; it's not bad. But you will feel guilty if you do it—you will feel that you have made a mistake.

Foreigners are not allowed in Juggernaut temple. Is that morally right?
They are not allowed because they do not believe in the Hindu religion. They are all Christians.

Suppose the foreigner had converted to Hinduism?
If he were a Hindu he would have been allowed to enter. If he believes in the Hindu religion he will be allowed.

Untouchables are not allowed in the temple. Is that morally correct?
I told you before about touchability and untouchability. Suppose we were untouchables. We would be feeling guilty. Because we have not taken our bath or washed our dress we are not entering the temple. Untouchables do not perform cleansing rituals—they don't keep to habits of purification. So they are not allowed in sanctified places.

Are all the practices, customs and traditions of Hinduism right?
The traditions of the Hindu religion are not bad but good.

The Indian population is increasing. Suppose the government passed a law that no family can have more than three children. Otherwise the child should be killed. Would that law be okay?
No. Such a law should not be obeyed.

Why should it not be obeyed?
Suppose a child is born. There is no way within the context of Hindu dharma to kill him. Take, for example, the case of a tree studded with fruit. It is a great sin to cut down that tree. If it is an obstacle or if it harms or gives some kind of pain then we are bound to cut it down. Otherwise one should not cut the tree. If we see it bending down on us, then we cut it. Imagine the government saying: "You have five or six children but you may not keep them!" There's a lot of difference between the age of the Gods and our age, between the age of the epics and the present age.

Why do you think that stealing is forbidden in Hindu dharma?
If one steals, in the next life who knows what form he will take? Any man who realizes this will not steal. That's why it is restricted.

Are the punishments the same for different kinds of stealing?
Yes.

What about someone who steals to save a life?
His punishment should be less. But it is a matter of dharma. We cannot steal and it is not us who gives punishment. God is considering their case. There was once a king. He was always offering things to Brahmans—he offered hundreds of thousands of cows as donations to Brahmans. Once one of the donated cows "played hookey" and returned to the king's cowshed. The king was not aware of this fact. So by mistake he again donated that particular cow to a different Brahman. Soon the first owner of that donated cow saw that cow while the second Brahman was taking it with him. He recognized the symbols on the cow's tail and the turmeric spot. So he proclaimed that the cow had been a gift of the king to him. He told the second Brahman to go to the king. When the king saw them coming he shivered. He wondered why the two Brahmans had come to him with a cow. Both of them put forth their claim. The king told the second Brahman: "You see I have already donated this cow. You return it to the first Brahman and I will donate a hundred thousand cows to you." But the second Brahman said: "No. I must take this cow because you have donated it to me." So both of them started quarrelling with each other over the ownership of the cow. The quarrel lasted so long that at last the cow died.

But even though the king had unknowingly redonated the cow he had to shoulder the sin. On the other hand, the king had donated hundreds of thousands of cows and even golden-made cow horns. When Yama [the God of Death] saw him, he said: "This king has done so many virtuous things and but one vice—unknowingly redonating that cow. So his mistake is only one percent. Still, he had to undergo the effect of sin." Yama asked the king: "Would you like to enjoy first the sin or first the virtue?" The king said: "I have not done this knowingly. Still, since I have committed a serious mistake, I will first experience the sin and then the virtue." Then Yama uttered the word "Kukulash" ("lizard") and threw the king into a well in the jungle.

How can the king be saved? When Krishna will go that place, then only will the king get salvation. Otherwise no one can remove him from the well. So even if we do something unknowingly, it can be wrong—from the point of view of dharma it is a mistake.

Ashok did break into the store. He stole the drug and gave it to his wife. Ashok was arrested and brought to court. A jury was selected. The jury's job is to find whether a person is innocent or guilty of committing a crime. The jury finds Ashok guilty. It is up to the judge to determine the sentence.

Should the judge give Ashok some punishment or should he let him go free? Why?
According to law—when he has stolen he should be punished. Ashok has created a family in this world. God gave him hands and legs yet he has not saved money by working and laboring. Now he has no money and cannot buy the medicine or cure the disease. With all his lethargy he did not think of his wife getting ill before. So if he steals now, he has to bear the punishment.

Thinking in terms of society, should people who break the law be punished?
It is written in our Hindu sacred scriptures that whatever may be the religion, be it Muslim or Christian, it is wrong to denigrate or blame other religions. God has not said I have one particular name. Whoever prays to him in any name—one should not think him wrong. But if someone is about to destroy Hindu dharma or break Christian dharma then he should be punished. The destruction of Hinduism is not the point; it's the destruction of any dharma.

How does this apply to how the judge should decide?
The case should be considered. He was involved in stealing. On the other hand we have to look carefully at the law. Why was that pharmacist demanding fifty rupees for a drug that cost five rupees? So, the pharmacist has done wrong. He should get punished.

Ashok acted out of conscience. Should a lawbreaker be punished if he is acting out of conscience?
Yes. He should get punished.

Should he get the same punishment from the judge as the person who steals for his own benefit?
Yes, the same punishment. It is our law that one cannot forcibly enter into another's house.

One man steals for himself and another steals to save a life. In the next life will they be reborn in the same way? Will God give the same kind of punishment for both offenses?
They'll get different kinds of punishment.

Then why shouldn't the judge give less punishment to the person who steals to save a life?
What's the same is that they get punished—the means is the same. The degree can differ. One person gets fined two rupees for taxation punishment. Another is fined five rupees. Not everyone gets six months imprisonment. Some get one year. The judge will consider the type of stealing in deciding on the punishment. Suppose I kidnapped a girl and another person being hungry stole away some black-gram cutlets. In both cases it is stealing but there is a difference between the degree of stealing. Before the creation of the world the Formless One created these three—Brahma, Vishnu and Siva. During that time there were demons in the world. The Formless One decided to kill the demons and create the world. The world was full of water all around. Seeing this Vishnu plucked a hair from his body and threw it away. It created a mountain on the earth. This trinity, Brahma, Vishnu and Siva lived on the mountain and created a flower garden. They thought about all the things they would

create. Meanwhile, many days passed, and the Formless One wondered where the three had gone and why they had not returned. He told this to the First Mother, and asked her to go and see what the three are doing. When she reached the mountain Brahma and Vishnu had gone somewhere; only Siva was there, alone. The garden was all decorated. Seeing the First Mother Siva became excited and starting have sexual intercourse with her. Brahma and Vishnu returned and saw it all. They abused the First Mother—so she cursed them and told them they will suffer after being born in the womb of the mother they were now abusing. Being cursed this way, Brahma and Vishnu went to the Formless One and told him all the facts. Hearing about it the Formless One cursed the First Mother and made her take birth as a cow on earth.

So the First Mother has sinned. Lingaraj [the reigning deity of Bhubaneswar] and other Gods and Goddesses have also sinned from time to time. But has the First Father done any sin?
No. He has never sinned!
Is there anything more valuable than life?
No.
Then if Ashok can save a life by stealing what is the harm of it?
He should have saved her life by virtue of labor. Whatever may be he should not steal. It is a wrong to steal and you will get punished. Ravana [the villain of the epic the *Ramayana*] was a great learned man before he kidnapped Sita [Ram's wife in the *Ramayana*]. When he stole away Sita he sinned. He was cursed for it and he was killed for it. Saving a life by means of stealing is not the only way out.

Ram is 14 years old. He wanted a bicycle. His father promised him that he could have a bicycle if he saved the money. So Ram worked hard and saved money, a little more than the cost of a bicycle. Before he purchased the bicycle his father changed his mind. His father's friends decided to go to Delhi to see the Asia Games. Ram's father was short of funds to go to Delhi. So he ordered Ram to give him the money he had saved for the bicycle. Ram did not want to give the money to his father. So he thinks of refusing to give the money to his father.

Should Ram refuse to give his father the money? Why?
The father wants to spend the money visiting the games; it is money ill-spent. So the son has done the right thing refusing to give him the money. If they were hungry in the house. If they have no food to eat. Had the father asked for the money for food. If the family loan has to be repaid. If the house is going to be auctioned. If in such cases the father had asked and the son had refused, then it would have been wrong. But for visiting games it is the father who has not done right to ask for the money.

Why should Ram refuse to give the money to his father?
Buying a cycle is beneficial. It will be easier to go to the market and other places. He can be equal with others. It is not necessary to spend money visiting games.

Does the father have the right to order Ram to give him the money?
When the father has given birth to a son he has the right to ask for anything. The father has every right over his son. But the son also has rights over his father. Why hasn't the father bought a cycle for the son? It's wrong for the father not to buy the cycle for the son. Otherwise the child may go astray. What if the son is going to a far-away school? It must be a pain to walk such a distance. If the son has saved money to buy a cycle and finds himself short of money, then the father ought to fill in the deficit. Or else there's no point being a father. If the father doesn't do it then the son may steal. Under such circumstances the father should buy a cycle for his son even if it means the father must stop eating food for awhile.

Does giving the money have anything to do with being a good son?
He is a good son if he gives money for true purposes. For bad purposes, he is a good son if he does not give.

Is the fact that Ram earned the money himself important in the situation?
It was right for the father to do it that way. So that the son can learn how to save. If he can save a little each day out of his daily expenses then he will be able to easily get his work done.

Is the fact that the father promised the most important thing in the situation?
If you have given your word you should keep it. You have created a hope in your son's mind. To break your promise is an act against dharma. Your son may become frustrated. He may have many thoughts come to his mind. He may curse you, and it may become true.

Should a promise be kept? Why?
One should keep his word. You should not speak your word until after you have thought it over. God has given intelligence to the individual to think before making a decision.

What is the most important thing a father should be concerned about in his relationship to his son?
The father–son relationship should always be a good one. If the father has a bad habit, like smoking ganja, then he should not smoke it before his son. Because the son will observe father's bad habit. The father should show affection to the son and always lead him to the way of truth.

Why should a father do these things? What good is it for the father?
There is a saying: "If you throw a small stone, then there must be a bigger stone for you." If the father does not lead the son on a good path then the son will be naughty and ultimately he will put his father into difficulty and defame him. When we will be lying dead, the son will kick us and go away. He won't live with us. There won't be any relationship between father and son. Therefore father always wants to give good advice to his children.

In general, what should be the authority of the father over his son?
The father should always give good advice to his son; always!

Suppose the father gave bad advice to his son and the son knew it was bad advice. What should he do?
If the son were to obey the father's bad advice it would be worry for both the father and the son. When you plant a tree you think about how to get good fruit. If I do bad work, how can I lead my son to a good path? How can he do the work of dharma if I give bad advice? A father who gives bad advice knows he will be punished for his ill-doings.

What do you think is the thing a son should be most concerned about in his relationship to his father?
It is always the duty of the son to obey his parents. After the son is educated he should try to lead his father on a good path, if his father has some bad habits. However bad the father may be, the son should recognize him and accept him as a father. The father has brought him into the world, given him life. The son will not suffer if he gives respect to his father. It is written in sacred scriptures as follows: Hiranya was a great devotee of Siva. Initially he was a devotee of Vishnu but he observed that it takes a long time to have an audience with Vishnu. So he worshipped Siva instead of Vishnu. Once Hiranya's son asked his school master: "Who will give salvation?" The school master told him that only Vishnu can offer salvation. Only Vishnu has that power. So the son questioned why his father is worshipping Siva and ordering

everyone to worship Siva throughout his kingdom. Then for the sake of his own salvation the son started worshipping Vishnu. When the father heard of this he tried to kill his son in so many ways. But each time God saved the son. Finally Hiranya asked his son to show him where is his God. The son pointed at a pillar and said, "God is inside it." Then Hiranya broke down the pillar. Out of the pillar Vishnu came in the guise of a lion, and he killed Hiranya. At that time, the son of Hiranya requested Vishnu to relent so that his father could get salvation. So, whatever harm the father has done to the son, at his last breath the son prays to God for his father.

When a person sins who is it that will be punished, the person who sins or his family members?

The one who sins will be punished. The sin committed by the left hand will not come to the right hand, or vice versa. If the husband sins, the wife will not suffer.

CHAPTER 8

Social Interaction as Practical Activity: Implications for the Study of Social and Moral Development

MARTIN J. PACKER

The aim of this chapter is to sketch (sometimes in rather sweeping strokes) the outline of an interpretive or hermeneutic approach to the study of social interaction, and to social and moral development. What shall be described here is a broad program within which only preliminary moves have been made, in terms of both planning and research. And since the hermeneutic approach is one with which most readers will have as yet little familiarity, some of what is said may seem obscure. The interested reader is referred to the author's and others' introductions to hermeneutics and its significance for the social sciences (Bleicher, 1980; Packer, 1985c; Palmer, 1969; Rabinow & Sullivan, 1979).

We shall begin by arguing that social interaction (indeed, human action in general) has certain unique and peculiar characteristics that require a method of research investigation (and an understanding of the research enterprise) that is radically different from the empiricist and experimentalist approaches psychologists generally employ, different from the formalist program that characterizes much of cognitive science (Gardner, 1985), and different from the methods of cognitive-developmental study of social and moral thinking. Nonetheless action seems to be the proper place to begin to study social and moral development, so we are obliged to confront these methodological requirements.

We shall discuss the characteristics of social action that we take to be unique with reference to a distinction first made by Heidegger between three modes of engagement people have in the world. These modes have been described in more detail elsewhere (Packer, 1985c), so the discussion here will be relatively brief. To anticipate the argument, it will be suggested that social interaction is best considered to be a practical activity, a definition that will be elaborated on. In the chapter's second section, two research projects will be described in which a hermeneutic approach was emphasized, which throw light on the general theme of this book: influences that interactions among people have on their social and moral development. The first project examined exchanges between an infant girl and her mother; the second involved the interpretation of confrontations between young college students over a minor occasion of betrayal. Taken together, these studies point up one candidate social process—practical deliberation—as a social and psychological process in everyday social interaction that seems likely to influence social and moral development. The third section of the chapter addresses more speculatively the general form that an account of moral and social development might have, approached from the hermeneutic perspective. Here the interpretive approach is contrasted with the cognitive-developmental program and with Kohlberg's views of philosophy. Kierkegaard's analyses of spheres of ethical development are used to illustrate several aspects of what an interpretive-developmental account might look like.

SOCIAL ACTION AS PRACTICAL ACTIVITY

The preparation of this book signals a growing recognition that social and moral development are not the results of solitary construction by individual minds, but are fostered and organized by the social interchanges that people are constantly engaged in together. For the past 25 years social and moral *thinking* have been the focus of developmental research, as this has been defined by the cognitive–developmental paradigm. Reasoning about moral and social situations and issues has been the most frequent object of inquiry, with moral and social beliefs and attitudes a close second. But if social processes influence development then we need to conduct research on people's action together as well as their reasoning and their knowledge. However, there is much confusion as to just what this means. Blasi (1980) describes two distinct approaches to the study of action: a behaviorist and a formalist, cognitive–developmental one. It has been argued by the author (Packer, 1985c) that these are both inadequate; the limitations of behaviorist approaches to human behavior are well known, and there are also many difficulties in conceptualizing human action within the cognitive–developmental paradigm (e.g., Locke, 1983). The ideas discussed in this chapter all rest in a particular account of the character of social action: Social interaction is viewed as a kind of practical activity. The account of practical activity that will be given here is based on Heidegger's work (1927/1962), although similar accounts can be found in the writings of other recent philosophers in less articulated forms: Wittgenstein (1972), Merleau-Ponty (1942/1963) and Suzanne Langer (1967) are three examples. These thinkers turned to the examination of human practical action in response to the shortcomings they found in the formalism that characterizes rationalist philosophy. A similar formalist zeitgeist greatly influences current psychological theory, in a variety of forms. Structuralism, cognitive developmentalism, information processing theory, computer models; each continues to hold formalist or rationalist assumptions about the structure and the sources of knowledge (Packer, 1985c). Consequently, our research methods are biased toward reading logic and formalism into human phenomena that have a very different kind of organization.

Social action has a special ontological status. Unlike biological processes such as differentiation, growth, or digestion, it has a *semantic* level of organization to it. Social events and actions have influence and significance by virtue of the meanings people find in them, not by virtue of material causation, or logical necessity. Consequently practical activity is different from the formal, logical organization that characterizes abstract systems of systematic reasoning: axiomatic mathematics, programming languages, formal decision rules and procedures. One particular consequence of this semantic character is central to the argument of this chapter: Practical activity is intrinsically polysemous or ambiguous. Every social act can be understood in a variety of different ways, depending on the perspective from which one views it, and the context in which one encounters it. This is not to say that *any* interpretation can be made of an action; there are limits to the semantic range of a specific act. But in general any human action or event is open to being understood in a range of possible ways. Yet this central characteristic of human behavior is denied or ignored by the majority of methodologies currently employed in psychological research. Positivist methodologies insist that there are "facts" to human behavior: elements of behavior that can be observed and identified in an interpretation-free manner. An obsession with reliability and objectivity has motivated attempts to reduce human action to a minimalist set of objective elements.

An interpretive method of investigation is needed if social interaction is to be studied appropriately by psychologists and other social scientists. Several characteristics of action necessitate this move. There is an intrinsic temporal organization to social episodes, lost entirely by empiricist correlational study, and distorted into a preorganized plan by sequential statistical analyses. Furthermore, social acts and events gain their meaning in a specific context or social setting that cannot be captured by operationalized coding schemes. Social exchanges are complex, intricate, and confusing. We can make sense of them only progressively, in an inductive manner that is ruled out of court by the traditional hypothetico–deductive research canons. More broadly, social interactions make sense to us as researchers, and are comprehensible as involving events of particular kinds, only because we are social beings and members of a shared culture. Our preunderstandings and prejudices are what make it possible for things to "count" for us in a social episode (Gadamer, 1976). However, since we are prejudiced we are capable of misunderstanding as well, and we need to introduce into our research ways of correcting the misinterpretations that inevitably arise.

To say that social interaction is a practical activity is to claim that it involves a certain kind of involvement between people. Following Heidegger, we shall distinguish between three modes of engagement people have with the world: the ready-to-hand, the unready-to-hand, and the present-at-hand. In their everyday practical activity people are in the ready-to-hand and the unready-to-hand modes. When they reason about abstract moral or social problems, when they speculate about hypothetical dilemmas, they are in a distinct detached mode, the present-at-hand.

The Ready-to-Hand

The ready-to-hand is the most fundamental of the three modes of engagement. The unready-to-hand is a mode of breakdown in activity while the present-at-hand is in contrast a derivative mode, one of detached contemplation. These modes cut across the social and nonsocial realms; they are found in manipulatory acts such as hammering as much as in social activities such as casual conversation, selling a used car, or joking with a neighbor. When we are engaged in unproblematic forms of practical activity, when we are caught up in familiar patterns of action, we are in the ready-to-hand mode. Our way of dealing with events in this mode is not mediated by reflection, deliberation, or calculation. Our action is guided by social know-how, not by explicit knowing-that. The ready-to-hand mode is one of active engagement in practical projects in the world, such as using a hammer, asking to borrow a pencil, teaching a class, playing a game of darts. It is the mode of unreflective practices, of skills and habits, and it is the mode exemplified by the forms of understanding characteristic of emotions and moods. Although they are unreflective, or prereflective, ready-to-hand practical activities are ongoing social constructions, the results of smooth and fluent interaction between skilled members of a culture (cf. Giddens, 1976).

In any ready-to-hand practical activity, our perception or way of understanding our world is essentially holistic: We are aware of the situation in which we find ourselves in an unreflective, absorbed manner. In ready-to-hand activity we don't experience ourselves as distinct individual agents; we don't act as though we are separate from a physical universe we are acting upon; instead we are acting *within* a world that we are always at home in and part of. We have no separate awareness of self, others, or tools: All these are fused into our activity or, more accurately, our activity is the single structure out of which we shall later be able to distinguish self, others, and tools. During an evening with a friend, for example, we experience not two individual selves, isolated egos, exchanging messages or acting instrumentally upon each other. Instead, our primary experience is of the pleasures and interests of a joint project (going to a movie, say) and only subsequently, analytically, can we dissect out self and other, plan and social goal, instrumental communication, and other apparently discrete elements. And this dissection can be done only when our mode of engagement is no longer one of practical involvement.

The kind of engagement characteristic of ready-to-hand practical activity has been noticed by psychologists, but there has been a tendency to project upon it certain assumptions about the way it is organized. This tendency is a general one in human reflection, not an aberration peculiar to social scientists. We tend to assume that rules and procedures or rigid causal connections characterize the mode of ready-to-hand engagement. Human behavior has always been understood by analogy with the most modern forms of technical apparatus: clockwork mechanism, telephone exchange, digital computer. If, instead, we undertake a systematic description of the ready-to-hand mode of engagement in its own right, it turns out to have a very different kind of organization. Practical activity is not guided by means–ends planning; it is an ongoing response to the environment, within the boundaries of a flow of a chosen activity. It *can* be viewed in means–ends terms, but this is a *mis*interpretation, a reading in of the characteristics of detached theorizing and contemplative planning that arise, we shall see, only in the present-at-hand mode.

Breakdown: The Unready-to-Hand Mode

Practical activity can shift to a second mode of engagement: the unready-to-hand. This is the form our engagement takes when something has gone amiss, and a breakdown of some kind has occurred in our smoothly flowing activity. If I have, naively, gone into a city lending library seeking a copy of *Carmichael's Manual*, I will most likely find myself talking to a puzzled librarian. I will find myself, hitherto absorbed in a taken-for-granted course of action, suddenly brought up against the librarian's bewilderment, and I will cast about to try to understand what has happened and repair the breakdown. If a child at preschool innocently reaches out for a toy that another child has put aside only temporarily, she is likely to find herself faced with an indignant peer. Suddenly an unanticipated problem has occurred, though at first the child will recognize not the precise form of moral or social wrong that has taken place, but instead an undifferentiated breakdown in the ongoing social activity.

Experience in the unready-to-hand mode has a structure analogous to the figure–ground structure the Gestalt school found in visual experience: Particular problematic aspects of the whole situation stand out, but they are still embedded in the background to the project they form part of, and in the interests and involvements guiding it.

The primary response to breakdown in the smooth flow of social interaction is not one of calculation and reasoned evaluation. Instead, we respond to breakdown in a particular and situated manner, in the search for a handy solution. Heidegger points to a special, engaged kind of reflection that occurs on occasions of breakdown. He calls this practical deliberation, but says little about its details. Much of this chapter will circle around the question of the nature of practical deliberation in social interactions.

Disengagement: The Present-at-Hand Mode

The sort of engagement that characterizes the third mode, present-at-hand engagement, is actually *dis*engagement. This is our mode of drawing back and detaching ourselves from the ongoing flow of a project or social activity. This often occurs when we are unable to find a direct and circumspect solution (by deliberating) to a breakdown in that project. On such occasions we have to "step back," reflect and theorize, and try to solve the breakdown by turning to tools that are more general and abstract, and so more situation independent; tools such as logical analysis and formal calculation. We now perceive the situation and interchange in terms of discrete, definite, and measurable properties, a type of perception distinct from the situated aspects that characterize experience in the unready-to-hand mode. For example, we perceive social events in terms of roles, social strategies, institutions, and norms that appear to have an existence independent of particular people's social situations, culture, and history.

This detached mode of engagement can come from leisure as well as from unresolved breakdown. In the comfort of an armchair we can contemplate our projects, carve them into plans and goals, roles and agents, means and ends. We can find rules and principles within them. Present-at-hand engagement is also encouraged as a type of scientific attitude. It provides the title of Nagel's (1986) book *The View from Nowhere*. Nagel explores the relationships between this kind of detachment and the forms of understanding that are tied to specific human viewpoints. His aim is to avoid the problem that in the present-at-hand, objective mode "one will get a false objectification of an aspect of reality that cannot be better understood from a more objective viewpoint" (p. 4), which he calls the problem of excessive objectivity.

Generally the investigation of influences of social interaction on development has been of this objective type, too. Research efforts have involved the application of traditional research methodologies: experimental manipulation of operationally defined variables that reflect group processes, coding schemes for the identification of typologies of social behavior, and so forth. Such research approaches assume (tacitly or explicitly) that social acts are objectively categorizable events that form series of causal connections or that are generated by internal formal or logical reasoning processes.

Social actions do not submit readily to this sort of treatment. They are understood by the participants themselves from involved perspectives, points of view, and positions, which means that different people will understand the same act or event differently (though, as stated, not in an unbounded number of ways). Every activity takes place in a context that we can view as a holistic network of interrelated projects, possible tasks, and thwarted potentialities. This network is not laid out explicitly but is present as a "background" to an interaction. Because of this embeddedness of meaning in a context or setting, once a social act (e.g., an utterance in a conversation) is removed from its original context (by a researcher employing an objectifying methodology, say) it becomes *multiply* ambiguous (Gergen, Hepburn, & Comer, in press).

We must allow that psychologists' ability to understand other people's actions is only human. We can comprehend only part of what we see, and we inevitably assimilate it to our preconceptions. Since the work of Freud and Marx, we can no longer assume that what goes on around us is just as it seems. Social and productive factors influence our lives and our behavior without our being explicitly aware of them, and our actions include parapraxes, intentions only half-uncovered, and ambivalences. Any claim by social scientists to be able to observe and analyze social action in some apodictic objective manner, some way that isn't filled through and through with judgments and interpretations, must be viewed with skepticism. An acknowledgement of these intrinsic limitations to the study of human action is not an admission of inadequacies in our research methods so much as it is the first step toward adopting a method of study that is adequate to the phenomena of practical social activity. The answer is not to strive somehow to achieve "objectivity," in the sense of a value-free description of indisputable "facts." Instead we must incorporate a reflexive component into our research; we must recognize our partiality, and acknowledge and do justice to the interpretation-loaded character of action.

Adopting a Particularist Perspective: The Hermeneutic Paradigm

It is important, then, to try to find a way of characterizing and describing practical activity that does not impose upon it categories from formal or causal present-at-hand reflection and contemplation. The analytic task of hermeneutics is one of characterizing ready-to-hand activity, and describing the shifts between the ready-to-hand and unready-to-hand modes of engagement. Social interactions are typically oriented to particular practical ends, to the mundane and trivial accomplishment of routine daily tasks, and as socially competent beings we are actively involved in these continuous accomplishments.

Hermeneutic methodology takes this ready-to-hand practical activity to be the *primary* origin of our understanding of the social world. People's spontaneous everyday practical involvement with other people, with equipment and social artifacts, provides the foundation for all our organized knowledge about society, psychological development, history, and so on. Theorizing and abstract speculation would be impossible if we did not already have practically grounded ways of understanding our world. The ready-to-hand mode, then, gives us the most primordial and direct access to human phenomena. The kind of access of the ready-to-hand—emotions, habitual practices, and skills—is radically different from the access to phenomena provided by theoretical reflection: As Heidegger puts it "the ready-to-hand is not grasped theoretically at all" (p. 99). People both constitute and are constituted by the cultural and bodily skills and practices of their everyday activity. Practical activity—both ready-to-hand and unready-to-hand—has a structure distinct from that of reasoning and theory construction. Our studies of social processes must be able to characterize practical social activity as kinds of ready-to-hand and unready-to-hand practical engagement. This is not a trivial task, since practical activity does not make reference to context-free elements, which could be defined in an interpretation-free manner. Practical activity is tricky: it is intrinsically polysemous, historically situated, context bound, and totally ambiguous when removed from its context, and for the large part it is as yet uncharted.

The approach that needs to be adopted is, as the author has argued elsewhere, a hermeneutic or interpretive one. Selman and Yeates and Shweder and Much also discuss aspects of this approach in their chapters in this volume. The general aim has been to develop a research methodology that takes account of and is sensitive to the particular characteristics of social action. Selman and Yeates see their method as being one that allows them to characterize with sensitivity the understanding they gain of children's social styles and strategies as a consequence of close clinical involvement with them over an extended period of time. Such involvement gives one access to the recurrent themes that develop as the children interact together. The hermeneutic approach avoids the decontextualization that positivist and formalist methods produce, as they abstract behaviors from their historical and personal situation.

For Shweder and Much, hermeneutics is a matter of making explicit what remains "unsaid" in everyday discourse. What is said in discourse can be contrasted with what is implied, suggested, or accomplished in that discourse. This side of social interaction is itself, they argue, skilled, facile, and developmentally advanced, and involves a type of rationality that is as valid as formal reasoning. While agreeing with most of their position, we differ from Shweder and Much in maintaining that what is revealed in a hermeneutic analysis of discourse is not what they call propositions about the moral order, but accounts of practices and ways of comporting oneself socially that are not hidden so much as taken for granted. To express the unsaid in propositional terms may not be the appropriate level of description: It is applying present-at-hand categories to ready-to-hand phenomena.

Broadly speaking, the kind of empirical program one engages in when adopting the hermeneutic paradigm as a developmental psychologist is one of studying, describing, and interpreting episodes of social interaction in relevant situations in naturally occurring or analog settings. This program matches hermeneutic research in other disciplines, for example, Geertz's (1972) study of the Balinese cockfight and Kuhn's (1977) analysis of scientists' paradigms of understanding and research. More specifically, our aim has been to look at interactions among children and adults over substantive social and moral concerns. As Shweder (1982, p. 412) suggested, we need to "take talk seriously" not as the outcome (viewed as mere performance) of internal cognitive structures and processes (competence), not as post facto rationalization of processes determined by factors outside individual agency, but as a substantive, structured, and structuring activity with intrinsic developmental significance.

THE DEVELOPMENTAL SIGNIFICANCE OF PRACTICAL ACTIVITY

We shall explore further the notion that social interaction has intrinsic developmental significance, and that this becomes apparent when one examines interaction hermeneutically, as practical activity. We shall do this by discussing two studies of developmentally relevant social exchange that were conducted from the hermeneutic perspective. The first was of infant–adult interaction, the second of moral confrontation among young adults.

Exchanges Between Infant and Adult

In the first study we were interested to consider what was accomplished during exchanges between an adult and her very young child. In particular, we wondered what developmentally significant influences might be uncoverable in such exchanges. This study involved repeated visits with a firstborn girl and her mother, between 6 weeks of age and 12 months. Videorecordings were made of semistructured interchanges between the two, once each month. Written narrative transcripts were developed from repeated viewing of the videotapes, and these and the tapes formed the basis for an interpretive analysis (see Packer, 1983, for a detailed account). The analysis was guided by intentions to describe the social interaction as negotiated exchanges between the two people involved. We were also interested in seeing to what extent the form the exchanges took could be adequately explained within an instrumental theory of communication in early infancy, such as the theories of Bates (1976), Stern (1977), and Ainsworth (1969). Three central assumptions are made by these and many other theorists: that communicative interaction is essentially instrumental; that meaning is transparent and unambiguous; and that development in communicative ability is the result of changes occurring in other cognitive "systems" such as operational thinking. These three assumptions follow if one uncritically takes the present-at-hand mode of engagement as characteristic of social interactions, since an information transfer account of interaction and communication and a means–ends instrumental account of social relations rest on a view of individuals as isolated entities exchanging context-free messages. And this, as was argued earlier, is a present-at-hand account of social activity.

It became apparent on examination of the videotaped exchanges of infant and adult that one could understand very little by viewing what occurred as being on the infant's part either instrumental (aimed at producing a specific effect on the adult) or deliberate (consciously planned). The infant was caught up in forms of social exchange by virtue of the fact that the adult structured the interaction in such a way as to involve her, so one could hardly view the infant's engagement as deliberate. Furthermore, exchanges frequently ended not in the accomplishment of some concrete goal, but in a consensus (in the original sense of "feeling together"): a shared emotion, such as a feeling of excitement and satisfaction, an outcome that was not aimed at in an instrumental manner by either participant. (In their chapter of this volume Selman & Yeates also describe shared affect as a highly important component of significant social exchanges.)

The semantic organization of the interaction was salient, too. The meanings of the infant's actions were often ambiguous and problematic. Her mother frequently failed to understand fully what an act on her daughter's part meant; what it indicated about the infant's wishes. The following is a brief segment from the transcripts, illustrating this phenomenon:

Sarah lifts Jenny into a standing position and supports her by holding her hands. The posture necessitates that Jenny actively maintain her own balance, and in doing so her face turns to the front, toward Sarah. But she immediately looks away again, this time to the other side. Sarah asks again, "What's wrong?" She tries to keep Jenny upright, but Jenny bends at the waist, looking down. Sarah now looks irritated. She asks, "Do you want to sit up?" and sits Jenny down on her knee. Jenny looks impassive, and Sarah says, "I don't know what you want to do."

The adult is clearly strongly motivated here to make sense of her child's acts, and is engaged in a kind of hermeneutic endeavor in order to do this. It is equally clear that she finds her daughter's actions obscure. So she finds meaning in the actions, but not a transparent, obvious meaning. The way Sarah deals with this is interesting: She makes repeated attempts to disambiguate the infant's actions by working out in practice what they mean; what they tell her about what Jenny "wants to do." One way of doing this, as the example illustrates, was to hold Jenny in a series of physical postures each of which was appropriate as a possible way of understanding what the child wanted. The adult provided a series of contexts in which Jenny's actions might make sense, to see which one allowed their interaction to proceed successfully.

In the course of these exchanges with her daughter, Sarah was doing several things that are of consequence to a social developmental psychology. First, she was encouraging the infant in certain fundamental forms of conduct: standing upright; delaying gratification; maintaining an en face orientation. Second, she was channeling her child's interests and needs into their social interaction, although the child sometimes resisted. In both of these ways, the adult's actions played a structuring role in her interaction with the infant. The third way in which the adult structured their interaction is the most important for our discussion here. Sarah tacitly attributed to her daughter forms of social competence that Jenny did not as yet fully possess. She ascribed credit and agency to the infant for significant events and occurrences in their exchanges. For example, on one occasion she interpreted Jenny's tongue protrusion as a competent conversational bid in an exchange between them:

Sarah says, "I've never seen you do that before with your tongue, what is that?" Jenny sticks her tongue out once more, and smiles again. Then her smile goes, she becomes serious and looks down at Sarah's mouth. This time we see clearly that Sarah is sticking her tongue out at Jenny. Jenny continues looking intently at this, then she opens her own mouth slightly, and tongues a little. Although this tongue protrusion is smaller than those that preceded it, Sarah picks up on it immediately: "*Yes*, that's your *tongue!*" Jenny smiles, grins, apparently happy at what has occurred. Sarah laughs at her. Jenny throws her head back, waves her arms, and vocalizes "uuh!"

The consequence of this ascription is that the adult and infant together produce interactions that are not possible for the infant alone. Structured exchanges are actualized that are beyond Jenny's abilities in their initiation and organization. As a consequence of the form the interaction takes Jenny can appear to be, can be interpreted as, the initiator of key events. It is possible to perceive and describe the exchanges (to punctuate them, using a term from Watzlawick, Beavin, & Jackson, 1967) in such a way that Jenny has active skillful and constituting agency. This means that, inasmuch as the infant can appreciate what has occurred, she also will grasp a regularity in the social structure that she is the agent of. Once this agency is grasped, the possibility is created that the infant can subsequently initiate a structure of interaction that she has hitherto only participated in. Consequently, it would be possible for the infant, as a result of examining her exchanges with the adult, to gain mastery of those social activities that they do together, and that she has been engaged in. We are suggesting that the infant can appropriate social practices by finding an agency in them—her own—by virtue of their openness to reinterpretation.

Now clearly the way an infant does what we have called appreciating her agency in those social interactions she has been engaged in by adults is not by abstract reflection (still less by giving verbal accounts of them, as older children and adults can). Presumably her appreciation of her action is itself at the level of action. She will understand her actions in a ready-to-hand manner, and in part her understanding will take the form of moods and emotions. This is, perhaps, why the shared affect between Jenny and Sarah is important: The infant's glee and satisfaction may constitute a prerational appreciation of her own competence and agency.

It is worth saying a little more here about the ambiguity of responsibility or agency that makes this appreciation possible. Earlier the semantic ambiguity of practical activity was mentioned; one central aspect of this ambiguity is the polysemy of agency and responsibility in human action. This ambiguity is clearly apparent in our everyday experience, once we look for it. It is one of the reasons that we have a legal system, soap operas, gossip, and psychological clinicians. Trying to work out who did what, and why, to whom is something we all spend much of our time doing, and doing socially, talking and perhaps arguing together to get it straight. This fascinating but frustrating practice would not be necessary if agency were not a polysemous matter: if it were not the case that the nature of a person's responsibility for an act is generally a matter of interpretation. This is not to deny that we generally have an unproblematic and doubt-free understanding of people's responsibility (including our own) in our everyday ready-to-hand practice. Agency and responsibility are contextual: They are unproblematic in the single context one has when engaged in a ready-to-hand project, but polysemous if one considers alternative contexts, in an unready-to-hand mode. Both gossip and the law courts deal with breakdowns in social practices. (And if all context is removed, agency becomes totally opaque and ungrounded, as happens in present-at-hand psychological and philosophical theories of determinism or free will.)

The way adults influence young children through their interactions with them has been described, by Bruner, Cole, and others, in terms of the metaphor of "scaffolding." As Damon and Colby point out in Chapter 1 of this volume, the metaphor is not fully adequate, because the infant, viewed as the "building," is not conceived as being active in the developmental construction process. Literally, scaffolding is a framework that holds a passive structure in place until external efforts to construct it have been completed. The metaphor here is a mechanical one, less adequate even than the organic, biological metaphors (accommodation, differentiation, etc.) used by cognitive developmentalists. Both mechanical and biological metaphors miss the semantic character of human action; physical and organic systems have no equivalent to this psychological level of organization (Langer, 1967). An appreciation of the semantics of action, and the consequent polysemy and perspectival nature of social activity, is essential to the understanding of social development. Only when we recognize the intrinsic plurivocality of social exchanges—their necessary openness to several interpretations—can we begin to understand how the infant can appropriate and take over agency and expertise in social interaction. The infant is not "tricked into believing that this agenda arose spontaneously from within," as Damon and Colby critically describe attribution-theoretic conceptions of social change; she spontaneously and creatively gains increased control over forms of interchange she constructs together with her mother. On the other hand, if we continue to view social interaction in mechanical or biological terms, then we will be unable to find any sources of agency within it. Agency in an interaction can be appropriated by a socially naive infant only because a social episode can be opened to new ways of understanding it, and this is a semantic phenomenon that would not be possible if social exchanges were simply sequences of objectively describable events.

I want to go a little further and suggest that the infant develops her social agency and her independence as a skillful social being as a consequence of being involved in deeply intimate exchanges; so intimate, in fact, that there is great ambiguity about who is responsible for the course that interaction takes. This implies that the two themes that Selman and Yeates (Chapter 3, this volume) call autonomy–agency and intimacy–sharing are indeed, as they argue, closely interrelated in their developmental significance. Skillful agency or social expertise is always a development that is relative to a particular social group (as anyone traveling to a foreign culture rapidly appreciates), and it is a construction that only intimate membership in that group makes possible.

Moral Confrontation Among Young Adults

The second study to be described was an interpretive look at confrontations occurring among college students. The young adults participated, in groups of eight friends assigned to two teams, in an analog task in which they played a modified version of the Prisoners' Dilemma game (cf. Haan, Aert, & Cooper, 1985, for procedural details and a quantitative analysis of the sessions; the results of the author's interpretive analysis have been described in Packer, 1985b). As in the infant study, videorecordings were the basis of a hermeneutic analysis. The aim was to examine several occasions of a particular kind of confrontation that occurred when an agreement to cooperate was made and then broken by the team that was winning the most points. On these occasions the young adults were faced with a breakdown in their joint social activity.

First, three ways of understanding action were reviewed: as a unique mode of engagement in the world (the ready-to-hand); as aspects of emotion; and as rhetorical, having a social influence on others. From these common threads were drawn that provided a methodological focus: vertical and horizontal "movements" in social interaction, movements that involve changes in certain fundamental structures of social exchange. The first of these structures is the *intimacy* among the people involved; the second is the *social and moral stances* people adopt. These structures or aspects of social activity, among others, have been examined and described in detail by de Rivera and his students (de Rivera, 1977, 1981). They seem to be fundamental to our social interactions and social worlds. In their chapter of this volume Selman and Yeates also attend in their research to distancing and intimacy movements that are the result of the social strategies children employ in pair therapy. A third methodological focus was the "mythology" of the discourse: the way events were described in participants' accounts. Here particular attention will be paid to the rhetorical aspects of social action in these confrontations: to the way in which people's actions moved and influenced one another, not necessarily in a planned and deliberate way. This aspect of social action is most closely tied to the topic of the influences, especially the developmental influences, that social interaction has upon the people engaged in it.

This study provided some further indications about the way people take stock of their own actions when a breakdown occurs in ongoing practical activity. We have suggested that a reflexive attitude vis-a-vis one's own actions, in combination with the inherent ambiguity of all social action, together with the fact that socially skilled people inevitably engage others (sometimes naive and unskilled, like the infant) in their cultural and subcultural practices, can be a source of social development. Unlike reflection upon the physical realm, reflection on social action always involves the possibility of reinterpretation; of reascribing agency, and reinterpreting events that have taken place. The term *reflection* is misleading when we are discussing this examination of action because the word suggests that we can accurately "mirror" something when we turn to look at it. With a semantic domain such as practical social activity this could never be done; every description, every look at a social episode is an interpretation and reinterpretation.

Let us sketch the circumstances in which the college students found themselves, and the typical course of events in a session. The young people had been playing the Prisoners' Dilemma (for points worth one cent apiece), modified to allow much interaction among participants, in a psychology experiment at the University of California, Berkeley, campus. Within a short time one team had rapidly pulled ahead in points (this was a consequence of the contingencies of the "payoff" matrix used in Prisoners' Dilemma), and the losers soon started to feel bored and frustrated. Shortly afterward they decided that the best way for both teams to gain points was to cooperate. The teams talked together and agreed that they would play cooperatively. Then, in 4 of the 10 sessions I examined, the team of winners very rapidly broke this agreement, playing competitively so that they gained points at the losers' expense (the losers had points taken away from them).

This was a trivial and minor moral confrontation, of course, for obvious ethical reasons that we need not go into, but it is one that is still of interest. One reason for not dismissing it is that those involved in the confrontations gave many indications that they themselves took it seriously. Another reason it is an interesting situation is that the motivation on the part of the team of winners is a little harder to understand than it is in the couple of occasions where the losing team cheated. There, "everyone" understood that they did this simply *because* they were losing. In such cases their status in the game justified their action, which was consequently not seen as a problem morally. With the winning team cheating, the students seemed to be thrown into a much more problematic moral confrontation. This was largely because (to explain things in terms of discoveries that actually were made only far along into the analysis) the ways the two teams understood the "burning" were very different. The teams had divergent interests in the way the game should end, and these provided incommensurate contexts within which the broken agreement was taken up and understood very differently.

But having said this, it is crucial to add that the young people themselves did not appreciate this basic aspect of their situation and interaction. And this initial lack of appreciation of the multiple ways of understanding the situation in turn forced them to examine that situation, and their interactions up to that point. It is the nature of this deliberation on events that we shall describe. To anticipate, the major phenomenon of interest will be the manner in which *concerns* that were apparent to the researcher at the beginning of the confrontation at the level of unreflective action and the *interests* members of the two teams had developed in the game became, toward the end of confrontation and the beginning of resolution, issues that were explicitly talked about by the participants. Here again, we shall suggest we are seeing that people's "appreciation" of their interactions, their deliberation about it, has significant developmental influence.

Phase One

The initial form of the confrontation was a rapid and thorough reorganization of the interactants' participation—both their action and their way of understanding what was going on. The losing team withdrew rapidly from their involvement in the game and from their participation with the other team, showing a rapid change in their mood. They refused to continue to play the game, and they sometimes refused to talk to the winning team, resorting instead to an occasional shouted sarcastic remark. Their uptake of the burning was one of outrage, disbelief, and shock. Any doubt we might have about whether the burning really constituted a breakdown in the ongoing practical activity for the teams was banished by the character of this first reaction.

Note that the withdrawal in response to the breakdown that the burning constituted was not one in which the teams stepped back and detached themselves, contemplating the event in a theoretical manner. This would have been a move to the present-at-hand mode, and we have argued that this does not happen while practical activity continues (though it is the mode upon which cognitive developmentalists base their theories of moral thinking and action). Although the losing team withdrew from their previous course of practical activity, their withdrawal was itself unreflective, structured by strong emotion, and took the form of rapid interpersonal and social movements of distancing and superiority. In this initial phase there was very little in the way of reflective "glossing" by participants: They did not make comments upon or describe to one another what they were doing. Comments during this phase were typically inarticulate; there had been no time (or need) to examine and articulate what was happening. For example:

Well, that shows a lack of. . . . eh. . . . [He points at the winning team.]

No reasons are offered in accounts such as these (nor, it seems, were they considered necessary); instead the losing team acted in an immediate way, showing distrust and disdain. These movements correspond (in the language we slowly developed to talk about this) to two concerns, over trust and responsibility. By *concern* we mean a problematic aspect of the others' actions. Trust was a concern because, colloquially, it had been broken. It was not clear what the winning team would do next; whether they could be trusted. Responsibility was a concern because it was unclear in what manner the winning team had acted. Was it malevolence, foolishness, or prankishness? These concerns were apparent in the losing team's action towards the burners; their anger, rejection, and self-protective withdrawal:

Session leader: The winning team wants to negotiate; does the losing team?
Gail (losing team): No more, no more.
Pat (losing team): We don't trust them.
Gail: We're not playing anymore

Phase Two

The losing team's understanding of the burning was very different from that of the winning team. They placed the "immoral" act (or found it) in a different context. However, the teams themselves did not recognize this divergence: Each took for granted that their way of understanding was the "real" one. Phase two involved a progressive articulation by each team of aspects of their own understanding. In some sessions this proceeded until the teams gained an appreciation of the others' grasp of events; the first manifestation of this was the granting that the others' accounts were not "wrong" descriptions of the "facts," but were alternative and so at least provisionally valid ways of grasping things.

The teams' motivation for giving accounts to one another was a practical one: Each team had a notion of what should be done next in the session. The losing team wanted the burners to compensate for breaking the agreement, while the winning team wanted the losing team to continue playing the game, and not make such a fuss about the burning. Since these lines of action were incompatible, members of both teams needed to give accounts to the others that justified their own course of action. The losing team, faced with the winning team's seeming recalcitrance about undoing the wrong they had done, began to formulate accusations of the burners that were increasingly explicit and articulated. In some sessions members of the losing team demanded restitution; in others they were contemptuous. In response members of the winning team were generally dismissive of these accusations, and frequently joked. However, as the impasse continued, the winning team felt an increased pressure and irritation. Consider, for example, the following remarks, all made over a short period of time by Bob, a member of the winning team, talking to an angry losing team:

We only did it for the humor of it. We'll give you a. . . . we'll give you a certain amount of points, then we. . . .
We feel shitty about this.
You're not very logical about this.
Well, this is, hey! Like, we gotta negotiate. We'll give you all of the points that you lost.

Bill, on the losing team, simply replies: "Shine on!"
Talk such as this did not take the form of appeals to justificatory principles, and was not reasoned justification in the sense of logical argumentation. Generally justifications took the form of descriptions of the events that had occurred; of the "facts of the matter" that each team understood had taken place. What seemed to be happening was that each team took for granted their own understanding of events, although this understanding was structured by the interests (as winners and losers) that had arisen in the game, and by the concerns (over trust and responsibility) that the burning gave rise to. Consequently, for each team their justification to the others needed only to point out the "salient facts" of what had happened.

This lack of any doubt of the veracity of their understanding should not be surprising; the young adults were only beginning, as they tried to move one another, to articulate the way they had prereflectively understood things. As a consequence, however, while the concerns seen in the first phase were perhaps even more apparent to an observer in the actions of phase two, and could be seen structuring the discourse between the two teams, they were not themselves talked about. Instead, the major issue the teams talked about was the number of points they had won or lost. Even here, on this apparently entirely objective matter, there were different interpretations. Generally both teams gave accounts that presumed they had lost points. In one session, for example:

LM1 We want the points back, like, we got burnt the second time.
WM2 We would have more points. We didn't realize that we would have more points [i.e., if they hadn't burned again].

So in the second phase there was examination of events, and the beginning of giving persuasive accounts, both of which built upon the unreflective withdrawal of phase one. As yet the accounts were about the "facts" of what had occurred, with no move by the teams to uncover and examine their taken-for-granted way of understanding their interaction.

Phase Three

In the third phase the ambiguity of what had transpired, and the perspectival character of the teams' accounts of it, became appreciated for the first time by the young people themselves. This recognition seemed to be a sudden one, and it was marked in several ways. The accounts of "facts" suddenly became conditional, phrased as involving a supposition now understood as questionable, possibly counterfactual. The "issue" of the second phase, that of points won and lost, vanished to be replaced in some of the sessions by new issues: the hypocrisy of the losing team, the winning team's motivation in the game (to "play" or to "make money"), whether broken trust can be restored, and the differences in status (as "winners" and "losers") at the start of the game. These issues all involved a new way of understanding events, with a variety of dimensions of motivation becoming suddenly ambiguous and at issue. The issues corresponded to the concerns acted upon in the earlier phases. Needless to say, they were not raised in a calm, reflective manner; they were hot topics of accusation and remorse.

To summarize, the confrontation among the students took the form of each team's attempting to move the other to act in the way that team found morally appropriate. This led to an articulation of the "facts," and an increased spelling out of events, starting from an understanding of what had happened that was holistic and almost inarticulate. This response to the breakdown and to the reorganized situation after the burning involved what we have called practical deliberation: an articulation of accounts of events, describing events in a way that purported (in linguistic structure and manner of presentation) to be objective and neutral, but that involved, from an observer's perspective, understanding that was organized by the interests and concerns people had come to adopt, due to the tasks and kinds of engagement in their social situation. People's accounts of what had happened started as global, undifferentiated descriptions ("You guys screwed off!"), but became more articulated statements of the events that stood out. The accounts were at first about the "facts of the matter," and only later did some of the young adults begin to recognize that there were at least two discrepant ways of understanding events, two perspectives on their social praxis, and so come to appreciate the ambiguity of their own interaction. And as this took place, the concerns and interests that had structured activity became talked about as issues, no longer acted upon in an unreflective, unquestioned manner.

Practical deliberation such as one sees here is a form of reflection in practical social activity that cannot be regarded as an appeal to logical or moral principles or as transactive reasoning, that cannot be accurately described in terms of logical argumentation. Yet deliberation has an organization that makes it a strong candidate as motivator of social and even moral development. Put simply, what goes on is that people (motivated by the practical problems of a confrontation with others) look back at, describe, and inevitably interpret what they have done. In doing this, they begin to recognize the interests that played a structuring role in their initial understanding of events, and they begin to appreciate that there are other possible ways of understanding things.

Again the plurivocality of social action is central here. But notice that, while action is ambiguous when one turns and deliberates upon it, it is unambiguous while one is absorbed in a practical project. The college students' action was unproblematic before the burning occurred. Here the teams had a common project, which provided a common perspective to their action. After the burning the teams' actions clashed. The confrontation led to a reinterpreting and reappropriation of what had taken place, recognizable only if one understands practical activity to be perspectival. In this case the students' different uptake of the burning and of their own activity was the result of being "winners" or "losers" early in their interaction.

It seems that this "uncovering" of concerns and interests is one way in which people deal with a confrontation. What might be its developmental consequences? At the least, this deliberation and uncovering appear to foster resolution of the confrontation; renewed action in the game generally occurred in those sessions where the teams came to appreciate the existence of each other's interpretations of events. Some teams avoided deliberation; some, for example, decided to play on at random rather than address the betrayed agreement. In such cases, confrontation persisted in the form of maintained distance and distrust.

The strategy in this section has been not to attempt to demonstrate that practical deliberation upon action has actually stimulated development (which would require a longitudinal research strategy), but instead to look to see whether the *conditions* for development could be found, the seeds, as it were, in the course of significant episodes of social interaction. One important consequence of viewing social interaction or social process as practical activity is a rethinking of the relationship between action and thinking or reflection. Deliberation about social conflicts and social relationships does not occur in a contextless setting. We never come to a moral issue in an uninvolved manner, without prior history. Deliberation on a social process or a moral concern starts with what has already happened, and is an articulation or the giving of an account of events in context. Accounts are articulated as part of the ongoing social interaction: Deliberation is itself a social activity. Accounts are oriented toward other people; they are directed toward pragmatic persuasive purposes, and they are built on ways of understanding events that are necessarily not impartial. Deliberation is not theorizing; understanding sociamainteraction is not like formulating a theory. There is a tendency to assume, when confrontations such as these occur, that they are well-defined disagreements to which explicit decision-making rules can be applied. But is there a clearly defined problem in the confrontations between the young students? Surely it changes its character several times, from phase to phase. At one time the problem is to get reparation for the burning; at another to decide upon a fitting course of action to recommence the game; at still another to convince others that they have misunderstood things. And the problems faced by the losing team are not the same as those the winning team have to deal with; they are complementary rather than identical. And they are at all times practical problems, not theoretical disagreements, or differences of opinion. The endpoint of these confrontations resembles the beginning of a Kohlbergian hypothetical dilemma: The interests and concerns of the parties involved are finally laid out in an articulate manner, albeit preliminarily. And this in itself seems to foster a resolution of the conflict, rather than being the starting point for argumentation.

TOWARD AN ACCOUNT OF SOCIAL AND MORAL DEVELOPMENT

Any account of development has three components. The first is a view of the relationship between people and their world; the second is the telos or direction in which development is considered to move; the third is a mechanism, a force, a process or activity that drives, motivates, causes, or generates that movement. (The multiplicity of terms reflects the diversity of levels—mechanical, organic, individual, social—on which this third component has been placed.) These three will be interrelated: The course of development can reasonably be viewed as more adequate functioning of the relationship with the world and the telos must be furthered by the process that results in development.

In this third and final section an attempt will be made to construct, rather speculatively, an account of social and moral development that does justice to the view of social interaction that has been described. Obviously any such account must be tentative, since little developmental research has thus far been conducted within a hermeneutic perspective. We want to explore the question of what a general account of social development looks like if we adopt the view that social interactions are forms of practical activity, and are structured in the ways described above. In doing so we want to propose the general outlines of an alternative to the structuralist account of development (and formalist approaches in general). On the other hand we don't want to hold to one alternative way of thinking about development that seems to be reappearing: the accretion view, in which children differ from adults in the size of their knowledge base, but not in the qualitative ways that Piaget above all grasped so well. We will then fit this account of social development into an overarching account of the development of moral concerns and practices, proceeding here by interpreting an already existing account of ethical development—that of Soren Kiekegaard—in terms of fluent practical activity. But first it is helpful to sketch the three developmental components described as they appear in cognitive developmentalism.

Cognitive Developmentalism

If we examine Piaget's account of cognitive development in terms of these components, we find that he conceived of people as individuals who are acting instrumentally on the world, and who consequently come to construct systems of knowledge about the world. He viewed the endpoint to cognitive development as achieving knowledge about the world similar in form to the operational intelligence that he took physicists to have: the result of planned operations upon objects, guided by theory and by the generation of hypotheses.

It is useful here to consider Piaget's work in the light of the Kantian philosophy that guided it. Piaget intended to give a developmental extension to Kant's notion that our experience is structured by transcendental categories of space, time, causality, and object. Piaget's earlier studies traced the construction of these categories in the instrumental actions of infants, and his later work was a continuation of this project. Piaget, like Kant, regarded knowledge as having an epistemological priority over action; as a result his account of the relationship between person and world has troublesome aspects. Kant described himself as a transcendental idealist, but at the same time an empirical realist. On the one hand "our experience is not limited to the private domain of our own representations, but includes an encounter with 'empirically real' spaciotemporal objects" (Allison, 1983 p. 7). On the other hand there are "subjective conditions in terms of which alone the human mind is capable of receiving the data for thought or experience" (Allison, 1983 p. 7). Objects are ideal in that they cannot be described independently of these conditions. "We assert, then, the empirical reality of space. . . . and yet at the same time we assert its transcendental ideality" (Kant, 1781/1965, p. 72, cf. p. 79).

This combination of (transcendental) idealism and (empirical) realism, while consistent as an ahistorical epistemology, translates problematically into a developmental psychology. The idealist aspect gives mind a priority over world that would seem to preclude changes in mental categories or structures. If the categories are genuinely transcendental they will not change (save perhaps in a preordained unfolding unrelated to experience, as in Chomsky's interpretation of rationalist epistemology). Piaget's world alternates unhappily between an unknowable realm of things–in–themselves and a concrete objective universe, a naive scientistic realism. Although Piaget gave strong theoretical emphasis to the interaction between subject and environment, this underlying naive realism leads to an odd equivocation in his statements about just what kind of organization the environment has. Is it made up of atomistic sensations? He sometimes talked that way. Or do objects have, in some subject-independent way, organization such as mass, length, and duration? It is hard to see how a new experience can resist assimilation to an old scheme, and require accommodation of that scheme, unless it has some structure of its own; something that resists assimilation by mind. But, on the other hand, how can we describe a structure that is intrinsically unknowable? One might say that, paradoxically, assimilation and accommodation always occur, for Piaget, as processes of interaction between a knower and the unknown. Damon and Colby are making, I think, a related point in their chapter in this volume when they point to an apparently unbridgeable gulf between pattern alpha and pattern beta; how can the mind accommodate to an unknown object?

For Kant this was less of a problem: The mind imposed categories upon our experience of things, while the things–in–themselves, although they must be considered real, were forever unknowable. Kant was not concerned with the possibility of historical or personal changes in these categories. As soon as one tries to fit such changes into the epistemological position Kant adopted, one runs into the problem of explaining how the "unknowable" influences (and forces accommodation of) the structures of knowledge. This epistemic split between subject and object shows the present-at-hand nature of the theories of both Kant and Piaget, and explains the difficulty of extending them to social understanding and social action. Ironically, Piaget gave us detailed and sensitive descriptions of ready-to-hand activity in his three studies of infancy (1951, 1952, 1954). There, he traced the Kantian categories—space, time, causality, and object—in the practical activity of children in their first 2 years: the sensorimotor stage. Unfortunately, in subsequent stages sensorimotor knowledge is, according to Piaget, reconstructed at new levels of representation, and he generally talks as though it is superseded and replaced. (And even in the sensorimotor stage children's activity is, for Piaget, instrumentally oriented and an individual construction.)

There is a parallel ambiguity to the development of knowledge in the cognitive–developmental scheme of things. Development is the progressive construction of representations of reality. Although nominally this is both a logical and an empirical process, at the same time it frequently has the connotation of a movement toward reconstruction of a fixed, objective reality (Bruner, 1986; Shweder, 1982). Adequately equilibrated cognitive constructions are, paradoxically, representations of an autonomous and defined real world. Piaget emphasized the development of reversibly applied cognitive operations, which he saw growing out of a reflexive abstraction from the instrumental nature of interaction with the material world. The mature form of representation of the world, seen from the cognitive–developmental perspective, explicitly parallels that of the physical or biological scientist. Piaget finds it helpful to "compare the elementary processes of the child's intelligence to those used by scientific thought" in understanding the object concept (1952, p. 87), and he finds three common methods: anticipation (prediction); experimentation; and production of the totality of a deductive system. So in the Piagetian model, cognitive development is a movement toward formal (and formalizable) operational intelligence, which has constructed an understanding of reality that is (in a covered-up way) in true correspondence with a real material world.

One test of the hermeneutic approach will be whether it can solve problems such as these. In place of instrumental, technical action, and instead of reflection as a rational reconstruction of this action into formalized, abstract representational structures, can we find an account of development, its telos and motive, that better explains empirical evidence and has increased internal coherence?

A Hermeneutic Account of Social and Moral Development

Relationship in the World

First, how shall we understand the interaction between people and their social world? This is the topic of the first section of this chapter; the view I have proposed is that people are reflective practitioners (the phrase is Schon's, 1983); they are always engaged in practical activity of a variety of kinds, and this is their primary mode of engagement in the world. Social reality is not an objective matter: It rests on and is constituted by the beliefs, wishes, interpretations, and actions of its members. Yet at the same time it has an objective aspect: "An institutional world is experienced as an objective reality. It was there before [the individual] was born, and it will be there after his death. He must "go out" and learn about [it], just as he must learn about nature. This remains true even though the social world, as a humanly produced reality, is potentially understandable in a way not possible in the case of the natural world" (Berger & Luckmann, 1967, p. 60).

We can contrast the sorts of conflicts that arise on the practical level, for someone engaged in practical social projects, with those experienced by a Kantian or Piagetian intellectual subject. Breakdown of ready-to-hand practical activity discloses structures of practice, and conflicts in practices, which are not the products of individuals, or of thought alone. As social agents, we cannot simply construct our world the way a transcendental ego could. The social world resists in tangible ways our efforts to impose structure on it, because it is a joint social construction that we as individuals are partly able to structure but that also structures us (Giddens, 1976, terms this the double structuration of social reality).

Breakdown of a variety of kinds inevitably occurs in social interactions of any duration and complexity, and motivates the move from the ready-to-hand mode to that of the unready-to-hand. These are occasions where action becomes problematic. Such breakdown and conflict may spur development in the realm of practical social activity, just as we think forms of logical conflict do in intellectual development. However, the kinds of conflict that occur as breakdowns in social activity are very different from intellectual conflicts, though we tend to use the latter as our base metaphor for conflict. Even reasoned intellectual discussion, though it makes reference to the fruits of detached theoretical reflection, does so while embedded in ongoing practical social activity. And disagreements that are apparently "objective"—over "the facts of the matter"—are not just surrounded but actively structured by interests and concerns.

The Telos

In what direction do social and moral developments proceed, in their practice (as distinct from thinking)? The telos I want to emphasize is that of becoming increasingly skilled and fluent in social practical activity. I want to propose that social fluency is at least as important a telos for social development as is the formation of explicit theories, principles, and hypotheses about the social world. (I say "at least" because I believe we cannot formulate good theories *unless* we have practical social understanding.) More explicitly, social development consists in increasingly broadened fluency: becoming socially fluent in an increased range of situations or subworlds; the family, the workplace, and so on (cf. Schutz & Luckmann, 1974, for an exploration of the concept of the many distinct worlds that people act in).

Cognitive developmentalists have applied Piaget's conception of development to the social realm also, and looked for and theorized about the kind of development that involves becoming more and more explicitly aware of the fixed features of an objectively describable social reality. As a consequence, I think, these researchers have tended to focus on one kind of social development to the exclusion of another equally important kind. The mature individual, it is assumed, is explicitly aware of, and can form theories about, the habits and practices, the roles and norms of individuals, organizations, and cultures.

There is more to this focus than a simple analogizing between physical and social cognition. We value the development of principled reasoning because we believe that it frees us from internal contradictions and logical conflicts, in both the interpersonal and instrumental realms. Perhaps because this is what we value in our professional lives, as psychologists and social scientists, we have tended to look for the same burgeoning ability in children and young adults. We look for lucid, clear, and noncontradictory explanations of social events, coupled with principled reasoning about social action and moral dilemmas. Consider, for example, the table of Transacts ("reasoning about another's reasoning") in Berkowitz, Oser, and Althof (Chapter 11, this volume). Reading through the glosses they provide of paradigm examples of the different acts, one has a sense of overhearing a polite intellectual disagreement in the faculty club:

Do you understand or agree with my position?
No, what I am trying to say is the following . . .
Would you go to this implausible extreme with your reasoning?

. . . and so on. Of course Berkowitz and Oser code very different kinds of utterance when they study young children; my point is that this is the kind of conversation that is the model against which children's talk is compared. As academics we have been socialized into practices such as these, and take them for granted. This is a valuable kind of social development, and one we should continue to study and foster, but there is a danger of ignoring its complement. For social development is also occurring when children become skilled in various forms of social action to the extent that these practices become habitual: that they become, so to speak, socially fluent at performing them. This is development even though the children become no more explicitly conscious of those skills; even though they do not behave like social scientists, if by that one means forming theories, testing hypotheses, and generally adopting an instrumental stance toward the social world.

The telos of development must not be confused with a final endpoint; this would be misleading. Human development is historically open ended: Its highest achievements change over history. Development cannot anticipate its ending; it cannot even anticipate a specific historically grounded final form; to anticipate it would be to have already achieved it in some preliminary form. Development as a process can only deal with *local* improvements and with proximal change. So to say that the telos of development is fluency is to say not that this fully defines the *outcome*, but that this is what is proximally sought.

We are socially fluent when our actions form a coherent unity; when they are organized by an underlying concern (e.g., as was the case with the young college students before the burning took place). A persisting concern gives us a project, structure, or organization to our actions, and enables a clear identification of the "facts," precisely because they are always aspects of a perspectival frame of understanding that has not been uncovered as the basis for action. Fluent action is action structured by a concern.

Accomplished social conduct has similarities, then, to habitual skills like touch typing or playing the piano (Sudnow, 1978), but it is a far more complex and subtle phenomenon. A variety of different kinds of concern arise in practical social activity: concerns over moral responsibility, intimacy, and doubtless many others. Emotions play a central role. Multiple social worlds must be smoothly recognized, entered, and left (Berger & Luckmann, 1967; Schutz, 1970). Meaningful social networks must be creatively modified. Accounts must be articulated, excuses made, descriptions given, reasons provided. Each of many social subworlds— classroom, playground, research laboratory, boardroom, bedroom—has its unique practices that "count." Certain characteristics will be common to all of them: the structuring role of emotionality, movements of intimacy, movements of responsibility and status.

Now, in each subworld fluent action will be possible only insofar as one finds forms of practice lead that to success. Fluency in practical activity occurs when one's practices are meaningfully connected. For some activities (e.g., tennis) success criteria have been laid down by prior consensus. For other activities (e.g., teaching) what counts as success is more open to interpretation. Nonetheless, fluency is a value-laden concept, and a value-laden phenomenon: to achieve fluency is to know how it is to do things right.

Several areas of research bear directly or indirectly on my notion of social fluency, including studies of habits and skills in sport (e.g., Neisser), and studies of experts and novices in a variety of domains (e.g., Benner, 1984; Dreyfus & Dreyfus, 1986). These studies have shown that experts have a perception or way of understanding the subworld of their expertise that is qualitatively different from that of novices. There is a spontaneity to expert and skilled performance that is the consequence of having developed a creative understanding of the demands of a situation. There is a "flow" to fluent practical activity that cannot be accurately cut apart into goals and instrumental actions, nor does it need to be. Consider tennis, or teaching, or bridge, or lovemaking. Basic principles, in the logical sense, enter into none of these. People who are learning a new skill do not employ or refer back to formal principles. Instead, they begin their learning by applying rules of thumb and maxims ("third hand high" in bridge, " weight on the leading edge" in skiing, "put on your best face" in a job interview) and a few exemplary prototypical actions. As they become familiar with the domain of the skill, they become able to organize greater spans of action, and their understanding of what they are doing becomes more holistic: Relevant aspects of the situation stand out apparently of their own accord, and do not need to be searched for. For example, beginning science teachers appear to move through several forms of practical activity in their first year in the classroom. Each is organized by a distinct predominant concern: problems carried over from preservice training; survival in the classroom; how to teach; how it is that students learn (Russell, 1986).

The Influence on Development of Social Interaction

I want to propose that the influence that social interaction has on social and moral development stems from the practical deliberation that this interaction fosters. The role of interaction in development of fluent social practice has been the topic of research in a number of subworlds, including those of nursing, architecture, psychotherapy, and teaching. For example, Schon (1983) analyzed exchanges between expert and novice in several areas of expertise, including architectural design and psychotherapy. Development here is acquisition of skill in the practices constituting competent professional performance.

Experience alone is not enough to bring about the development of social fluency, and the move from one of these stages to the next. What has to happen, it seems, is that the frame that organizes action at each stage has to be uncovered. The student teachers studied by Russell (1986), for example, have to appreciate the concern that organizes their action at one level before they are able to move beyond that way of acting to a new stage. By *appreciate* I don't mean necessarily conscious awareness; what is required is that the concern either is fulfilled or fails; in either case it can be (perhaps must be) abandoned. A teacher can feel that concern over surviving—generally managing a class so that chaos is staved off—dissolves because he or she can generally keep classes in control, or this concern may be abandoned as an inadequate way of organizing teaching activity, because it ignores the actions that constitute "teaching" (the concern of the next stage). Fulfillment and failure can occur together: Once a concern is satisfied its inadequacy at a higher level may become appreciated.

This is where telos and "mechanism" converge. Concerns become addressed and uncovered by practical deliberation. We can see this with the college students. Deliberation together led to an articulation and explicit entering into discourse of the concerns manifest in action, and of other components of the framework organizing that action: the emotions consequent on the burning; interests in the outcome of the game. When expert practitioners supervise novices, one central thing they do is surface and criticize the novice's framing of a practical situation, and talk themselves in a way that frames events in a more adequate manner (Schon, 1983). In such cases deliberation is guided by an expert. For the college students' interactions, no expert was present and consequently deliberation took a more serendipitous course, with the result that only in some sessions did concerns become uncovered. It was suggested earlier that young children develop forms of expert conduct not in a deliberate and planful manner but, first, because they find themselves already involved in meaningful social practices: the culture's forms of conduct that accomplish the myriad of everyday social tasks. It is impossible for a child not to be caught up and engaged in social praxis, short of autistic withdrawal. Children ultimately take up and acquire some degree of control and guidance over actions they find themselves already doing.

The General Form of an Account of Moral Development

Finally, moral development also can be understood as a sequence of forms of practical activity, and as motivated by a search for meaningfulness, expertise and fluency in practical action.

We shall begin to justify this claim by examining an account of ethical development that is very different from the view of moral judgment central to cognitive developmentalism: the account to be found in the writings of Soren Kierkegaard (1968, 1971). Kierkegaard's writings involve a conception of moral development that is an existential opposite in several respects to rationalist theories such as Piaget's and Kohlberg's. Kierkegaard described ethical development as the progressive movement through distinct ways of living or "spheres." This account can be interpreted (without, it is to be hoped, too great a distortion) in the same terms as the developmental account that has been given: Social fluency is the telos, social reality is viewed as co-constructed, and deliberation on action is the motivator of development.

Kierkegaard distinguished four spheres, which he named the Aesthetic, the Ethical, Religiousness A, and Religiousness B. In addition there is a preliminary undifferentiated stage, the Present Age. These four resemble stages that a structuralist would recognize in that, as Kierkegaard describes them, they form an ordered sequence of maturity, self-development, and understanding, and are qualitatively distinct from one another, each involving a reorganization and a loss of the forms of activity of the previous way of living.

But there are several important differences between Kierkegaard's description and a structuralist characterization of developmental progression. Development for Kierkegaard is a matter of the struggle to form a self, a praxis that is correlative with the search for a meaningful way of living. Each sphere is a temporary solution to these problems; each fails precisely when it is lived to the fullest, in the most committed manner. In Kierkegaard's account the move from one sphere to the next and progression within a sphere are emotional and valuative movements. The impetus to move on is provided not by logical contradiction or cognitive conflict, but by a leveling out: a meaninglessness and loss of significance to the world that is experienced as despair, and that renders action impossible. At the end of each sphere, a form of life whose telos was finding a coherent scheme of meaning to the world and to action results, instead, in a breakdown of coherence. Each sphere ends in despair, when it is discovered that the way of organizing one's life that it entails has failed to fulfill the search for coherent and meaningful social relations. The transition to the next sphere requires a leap, with associated anxiety and fear, rather than being a smooth and logically necessary transition. Each leap is intrinsically unreasonable, since reasons are always defined by a sphere, and the sphere that one must leap out of has ceased to provide good reasons. And since it is a leap into a new form of ready-to-hand action, one has no reflective awareness of what is to come. A further difference from the cognitivist stage progression view of development we have come to take for granted is Kierkegaard's view that the fourth sphere —Religiousness A—can itself fail, and the only move then is a return to the superficialities of the Present Age. As an example of a nonformal account of ethical development, Kierkegaard's work could well bear further examination by developmental psychologists.

Interpreted in this light, Kierkegaard's spheres represent a series of distinct forms of social fluency; of coherent and meaningful practice. Each involves a central project that provides a point of view (or, in some sense, *is* a point of view) within which situations are coherently understood. Each sphere is, at its best, a coherent way of living, a style of acting, that is fluent and meaningful. Each has its own unique central concern, providing focus and clarity to the world and enabling action to be conducted in an unproblematic manner. Fluency of action is the telos each sphere pursues, and action is fluent when it is organized as a whole project, as a coherent style of practical activity. The achievement of this fluency is what makes each of the spheres; the ultimate failure to sustain fluency leads to despair and the leap to a new sphere and lifestyle.

Now each of the spheres will be outlined in turn.

The Present Age

This is a way of living where the concerns over meaning that characterize later spheres have not become acted on. It is living and acting entirely in terms of the commonly accepted norms of one's social milieu, it is a routinization of activity rather than expert fluency of action. Kierkegaard picked the newspapers of nineteenth century Sweden as exemplifying the trivialized, gossipy form of interchange characteristic of such a life; television would now surely be the object of his attack. The Present Age—even as Kierkegaard saw it then—is one of fashion and trends; of rapidly and meaninglessly changing norms of dress, appearance, and behavior. It is a way of living and of social action characterized by superficiality, where gossip about topics and evanescent events holds more weight than careful examination of moral and social issues.

The Aesthetic Sphere

This is the first kind of search for an escape from the triviality of the Present Age. Meaning is sought through a life-style of aestheticism, where the experience of pleasure is sought, together with the avoidance of pain. The aesthete finds good divided from bad on the basis of the pleasure or displeasure involved. This first sphere breaks down because the search for pleasure requires that one be open to experiencing it, and such openness necessarily involves an absence of defense against pain. Since the world is such that we have little control over the appearance or duration of pleasurable experiences, the aesthete finds pain and disappointment as corollaries of pleasure. The best way to avoid pain is to avoid pleasure also. The interdependence of pleasure and pain and the consequent lack of any way of living that captures the first while escaping the second are what drives the aesthete to a depairing recognition of the failure of his or her projected life-style.

The Ethical

In this sphere, planning and control are the mainstays of a life-style. A person living in this sphere attempts to determine rationally how to choose the best course of action. The ethical is the sphere of trying to apply to everyday practice the fruits of detached contemplation: a concern with social roles and duties, principled and universal rule following. Standards are sought upon which decisions can be based, allowing courses of action to be followed and right to be distinguished from wrong.

The importance of choosing, of making a decision that is the "reasonable" one, is central here. The concern is not with the particularities of *what* is done, but instead with *how* it is done. Clarity of reasoning and freedom from ambiguity and impulse are seen as the way toward making morally right choices. The rational justification of one's action to other people is also central. Once a decision is made strength of will is what will bring about the correct action.

The ethical sphere collapses because coherent universal principles cannot be found, and the consequent arbitrary nature of choice undercuts the individual's ability to act. The more clarity one obtains by becoming detached and rational, the more one begins to see that any practical situation has many sides, among which no rational basis for choice among right and wrong can be found.

Religiousness A

The attempted solution to this is the sphere of Religiousness A. The person in this sphere gives up the attempt to get security through either pleasure or intellectual clarity, seeing both as futile. Absorption in the moment is the solution of this sphere, not in the hedonistic manner of the aesthetic sphere, but in giving up all efforts to control outcomes and ends. Happiness is not guaranteed by such a life-style, but the fortunate events that happen can be appreciated and enjoyed, where in the aesthetic sphere they became spoiled through anxiety over their inevitable loss.

This sphere fails in its attempt to suppress or deny one's concrete desires and wishes. Giving them up is necessary if one is to accept things, good and bad, as they come, and so be able to experience them as meaningful. But as desires are sloughed off, the distinctions between good and bad, pleasant and unpleasant, right and wrong are lost also. This leveling of significance leads again to a despair that motivates the leap to a new way of acting.

Religiousness B

The final sphere differs from the previous ones in that it gives up the attempt to achieve a coherence of action, a meaningful life-style, by developing a particular kind of internal relationship, such as aestheticizing pleasure, developing clarity, or renouncing desire. In Kierkegaard's Religiousness B one develops a constituting relationship to something outside oneself: a paradigmatic person or project that exemplifies a form of practice one can emulate. For Kierkegaard, it was Christ who was the prototypical paradigm, but the organization of this sphere would be the same with a different object of emulation. The paradigmatic project or person provides a clarity to one's actions that is quite unlike the lucidity of internal reflection that the ethical sphere seeks.

Kierkegaard's writing is an account of moral development that places meaningful action in a central position, as we have tried to do when discussing social development. As a result, we can consider the way in which moral development and social development might be interrelated, and our account goes somewhat as follows. Grounding the many social subworlds in which a person has more or less expertise we can articulate a more general level of description, and a more general concern: that of living a good life. What Kierkegaard's theory points out is that this too is a matter of fluency. Coherent and skillful action is possible in a social subworld only when a particular concern structures one's activity. Some concerns are evanescent; others have duration. Similarly, a coherent moral life-style is possible only by finding or creating an overarching concern, which provides a division between right and wrong, good and bad. Kierkegaard points out four different forms this concern can take, one for each of the spheres: the concern with pleasure; the concern with clarity and justice; the concern with openness to experience; and the concern found in a paradigmatic project accepted as one's own. Each of these concerns provides action with coherence. In contrast, one can have none of these concerns, have no concern with living the good life, have no unity to one's subworlds, and be swayed in one's action by fads and trends instead. This is what Kierkegaard called the Present Age.

Kierkegaard's account makes an interesting claim. This is that, when it comes to moral development and moral action, fluency can be achieved only temporarily. No matter which of his spheres we find ourselves trying to live fully, there is always the possibility that meaningfulness will be lost and expertise will collapse. While this may seem a pessimistic account of morality, I think it realistically reflects our sense that moral development is unlike cognitive development; its accomplishments are not automatically sustained. Both individuals and cultures are unlikely to regress in their level of cognition, but the same is not true of their ethical status. Loss of commitment, failure of nerve, weakness of the will: all these are phenomena of moral reversal, decline, and even collapse.

Interestingly the first two of Kierkegaard's spheres show similarities with the content of Kohlberg's earlier stages. But where Kohlberg then sees development proceeding to increased formalism, prescriptivism, and universalizability, for Kierkegaard it is the attempt to actualize these goals that leads to the demise of the Ethical sphere. Kierkegaard's spheres move instead to increased individualism and particularism. Is this unrealistic or unreasonable? We think not. Philosophers have by no means been able to settle on any sort of ethical "calculus" or set of principles whereby judgments of appropriate action can be made. On the contrary, recent analyses have focused on the *discord* in moral theorizing. MacIntyre (1984a, 1984b) places current ethical theory in a historical context, and argues that as an intellectual enterprise it is based on a contradiction of efforts (cf. Packer, 1985a). Consequently, those of us interested in moral development find ourselves without a rational philosophical theory of ethics. The consequence of this, though, is by no means to return to philosophically naive empiricism. Instead, we must examine the possibility that a *rational* ethical theory is an impossible achievement, for a number of reasons. The separation of psychology and philosophy as academic disciplines notwithstanding, both are the products of human efforts. Rationalist philosophy, like rationalist psychology, assumes the priority of a present-at-hand, detached, calculative kind of engagement with the world. Consequently it assumes (but does not examine) morally relevant practices such as trusting, cooperation, even betrayal.

Like Kohlberg we think there is a place where philosophy and psychology converge. Kohlberg (1971) made the claim, controversial then and now, that a philosophical theory of the adequacy of one form of ethical reasoning over another and a psychological theory of the development from one stage to the next were "one and the same theory extended in different directions" (p. 154) (just as, for Piaget, development was a matter of logic: Rational appreciation of a system's inadequacy promoted the generation of a higher-order system of greater consistency and completeness). The parallel we want to point out is between hermeneutic inquiry, as a form of philosophical activity and a basis for a psychological method, and practical deliberation, something people do with their own actions. In other words, interpretation, the articulation of accounts of one's own unreflective actions, is, rather than logical reasoning, what unites psychology and philosophy, as we are interpreting them, and finds a link between both of them and ordinary everyday human activity. Theorizing grows out of practical activity, and surpasses it in its application across different content areas and in its transcendence of temporality. But practical activity surpasses theorizing in its appreciation of the social and personal context in which practical problems appear, and its essential role in the initial *identification* of a problem.

One theme running through the chapters in this book is an interest in alternatives to a universalistic type of morality. Friendship, for example, is mentioned on several occasions. Particularistic relations are discussed as an important source of morality. Commitment and caring in these specific relationships are described as valid content in a morality (cf. Kohlberg & Higgins, Chapter 4, Youniss, Chapter 5, this volume). The detached objective universalistic perspective and the involved, participating particular perspective are clearly distinct modes of engagement in the world. An important question is which one of them has ontological or moral priority. The dominant view has been that the universalistic is primary, but there is what one might call a growing suspicion that this view is misguided, and that the particularistic mode is the primary one. But we are minimally equipped—intellectually, methodologically, or personally—to deal with this. John Gardner confronted this theme recently in fictional form, in *Mickelsson's Ghosts*. Here a professor, a philosopher of ethics, going through a profound personal crisis, finds that the intellectual tradition he has been trained in provides him with no basis for making the moral choices necessary for his life to become meaningful again. With the demise of God as a source of universally valid moral values and injunctions, various attempts have been made to find a Godlike perspective from which humanity can achieve a similar system. These attempts have failed, and Mickelsson finds himself instead growing acutely aware of his own past, and the social context of his immediate social world; of ways of understanding others that a community of people develops, scarcely graspable in a rational manner. But, in Gardner's account, Mickelsson has no way of successfully living in this new mode, and he descends into the irredeemable insanity that Nietzsche predicted would follow from the death of God. Perhaps Gardner paints too gloomy a picture of our intellectual moral condition, but the problems Mickelsson lives out and deliberates on in anxiety and guilt are genuine ones. We need, perhaps, to look beyond ideals of rationality, confront the plurivocality of everyday activity in our various social worlds, and begin our psychological study there. The approach to social development that we have sketched here focuses our attention not on the acquisition of knowledge of social phenomena, or on patterns of thinking about the world, but first of all on the development of skillful social practices.

REFERENCES

Ainsworth, M.D.S. (1969). Object relations, dependency and attachment: A theoretical view of the infant–mother relationship. *Child Development, 40*, 969–1025.

Allison, H. E. (1983). *Kant's transcendental idealism: An interpretation and defense.* Yale University Press.

Bates, E. (1976). *Language and context: The acquisition of pragmatics.* Academic.

Benner, P. (1984) *From novice to expert: Excellence and power in clinical nursing practice.* Addison-Wesley.

Berger, T., & Luckmann, T. (1967). *The social construction of reality.* Penguin.

Blasi, A. (1980). Bridging moral cognition and moral action: A critical review of the literature. *Psychological Bulletin, 88*, 1–45.

Bleicher, J. (1980). *Contemporary hermeneutics: Hermeneutics as method, philosophy and critique.* Routledge & Kegan Paul.

Bruner, J. (1986) *Actual minds, possible worlds.* Harvard University Press.

de Rivera, J. (1977). A structural theory of the emotions. *Psychological Issues, 10* (40).

de Rivera, J. (Ed.). (1981). *Conceptual encounter: A method for the exploration of human experience.* Washington: University Press of America.

Dreyfus, H. L., & Dreyfus, S. E. (1986). *Mind over machine: The power of human intuition and expertise in the era of the computer.* Free Press.

Gadamer, H-G. (1976). *Philosophical hermeneutics.* University of California Press.

Gardner, H. (1985). *The mind's new science: A history of the cognitive revolution.* Basic Books.

Gardner, J. (1985) *Mickelsson's Ghosts.* New York: Random House.

Geertz, C. (1972). Deep play: Notes on the Balinese cockfight. *Daedalus, 101* (1).

Gergen, K.J., Hepburn, A., & Comer, D. (in press) The hermeneutics of personality description. *Journal of Personality & Social Psychology.*

Giddens, A. (1976) *New rules of sociological method.* New York: Basic.

Haan, N., Aert, E., & Cooper, B. (1985) *Practical morality: Self and situation in everyday morality.* New York University Press.

Heidegger, M. (1962). *Being and time* (J. Macquarrie & E. Robinson, Trans.). Harper & Row. (Original work published 1927)

Kant, I. (1965). *Critique of pure reason.* New York: St. Martin's Press. (Original work published 1787)

Kierkegaard, S. (1968) *Fear and trembling, and the sickness unto death.* Princeton University Press.

Kierkegaard, S. (1971). *Either/or.* Princeton University Press.

Kohlberg, L. (1971). From is to ought: How to commit the naturalistic fallacy and get away with it in the study of moral development. In T. Mischel (Ed.), *Cognitive development and epistemology.* Academic Press.

Kuhn, T. (1977). *The essential tension.* Chicago: University of Chicago Press.

Langer, S. K. (1967). *Mind: An essay on human feeling* (Volume I). Baltimore and London: Johns Hopkins University Press.

Locke, D. (1983). Doing what comes morally: The relation between behavior and stages of moral reasoning. *Human Development, 26,* 11–25.

MacIntyre, A. (1984a). *After virtue: A study in moral theory.* University of Notre Dame Press.

MacIntyre, A. (1984b). Bernstein's distorting mirrors: A rejoinder. *Soundings, 67,* 30–41.

Merleau-Ponty, M. (1963). *The structure of behaviour.* Methuen. (Original work published 1942).

Nagel, T. (1986). *The view from nowhere.* Oxford University Press.

Packer, M. J. (1983). Communication in infancy: Three common assumptions examined and found inadequate. *Human Development, 26,* 233–248.

Packer, M. J. (1985a). Concealment and uncovering in moral philosophy and moral practice. *Human Development, 28,* 108–112.

Packer, M. J. (1985b). *The structure of moral action: A hermeneutic study of moral conflict.* Basel: Karger.

Packer, M. J. (1985c). Hermeneutic inquiry in the study of human conduct. *American Psychologist, 40,* 1081–1093.

Palmer, R. E. (1969). *Hermeneutics: Interpretation theory in Schleiermacher, Dilthey, Heidegger and Gadamer.* Evanston, IL: Northwestern University Press.

Piaget, J. (1951). *Play, dreams and imitation in childhood* (C. Gattegno & F. M. Hodgson, Trans.). New York: W.W. Norton Co.

Piaget, J. (1952). *Origins of intelligence in children.* Basic.

Piaget, J. (1954). *The construction of reality in the child.* Basic.

Rabinow, P., & Sullivan, W. M. (Eds.). (1979). *Interpretive social science: A reader.* Berkeley: University of California Press.

Russell, T. L. (1986). *Beginning teachers' development of knowlege-in-action.* Paper presented at the annual conference of the American Educational Research Association, San Francisco.

Schon, D. A. (1983). *The reflective practitioner: How professionals think in action.* Basic.

Schutz, A. (1970). *On phenomenology and social relations.* Chicago: University of Chicago Press.

Schutz, A., & Luckmann, T. (1974). *The structures of the life world.* London: Heinemann.

Shweder, R. A. (1982). Beyond self-constructed knowledge: The study of culture and morality. *Merrill-Palmer Quarterly, 28*, 41–70.

Stern, D. (1977). *The first relationship: Infant and mother.* Fontana/Basic Books.

Sudnow, D. (1974). *Ways of the hand: The organization of improvised conduct.* Harvard University Press.

Watzlawick, P., Beavin, J.H., & Jackson, D.D. (1967). *Pragmatics of human communication.* Norton.

Wittgenstein, L. (1972). *On certainty.* Harper & Row.

PART 5

Social Process Perspectives

CHAPTER 9

The Distinctive Features of Conversations Between Friends: Theories, Research, and Implications for Sociomoral Development

THOMAS J. BERNDT

Preparation of this paper was supported in part by grants from the W. T. Grant Foundation, the National Institute of Mental Health, and the Spencer Foundation.

In this chapter, current theories and research are used as a basis for three conclusions about the distinctive features of conversations between friends. First, friends' conversations generally are marked by greater mutuality than conversations between peers who are not close friends. Mutuality may be reflected in the amount of conversation between two children, the connectedness of their conversation, or their degree of intimate self-disclosure. Second, friends' conversations generally are more emotionally intense, in both positive and negative ways, than conversations between nonfriends. Compared to nonfriends, friends show more smiling and agreement but also more disagreement and criticism. Third, friends show more concern with equality than nonfriends do. This concern is most apparent in situations that encourage comparisons of relative performance. Friends may respond to their concern with equality by helping or sharing with each other and responding readily to each other's requests, or by competing with each other and refusing to comply with requests. The implications of these findings for current theories and future research on peer relationships and sociomoral development are discussed.

Most developmental psychologists assume that children's friendships have a strong and distinctive influence on their social and personality development (see Hartup, 1983; Selman & Yeates, Chapter 3, Youniss, Chapter 5, this volume). There is little reason to doubt that this assumption is largely valid. Nevertheless, there are relatively few studies that clearly show the special significance of friendship. Many studies that are commonly viewed as demonstrating the significance of friendship do not include any measures of friendship. These studies primarily establish that a poor reputation with peers, or low status in the peer group, is symptomatic of pervasive and long-term difficulties in social adjustment (Hartup, 1983). Few investigators have looked not only at problems that involve the peer group as a whole, but also at problems in close friendships (for an exception, see Maas, 1968).

Similarly, the theories commonly used to bolster the case for the significance of friendship do not always refer to friendship per se. Piaget (1932/1965), for example, wrote at length about the importance of mutual respect between peers for the development of rational discussions and mature moral judgments, but he said little about close friendships. Most of his examples involved a large peer group (e.g., when he discussed his own school experiences) or interactions among peers who may or may not have been close friends (e.g., when he observed children playing marbles).

There is a small amount of theoretical and empirical work that does focus on friendships per se. For instance, Sullivan (1953) emphasized the special features of close friendships in later childhood and early adolescence. He suggested that friendships at these ages are marked by a high degree of intimacy and sensitivity to each other's needs and desires (see also Youniss, 1980; Youniss & Smollar, 1985). Partly following Sullivan's lead, several researchers have directly compared interactions between friends and interactions between peers who are not close friends. In most studies, the comparisons were based primarily on measures of verbal interaction, or conversation, between friends and nonfriends.

In this chapter, the existing theories and research are used to raise questions about the distinctive features of conversations between friends. Three themes are emphasized. First, friends' conversations appear to be more mutual than those between peers who are not close friends. *Mutuality* refers to various aspects of a conversation, from the sheer amount of verbal interaction to the degree to which children are involved in a conversation and "in tune" with each other. Second, friends have more emotionally intense conversations than nonfriends, with more frequent expressions of both positive and negative emotions. Third, other features of friends' conversations are strongly affected by the situational context. Situations are important because they affect the social goals and means that friends perceive as salient. In situations that allow children to evaluate their relative performance, friends seem more concerned than nonfriends about the equality of their performance. In situations where relative performance is not an issue, differences between the conversations of friends and those of nonfriends are influenced by other goals; for example, children's attempts to get acquainted or to "make friends" with a stranger.

Because the situational context has such powerful effects, this chapter is organized around the types of situations that have been studied most intensively. The first section focuses on friends' conversations in situations that involve explicit assessments of individual children's performance. The second section focuses on friends' conversations in less structured situations, where the only explicit instruction was for children to be sociable to each other. The third section focuses on situations in which friends were asked to discuss a question or topic and try to reach a consensus. In a final section, the evidence from all types of situations is used as a basis for conclusions about the special features of friends' conversations and the effects of these conversations on children's social and moral development.

TASK-ORIENTED CONVERSATIONS BETWEEN FRIENDS AND OTHER CLASSMATES

Interactions between friends and nonfriends have often been observed as children worked on specially designed tasks. In some cases, pairs of children worked together on a single task; in other cases, two children worked at the same time at separate tasks. The children usually were told that they would receive a reward that depended on how well they did their own part of the task. Under these conditions, children were likely to be concerned about their absolute level of performance and their performance relative to that of their partner.

Cooperative Problem Solving

In two studies (Newcomb & Brady, 1982; Newcomb, Brady, & Hartup, 1979), pairs of friends or other classmates were asked to work together to build a tower with blocks or to explore a puzzle box. These tasks were designed to assess the children's social problem solving. Because the children worked with a partner rather than by themselves, the tasks can also be viewed as assessing cooperative problem solving. As in most studies of this type, the children were told that they would receive rewards for how well they did on their task. The rules for allocating rewards varied during different time periods, but these variations had little effect on the children's behavior. Regardless of the reward allocation procedure, children appear to have interpreted the situation as one in which they were expected to cooperate with their partners.

The study with the tower-building task (Newcomb et al., 1979) included boys and girls from the first and third grades. The study with the puzzle box task (Newcomb & Brady, 1982) included only boys from the second and sixth grades. The children's behavior varied little with grade or sex, however, and the findings of both studies were similar. Three major sets of findings were obtained.

First, friends showed more concern than other classmates about the equality of their efforts and outcomes. When building the tower, friends referred to equity or reciprocity norms more often than other classmates. When reporting what they had discovered about the puzzle box, friends more often shared the credit for their discoveries. These findings imply that friends were particularly motivated to treat each other as equals and, during their conversations, to remind each other that they expected to be treated as equals.

Second, friends spent more time in interaction or conversation with each other than nonfriends. In both studies, friends talked more than other classmates. In the second study, friends discussed the task more frequently. Friends also showed more affective behaviors such as laughing, smiling, and touching. Simultaneous or matching affects were examined in the second study, and friends showed more matching affects than other classmates. For example, the friends smiled more often at the same time. In other words, the friends not only conversed more with each other, but also were more affectively "in tune" with each other during their conversations.

Third, friends and classmates differed in their techniques for influencing each other's behavior. Compared to nonfriends, friends gave more mutually directed commands (e.g., "Let's put that block here") and fewer individually directed commands (e.g., "Leave that one where it is"). This difference might be described, in Piaget's (1932/1965) terms, as an indication of greater mutual respect between friends than nonfriends.

In both studies, friends showed more compliance with mutually directed commands than nonfriends. In the first study but not the second, friends showed more compliance with individually directed commands than nonfriends. These data suggest that friends were especially responsive to each other's commands or suggestions, as Sullivan (1953) had proposed. The data would be more convincing, however, if the measures were not for the sheer frequency of compliance with commands, but for the proportion of commands to which children complied. Friends might have had a higher frequency of compliance with mutually directed commands, for example, simply because they issued more commands of this type. Thus any conclusion about responsiveness to commands among friends and nonfriends must be considered tentative.

Compliance with Requests to Share

Sevevel other studies were done to test the commonsense hypothesis that friends are more generous, more helpful, and more responsive to each other's requests for prosocial behavior than nonfriends. In most studies, prosocial behavior was measured by children's sharing a crayon (or another drawing implement) as they colored a picture or design. Often, the only measures of children's conversations were the frequencies of requests for the crayon and refusals to share the crayon. A conversation consisting entirely of requests and refusals is highly constrained and somewhat unnatural. Yet because compliance with requests provides an important indicator of friends' responsiveness, these studies deserve some attention.

Nearly all the recent studies of sharing by friends and nonfriends relied on essentially the same experimental paradigm. Samples of children were paired either with a close friend or with another classmate whom they liked a moderate amount. The pairs of children were asked, next, to color a design or draw a picture. In contrast to the tasks discussed earlier, each child worked on his or her own design or picture. The children were told that they would receive a prize for their work, and that the child who did a better job would receive a better prize.

The children were allowed to use only one crayon at a time, so they needed to share it. There was a cost to sharing, because the child who shared for a longer time had less time to color and so was likely to get fewer rewards than his or her partner. When tasks are arranged in this way, the amount that children share can be used as a measure of their self-sacrifice or altruism toward their partner. Recent studies have shown, however, that children themselves perceive such tasks rather differently (e.g., Berndt, 1985). They view their primary options as trying for equality in rewards or treating the task as a contest that they can win by competing. If they aim for equality in rewards, they share the crayon equally; if they see the task as competitive, they limit their sharing so that they can work more on their own design or picture.

In one study (Berndt, 1981a), pairs of first and fourth graders were told that they would receive more rewards than their partner (three nickels versus one nickel) if they colored more on their design than their partner, but that they and their partner would receive the same number of rewards (two nickels) if they colored the same amount. An identical reward structure was used for a second task in which children had opportunities to help their partner The rewards were arranged in this way so that children could achieve equality in rewards on each trial if they spent roughly half the time helping or sharing with their partner.

The pairs of children worked on the tasks for the first time during the fall of a school year, when they were all close friends with their partners. The tasks were repeated in the spring of the year with the same pairs of children, regardless of whether or not they had remained close friends. In both the fall and the spring, fourth graders helped their partners for a longer time, and less often refused to share with them, than did first graders. These differences are consistent with Piaget's (1932/1965) hypothesis regarding an increase in mutual respect between peers. The findings should not be construed as evidence for an age change in friends' interactions because the differences were as large in the fall as in the spring, even though some pairs who were close friends in the fall were no longer close friends in the spring.

For the measures of sharing and refusals to help, grade differences were absent in the fall, but in the spring fourth graders shared for a longer time and less often refused to help their partners than did first graders. Other data from the study indicated that first graders' friendships were less stable than those of fourth graders. Thus by the spring, more first graders than fourth graders had partners with whom they were no longer close friends. The differences in first graders' and fourth graders' behavior in the spring suggest that children who were closer friends were more generous toward each other and more often complied with each other's requests for help.

Strikingly different results were found when the rules for distributing rewards were changed. The children in another study (Berndt, 1981b) were told that they would receive two nickels for each trial on which they colored more than their partner and one nickel for each trial on which they colored less. They were not given the option of equality in rewards on each trial. Under these conditions, girls shared fairly equally with close friends and with other classmates, and rarely refused or ignored requests for the crayon from either friends or other classmates. By contrast, second grade and fourth grade boys shared *less* with friends than with other classmates, although these differences were qualified by a higher-order interaction. Boys' requests for the crayon tended to be less successful when they were paired with a close friend than with another classmate, although the Sex x Friendship interaction for unsuccessful requests was only marginally significant.

Additional evidence that boys under certain conditions share less with friends than with other classmates was obtained in a second study published in the same year (Staub & Noerenberg, 1981). As in the previous study (Berndt, 1981b), the findings for sharing were comparable to those for a measure of refusals to share, but for each measure the friend–nonfriend difference was qualified by higher-order interactions.

Berndt (1982) argued that the boys' behavior in these two studies was a manifestation of the importance of equality in friendship. Because children view themselves as equal to their friends in all important respects, they are especially concerned about their performance relative to that of a friend. If placed in a situation where sharing creates a risk of seeming inferior to a friend, by getting fewer rewards than he or she, children are likely to limit their sharing so that they can be assured of getting more rewards than the friend (cf. Tesser, 1984). That is, children are likely in such situations to compete with friends rather than to share equally with them. Competition may be most obvious among boys, because boys have more positive attitudes toward competition

(Ahlgren & Johnson, 1979), but girls will also compete with friends when they view the outcome of a task as personally important (Berndt, Hawkins, & Hoyle, 1986; Tesser, 1984).

Summary

The hypothesis about friends' concern with equality helps to tie together the findings from all studies of task-oriented interactions. Four conclusions can be drawn from the findings. First, the commonsense hypothesis that friends always show more prosocial behavior toward each other and more responsiveness to each other's requests than do peers who are not close friends is false. The general hypothesis is disconfirmed not only by the recent studies, but also by other studies dating back to the 1940s (see Hartup, 1983). The research suggests instead that friends' prosocial behavior depends primarily on the process of social comparison between friends, and the importance of equality in friendship. Children share more with friends than with nonfriends when they believe they can achieve equality through sharing (Berndt, 1981a; see also Staub & Sherk, 1970). Children share less and compete more with friends than nonfriends when they believe that by sharing they may end up losing an important game or contest.

More recent studies (Berndt, 1985; Berndt et al., 1986) suggest that adolescents have a stronger preference for equal sharing over competition with friends than do younger children. These findings are consistent with Sullivan's (1953) hypothesis that friends' sensitivity to each other's needs and desires increases in later childhood and early adolescence. They are also consistent with Youniss's (1980) proposition that the increase in sensitivity is motivated by a desire for equality between friends.

Second, the characteristics of particular situations have a marked impact on what children decide to do, because these characteristics affect children's opinions about how they and their partner can achieve equality in rewards. The evidence on friends' prosocial behavior demonstrates once again the necessity to understand children's own definition of an experimental situation (cf. Bronfenbrenner, 1979). Clearly, the children in previous studies did not view their tasks simply as providing them with opportunities to share with each other. They saw each task as a game or contest that they could lose if they shared a great deal, win if they shared relatively little, or, when the task allowed it, end up in a tie with their partner if they shared equally.

Third, in most studies the pattern of results for sharing or helping paralleled that for refusals or unsuccessful requests. The parallels imply that in general, friends' conversations will vary as a function of processes such as social comparison and motives for equality, in interaction with the characteristics of specific situations. There cannot be a single theory of friends' conversations, just as there cannot be a single theory of friends' prosocial behavior. Instead, theories must be tailored to particular situations and refer to the definition of those situations to the children involved.

Finally, the differences between friends' and nonfriends' interactions should not be exaggerated. In many studies, friend–classmate differences were either marginally significant, significant for some measures but not others, or complicated by higher-order interactions. Although comparable results have been obtained in studies with comparable procedures (Berndt, 1981b; Berndt et al., 1986), there also appear to be effects of apparently minor variations in procedure. In one recent study (Jones, 1985), for example, school-aged children shared more with friends than with other classmates when working on a crayon-sharing task. In this study, the rules for distributing rewards were like those that, in previous research (Berndt, 1981b), led to less sharing between friends than between other classmates. Tokens were used as rewards, however, not the nickels used in previous research. The shift from nickels to tokens may have reduced the perceived importance of the task and so reduced friends' concern about their relative performance. In addition, sex differences in behavior were not examined, despite their significance in previous studies.

On the other hand the general conclusion about the magnitude of friend-classmate differences is confirmed by the findings of the recent study (Jones, 1985). Although friends and classmates differed in how much they shared the crayon, they did not differ in their number of requests for the crayon or the proportion of successful requests. When children refused to pass the crayon, they were more likely to present an "expanded" refusal to a friend than to a nonfriend, often by saying that they would pass the crayon in a short time. Children were more likely to respond with a simple "no" to a nonfriend's request. These findings imply that the differences between friends' and nonfriends' verbal interactions may often be quite subtle.

SOCIABLE CONVERSATIONS BETWEEN FRIENDS AND NONFRIENDS

A few researchers have investigated friends' interactions under more natural conditions than those in the research with specially designed tasks. These researchers have either recorded spontaneous conversations between children and their friends in their homes, or recorded relatively unstructured conversations between friends in a university laboratory setting. The friends' conversations have been compared with conversations between strangers or conversations between classmates who were not close friends.

Preschoolers' Conversations with Friends and Strangers

The first major study of friends' conversations was reported by Gottman and Parkhurst (1980). They studied 13 children who ranged in age from 2 to 6 years. The mothers of the children recorded conversations that the children had with their best friends in their own playrooms. At a different time, the mothers recorded conversations that their children had as they played with another child who initially was a stranger. That is, each "host" child interacted with a best friend and with a stranger. The study is unusual and perhaps unique in thus making friendship a within-subject factor. The study is also unusual in that several pairs of friends and strangers were mixed sex rather than same sex.

The children's conversations were transcribed and coded in multiple ways. The codes were adapted from those used by Piaget (1926/1955) in his early research on egocentric speech and those used by Gottman (1979) in his research on the conversations of husbands and wives. The final set of codes was designed to assess various social processes that were assumed to influence friendship formation and maintenance. A few social processes were assessed by the proportion of statements falling into a specific category. For example, the proportion of statements falling into Piaget's category of collective monologue served as the primary indicator of connectedness in conversations. Conversations with a lower proportion of collective monologue were judged to be more connected.

Other social processes were indexed by particular sequences of codes. For example, communication clarity was indexed by the frequency with which a request for clarification of a statement was followed by a clarification. In other words, the critical indicator of the process was the conditional probability of a clarified message given a request for clarification. These conditional probabilities were reported separately for friends' conversations and for strangers' conversations. In addition, conditional probabilities were reported separately for the eight pairs in which the host child was under 5 years of age and the five pairs in which the host child was 5 years old or older. The probabilities were also reported separately for statements by the host children and statements by their guests. Finally, several code sequences were usually designated as indicators of the same social process.

The findings most relevant for this paper concern the differences between friends' and strangers' conversations. Standard significance tests were used to examine hypotheses about the proportions of specific types of statements. For the processes indexed by particular sequences of codes, friend–stranger differences are considered significant when the conditional probabilities for a given code sequence differed significantly (using as a criterion for significance a difference in z-scores greater than 1.96) for friends and strangers for statements by both hosts and guests. Because the selection of hosts and guests was random and has little theoretical interest, differences that were found for either hosts or guests but not both are considered unreliable.

As expected, friends had more connected conversations than strangers. That is, the proportion of statements classified in Piaget's category of collective monologue was lower for friends' conversations than for strangers' conversations. Friends also engaged more than strangers in fantasy talk—more talk in fantasy roles and more talk related to the development of fantasy or dramatic play. These two differences confirmed the hypotheses of Gottman and Parkhurst about the importance of connected conversations and fantasy play in the friendships of young children. The differences also suggest that the children defined the situation as one calling for sociable interaction and dramatic play with their partners. Apparently, friends were more sociable and more involved in their play together than were strangers.

The code sequences that served as indicators of the process of communication clarity also showed a fairly consistent pattern of friend–stranger differences. Communication clarity was indexed by appropriate responses to requests for information and requests for clarification of a previous statement. These data were reported only for requests by guests, because the frequency of such requests by hosts was too low to allow interpretable analyses.

Unclear communication, as indexed by failures to respond to requests for information or clarification, was less common for friends than for strangers among the younger pairs of children. Among the older pairs, failures to respond to requests for clarification were again less common among friends than among strangers, but the reverse was true with requests for information. Gottman and Parkhurst (1980) suggested that younger children may be more responsive to their friends than older children, although this explanation does not account for the inconsistent findings for the two indicators of communication clarity. Perhaps a more cautious conclusion is that friends usually are more responsive to each other's questions during a sociable conversation than strangers. Their greater responsiveness may be another manifestation of their greater mutual involvement in their play.

For the other social processes described by Gottman and Parkhurst (1980), few consistent differences between friends and strangers were found. Among the older children, for example, conflict resolution appeared to be more rapid for friends than for strangers. That is, the child who started a quarrel with an initial disagreement was more likely to continue to disagree, even after hearing the other child's response, when the children were strangers rather than friends. Among the younger pairs of children, reactions to a disagreement did not differ significantly for friends and strangers. Consequences of more serious disagreements, coded as *squabbles*, also appeared to be similar for friends and strangers.

Finally, compliance with commands and suggestions, which was used as an indicator of the process of control, was significantly greater for friends than for strangers in some comparisons, but the differences often held for only one age group. Occasionally, strangers appeared to be significantly more responsive to each other than friends.

In a second report, Gottman (1983) presented additional data from the study of preschoolers' conversations. He noted that the proportion of statements by guests that were coded as *agreements* was greater for friends than for strangers. On the basis of this difference and other data, he proposed that guest agreements could be viewed as an indicator of progress toward friendship, or movement from being strangers to being acquaintances to being friends.

Previous research has clearly demonstrated the importance of positive interactions for the formation and maintenance of friendships (e.g., Masters & Furman, 1981). Nevertheless, the selection of the code for guest agreement as the single criterion of progress toward friendship may be premature. For reasons that are not clear, the proportion of *disagreements* by guests was also higher for friends than for strangers. Nevertheless, few people would view disagreements as a reasonable criterion of progress toward friendship. In addition, it is worth noting that neither agreements by hosts nor disagreements by hosts differed significantly for friends and strangers.

Gottman (1983) proposed the use of guest agreements as the criterion of progress toward friendship in a report on a study of 18 children ranging from 3 to 9 years of age. At the beginning of the study, the children were paired with strangers roughly the same age. Then each pair of children had three play sessions over a period of a few weeks at the home of one child. The children's conversations were recorded during these play sessions. Analyses of the conversations were designed to answer questions about how strangers become acquainted with each other, and why some pairs of strangers began to form friendships with each other. The most relevant data on these questions are the correlations of guest agreements with indicators of the social processes assumed to be important in friendship formation. These correlations were presented not only for the new sample in the second study, but also for the pairs of children in the first study who were strangers to each other. Because the choice of guest agreements as the criterion of progress toward friendship is problematic, the correlations must be interpreted cautiously. On the other hand, the extent to which other aspects of a conversation are related to statements of agreement is of some interest.

Only a few correlations were significant for both the children who were hosts and the children who were guests. For the strangers in Study 1, agreement was associated with reciprocity in joking, that is, episodes in which one child responded to the other child's joking comment with another joking comment. For the first session in Study 2, agreement was associated with reciprocity in fantasy, that is, episodes in which one child talked in a fantasy role and the other child reciprocated. These correlations illustrate that reciprocity in affective behavior and dramatic play was associated with more harmonious interactions.

The correlations of agreements with reciprocity in fantasy were not significant for the second and third conversations of the pairs in Study 2. Indeed, no indicators of the hypothesized social processes correlated significantly ($p < .05$) with agreements in all three sessions. There were significant or marginally significant ($p < .10$) correlations of agreements with the proportion of information codes in all three sessions. The information code was used for statements of factual information (e.g., "White and red makes pink"), statements about the other child and his or her actions (e.g., "You have big trucks"), and inferences about feelings (e.g., "That must have hurt"). These statements may reflect the sheer amount of conversation between two children, and establish that children who are more agreeable with each other also talk more to each other.[1]

Intimate Self-Disclosure in Children's and Adolescents' Conversations

Taking a different approach, Mettetal (1983) explored the content of friends' conversations. She examined one type of content mentioned by Gottman, — fantasy talk,— but she also examined the frequency of gossip and intimate self-disclosure in the conversations of best friends and other classmates. Her study included 90 girls ranging from 6 to 17 years of age. Each girl was paired with her best friend or with an other classmate whom she reported not knowing very well. Each pair of girls was brought to a room in a university psychology laboratory that was furnished like a typical living room. The girls were asked to talk about whatever they chose for 30 minutes, while the experimenter was absent.

Friends and classmates did not differ in the frequency of fantasy talk, gossip, or self-disclosure that was low in intimacy. Friends displayed more highly intimate self-disclosure than other classmates, but highly intimate self-disclosure was rare (less than 5 percent of the units of conversation) in all groups except the 16- and 17-year-old girls paired with friends. These findings were inconsistent with Mettetal's hypothesis that fantasy talk and gossip would be more frequent among friends. Indeed, Mettetal concluded that the content of the girls' conversations was very similar for friends and other classmates.

Summary

The evidence on sociable conversations between friends and nonfriends suggests three major conclusions. First, friends typically are more mutually involved in their conversations than are strangers. In Gottman and Parkhurst's (1980) study, friends had more connected conversations and more conversations concerning fantasy themes than strangers. Friends were generally more responsive to requests for clarification or information than were strangers. On the other hand, friends were not generally more responsive to commands or suggestions. In other words, friends did not show more compliance than strangers with each other's requests.

The importance of mutual involvement is also suggested by Gottman's (1983) more recent report. The children who initially were strangers to each other tended to have more positive interactions, reflected by more agreements by guests, when they showed more mutual fantasy, mutual joking, and exchanges of information. Although agreements by guests is not a fully satisfactory index of movement toward friendship, these findings are consistent with the general conclusion suggested by the original study.

Second, friends typically have conversations that are more emotionally intense than those of strangers. In Gottman and Parkhurst's (1980) study, guests who were close friends showed more agreements and more disagreements than guests who were strangers. Thus friends and strangers differed in the expression of positive emotions (agreements) as well as negative emotions (disagreements). This conclusion about the emotional intensity of friends' conversations must be regarded as tentative, however, because agreements and disagreements by friends and strangers differed only for guests and not for hosts.

Third, by late adolescence friends appear to have more intimate conversations than nonfriends. Although this conclusion rests on a single study of friends' conversations (Mettetal, 1983), it is consistent with theoretical writings and previous research on friends' reports about their friendships (see Berndt, 1982). Aside from the difference in intimate self-disclosure, the content of friends' conversations is similar to the content of other classmates' conversations.

DISCUSSIONS AMONG FRIENDS AND OTHER CLASSMATES

Further evidence on friends' conversations has been obtained in a third type of situation that involves true discussion, defined as an exchange of opinions on an issue in an attempt to reach a decision. Despite the importance that Piaget (1932/1965) attached to discussions with peers, only a few researchers have examined such discussions directly. Moreover, most studies have focused on discussions of cognitive tasks (e.g., Perret-Clermont, 1980) or moral dilemmas (e.g., Berkowitz, Oser, & Althof, Chapter 11, this volume; Berndt, McCartney, Caparulo, & Moore, 1983–1984; Damon & Killen, 1982). These studies involved peers who were not necessarily close friends. Apparently, discussions between friends have been compared with discussions between nonfriends in only two studies.

In the first study (Nelson & Aboud, 1985), third and fourth graders were paired either with a best friend or with another classmate. Then the pairs of children were asked individually to answer items from the WISC-R Social Comprehension subtest. After they answered the items for themselves, they were asked to discuss them and try either to reach agreement on the best answer or to generate many different answers. After the discussion, the children were asked individually to answer the same items again. Consequently, changes in responses as a result of the discussion could be evaluated.

The transcripts of the discussions were coded using a system with 29 categories. Analyses were reported only for the 9 categories that had the highest loadings on each of 9 factors that emerged from a factor analysis of all categories. Differences between friends and other classmates were found for 3 of the 9 categories. Friends gave more explanations for their opinions and more often criticized each other. When they initially agreed on an item, friends sought more information from each other than did nonfriends. Friends and nonfriends did not differ in the frequency of praise or agreements, responses to commands, or other variables coded from the discussions.

The difference in explanations by friends and classmates illustrates the more extensive exchange of information that occurs between friends (e.g., Gottman & Parkhurst, 1980; Newcomb & Brady, 1982). The difference in criticisms may reflect an emphasis on honesty rather than politeness in friends' interactions. Apparently, the friends who disagreed tried to change each other's opinions by explaining their own views and criticizing their partners' views. In support of this interpretation, changes toward the correct answers on the items were most common among pairs of friends who initially disagreed about their answers. In other words, the discussions by disagreeing friends led to the greatest improvement in children's answers.

In the second study of friends' discussions (Berndt, 1986), third and seventh graders were paired with a close friend or with another classmate whom they neither strongly liked nor strongly disliked. Then the children were asked individually to indicate their opinions on various topics. For example, they were asked to rank their preferred after-school activities. After completing their own rankings, the children were asked to discuss each topic until they reached a consensus. For example, they were asked to discuss the list of after-school activities until they could reach agreement on which ones kids their age preferred most.

Two coding systems for the children's discussions were devised. The first set of seven codes concerned the content of the children's conversations. Statements directly relevant to the task were distinguished from statements about oneself, one's family, the partner, the experimental setting, teachers or other classmates (i.e., gossip), and other topics.

Friends were expected to engage in more intimate conversations, particularly conversations about themselves and their families, than other classmates. The results did not support this hypothesis. As in Mettetal's (1983) study, the frequency of statements coded into each content category was similar for friends and for other classmates. There were differences, however, in the intercorrelations of the categories for friends and classmates. For the classmate pairs, categories that reflected more intimate conversations—those involving statements about oneself, one's family, the partner, and gossip—were all significantly correlated. For the pairs of friends, only the self and family categories were correlated. These differences suggest that some pairs of classmates used the discussions as an opportunity to get to know each other, and perhaps to take a first step toward friendship. Friends did not react to the conversations in the same way, probably because they already knew each other well.

The second coding system was adapted from that devised by Gottman and Parkhurst (1980). The definitions of the codes were generally broader than the definitions of Gottman and Parkhurst, however, to insure that the frequencies for each code were large enough to allow interpretable analyses. The final set of six codes included agreements, disagreements, suggestions stated in "we" form (e.g., "Let's make this our most favorite"), commands, whispers, and questions.

Only disagreements differed significantly for friends and other classmates at both ages. Friends disagreed with each other roughly twice as often as other classmates (i.e., M's = 1.65 and .84). To shed more light on the reasons for this difference, the statement that preceded each disagreement was examined in a secondary analysis of code sequences. Sequences consisting of a statement about the task followed by a disagreement and sequences consisting of a question about the task followed by a disagreement were more common for friends than for other classmates. These sequences suggest that friends were more willing than other classmates to state their views honestly, and tell their partner when they had a different opinion about the task or the decisions that they were making.

The friends' disagreements seem not to reflect honesty alone, however, because sequences consisting of a disagreement followed by another disagreement were also more common for friends than for other classmates. These sequences are likely to represent real conflicts, not merely the expression of opposing views. Moreover, among seventh graders but not third graders, agreements were more commonly expressed by classmates than by friends. This difference further suggests that friends' discussions were marked by more conflicts than classmates' discussions.

Among third graders but not seventh graders, whispering occurred more frequently between classmates than between friends. Whispers and commands were highly correlated for classmates ($r = .83$), but not for friends ($r = .27$). Commands were usually expressed when children felt their partners were getting off the topic and needed to get back to the task. In addition, children who rarely agreed with each other expressed more commands, which supports the assumption that commands reflected conflict between partners. The friend-classmate difference in whispering thus implies that third graders were more willing to reveal their conflicts and state commands openly (i.e., without whispering) when interacting with friends than with classmates.

Summary

Taken together, the two studies of friends' discussions offer additional support for the earlier conclusion that conversations between friends and conversations between classmates who are not close friends are fairly similar in their content. The evidence further suggests that the similarity is due partly to children's taking advantage of the opportunity to make friends with classmates whom they did not know very well. The desire to make friends may also explain why children seemed especially polite when engaged in a discussion with nonfriends. When trying to reach a consensus on a topic, nonfriends were less critical and less often disagreed with each other than friends did. These differences may perhaps reflect the greater honesty of friends with each other, but this honesty often seems to create real conflicts. The greater frequency of negative comments by friends was not balanced by a greater frequency of positive comments or agreements. Nevertheless, friends' conflicts may be more beneficial than harmful, because they appear to promote more positive effects of a discussion on individual children's reasoning.

GENERAL CONCLUSIONS AND IMPLICATIONS

When the evidence from all three types of situations is considered together, the combined data base is far from ideal for drawing conclusions about friends' conversations and their significance. Overall, few studies have been reported; the number of studies on each specific type of situation ranges from a handful to a couple. In addition, the three types of situations that have been investigated up to now are not a comprehensive or even representative sample of the situations in which friends' conversations occur.

Most studies have included school-aged children (e.g., Newcomb & Brady, 1982), but a few have included preschool children (Gottman & Parkhurst, 1980) or late adolescents (Mettetal, 1983). Many studies include children from a small age range that overlaps little with the age range in other studies. Consequently, questions about developmental changes in friends' conversations are difficult to state with any specificity. Furthermore, several key studies had small samples of children, or very brief samples of friends' conversations.

Coding systems varied greatly across studies. Even codes given the same label (e.g., refusals) often were operationally defined in quite different ways. For all these reasons, the findings of various studies are difficult to integrate.

Nevertheless, the research clearly suggests three conclusions that seem both reasonable and an advance on the conventional wisdom about children's friendships. First, conversations between friends are marked by greater mutuality than conversations between nonfriends. How mutuality is reflected in friends' conversations depends partly on the situational context and partly on the age of the children involved. When school-aged children are not explicitly told to talk with each other and they are working on a task that does not require a great deal of talking, friends talk more with each other than do other classmates (Newcomb & Brady, 1982). When a situation calls for sociable conversation, preschool children who are close friends show more connected conversation, more conversation about fantasy or dramatic play, and more responsiveness to each other's requests for information than preschoolers who are strangers (Gottman & Parkhurst, 1980). In the same type of situation, older adolescents who are close friends show more intimate self-disclosure than adolescents who are merely classmates (Mettetal, 1983). Finally, when a situation calls for discussion of opposing views, school-aged children are likely to explain their own views more frequently to a friend than to another classmate (Nelson & Aboud, 1985). A difference in mutuality between friends and nonfriends may not be apparent, however, when nonfriends treat a conversation as a chance to become better friends with each other (cf. Berndt, 1986; Mettetal, 1983).

Second, conversations between friends are often marked by greater affect, both positive and negative, than conversations between peers who are not close friends. When working cooperatively on a task, friends smile more often and show more simultaneous smiling than do other classmates (Newcomb & Brady, 1982). When engaged in a sociable conversation, friends tend to express more agreement and more disagreement with each other than nonfriends (Gottman, 1983). During a discussion, friends are likely to disagree with each other and express more criticism of each other than nonfriends do (Berndt, 1986; Nelson & Aboud, 1985). The disagreements between friends could be viewed simply as reflecting their honesty and openness with each other. This proposition is plausible, but it does not necessarily imply that the disagreements are unimportant. Scattered evidence suggests that children regard interactions with friends as unpleasant or unsatisfying when they frequently disagree with their friends (Berndt, 1986) or the friend is unresponsive to their requests for prosocial behavior (Berndt et al., 1986). Overall, the evidence suggests that the emotional intensity of conversations is generally greater for friends than for nonfriends. In other words, conversations with friends have more affective impact than conversations with other peers: The highs are higher and the lows are lower (Larson & Csikszentmihalyi, 1980).

Third, friends show greater concern with their equality than nonfriends, but this difference is apparent primarily in situations that allow or encourage comparisons of performance. In such situations, friends may try to achieve equality in performance by helping or sharing with each other, or by competing with each other. The choice between prosocial behavior and competition depends on other characteristics of the situation, for example, how easily friends can achieve equality. Children's motives in a particular situation in turn affect their conversations. The effects of children's motives on their responsiveness to friends' requests for generous or helpful behavior have been studied more extensively. When children are cooperating with each other, responsiveness is typically greater for friends than for other classmates (e.g., Newcomb et al., 1979). When children are competing with each other, responsiveness is typically lower for friends than for other classmates (e.g., Berndt, 1981b). That is, friends do not always show greater mutual responsiveness than nonfriends (cf. Sullivan, 1953).

These conclusions about friends' conversations have implications for an understanding of friends' influence. That is, they suggest ways in which conversations between friends may affect children's social and moral development. Specific hypotheses about these effects can be generated by linking the research on friendship to the larger body of research on social and moral development. In the larger literature, the critical features of conversations are defined differently than in this chapter, but a closer inspection reveals the underlying similarities.

For example, a number of researchers have discussed constructs analogous to mutuality in conversations. Berkowitz and his colleagues (Chapter 11, this volume) have shown that moral discussions lead to greater changes in moral reasoning when they are marked by a high frequency of transactive statements. Paraphrases, clarifications, criticisms of another's reasoning, and other types of statements about another's reasoning are defined as transacts. The frequency of transacts in friends' and nonfriends' conversations has not been examined, but the data on several indicators of mutuality suggest that transactive discussion is more likely between friends than between nonfriends. Friends have more connected conversations, are more responsive to each other's requests for information, and more often give an explanation of their own views than nonfriends do. Thus friends' conversations may facilitate greater advances in moral reasoning than do nonfriends' conversations, just as is true for nonmoral reasoning (Nelson & Aboud, 1985).

Different aspects of the broad construct of mutuality are emphasized by other theorists. Selman and Yeates (Chapter 3, this volume) proposed that the benefits of pair therapy for children's social behavior and adjustment are due partly to the intimate self-disclosure that takes place once children have established a relationship based on trust. Youniss (Chapter 5, this volume) showed that intimacy is especially intense and especially important in adolescent friendships. He also revived and extended Piaget's (1932/1965) and Sullivan's (1953) hypotheses that intimate self-disclosure between friends is essential for the development of personality, social understanding, and morality (Youniss, 1980; Youniss & Smollar, 1985).

The other features of friends' conversations also have implications for children's sociomoral development. Gibbs (Chapter 10, this volume) argued that the effectiveness of moral discussion programs depends critically on the affect that is aroused and expressed during the discussions. This hypothesis suggests that the emotional intensity of friends' conversations would contribute to greater progress after a moral discussion than does the more polite but emotionally restrained conversational style of nonfriends.

The emphasis of friends on equality parallels the emphasis on autonomy in the early phase of pair therapy (Selman & Yeates, Chapter 3, this volume). This phase is marked by extensive social comparison, competition, and negotiating for an acceptable balance of power and control. During this phase, children appear to be trying to determine whether they can satisfy the first requirement for friendship, which is to treat each other as equals. Learning to do so may be essential for forming egalitarian relationships with peers in other settings and forming mature social relationships in adulthood (Youniss, 1980).

In summary, the current theories and recent research converge in suggesting that conversations with friends are particularly significant for children's social and moral development. Yet in a recent review, Berndt (1982) pointed to the relative scarcity of research on the effects of friendship. When studying peer interaction, most researchers have ignored the existing network of friendships among the children in the sample or have deliberately selected for observation peers who were not close friends. The reasons for these methodological decisions are not often stated explicitly, but many researchers seem to have considered friendships as a small and rather atypical subset of peer relationships. In other words, the researchers ignored friendships in an attempt to understand "generic" peer relationships.

The data from the recent research on friends' conversations could be seen as justifying these methodological decisions. Although significant differences between friends' and nonfriends' conversations have been found, the differences are often small. In many studies, the differences were significant for only a fraction of the dependent measures or were not replicated across similar measures.

Nevertheless, there are two important disadvantages to such an approach. First, the failure to distinguish between close friendships and other peer relationships may also blur the distinction between the effects of close friendships and the effects of interactions with members of the larger peer group. Children's behavior, their moral reasoning, and other aspects of their social and moral development may be influenced not only by their interactions with friends but also by the norms and behavior of the dominant peer groups in their schools (Coleman, 1961; Kohlberg & Higgins, Chapter 4, this volume). To understand these effects, the distinction between close friendships and the peer group as a whole must be retained.

Second, children interact more frequently with close friends than with other classmates (see, e.g., Berndt & Perry, 1986). For this reason, research on friends' interactions has greater ecological validity (Bronfenbrenner, 1979) than research on nonfriends' interactions. Stated differently, friendship is a special relationship but is also the prototypical peer relationship. Moreover, because of their distinctive features, friends' conversations are likely to have a greater impact on children's reasoning and behavior than conversations with nonfriends. Consequently, researchers will obtain the most powerful and most valid tests of hypotheses about the contributions of close peer relationships to sociomoral development when they focus on interactions between friends.

REFERENCES

Ahlgren, A., & Johnson, D. W. (1979). Differences in cooperative and competitive attitudes from the 2nd through the 12th grades. *Developmental Psychology, 15*, 45–49.

Berndt, T. J. (1981a). Age changes and changes over time in prosocial intentions and behavior between friends. *Developmental Psychology, 17*, 408–416

Berndt, T. J. (1981b). The effects of friendship on prosocial intentions and behavior. *Child Development, 52*, 636–643.

Berndt, T. J. (1982). The features and effects of friendships in early adolescence. *Child Development, 53*, 1447–1460.

Berndt, T. J. (1985). Prosocial behavior between friends in middle childhood and early adolescence. *Journal of Early Adolescence, 5*, 307–317.

Berndt, T. J. (1986, August). *The distinctive features of conversations between friends.* Paper presented at the annual meeting of the American Psychological Association, Washington, D.C.

Berndt, T. J., Hawkins, J. A., & Hoyle, S. G. (1986). Changes in friendship during a school year: Effects on children's and adolescents' impressions of friendship and sharing with friends, *Child Development, 57*, 1284–1297.

Berndt, T. J., McCartney, K., Caparulo, B. K., & Moore, A. M. (1983–1984). The effects of group discussions on children's moral decisions. *Social Cognition, 2*, 343–360.

Berndt, T. J., & Perry, T. B. (1986). Children's perceptions of friendships as supportive relationships. *Developmental Psychology, 22*, 640–648.

Bronfenbrenner, U. (1979). The *ecology of human development.* Cambridge, MA: Harvard University Press.

Coleman, J. S. (1961). *The adolescent society.* New York: Free Press.

Damon, W., & Killen, M. (1982). Peer interaction and the process of change in children's moral reasoning. *Merrill-Palmer Quarterly, 28*, 347–368.

Gottman, J. M. (1979). *Marital interaction: Experimental investigations.* New York: Academic.

Gottman, J. M. (1983). How children become friends. *Monographs of the Society for Research in Child Development, 48* (3, Serial No. 201).

Gottman, J. M., & Parkhurst, J. T. (1980). A developmental theory of friendship and acquaintanceship processes. In W. A. Collins (Ed.), *Minnesota Symposium on Child Psychology* (Vol. 13). Hillsdale, NJ: Erlbaum.

Hartup, W. W. (1983). Peer relations. In E. M. Hetherington (Ed.), *Handbook of child psychology* (Vol. 4). New York: Wiley.

Jones, D. C. (1985). Persuasive appeals and responses to appeals among friends and acquaintances. *Child Development, 56*, 757–763.

Larson, R., & Csikszentmihalyi, M. (1980). Mood variability and the psychosocial adjustment of adolescents. *Journal of Youth and Adolescence, 9*, 469–490.

Maas, H. S. (1968). Preadolescent peer relations and adult intimacy. *Psychiatry, 31*, 161–172.

Masters, J. C., & Furman, W. (1981). Popularity, individual friendship selection, and specific peer interaction among children. *Developmental Psychology, 17*, 344–350.

Mettetal, G. (1983). Fantasy, gossip, and self-disclosure: Children's conversations with friends. In R. N. Bostrom (Ed.), *Communication yearbook* (Vol. 7). Beverly Hills, CA: Sage.

Nelson, J., & Aboud, F. E. (1985). The resolution of social conflict between friends. *Child Development, 56,* 1009–1017.

Newcomb, A. F., & Brady, J. E. (1982). Mutuality in boys' friendship relations. *Child Development, 53,* 392–395.

Newcomb, A. F., Brady J. E. & Hartup W. W. (1979). Friendship and incentive condition as determinants of children's task-oriented social behavior. *Child Development, 50,* 878–881.

Perret-Clermont, A. N. (1980). *Social interaction and cognitive development in children.* New York: Academic.

Piaget, J. (1955). *The language and thought of the child.* New York: World. (Original work published 1926.)

Piaget, J. (1965). *The moral judgment of the child.* New York: Free Press. (Original work published 1932.)

Staub, E., & Noerenberg, H. (1981). Property rights, deservingness, reciprocity, friendship: The transactional character of children's sharing behavior. *Journal of Personality & Social Psychology, 40,* 271–289.

Staub, E., & Sherk, L. (1970). Need for approval, children's sharing behavior, and reciprocity in sharing. *Child Development, 41,* 243–252.

Sullivan, H. S. (1953). *The interpersonal theory of psychiatry.* New York: Norton.

Tesser, A. (1984). Self-evaluation maintenance processes: Implications for relationships and for development. In J. C. Masters & K. Yarkin-Levin (Eds.), *Boundary areas in social and developmental psychology.* New York: Academic.

Youniss, J. (1980). *Parents and peers in social development.* Chicago: University of Chicago Press.

Youniss, J., & Smollar, J. (1985). *Adolescent relations with mothers, fathers, and friends.* Chicago: University of Chicago Press.

REFERENCE NOTE

1. Another code that correlated significantly with agreements for hosts and guests in Study 1 was for the probability of compliance with polite requests or suggestions. These correlations are difficult to interpret, because agreement was used as the indicator of compliance. The significant correlations may thus be partly artifactual, a consequence of correlating agreements with a code dependent on agreements.

CHAPTER 10

Social Processes in Delinquency: The Need to Facilitate Empathy as Well as Sociomoral Reasoning

JOHN C. GIBBS

This chapter addresses social processes in delinquency causation and treatment, arguing for the importance of studying affective as well as cognitive aspects of those processes. In terms of Kohlberg's primarily cognitive moral developmental theory, delinquents' antisocial conduct generally reflects egocentrism, immature sociomoral reasoning (relating to superficial empathy), and inadequate role-taking opportunities. In terms of Hoffman's primarily affective socialization theory, the antisocial conduct generally reflects the failure of empathy or anticipatory empathy-based guilt to inhibit aggressive impulses. Ineffective empathy and frequent aggressive impulses are in turn often attributable to a particular form of inadequate role-taking opportunities—namely, harsh, arbitrary power assertion—that fosters anger and the defensive derogation of others rather than empathic responsiveness and self-attribution (see Eisenberg, Chapter 2, this volume) of prosocial norms. A full account of social processes in delinquency causation must include the interaction of developmental and socialization processes with constitutional factors (e.g., child's temperament). The causal social processes described in Kohlberg's and Hoffman's theories have treatment implications. Small-group moral dilemma discussion programs have been found to reduce adolescent antisocial conduct (Arbuthnot & Gordon, 1986). I argue that the effectiveness of such programs is attributable to affective as well as cognitive processes; that is, inductions of empathic arousal as well as role-taking equilibrations (facilitating moral stage growth and reducing egocentrism). Developmental approaches to antisocial behavior should supplement the traditional emphasis on sociomoral reasoning with an analysis of empathic affect, and should systematically include empathy-enhancing techniques in small-group treatment programs.

Not only cognitive processes (e.g., attribution; see Chapter 2) but also affect—especially empathy—are critical to moral conduct. Feelings for others not only tend to prompt altruistic behavior (Hoffman, 1981) but also "may play a particularly significant role in the control of aggression" (Feshbach, 1983, p. 267; cf. Perry & Perry, 1974). If a delinquency treatment program is to reduce aggressive or antisocial behavior, one goal must be the inculcation of effective empathic motives and inhibitions (Kaplan, 1984). Students of antisocial behavior from the Kohlbergian sociomoral developmental perspective should supplement cognitive analyses with an analysis of the socialization of empathic affect, and should systematically include empathy-enhancing techniques in treatment programs.

DESCRIPTION

Stanton Samenow (1984; cf. Yochelson & Samenow, 1977) has provided a clinical analysis of antisocial youth through his and Yochelson's careful study of young adult criminal offenders. The two principal features of his description are respectively affective and cognitive: (1) empathic dysfunction; and (2) egocentric orientation (or "embeddedness in one's own point of view," Looft, 1972, p. 74; cf. Short & Simeonsson, 1986). Although certain antisocial individuals may be devoid of any potential for empathic responsiveness (the idiopathic or primary psychopath—Karpman, 1941), Samenow infers that the empathic affect problem for most offenders is more a matter of dysfunction than of total deficit (cf. Barahal, Waterman, & Martin, 1981; Ellis, 1982; Kaplan & Arbuthnot, 1985). Empathy is available in most offenders but is not readily elicited and tends to be either an isolated impulse or a mawkish sentiment. In either case, the empathy is superficial and erratic; when it lingers, it is readily suppressed by self-centered motives or aggressive impulses (which are highly charged and represent another aspect of the affective dysfunction), or neutralized by self-serving rationalizations. Hence the empathy is behaviorally ineffective: Although it may prompt an occasional impulsive act helpful to another, it does not motivate a stable consideration for others or inhibit aggression. For example, an antisocial individual's occasional adulation of his mother does not deter his continuing to "make her life hell" (Samenow, 1984, p. 166). Samenow gives several examples of the erratic nature of the antisocial person's empathy:

> Amazingly, a violent street thug became impassioned about sparing the life of a bug, ordering his wife not to squash it. A criminal who indulged in fantasies of knife-point rape and homicide said to his wife when she proposed that they go to a tree farm where they'd be allowed to chop down their own Christmas tree, "No, I will not destroy living matter." Even while en route to a crime, a criminal may perform a good deed. One man dropped by a bar, treated a down-and-out alcoholic to a meal, and, feeling pretty good about himself,[1] robbed a bank. (p. 164)

Empathy in such individuals may scarcely even be experienced once a self-centered motive or aggressive impulse arises, as indicated in the introspective comment of one of Samenow's subjects:

> "I do have feelings for other people. If I saw people trapped in a burning house, I'd experience a certain horror." The man continued, "And yet I really don't have any feelings for those I hurt. Were I to rape a woman, I wouldn't feel one second of her pain or anguish. I can't explain the contradiction between my pain for those in the burning building and my complete lack of feelings for my victims. I think it's because, where my own interests and pleasures are concerned, my feelings for others are automatically so totally suppressed and discarded as to be totally absent. I don't know. I only know that if I could appreciate the sufferings of my victims, they wouldn't be my victims. (p. 235)

The superficiality and ineffectiveness of antisocial youth's empathy becomes less surprising when one considers more fully their self-centeredness, or egocentrism. Although other people may be momentarily and superficially "felt for" in the absence of egoistic interests and pleasures (especially given overwhelmingly salient distress cues, e.g., people trapped in a burning building), empathic feelings can otherwise be suppressed and discarded at least partly because other people are not usually considered individuals in their own right, with their own needs and legitimate claims or expectations. They are instead thought of mainly in terms of whether they can further or frustrate one's egoistic wishes and aims. Similarly, Gough (1948) found antisocial behavior to involve a lack of "attention to the rights and privileges of others when recognizing them would interfere with personal satisfaction in any way" (p. 362). Antisocial people will demand fair play for themselves yet not accord it to others, and will act as if they are entitled to dominate others. Antisocial individuals are generally hostile or aggressively impulsive, and egocentrically attribute that hostility to everyone else; also, they fail to recognize their role in creating some genuine hostility by unfairly treating or exploiting others (cf. Dodge, 1980, p. 169). The hostile egocentrism generally precludes cooperative social interaction; the delinquent "does not know what friendship is because trust, loyalty, and sharing are incompatible with his way of life. [He] does not know how to hold a discussion. He says his piece and ignores or shouts down those who disagree" (Samenow, 1984, p. 61).

The antisocial individual's self-centered conceptualization of others as either pawns or potential obstructors, then, is incompatible with other-oriented feelings and hence serves to suppress empathy. If incipient empathy or empathy-based guilt cannot be totally turned off[2] or sufficiently suppressed, such feelings may be neutralized through the use of defensive and self-serving rationalizations (cf. Sykes & Matza, 1957). This defensive egocentrism can even transform incipient empathy into a feeling of retributive justice: "Said one 17-year-old about a recent break-in: 'If I started feeling bad, I'd say to myself, "Tough rocks for him. He should have had his house locked better and the alarm on"'" (Samenow, 1984, p. 115; cf. "externalizing" defenses, Achenbach & Edelbrock, 1978). Similarly, Wilson and Herrnstein (1985) note:

> Criminal and aggressive persons frequently defend their behavior by denigrating their victims. . . . as somehow deserving their fate (they are "jerks," or "suckers," or "people who don't deserve what they have"). . . . To the extent that the criminal feels that his offense is justified by some perceived inequity, then the rewards of committing the crime, far from being reduced by the bite of conscience, are enhanced by a sense of restored equity. (p. 59)

In short, the antisocial youth's empathy is not readily elicited; it is superficial and erratic. Their weak empathy is behaviorally ineffective particularly because their egocentric thinking patterns suppress and neutralize incipient empathy.

PERSPECTIVES ON CAUSATION

Developmental Theory

How are we to account for the ineffective empathy and egocentric orientation of antisocial individuals? Sociomoral–developmental theory analyzes the antisocial individual's egocentrism (and associated superficial empathy) as readily resulting from his or her delayed social cognitive development, especially immature moral judgment. Controlled comparisons of delinquent or conduct-disordered with normal children or adolescents (Bear & Richards, 1981; Blasi, 1980; Campagna & Harter, 1975; Gavaghan, Arnold, & Gibbs, 1983; Jennings, Kilkenny, & Kohlberg, 1983) indicate that, at least on production measures, significantly higher percentages of delinquent or conduct-disordered youths are at Kohlberg's (1984) sociomoral stage 2 (pragmatic exchanges and instrumental motives), and even stage 1, unilateral authority and simplistic labels, than are at stage 3 (mutual relationships and prosocial intentions) or stage 4 (social system practices and standards). The intrinsic amenability of stage 2 thinking to self-centeredness is clear in any scrutiny of stage 2 justifications. Although a stage 2 thinker may value, say, law and property norms, the valuation is contingent upon the individual's calculations and interests. Law and property norms may be valued by appeal to exchanges ("The law might help you if you help the law"), short-term preferences ("There might be a good law you don't want to break at the time"), practical needs ("Maybe you don't need to break any law"), or calculated advantages and disadvantages ("You might not get away with it"). Such appeals can be readily redirected to support *breaking* the law, however, if one decides that a given law is *not* helping one, that one *does* wish or need to break a law, or that the likelihood of detection and punishment is actually quite low. The individual's criteria for moral values and action, then, tend to be self-centered or egocentric.

In contrast mutualistic thinking or third-person perspective taking (stage 3; see table in Selman & Yeates, Chapter 3, this volume) is less subvertible to antisocial behavior since it features role reversal ("How would you feel if someone stole from you?") and empathic role taking ("Other people's things mean so much to them"); that is, genuine socioemotional considerations of the other person's feelings and legitimate expectations in an abstractly or ideally valued relationship. Furthermore, one anticipates adverse self-judgment for transgressing against the values of a relationship ("It would be on your mind that you've hurt their trust"). Hence taking advantage of another individual is not ethically permissible even given the "right" narrow calculations and interests.[3] As children enter adolescence, those who have not achieved at least a stage 3 understanding of human social life (age normative for adolescents) are left with a worldview (stage 2) that renders them amenable to behavior that is self-centered and antisocial—and dangerous, given the size, strength, independence, sex impulses, and ego capabilities of adolescents.

The antisocial youth's egocentrism, then, is linked in the developmental view to certain sociomoral–cognitive immaturities or delays. These delays are in turn seen as attributable to inadequate social role-taking opportunities at school, at work, at social gatherings, and especially at home. Without role-taking opportunities, the coordination of social perspectives that leads to sociomoral growth and maturity cannot take place. Antisocial youth disproportionately evidence physically harsh, disharmonious, and neglectful parental histories (e.g., Farrington, 1978; Welsh, 1976). When parents do not explain to their children why their transgressions were wrong (especially by appeals to take the role or perspective of the victim), do not assign and insist on the performance of responsible family roles, and do not solicit the child's perspective in decisions of importance to the child or family—indeed, when the parents (or other socialization agents) simply threaten and punish the child—then the child is not given the opportunity to take anyone's role but his or her own (Kohlberg, 1969) and scarcely grows beyond concrete and superficial levels of sociomoral understanding.

Socialization Theory

This developmental analysis is helpful, but we are still left with some questions. Why is the offender's empathy not only superficial but also grossly ineffective in inhibiting aggression? Why is the offender's immature moral judgment so *intensely* egocentric, so defensive and antagonistic? In Samenow's terms, how does the hostile victim*izer* come to perceive himself exclusively as victim in a hostile world? These questions point to individual differences in temperament and in socialization history, factors that are essential for a full understanding of prosocial or antisocial behavior (Gibbs & Schnell, 1985). The conduct-disordered adolescent's particularly hostile manifestation of egocentrism and unusually ineffective empathy will be considered mainly in the light of socialization theory, although the interactive role of temperament or predispositions will be noted.

Hoffman's (1983) socialization analysis, in providing a role for affect in moral learning and motivation, supplements in important ways Kohlberg's emphasis on cognitive role taking and understanding. (Indeed, whereas Kohlberg's theory is primarily cognitive, Hoffman's theory is primarily affective; see Gibbs & Schnell, 1985.) Also, whereas for Kohlberg the discipline encounter is but one of many role-taking opportunities, Hoffman grants it a central role in moral development. Hoffman emphasizes that moral behavior typically must occur in the face of egoistic desires; hence the moral learning and motivation derived from the discipline encounter are most important since that is principally where the conflict between moral norms and egoistic desires was first faced and negotiated. The kind of discipline that provides a role-taking opportunity (especially taking the perspective of the person suffering the adverse consequences of the child's act) is termed inductive discipline by Hoffman and Saltzstein (1967); simple punitive discipline is termed power assertion. Maccoby (1980) notes that the parents of delinquents are generally found to have "used discipline arbitrarily, with little explanation and sometimes considerable violence [cf. Welsh, 1976]. Clearly. . . without . . . additional conditions . . . such as close parental supervision and/or a reasonable level of affection . . . arbitrary power assertion is associated with both defiant and antisocial behavior" (p. 385).

Hoffman (1983) points out some important contrasts between power assertion and inductive discipline. These contrasts—concerning the nature of the induced moralities (externally oriented vs. internally attributed) and their associated affects—shed some light on the defensive egocentrism of conduct-disordered adolescents and their ineffective empathy. The first contrast concerns the differing moral orientations induced. Nonnurturant, arbitrary, and severe power assertion heightens the opposition-of-wills feature of the discipline (cf. Feshbach, 1983). Simple threats of physical or other punishment induce a defensive and antagonistic approach in morality because they direct the child's attention not to the child's transgression (and why it is wrong) but instead to the threatening, punitive parent. Morality comes to be perceived as a matter of externally imposed, arbitrary demands oppositional to one's desires; and the main moral "norms" inferred are that one should resolve social conflict violently, and should avoid getting caught next time by those who are more powerful. As the consequences of their transgressions for others receive no attention, these children come to perceive themselves not as occasional transgressors but instead exclusively as actual or potential victims. In other words, other persons come to be viewed defensively in terms of whether they, too, may be powerful enough to threaten or restrict the children's desires. If others are perceived as potential victimizers, such a perception could readily lead to the rationalizing tendency (noted earlier) to see others in derogatory terms, as probably deserving victimization.

In contrast, the focus in inductive discipline is on the transgression and its harmful (physical or emotional) consequences for the victim. Such a focus renders the discipline less arbitrary and alienating; models a rational, constructive approach to interpersonal conflict situations; and permits the parental source of the induction to be "low in salience" (p. 250). Hoffman argues that precisely because of this low salience, the parental source of the norm content tends to be forgotten with time and the normative prescription for considering or helping others comes to be self-attributed—a key factor in autonomous moral behavior, as Nancy Eisenberg's chapter in this volume makes clear.

The second contrast concerns the differing roles of the associated affect in moral learning and motivation. Even if the threatening parent does prescribe a prosocial norm in the course of the threat, the child's level of affective arousal (intensities of fear, rejection, anger, resentment) may be too high to permit attention to and processing of the disciplinary teaching. The child may be too afraid to express resentment by striking back at the parent, but may displace his or her anger onto weaker persons, typically, siblings or younger peers. Also, the child may egocentrically attribute to everyone else his or her own feelings of hostility and anger (Short & Simeonsson, 1986, p. 173). This displaced and egocentrically-projected anger probably further enhances the noted tendency to rationalize that other people deserve victimization.

It should be noted that effective inductive discipline does require some affective arousal; children simply do not attend to blandly communicative parents, no matter how "inductive" or socially enlightened their intended message (Zahn-Waxler, Radke-Yarrow, & King, 1979). The inductive parent studied in the literature, however, is typically also a warm, nurturant parent, who arouses through tone and expression the child's concern for the relationship and the parent's continued approval. Even power assertion plays a role. Hoffman (1983) notes:

> The occasional use of power assertion as a means of letting the child know that the parent feels strongly about a particular act or value, or as a means of controlling the behavior of a child who is acting in an openly defiant manner—by parents who usually employ inductions—may make a positive contribution to moral socialization. (pp. 246–247)

Even on these occasions, however, the level of affective arousal involved in inductive discipline may not be so intense as to disrupt the child's learning of the prosocial norm, for example, by generating anger. Hoffman stresses, then, the importance of an intermediate or optimal level of affective arousal in the child: The communication should be neither so bland that the child pays no attention to the disciplinary teaching nor so harsh that the child is too disrupted emotionally to attend.

If harsh, arbitrary power assertion generates displaced anger, inductive teaching tends to cultivate empathy. In Hoffman's terms, the inductive focus on a victim's distress tends to elicit "a motivational resource that exists in the child from an early age, namely, the child's capacity for empathy, defined as a vicarious affective response to others" (p. 252). The elicited empathy and empathy-based guilt (i.e., the combination of the child's empathy with the child's induced awareness of being the cause of the other's distress,—Thompson & Hoffman, 1980) "suffuse" the induction, rendering it "emotionally charged," or "hot" (p. 261). In other words, the inductive cognition gains motivational properties through classical conditioning with empathic affect. Hoffman (1981) argues that empathic affect represents a biologically rooted predisposition for altruistic behavior—but that the predisposition must be developed through inductive discipline and social cognitive maturity (Hoffman, 1978) into a stable, appropriate, discerning, and broadly applicable consideration for others. Effective socialization means, then, that empathy and anticipatory empathy-based guilt enable the induction-guided behavior (at least usually) to overcome self-centered motives or aggressive impulses. At best, behavior that considers others is accomplished even in the face of self-centered motives or aggressive impulses; but at least, aggression against others tends to be inhibited by vicarious distress.

The child whose home situation has generated defensiveness and anger rather than a self-attributed norm of consideration for others and empathy then approaches peer play situations in ways that only worsen matters (cf. Dodge, 1980, p. 169). The child threatens and tries to dominate others just as the parent dominates and threatens him or her. Such a child's anger displacement and physically confrontational approach to conflicts (as modeled by the parents) tragically preclude opportunities to take others' roles in peer interaction—opportunities that might have compensated for the inadequate opportunities at home.

The explanation of antisocial behavior is clearly implied. High-risk children are those who have experienced harsh, arbitrary power assertion and little or no inductive discipline, with no compensating role-taking opportunities at school or elsewhere. They not only remain at primitive moral judgment levels, but develop an external, avoidance-of-sanctions moral orientation (interestingly, Maccoby [1980, p. 343] speculates that Hoffman's external orientation is interpretable in terms of Kohlberg's stages 1 and 2). External morality may induce a defensive perception of others as would-be obstructors who probably deserve victimization, a perception intensified by the displaced and egocentrically projected anger stemming from the harshness of the power assertion. Such children have not been directed to attend to others' distress and their role in causing that distress. Hence their empathy remains undeveloped, a matter of isolated impulses or sentiments that are superficial and erratic—ineffective against their self-centered impulses, to say nothing of their anger and defensive egocentric tendencies. Superficial and ineffective empathy, defensive egocentrism, immature sociomoral reasoning, and displaced anger all mean that the antisocial youth's impulses and frustrations can readily lead to action at the expense of others.

Constitutional Factors

I have suggested that the empathic dysfunction and hostile egocentrism of antisocial youth are amenable to both cognitively oriented developmental and affectively oriented socialization analyses. It should be noted that both kinds of analyses are insufficient insofar as they neglect the antisocial individual's own contribution to his or her adverse family background. Wilson and Herrnstein (1985) are probably correct in stating that antisocial behavior "cannot be understood without taking into account individual predispositions and their biological roots" (p. 103; cf. Rowe & Osgood, 1984). Parents may use arbitrary and harsh power assertion not simply because of skill deficiencies in parenting and socioeconomic stress, but also because the child is temperamentally difficult and provocative (see Samenow, 1984, Chap. 4; cf. Spivack, Marcus, & Swift, 1986, pp. 128–129). Research on infant temperament (Buss & Plomin, 1984; Thomas & Chess, 1984), longitudinal and retrospective studies of aggressive behavior (e.g., Farrington, 1978; Kagan & Moss, 1962; Mitchell & Rosa, 1981; Robins, 1966; Taylor & Watt, 1977; Wolfgang, Figlio, & Sellin, 1972), twin and adoption studies (Bohman, Cloninger, Sigvardsson, & von Knorring, 1982; Christiansen, 1977; Mednick, Gabrielli, & Hutchings, 1984; Rowe, 1983), and conditioning experiments with psychopaths (e.g., Hare, 1975; Mednick, Volavka, Gabrielli, & Itil, 1981; Siddle & Trasler, 1981) suggest if considered together that heritable and constitutional factors do play a role in the etiology of antisocial behavior (see Wilson & Herrnstein, 1985, Chaps. 4, 5, 6, & 7).

In an extreme nativistic position, antisocial individuals are considered to be simply born without the capacity for empathic responding (e.g., Cleckley, 1964), perhaps because of a general hypoarousal and poor conditionability (e.g., Eysenck & Eysenck, 1978; Hare, 1975; Quay, 1965). Along a continuum of individual differences in temperament and natural disposition, individuals with something approximating empathic incapacity do exist (albeit as a small percentage even of designated psychopaths; Karpman, 1941). Although such individuals may accomplish nonegocentric thinking in a strictly cognitive sense through role-taking opportunities, they would not accomplish empathic motivation for their possible consideration of others even with the best inductive discipline; hence even the best parenting might be to little or no avail. For such individuals, egocentrism is a matter of inclination, not incapacity or developmental delay. (The converse of such person–environment situations may be the case of so-called invulnerable or resilient children, those who have managed despite extremely adverse parental and other environmental circumstances to survive by one means or another and to thrive as responsible contributors to society–Garmezy, 1983; Werner & Smith, 1982.)

Since most offenders do evidence some empathic potential (Samenow, 1984), however, a causal account addressing the interaction between person and environment variables would seem to be generally warranted. As Patterson's home observational studies (Patterson, 1976, 1982; Patterson & Cobb, 1971; Patterson & Reid, 1970) suggest, inadequate role-taking opportunities and harsh, arbitrary power assertion arise most typically in the course of vicious circles of worsening interaction between temperamentally difficult, active children who are provocative (e.g., tend to be defiant) and unskilled, readily angered parents who are under stress (cf. Trickett & Kuczynski, 1986).

> [Defiant and other provocative] behaviors may not have their origins in hostile intent, [but] it is easy to imagine how such children quickly become involved in negative peer interchanges and angry adult reactions, all of which would quickly snowball, with increasing age, into the kind of behavior we label as antisocial. (Spivack et al., 1986, p. 128)

Consideration of the interaction of temperament with socialization means that, for the difficult child, more than the average amount of (nonrejecting) parental assertion and firmness is required if the child is to attend to any inductive teaching. It should be noted that Samenow (1984) at some points seems to prefer over an interactionist position an exclusive focus on the individual's free will:

> From an early age [beginning as early as the preschool years], each [predelinquent] begins making a series of *choices to live a life* that he considers exciting, a life in which he is determined to do whatever he wants, a life in which he ignores restraints and eventually turns against his family and scoffs at those who live responsible lives. (pp. 25–26; emphasis added)

Since it is scarcely tenable developmentally to attribute conscious life-style choices to a preschool-age child, however, the interactionist position at least for the early years would seem to be more plausible.

TREATMENT

Developmental and socialization analyses of antisocial behavior also have treatment implications. My basic treatment approach is developmental, although I will argue that developmental treatment programs can and should encompass the treatment implications of the socialization analysis. In the sociomoral–developmental approach, treatment of antisocial behavior is a matter of remediation. Provision of compensatorily concentrated dosages of role-taking opportunities may enable delayed juveniles or young adults to catch up to age-appropriate levels of sociomoral judgment. The sociomoral-developmental approach has entailed strategies aimed at providing an opportunity for subjects to consider the perspectives of others vis-a-vis their own perspectives. Remedial role-taking opportunities are provided in terms of either macro- or microintervention strategies. In the former strategy, attempts are made to restructure the institution (school, correctional institution) in accordance with principles of democracy and justice, such that subjects (students, inmates) participate as much as is feasible in the rule-making and enforcement processes that affect institutional life (e.g., Hickey & Scharf, 1980). In the narrower microintervention strategy, there is an exclusive focus on challenging group discussions of relevant sociomoral dilemmas as a technique for stimulating perspective-taking experiences. In effective "dilemma session" programs, subjects must justify their reasons for their dilemma decisions in the face of challenges from developmentally more advanced peers and Socratically questioning session leaders (e.g., Gibbs, Arnold, Ahlborn, & Cheesman, 1984; see also literature reviews by Lockwood, 1978; Schlaefli, Rest, & Thoma, 1985).

Where the exercise of power in a given institution is typically arbitrary and severe—inducing, not surprisingly, an "externally" oriented or stage 1/stage 2 sociomoral climate—whatever sociomoral progress is achieved through microintervention tends eventually to be undermined by the conditions of institutional life. Fortunately, many institutions incarcerating or detaining antisocial juveniles are therapeutically oriented and may not be perceived by the delinquents as grossly unjust and arbitrary. Under these conditions, substantial and stable sociomoral–developmental gains may be realizable from small-group programs in both cognitive (moral judgment) and behavioral terms.

Stable behavioral gains from a dilemma session program have been reported by Arbuthnot and Gordon (1986). Antisocial juveniles (as nominated by teachers) evidenced not only moral judgment but also behavioral gains (in terms of disciplinary referrals, tardiness, and grades) on both short-term (2 to 3 weeks) and 1-year follow-up post test assessments relative to a randomly assigned, passage-of-time control group following a 4-month dilemma session treatment. Several experimental group–control group differences increased on the follow-up assessment (i.e., the group-by-time interaction terms were significant). Similarly, classroom conduct changes (according to rates of absenteeism and teachers' ratings) suggested a possible sleeper effect; that is, they did not indicate significant improvement for the experimental group relative to controls until the 1-year follow-up (although there was only a significant interaction term for teachers' ratings). Perhaps most significantly, internal correlations between moral judgment gain and improvement on all the behavior variables were significant on both the post test and follow-up.

I believe that such reductions in antisocial behavior take place through dilemma sessions not only for cognitive–developmental but also for affective–socialization reasons. In cognitive terms, as indicated earlier, the advent of stage 3 moral judgment through the coordination or equilibration of social perspectives—for example, through the "transactive" process described by Berkowitz, Oser, and Althof, Chapter 11, this volume—generates a deterrent against antisocial behavior: Mutualistic role taking (stage 3) is simply much less amenable to self-serving egocentrism than are contingent calculations (stage 2). Also, empathic feelings become less superficial as they become structured by mutualistic thinking. Furthermore, the very process of equality-based turn taking involved in a group discussion (especially as regulated by the session leader) effects some attenuation of egocentrism: The subject must listen as well as talk, give as well as take, and reach a resolution verbally instead of violently. The attenuation of egocentrism means in positive terms the accurate understanding and consideration of others' viewpoints, needs, rights, feelings, and so on. The "affective" point is that such consideration tends to elicit empathic feeling for those others. In effective dilemma sessions, consideration and empathy for others are also directly fostered by "inductive" session leaders who repeatedly step in at opportune points to challenge the subject and group to consider (in addition to one another's viewpoints) the distress of would-be victims given various consequences of action in a social dilemma. Indeed, as Hoffman (in press) notes, "most moral dilemmas in life. . . involve victims" and hence can "arouse empathy" even for "absent victims, future victims, and victims who are not members of one's own group." Essentially, the dilemma is serving as a vehicle for providing not only role-taking opportunities, but also something akin to inductive discipline (albeit in hypothetical rather than actual transgression circumstances and outside the parent–child relationship).

The inductive discipline comparison points up the need to consider arousal level in group sessions. Overly aroused (angry, intimidated, defensive) session participants will not learn and empathetically condition to any social cognition, just as they did not in their power–assertive homes. Dilemma session programs must also avoid underarousal; that is, the sessions must be interesting and ego involving if stimulation and disequilibration are to take place. Involvement is enhanced by the use of dilemmas entailing problem situations often faced by delinquents, and probe questions specifically geared to relevant transition stage 2/stage 3 issues. Involvement is also enhanced by controversy and vigorous discussion, the potential for which is established by heterogeneous group composition: Through pretesting on dilemma decision and moral judgment stage, one can insure that the group members will represent diversity in both respects. Composition of the group with an appreciable component (approximately 50 percent) of participants who can provide stage 3 challenges may be especially important. Hickey and Scharf (1980) noted with regard to their intervention: "The program showed great signs of distress whenever the majority of inmates did not possess at least *some* stage 3 reasoning" (p. 136). Finally, involvement is fostered if the members after several sessions start to jell as a group. In a cohesive group, subjects will especially attend to peer challenges and session leader inductions: Group members care about other group members' impressions of them, and about whether they can influence the group decision-making process and be respected as important contributors. (Conditions fostering group cohesiveness are discussed by Kohlberg & Higgins, Chapter 4, this volume.)

Samenow, too, claims to accomplish reductions in antisocial behavior—and even total reforms in behavioral life-style (pp. 250–251)—through a small-group discussion program. Samenow's program was innovated by his late mentor, Samuel Yochelson. Like the applied dilemma session program, the Yochelson–Samenow program involves vigorous small-group discussion by antisocial individuals of ethically relevant topics under the guidance of a group leader. Yochelson, too, was critically concerned with developing in the individual "new thinking patterns" (p. 257) involving "consideration of other people" (p. 231), so that he or she will learn "to live without injuring others" (p. 252).

Differences abound, however. Whereas dilemma session programs deal with the full range of antisocial behavior among youth or adults, the Yochelson--Samenow program focuses on severely antisocial behavior (e.g., adult criminal insanity cases; conducted at Saint Elizabeth's Hospital, Washington, D.C.). Also, the Yochelson–Samenow program is much more extensive: The sessions are lengthy (2 to 3 hours, vs. 1 hour for the usual dilemma session), take place almost daily (vs. several times a week), and last for a year or more (vs. several months). Even after offenders are released on parole, they must periodically report to the group. The ethically relevant material is not hypothetical moral dilemmas but instead recollected thoughts, feelings, and actions. Each inmate takes notes and reports to the group on seemingly insignificant incidents; Yochelson would identify several themes for discussion such as the offender's "expectations of other people [usually self-serving], his attempt to control others, his fears, and his anger" (p. 220). Furthermore, Yochelson's guidance was not Socratic but instead quite direct and didactic, "applying corrective concepts to everyone in the group, not just the man who was giving the report" (p. 218). This procedure would seem to go beyond even the teacher advocacy recommended by Kohlberg and Higgins (Chapter 4, this volume).

It is interesting that despite these and other differences the small-group processes in the Yochelson–Samenow program also seem to effect the attenuation of egocentrism, the inculcation of empathic motivation, and the reduction of antisocial behavior. Although Yochelson did not explicitly compose the groups in terms of developmental stage mixture, he did include individuals at different points in the process. ("Groups were organized in this manner so that a new man could see how others were functioning and the current members could see themselves all over again as they heard the questions, arguments, and excuses of a totally unchanged criminal" [p. 217].) Samenow notes that through the group discussion inmates "[find] out what a discussion is, witnessing that it is possible to disagree with a person without insulting him" (p. 237). Each subject, initially atop his "perch of solitary grandeur, ... gradually emerged from his own private universe into a world of sharing, teamwork, loyalty, and trust" (pp. 236–237).

It is probably important that something very much like inductive teaching takes place in the Yochelson–Samenow program. Samenow describes the experience of one subject named Leroy, as well as the inductive learning of others.

In Yochelson's program, the theme of the criminal's injury to others always hung heavily in the air. ... Leroy experienced new waves of awareness and then disgust as to the scope of the damage that he had inflicted in almost three decades as a criminal. Beyond physical suffering and financial loss, injury extends to the emotional damage, to the climate of fear engendered in the aftermath of a crime, and to the disruption of lives. A small violation has a far-reaching effect. If a man pays for a meal with a bad check, the business suffers a direct loss. But the customers are hurt too, because if enough of these losses occur, management will refuse to take checks and customers will have to pay by cash or credit card. Furthermore, because the cost of losses is passed on to customers, the offender's own mother will have to pay more in that very restaurant. One of the men in Yochelson's group had committed burglaries and had been in a few fights. But he hadn't fought or broken into any place lately. He asserted that he wasn't much of a criminal because "I only dealt drugs." Yochelson pointed out that there was no telling how much injury this man contributed to through his drug sales. The criminal did remember that one of his buyers, after purchasing some heroin, held up a store, terrorized the customers, and shot the lady behind the cash register. But never before had he thought about these or other injuries resulting from his drug trafficking[4] (pp. 235–236)

Note that as Leroy finally attends seriously to the consequences to others of his actions he experiences "new waves of awareness and then disgust," or as Hoffman might put it, empathy-based guilt. Empathy-based guilt is probably also the best interpretation of the nausea experienced during recollections by a veteran (Pete) of the Yochelson–Samenow program:

Pete had done well in sales and had received a promotion. Now he was authorized by management to attend an out-of-town convention. Pete picked up the phone book to look up the airlines number to make reservations. As he ran his finger down the page, he thought of the obscene phone calls he had made to clerks at nearly all the airlines, as he tried to find a female agent who would engage in sexual repartee while he clung to the other end of the line masturbating and fantasizing. As these recollections flashed through Pete's mind, he was revolted to the point of feeling physically nauseated. (pp. 237–238)

Gradually, repeatedly induced empathy and empathy-based guilt come to prompt and enhance spontaneous consideration of others' feelings and legitimate expectations in the course of the offender's erstwhile self-centered thinking and behavior. No longer can incipient other-oriented thoughts and feelings be so readily "shut down" as egoistic motives arise, or neutralized by self-serving rationalizations. Perhaps for the first time, empathy for a prospective (direct or indirect) victim emerges powerfully enough to suppress aggressive impulses or inhibit irresponsible behavior; that is, to permit the accomplishment of self-control. An example from the case of Leroy:

One day in the group, Leroy reported that a "sexy looking thing" was waiting at the bus stop. Catching himself thinking, "She'd be a nice piece to have," he shifted his gaze, then boarded the bus and buried himself in the newspaper. She made her way down the aisle, plopped down beside him, and brushed her thigh against his. Leroy shifted his leg and responded politely to the conversation. Deciding to keep things light, he discussed the weather and bus breakdowns. When he got off, he thought he was a "damn idiot" for not taking her phone number. But as he walked to his office building, *he had an image of Mary, who had suffered so much in the past because of him. Now she was beginning to trust him, to plan a life with him as her husband and father of their two boys. He felt ashamed of his thoughts about the girl on the bus* and dug into the work piled up on his desk. (pp. 240–241; emphasis added)

Through experiences of successful self-control, a sense of integrity gradually emerges and comes to induce its own reward: "Perhaps what Leroy and others prized most was not so much the tangible accomplishments [e.g., job promotions] but rather the feeling of being clean" (p. 241).

Antisocial behavior may be particularly difficult to inhibit following frustration, when empathy must check a deeply ingrained violent response. Part of the offender's problem with frustration may be that he or she simply is not used to preparing and initiating constructive responses incompatible with destructive ones. Hence Yochelson also prompted each of the subjects to "learn to anticipate situations in which he might be angry and think them through in advance" (p. 226). An example of aiding anger inhibition by anticipating problems is provided in a group report by Mark.

> Mark, one of the men most advanced in change in the group, reported that he and his wife Liz were driving to the mountains for a holiday weekend. In the past, the two of them had had arguments, long, cold silences, tears, and bitter recriminations whenever they were together, but especially on vacation. Weekends and trips had totally fallen apart over the most inconsequential incidents because Mark had always insisted on having his way. He tried to control Liz, even to the point of deciding what she should order from the menu for dinner. This time Mark was trying to anticipate everything that could possibly go wrong—getting lost, car trouble, illness, dirty accommodations, cold weather, rain, weak coffee, inconsiderate people, crowds at recreational facilities, a wife wanting to do something he didn't have any interest in, her moving at a slower pace, her having her period and refusing sex. (pp. 229–230)

Yochelson's program in this respect has much in common with the self-instruction and "thinking ahead" procedures[5] of anger control training programs (Feindler & Ecton, 1986). Note, however, that empathic inductions probably play a considerable role even in this aspect of Yochelson's program: Anticipating problems includes anticipating the feelings, preferences, and needs that *others* might have. Presumably, Mark did in fact become less domineering and antagonistic as he genuinely listened to and empathized with "a wife wanting to do something he didn't have any interest in, her moving at a slower pace, her having her period and refusing sex."

It is possible to use the moral dilemmas as vehicles to accomplish some of these cognitive–behavioral benefits; for example, through role-play exercises (cf. Chandler, 1973; Staub, 1971). Short of actual role play, perspective-switching probe questions ("How do you think so-and-so felt?"; "If you were so-and-so, how would you feel if . . .?") may be effective in promoting empathy and altruistic or anger-inhibited behavior (cf. Thompson & Hoffman, 1980). Many of the dilemmas, for example, interpersonal problems linked to drug abuse, theft, or alcoholism, are only ostensibly hypothetical and can readily serve as springboards for subjects to reflect on personal responsibility for injury to others. Subjects can also learn to anticipate and cope with problems through the dilemmas: A dilemma can be presented at least initially as open ended, and subjects can then suggest various alternative solutions with consideration of their consequences (direct vs. indirect, short run vs.long range, destructive vs.

constructive, self-centered vs. considerate—cf. Spivack & Shure, 1974). Alternatively, one can utilize an eclectic program: for example, combining a dilemma session program with a program for controlling anger, as Goldstein and associates (1986) are doing.

The Yochelson–Samenow program per se would have to be substantially modified, however, before it would be appropriate for most antisocial youth. For one thing, Yochelson worked with volunteers, already at least fleetingly motivated by "disgust for the past and fear about the future" (p. 218) to try to change; those working with antisocial youth may not have the opportunity to work exclusively with volunteers, however. Also, in preliminary sessions before each subject was "permitted" (p. 217) to join a group, he or she was subjected to a frank personality assessment. Yochelson "did not worry about establishing rapport," because the aim was to make clear to the subject that Yochelson "would not fall prey to [his] diversions, excuses, and other attempts to mislead and confuse him" (p. 214). For example, Leroy sat "almost mesmerized while Yochelson picked him apart and presented him with a mirror image of himself" (p. 215):

> Bluntly, Yochelson told him that he was a thoroughbred criminal and that three options were possible: Leroy could continue in crime and experience the consequences; he could commit suicide, in which case society would be better off; or he could learn to live like a civilized human being and become a responsible person. (p. 216)

Although such a blunt approach may be necessary with Yochelson and Samenow's "thoroughbred" criminals, it is not so clear that such an approach would be advisable for less severe, less hardened youthful offenders, especially those who are anxious–withdrawn (Quay, 1979) or internalizing (Achenbach & Edelbrock, 1978). Told that "society would be better off," this type of delinquent might indeed choose suicide.[6] Also, recall that harsh power assertion and post optimal affect arousal are part of the *problem* in the backgrounds of many antisocial youths; the optimally arousing or nonthreatening but challenging atmosphere required for dilemma session inductions and other role-taking opportunities may be seriously undermined by such preliminaries. On the other hand (as noted), it may be important to focus at *some* opportune point in the dilemma sessions on each subject's personal responsibility for actual harm done to others, if a sense of empathy-based guilt is to be induced along with empathy and moral judgment development.

The most important feature of the Yochelson small-group program may be not the blunt preliminaries or the situational skills training, but the role-taking opportunities and inductions whereby subjects grow in sociomoral understanding and in feeling for other people. As Hoffman (1983) notes, cognitive, linguistic, and social–situational skills are themselves neutral with respect to moral versus immoral behavior, since "they can be useful in manipulating as well as benefiting others" (p. 269). We believe it is mainly the need to facilitate sociomorally *mature* and *empathic* "thinking patterns" that Samenow had in mind in writing: "To teach a criminal social skills without addressing lifelong thinking patterns is as useless as pouring a delectable sauce over a slice of burned, rancid meat" (p. 196). I have emphasized the need to transform empathy in antisocial youth from superficial and erratic sentiments or impulses into a stable feeling for other people, one that can inhibit aggression and even prompt altruism. We cognitive developmentalists, in theory if not in practice, have neglected this aspect of the remedial problem. In our therapeutic interventions with antisocial youth, we must respond to the pointed introspection of one of Samenow's subjects, quoted earlier:

> I really don't have any feelings for those I hurt. Were I to rape a woman, I wouldn't feel one second of her pain or anguish. . . . Where my own interests and pleasures are concerned, my feelings for others are automatically so totally suppressed and discarded as to be totally absent. . . . If I could appreciate the sufferings of my victims, they wouldn't be my victims. (p. 235)

REFERENCES

Achenbach, T. M., & Edelbrock, C. S. (1978). The classification of child psychopathology: A review and analysis of empirical efforts. *Psychological Bulletin, 85,* 1275–1301.

Arbuthnot, J., & Gordon, D. A. (1986). Behavioral and cognitive effects of a moral reasoning development intervention high-risk behavior-disordered adolescents. *Journal of Consulting & Clinical Psychology, 54,* 208–216.

Barahal, R. M., Waterman, J., & Martin, H. P. (1981). The social cognitive development of abused children. *Journal of Consulting & Clinical Psychology, 49,* 508–516.

Bear, G. G., & Richards, H. C. (1981). Moral reasoning and conduct problems in the classroom. *Journal of Educational Psychology, 73,* 644–670.

Blasi, A. (1980). Bridging moral cognition and moral action: A critical review of the literature. *Psychological Bulletin, 88,* 1–45.

Bohman, M., Cloninger, C. R., Sigvardsson, S., & von Knorring, A.-L. (1982). Predisposition to petty criminality in Swedish adoptees. I. Genetic and environmental heterogeneity. *Archives of General Psychiatry, 39,* 1233–1241.

Buss, A. H., & Plomin, R. (1984). *Temperament: Early developing personality traits.* Hillsdale, NJ: Erlbaum.

Campagna, A. F., & Harter, S. (1975). Moral Judgment in sociopathic and normal children. *Journal of Personality & Social Psychology, 31,* 199–205.

Chandler, M. J. (1973). Egocentrism and antisocial behavior: The assessment and training of social perspective-taking skills. *Developmental Psychology, 9,* 326–332.

Christiansen, K. O. (1977). A preliminary study of criminality among twins. In S. A. Mednick & K. O. Christiansen (Eds.), *Biosocial bases of criminal behavior.* New York: Wiley.

Cleckley, H. (1964). *The mask of sanity* (4th ed.). St. Louis: Mosby.

Dodge, K. A. (1980). Social cognition and children's aggressive behavior. *Child Development, 51,* 162–170.

Douglas, E. K. (1986). *The relationship of moral judgment, guilt, self-esteem, and conduct in institutionalized male delinquents.* Unpublished doctoral dissertation, the Ohio State University, Columbus.

Ellis, P. L. (1982). Empathy: A factor in antisocial behavior. *Journal of Abnormal Child Psychology, 10,* 123–124.

Eysenck, H. J., & Eysenck, S. B. G. (1978). Psychopathy, personality, and genetics. In R. D. Hare & D. Schalling (Eds.), *Psychopathic behaviour: Approaches to research.* Chichester, England: Wiley.

Farrington, D. P. (1978). The family backgrounds of aggressive youth. In L.A. Hersov & M. Berger (Eds.), *Aggression and anti-social behavior in childhood and adolescence.* Oxford, England: Pergamon.

Feindler, E. L., & Ecton, R.B. (1986). *Adolescent anger control: Cognitive-behavioral techniques.* New York: Pergamon.

Feshbach, N. D. (1983). Learning to care: A positive approach to child training and discipline. *Journal of Clinical Child Psychology, 12,* 266–271

Garmezy, N. (1983). Stressors of childhood. In N. Garmezy & M. Rutter (Eds.), *Stress, coping and development in children.* New York: McGraw-Hill.

Gavaghan, M. P., Arnold, K. D., & Gibbs, J. C. (1983). Moral judgment in delinquents and nondelinquents: Recognition versus production measures. *Journal of Psychology, 114,* 267–274.

Gibbs, J. C., Arnold, K. D., Ahlborn, H. H., & Cheesman, F. L. (1984). Facilitation of sociomoral reasoning in delinquents. *Journal of Consulting & Clinical Psychology, 52,* 37–45.

Gibbs, J. C., & Schnell, S. V. (1985). Moral development "versus," socialization: A critique. *American Psychologist, 40,* 1071–1080.

Goldstein, A. P., Glick, B., Reiner, S., Zimmerman, D., Coultry, T. M., & Gold, D. (1986). Aggression replacement training: A comprehensive intervention for the acting-out delinquent. *Journal of Correctional Education, 37,* 120–125.

Gough, H. G. (1948). A sociological theory of psychopathy. *American Journal of Sociology, 53,* 359–366.

Hare, R. D. (1975). Psychophysiological studies of psychopathy. In D. C. Fowks (Ed.), *Clinical application of psychophysiology.* New York: Columbia University Press.

Hickey, J., & Scharf, P. (1980). *Toward a just correctional system.* San Francisco: Jossey-Bass.

Hoffman, M. L. (1970). Conscience, personality, and socialization techniques. *Human Development, 13,* 90–126.

Hoffman, M. L. (1978). Toward a theory of empathic arousal and development. In M. Lewis & L. A. Rosenblum (Eds.)., *The development of affect* (Vol. 1). New York: Plenum

Hoffman, M. L. (1981). Is altruism part of human nature? *Journal of Personality & Social Psychology, 40,* 121–137.

Hoffman, M. L. (1983). Affective and cognitive processes in moral internalization. In E. T. Higgins, D. N. Ruble, & W. W. Hartup (Eds.), *Social cognition and social development: A sociocultural perspective.* Cambridge, England: Cambridge University Press.

Hoffman, M. L. (in press). The contribution of empathy to justice and moral judgment. In N. Eisenberg & J. Strayer (Eds.), *Empathy: A developmental perspective.* New York: Cambridge University Press.

Hoffman M. L., & Saltzstein H. D. (1967). Parental discipline and the child's moral development. *Journal of Personality & Social Psychology, 5,* 45–47.

Jennings, W. S., Kilkenny, R., & Kohlberg, L. (1983). Moral development theory and practice for youthful and adult offenders. In W. S. Laufer & J. M. Day (Eds.), *Personality theory, moral development and criminal behavior.* Lexington, MA: Lexington Books.

Kagan, J., & Moss, H. A. (1962). *Birth to maturity.* New York: Wiley.

Kaplan, P. (1984). *Developing affective empathy and moral reasoning skills in delinquent males.* Unpublished manuscript, Ohio University, Athens, Ohio.

Kaplan, P., & Arbuthnot, J. (1985). Affective empathy and cognitive role-taking in delinquent and nondelinquent youth. *Adolescence, 20*, 323–333.

Karpman, B. (1941). On the need for separating psychopathy into two distinct types: The symptomatic and the idiopathic. *Journal of Criminal Psychopathology, 3*, 112–137.

Kohlberg, L. (1969). Stage and sequence: The cognitive–developmental approach to socialization. In D. Goslin (Ed.), *Handbook of socialization theory and research.* Chicago: Rand McNally.

Kohlberg, L. (1984). *The psychology of moral development: Essays on moral development* (Vol. 2). San Francisco: Harper & Row.

Lockwood, A. L. (1978). Effects of values clarification and moral development curricula on school-age subjects: A critical review of recent research. *Review of Education Research, 48*, 325–364.

Looft, W. (1972). Egocentrism and social interaction across the life span. *Psychological Bulletin, 78*, 73–92.

Maccoby, E. E. (1980). *Social development: Psychosocial growth and the parent–child relationship.* New York: Harcourt Brace Jovanovich.

Mednick, S. A., Gabrielli, W. F., Jr., & Hutchings, B. (1984). Genetic influences in criminal convictions: Evidence from an adoption cohort. *Science, 224*, 891–894.

Mednick, S. A., Volavka, J., Gabrielli, W. F., Jr., & Itil, T. M. (1981). EEG as a predictor of antisocial behavior. *Criminology, 19*, 212–229.

Mitchell, S., & Rosa, P. (1981). Boyhood behaviour problems as precursors of criminality: A fifteen-year follow up study. *Journal of Child Psychology & Psychiatry, 22*, 19–33.

Patterson, G. R. (1976). The aggresssive child: Victim and architect of a coercive system. In L. A. Hamerlynck, L. C. Handy & E. J. Mash (Eds.), *Behavior modification and families. I. Theory and research.* New York: Brunner-Mazel.

Patterson, G. R. (1982) *Coercive family process.* Eugene, OR: Castalia.

Patterson, G. R., & Cobb, J. A. (1971). A dyadic analysis of "aggressive" behaviors. In J. P. Hill (Ed.), *Minnesota Symposium on Child Psychology, 5.* Minneapolis: University of Minnesota Press.

Patterson G. R. & Reid J. B. (1970). Reciprocity and coercion: Two facets of social systems. In C. Neuringer & J. L. Michael (Eds.), *Behavior modification in clinical psychology.* New York: Appleton-Century-Crofts.

Perry, D. G., & Perry, L. C. (1974). Denial of suffering in the victim as a stimulus to violence in aggressive boys. *Child Development, 45*, 55–62.

Quay, H. C. (1979). Classification. In H. C. Quay & J. S. Werry (Eds.), *Psychopathological disorders of childhood* (2nd ed.). New York: Wiley.

Robins, L. N. (1966). *Deviant children grown up: A sociological and psychiatric study of sociopathic personality.* Baltimore: Williams & Wilkins.

Rowe, D. C. (1983). Biometrical genetic models of self-reported delinquent behavior: A twin study. *Behavior Genetics, 13*, 473–489.

Rowe, D. C., & Osgood, D. W. (1984). Heredity and sociological theories of delinquency: A reconsideration. *American Sociological Review, 49*, 526–540.

Ruma, E. H., & Mosher, D. L. (1967). Relationship between moral reasoning and guilt in delinquent boys. *Journal of Abnormal Psychology, 72*, 122–127.

Samenow, S. E. (1984). *Inside the criminal mind.* New York: Random House.

Schlaefli, A., Rest, V. R., & Thoma, S. J. D. (1985). Does moral education improve moral judgment? A meta-analysis of intervention studies using the Defining Issues Test. *Review of Educational Research, 55*, 319–352.

Schnell, S. V. (1986). *Delinquents with mature moral reasoning: A comparison with delayed delinquents and mature nondelinquents.* Unpublished doctoral dissertation, the Ohio State University, Columbus.

Short, R. J., & Simeonsson, R. J. (1986). Social cognition and aggression in delinquent adolescent males. *Adolescence, 21,* 159–176.

Siddle, D. A. T., & Trasler, G. B. (1981). The psychophysiology of psychopathic behavior. In M. J. Christie & P. G. Mellet (Eds.), *Foundations of psychosomatics.* Chichester, England: Wiley.

Spivack, G., & Shure, M. B. (1974). *Social adjustment of young children: A cognitive approach to solving real-life problems.* San Francisco: Jossey-Bass.

Spivack G. Marcus J. & Swift M. (1986). Early classroom behaviors and later misconduct. *Developmental Psychology, 22,* 124–131.

Staub, E. (1971). The use of role playing and induction in children's learning of helping and sharing behavior. *Child Development, 42,* 805–816.

Sykes, G. M., & Matza, D. (1957). Techniques of neutralization: A theory of delinquency. *American Sociological Review, 22,* 664–670.

Taylor, T., & Watt, D. C. (1977). The relation of deviant symptoms and behavior in a normal population of subsequent delinquency and maladjustment. *Psychological Medicine, 7,* 163–169.

Thomas, A., & Chess, S. (1984). Genesis and evolution of behavioral disorders: From infancy to early adult life. *American Journal of Psychiatry, 141,* 1–9.

Thompson, R., & Hoffman, M. L. (1980). Empathy and the arousal of guilt in children. *Developmental Psychology, 15,* 155–156.

Trickett, P. K., & Kuczynski, L. (1986). Children's misbehaviors and parental discipline strategies in abusive and non-abusive families. *Developmental Psychology, 22,* 115–123.

Welsh, R. S. (1976). Severe parental punishment and delinquency: A developmental theory. *Journal of Clinical Child Psychology, 5,* 17–21.

Werner, E. E., & Smith, R. S. (1982). *Vulnerable but invincible: A study of resilient children.* New York: McGraw-Hill.

Wilson, J. Q., & Herrnstein, R. J. (1985). *Crime and human nature.* New York: Simon & Schuster.

Wolfgang, M., Figlio, R. F., & Sellin, T. (1972). *Delinquency in a birth cohort.* Chicago: University of Chicago Press.

Yochelson, S., & Samenow, S. (1977). *The criminal personality* (Vol. 2). New York: Aronson.

Zahn-Waxler, C., Radke-Yarrow, M., & King, R. M. (1979). Childrearing and children's prosocial initiations toward victims of distress. *Child Development, 50,* 319–330.

REFERENCE NOTES

1. Samenow suggests that such "isolated acts of kindness" as well as occasional "sentimentality," by supporting "the criminal's inherent view that he is a good person," actually contribute to his criminality: "He sincerely believes that any sin he might have committed is more than compensated for by the good he has done" (p. 168).

2. Samenow asserts that when "criminals commit a crime, they can shut off considerations of conscience as quickly and totally as they can shut off an electric light" (p. 163). Similarly, Hoffman (1970) found that children evidencing "externally oriented" (cf. stages 1 and 2) moral judgment show empathy-based guilt only fleetingly on pro-

jective tasks, leading him to infer that "externals" may have "developed defenses" against empathy "which are activated immediately upon experiencing it" (pp. 102–103).

3. Nonetheless, a minority of delinquents evidence stage 3 moral judgment; these juveniles may experience dissonance between their antisocial behavior or attitudes and their moral judgment maturity. Schnell (1986) has found that, although stage 3 delinquents endorse antisocial values more than do stage 3 nondelinquents, they also indicate more guilt-related anxiety responses (on the MMPI) than do stage 3 nondelinquents as well as stage 2 delinquents (cf. Douglas, 1986; Ruma & Mosher, 1967). It is likely that these delinquents would be classified as anxious–withdrawn in terms of Quay's (1979) typology.

4. Hoffman (in press) relates empathy-enhancing inductive teaching to the role of moral education:

It seems clear that one thing moral education can do is teach people a simple rule of thumb: Look beyond the immediate situation and ask questions such as "What kind of experiences does the person have in various situations beyond the immediate one?"; "How will my action affect him or her, not only now but in the future?;" and "Are there other people, present or absent, who might be affected by my actions?" If children learn to ask these questions, their empathic responses should be less exclusively confined to the here and now.

Hoffman also recommends "training in role-taking procedures that are vivid enough to generate empathic feelings for people in different circumstances than their own."

5. In the Yochelson–Samenow program, the offender must learn to think ahead by introducing against immediate impulses long-run considerations such as whether a momentary gratification of pleasure or revenge is "worth throwing away his life [i.e., everything he has begun to accomplish] and returning to the gutter" (p. 231).

6. Recently, Samenow (personal communication, Feb. 11, 1986) has abandoned this line even with adults because "it can be provocative unnecessarily." When working with adolescents, Samenow instead points out "the errors in suicidal thinking [if] the youngster indicates that he has such thoughts."

CHAPTER 11

The Development of Sociomoral Discourse

MARVIN W. BERKOWITZ, FRITZ OSER, AND WOLFGANG ALTHOF

The authors would like to express their appreciation to Joyce Caldwell and Sister Marie-Madleine Schildknecht for supervising the data collection of the American and Swiss cross-sectional samples, respectively.

As psychological and educational researchers and theorists have investigated sociomoral cognition, they have come to recognize that a critical factor in the development of such competencies is the nature of social interactions concerning social and moral issues, particularly verbal interactions. Recently, interest has turned to the investigation of sociomoral discourse itself, first as an independent variable affecting individual development, then as a process variable in the course of development. This chapter examines sociomoral discourse from a third perspective, as an independent variable; that is, it examines the development of sociomoral discourse. First, a brief history of the literature on sociomoral discourse analysis is presented. This includes a description of the theory of transactive discussion, a form of sociomoral discourse that has been shown to facilitate individual development of sociomoral cognition. Then the six existing studies relevant to the development of transactive discussion are reviewed. In this review, new data from a cross-cultural cross-sectional study of children and young adults 6 to 20 years old are presented. Additionally, a descriptive meta-analysis of the five studies of transactive discussion is employed to explore the development of transactive discussion. Finally, a preliminary stage model of the development of sociomoral discourse, based upon the theory of transactive discussion and upon the empirical and theoretical work of others such as Selman, Piaget, Habermas, and Powers, is presented.

Over the past two decades, theorists and researchers in cognitive structural developmental psychology have begun to investigate the social processes that impact upon individual cognitive growth. While Piaget (1932/1965a) has long argued that social relationships and interactions can facilitate or inhibit structural growth, it is only recently that serious empirical attention has been focused on this issue. Beginning with studies of children jointly attempting to solve conservation tasks (Miller & Brownell, 1975) and leading to similar studies in the sociomoral development domain (e.g., Berkowitz & Gibbs, 1983), such investigations have attempted to identify how social interactions can foment individual growth (cf. Berkowitz, 1985). These investigations have identified such variables as presentations of conflictual constructions (Miller & Brownell, 1975), reasoning about one's partner's constructions (Berkowitz & Gibbs, 1983), supportive styles of confrontation (Powers, 1982), and optimal stage disparity of sequential constructions (Taranto, 1984).

While these investigations have spanned early childhood (Damon & Killen, 1982; Miller & Brownell, 1975) to early adulthood (Berkowitz & Gibbs, 1983; Powers, 1982), there has been almost no consideration of the "second-order" developmental question; that is, how do the developmentally stimulating interactional processes themselves develop? In other words, we have focused on how the interactional processes lead to cognitive development, but not on how the interactional processes are formed. This question has both theoretical and practical significance. Theoretically, if developmentally stimulating interactional processes are dependent upon a specific level of cognitive development, for example, if certain social skills require a certain level of logical sophistication, then they should only be relevant for investigations of individuals in a limited developmental range. We therefore need to consider how the interactional processes may vary for individuals at different developmental levels. Practically, if such interactional processes are at play in natural development and in common developmental institutions, for example, the school and the family, then we need to know how to chart and facilitate their development in order to maximize the developmental richness of these milieux. Hence it becomes critical to study how the developmentally relevant features of social interactions develop.

In this chapter, we will examine the development of moral discussion, thus representing what has previously been termed the developmental perspective on sociomoral discussion (Berkowitz, 1986). In doing so, we will be focusing on the developmentally stimulating features of such discourse, but we will not focus exclusively on that aspect of the phenomenon. First we will present a brief history of the literature on sociomoral discussion analysis. Second, we will review the few existing studies of the development of sociomoral discussion, including results from a cross-sectional cross-cultural study of the development of sociomoral discussion behavior, while considering the developmental status of the subjects investigated. Finally, we will present a preliminary stage model for the development of sociomoral discussion.

THE STUDY OF SOCIOMORAL DISCUSSION: AN OVERVIEW

Sociomoral discussion originally was of interest as an educational intervention technique (Blatt & Kohlberg, 1975; Colby, Kohlberg, Fenton, Speicher-Dubin, & Lieberman, 1977). The use of peer discussion of sociomoral dilemmas was indirectly derived from the standard Kohlberg assessment technique (Colby et al., in press), which has recently been reconceptualized as a sociomoral discussion (Keller & Reuss, 1985). As the use of sociomoral discussion education proliferated, attempts were made to conceptualize the effective features of the technique (see review by Berkowitz, 1981). Nonetheless, most of these attempts were post hoc reflections or simply theoretical conjectures. Little empirical evidence was collected and that little bit was poorly designed and therefore less than illuminating.

The classic sociomoral discussion paradigm centers upon (1) a trained expert's (teacher's, researcher's, etc.) presentation of a sociomoral dilemma to a typically homogeneous group (usually school children or adolescents) and subsequently (2) the facilitation of a group discussion of the sociomoral implications of the problem under consideration, usually following at least loosely the guidelines of a class lesson plan or specific discussion procedure (e.g., Arbuthnot & Faust, 1981; Galbraith & Jones, 1976; Gomberg, Cameron, Fenton, Furtek & Hill, 1980; Reimer, Paolitto, & Hersh, 1983). The results are typically for the sociomoral discussion group to gain, on the average, about one third of a stage in Kohlberg's (1984) stage scheme while comparison groups (typically, "no discussion" conditions) do not change appreciably in their stages of sociomoral thinking. Then the investigators suggest what aspect of their manipulation was the likely culprit in inducing this change, for example, the discussion leader's style or the exposure to specific sociomoral arguments. Rarely have these features of sociomoral discussion been systematically controlled in a successful sociomoral discussion intervention program. Nonetheless, the use of "generic" sociomoral discussion has been successful in inducing sociomoral reasoning stage development and continues to be used extensively both in classrooms and in the laboratory as well as more recently in the family (Lickona, 1983) and the church (Caldwell & Berkowitz, in press). In order to better understand how sociomoral discussion leads to sociomoral reasoning development, Berkowitz and Gibbs (1983) began the study of transactive sociomoral discussion.

The theory of transactive discussion is predicated on the Piagetian assumption that discussion leads to development by means of the disequilibrating effects of the confrontation of incompatible constructions presented by two or more discussants (Piaget, 1965a). When one considers another's (alter's) construction in the context of one's own (ego's) construction and subjectively discovers incompatibility, one experiences disequilibrium, which is a necessary but not sufficient condition for stage growth. The more actively and fully one considers incompatible constructions, the more likely one is to experience disequilibrium. We have therefore defined transactive discussion as reasoning about another's reasoning (Berkowitz & Gibbs, 1983). We specifically were looking for features of moral discussions that we could empirically demonstrate led to the development of the sociomoral reasoning of the undergraduate same-sex dyadic discussants we studied, while at the same time fulfilling this definition. In the process we identified 18 categories of transacts grouped into lower-order (representational) types and higher-order (operational) types. The former are behaviors in which one simply represents alter's construction as in a paraphrase (see Table 11.1, transact 2). The latter are behaviors in which one cognitively "operates" on or transforms alter's construction as in a reasoning critique or integration (Table 11.1, transacts 14 and 17a). We have empirically demonstrated that the degree of transaction in a dialogue is related to the degree of sociomoral reasoning development of the lower-stage discussant and that this relationship is a stronger and independent predictor of development when compared to the stage disparity between the discussants or the absolute stage of the discussants. Finally, operational transaction seems to be more strongly related to development than is representational transaction. Hence we have empirically supported the theory of transactive discussion from the growth-facilitative perspective on sociomoral discussion (Berkowitz, 1986), that is, from the point of view of the developmentally stimulating aspects of sociomoral discussion. As noted earlier, in this chapter we are interested in the developmental perspective on sociomoral discussion, that is, how transactive discussion and sociomoral discussion in general develop. Let us therefore examine some more recent research on transactive discussion from the developmental perspective.

TABLE 11.1. Table of Transactions

A. Representational Transacts
    1. *Feedback Request* (R): Do you understand or agree with my position?
    2. *Paraphrase* (R):
        (a) I can understand and paraphrase your position or reasoning.
        (b) Is my paraphrase of your reasoning accurate?
    3. *Justification Request* (R): Why do you say that?
    4. *Juxtaposition* (R): Your position is X and my position is Y.
    5. *Dyad Paraphrase* (R): Here is a paraphrase of a shared position.
    6. *Competitive Juxtaposition* (R): I will make a concession to your position, but also reaffirm part of my position.

B. Hybrid Transacts
    7. *Completion* (R/O): I can complete or continue your unfinished reasoning.
    8. *Competitive Paraphrase* (R/O): Here is a paraphrase of your reasoning that highlights its weakness.

C. Operational Transacts
    9. *Clarification* (O):
        (a) No, what I am trying to say is the following.
        (b) Here is a clarification of my position to aid in your understanding.
    10. *Competitive Clarification* (O): My position is not necessarily what you take it to be.
    11. *Refinement* (O):
        (a) I must refine my position or point as a concession to your position or point (subordinative mode).
        (b) I can elaborate or qualify my position to defend against your critique (superordinative mode).
    12. *Extension* (O):
        (a) Here is a further thought or an elaboration offered in the spirit of your position.
        (b) Are you implying the following by your reasoning?
    13. *Contradiction* (O): There is a logical inconsistency in your reasoning.
    14. *Reasoning Critique* (O):
        (a) Your reasoning misses an important distinction, or involves a superfluous distinction.
        (b) Your position implicitly involves an assumption that is questionable (premise attack).
        (c) Your reasoning does not necessarily lead to your conclusion/opinion, or your opinion has not been sufficiently justified.
        (d) Your reasoning applies equally well to the opposite opinion.
    15. *Competitive Extension* (O):
        (a) Would you go to this implausible extreme with your reasoning?
        (b) Your reasoning can be extended to the following extreme, with which neither of us would agree.
    16. *Counter Consideration* (O): Here is a thought or element that cannot be incorporated into your position.
    17. *Common Ground/Integration* (O):
        (a) We can combine our positions into a common view.
        (b) Here is a general premise common to both of our positions.
    18. *Comparative Critique* (O):
        (a) Your reasoning is less adequate than mine because it is incompatible with the important consideration here.
        (b) Your position makes a distinction that is seen as superfluous in light of my position, or misses an important distinction that my position makes.
        (c) I can analyze your example to show that it does not pose a challenge to my position.

THE DEVELOPMENT OF TRANSACTIVE DISCUSSION:
A RECONSTRUCTIVE ANALYSIS

Six studies of transactive discussion are amenable to a developmental interpretation. They were not necessarily designed from the developmental point of view, but we can reconstructively interpret them in two ways that will help shed light on the developmental question. First, we can reexamine the findings of each study to see whether there is a developmental question embedded in the design. Second, we can engage in a comparative meta-analysis by examining the behaviors of the subjects of different ages in the different studies. Let us begin by examining two studies that contain developmental aspects.

Gibbs, Schnell, Berkowitz, and Goldstein (1983) tested the hypothesis that operational transaction is a formal logical skill and requires the development of Piagetian formal operational thought for its manifestation in sociomoral discussion. They argued that (1) operational transacts appeared to be logical reasoning acts and (2) Piaget (1972) had hypothesized that the advent of formal operations would herald similar changes in dialogue. College students were paired on the bases of (1) their levels of formal operational thinking (assessed by the *Test of Logical Thinking* [TOLT], Tobin & Capie, 1981) and (2) their disagreement on the action solution to a series of sociomoral dilemmas. Dyad members were in disagreement on the action solution to the dilemmas and were homogeneously either nonformal, transitional, or formal operational on the TOLT. While 76 percent of the formal operators used transactive sociomoral discussion, only 29 percent of the transitionals and 8 percent of the nonformal subjects used transactive discussion behaviors. These data strongly suggest that transactive discussion skills are based upon the prior acquisition of logical thinking skills.

Powers (1982), as part of a larger study of adolescent ego development, analyzed mother–father–adolescent trialogues about a sociomoral dilemma for transactive discussion. Her main interest was not in the development of transactive skills per se, but her data analyses shed some light on this question. In examining the correlations between one's stage of sociomoral reasoning and one's usage of transaction in the family discussion, there is a significant positive relation for both mothers and fathers of nonpsychiatric adolescents. Surprisingly there was no significant relation for their children. Thus there seems to be a relation between usage of transactive discussion behaviors and sociomoral development for adults but not for adolescents in this study.

We can now turn to the comparative analysis of evidence about subjects at different ages of the life span from six different studies. Four studies have examined the transactive discussion behaviors of adolescents and adults (Berkowitz & Gibbs, 1983; Gibbs et al., 1983; Leadbeater, 1986; Powers, 1982). Powers reports data only for the entire family discussion, comprising two adults and one adolescent. From her Tables 7 and 9, we can calculate that 52 percent of the total speech acts coded were transactive. We can further calculate that 29 percent were representational transacts and 23 percent were operational transacts. Leadbeater found no significant difference in usage of transaction between 20 high school (ages 15 to 17) and 20 adult (29 to 42) subjects, and

TABLE 11.2.   Comparative Analysis of Transaction at Varied Ages

Age	N	Study	Transaction Percentage		Total
			Operational	Representational	
7	24	Kruger and Tomasello (1986)	—	—	12.8
11	24	Kruger and Tomasello (1986)	—	—	13.4
Mean–19	80	Gibbs, Schnell, Berkowitz, and Goldstein (1983)	4	—	—
Mean–21	60	Berkowitz and Gibbs (1983)	16	7	23
Mean–24 (adolescent and young adult)	40	Leadbeater (1986)	—	—	20
12 to 16 with parents	59 118	Powers (1982)	23	29	52
Mothers of 7 and 11–year olds	24	Kruger and Tomasello (1986)	—	—	16.2

therefore only reports the grand mean of 20 percent of total statements being transactive. No data are reported on operational versus representational transaction. Berkowitz and Gibbs's subjects were college students. They reported a total of 23 percent transaction, with 16 percent operational and 7 percent representational. While Gibbs and colleagues also studied undergraduate dyads, they only coded operational transacts. They also employed very stringent coding criteria and overrepresented low cognitive ability subjects in their sample. They observed only 4 percent transaction. We can therefore see that as the mean age and the cognitive level of the subjects increase, so does the usage of transactive discussion behaviors (see Table 11.2).

There have also been two studies of children that have reported data on transactive discussion (Damon & Killen, 1982; Kruger & Tomasello, 1986). While Damon and Killen were successful in demonstrating a relation between use of transaction and sociomoral reasoning development in children in kindergarten through third grade, they only coded four transact categories (equivalent to categories 2, 9, 12, and 18 in Table 11) and did not report data on their degree of usage. Kruger and Tomasello observed 7- and 11-year-old children in dialogues with either a same-age peer or a parent. They did not report usage data for representational versus operational transacts, but did report the following mean percentages of total transaction for the 7-year-old, and adult groups, respectively: 12.8, 13.4, 16.2. Thus if we examine Table 11.2 we can see some suggestive patterns. There seems to be a trend for operational transaction to increase with increasing age and cognitive development across the three studies that report such data. With the exception of the mothers in the Kruger and Tomasello (1986) study, there is also a clear trend for total transaction to increase with age. We can conjecture that the Kruger and Tomasello data are affected by the fact that the adults studied were observed in discussions with their young children. As researchers have demonstrated, adults alter their discourse behavior when communicating with children of different developmental levels (Newport, 1977; Phillips, 1973). Hence the mothers observed here may well have lowered the sophistication of their discourse behaviors to accommodate to the perceived communication limits of their codiscussants (children). These data are nonetheless only suggestive, due to the variability of the data-gathering and coding techniques used by the different researchers. Furthermore, while these data impact upon the question of the development of discussion skills, they only impact on the question of the development of transactive discussion skills, most of which (i.e., operational transacts) have already been demonstrated to be related to the acquisition of formal operational thought (Gibbs et al., 1983). Therefore, the following cross-sectional study of the development of sociomoral discussion skills was designed. The first analyses we will report focused on the usage of transactive discussion throughout childhood and adolescence. Later in this chapter we will report a preliminary model of precursors to transactive discussion.

THE DEVELOPMENT OF TRANSACTIVE DISCUSSION: A CROSS-SECTIONAL STUDY

Separate samples of subjects from two cultures were observed in same-age, same-gender dialogues about one sociomoral and one religious dilemma. The two groups represented matching samples from Switzerland and the United States. Two male and two female dyads were observed in each culture at each of the following age groups: 6 to 8, 9 to 11, 12 to 14, 15 to 17, 18 to 20. The dialogues were transcribed and coded. Due to the difficulty of coordinating data collection in two different cultures on different continents, a number of potentially significant methodological differences should be cited. First, the Swiss team had access to videotaping equipment whereas the American team had to rely solely on audiotaping equipment. Second, the experimenter in the U.S. study was more intrusive in the data collection with the youngest age group. She served as a moderator and interviewer because the subjects did not interact sufficiently without her intervention. The Swiss experimenter did not employ such intrusive techniques. Third, the Swiss team used pictorial representations of the dilemmas along with the verbal accounts and the U.S. team did not. Finally, the U.S. study was done in English and the Swiss study was done in Swiss German.

In order to examine more directly whether transactive discussion increases with age, data were analyzed for the usage of transactive discussion at each of the different age groups studied. Both the religious dilemma discussion and the sociomoral dilemma discussion were coded for transactive statements and total statements. The transactive statements were also identified as either operational or representational. The dependent measures used for subsequent analyses are the percentage of total statements in a discussion that are (1) transactive, (2) specifically operational, or (3) specifically representational.

One 2 x 5 ANOVA was calculated on Culture (Swiss, American) and Age (6 to 8, 9 to 11, 12 to 14, 15 to 17, 18 to 20) for each of three dependent variables:

percentage of total statements that were transactive (PT), percentage of total statements that were operational transacts (PO), and percentage of total statements that were representational transacts (PR).

For total transaction, there was a significant Age effect. $(F [2,28] = 13.2; p <.001)$. The means for the five age groups, in increasing age order, were 2.2, 6.8, 13.5, 20.4, and 22.2. A Newman-Keuls analysis revealed that both of the two oldest age groups used significantly more transaction than each of the three youngest age groups. The same was true in comparisons of the middle group with the two youngest groups. There was no effect of Culture, but there was a significant Age x Culture interaction effect $(F [4,28] = 3.0; p <.04)$.

In order to examine further this interaction effect, one-way ANOVAs and Newman-Keuls comparisons were calculated on the Age variable for each culture separately. Age was significant for the American subjects $(F [4,13] = 6.15; p <.005)$. The youngest group (mean – 4.2) used significantly less transaction than each of the other groups with means of 11.9, 17.1, 16.5, and 19.4. Age was also significant for the Swiss subjects $(F [4,15] = 11.7; p <.001)$. Each of the two oldest groups (mean for 15- to 17-year-olds = 23.4; mean for 18- to 20-year-olds = 24.4) used significantly more transaction than each of the three youngest groups (means of 0.1, 1.8, and 9.9 in increasing age order). T-tests were also performed between cultures at each age level. Only the comparison for children 9 to 11 was significant, with the American children (11.9) scoring significantly higher than the Swiss children (1.8) $t [6] = 9.45; p <.001)$ (see Table 11.3).

To understand these results we must inspect the cross-sectional age trends for operational and representational transaction separately. The effect of Age on operational transaction was also significant $(F [4,28] = 12.1; p <.001)$. The respective means in increasing age order were 1.0, 4.5, 8.0, 15.4, and 15.1. Newman-Keuls comparisons revealed that the two oldest groups used significantly more operational transaction than the three youngest groups and that the middle group used significantly more than the youngest group (see Table 11.4). The effect of Culture was not significant and the Age x Culture interaction effect only approached significance $(F [4,28] = 2.3; p = .085)$.

TABLE 11.3.   Mean Percentage of Total Transaction (PT) by Age and Culture

Culture	Age				
	6 to 8	9 to 11	12 to 14	15 to 17	18 to 20
U.S.	4.2	11.9	17.1	16.5	19.4
Swiss	0.1	1.8	9.9	23.4	24.4
Total	2.2	6.8	13.5	20.4	22.2

TABLE 11.4.   Mean Percentage of Operational Transaction (PO) by Age and Culture

Culture	Age				
	6 to 8	9 to 11	12 to 14	15 to 17	18 to 20
U.S.	1.9	7.2	9.4	13.0	10.5
Swiss	0.1	1.7	6.5	17.2	18.6
Total	1.0	4.5	8.0	15.4	15.1

TABLE 11.5.   Mean Percentage of Representational Transaction (PR) by Age and Culture

Culture	Age				
	6 to 8	9 to 11	12 to 14	15 to 17	18 to 20
U.S.	2.3	4.6	7.6	3.6	8.9
Swiss	0.1	0.1	3.4	6.2	5.8
Total	1.2	2.4	5.5	5.1	7.1

Finally, analyses of representational transaction reveal two significant effects. The main effect for Age was significant, $F[4,28] = 6.1; p < .001$). Group means in increasing age order were 1.2, 2.4, 5.5, 5.1, and 7.1. Newman-Keuls comparisons revealed that the youngest group used significantly less representational transaction than each of the three oldest groups and that the oldest group also used significantly more than those 9 to 11 years old. The main effect for Culture was also significant ($F[1,28] = 7.0; p < .02$); American subjects used significantly more representational transaction (mean – 5.3) than Swiss subjects (3.1) did (see Table 11.5).

It appears that the use of transactive discussion increases with age, at least from 6 to 20 years of age. Furthermore, this trend is found for both lower-level (representational) and higher level (operational) forms of transactive discussion. Finally, these results are found in both an American sample and a Swiss sample. It appears, however, that American children use more overall transaction at ages 9 to 11 and generally more representational transaction across the entire sample.

These findings support our assumption that transactive discussion is a mature form of argumentative logic. It is a form that nonetheless is present in childhood, but one that becomes significantly more prominent in adolescence. Finally, transactive discussion is found in two cultures and has been coded in two languages. These data support the comparative data reported earlier and lead us to conclude that transactive discussion is relatively infrequent before adolescence. This raises the question of what forms of sociomoral discourse are present in the discussions of children.

STAGES OF SOCIOMORAL DISCUSSION

In his early work, Piaget (1932/1965a) discovered that children do not interact logically. He labeled the inability to coordinate judgments logically in an interaction *parataxical thinking*. He also noted that children construct only a vague and distorted overview of a discussion, a type of holistic intuitive thinking he has called *syncretic thinking*. Furthermore, he pointed out that children's justifications for a position tend to be less logical and more *psychological*. Despite these communicative limitations and distortions, children appear remarkably confident in concluding that they have accurately understood what another has said.

Piaget's conception of interactional logic rests on two principles. (1) The *principle of identity* states that a person must securely assert and maintain his or her position in the context of the claims of another. (2) The *principle of contradiction* states that a person has to support or reject the truth of another person's claims. The principle of identity implies maintenance and defense of ego's position while the principle of contradiction implies consideration of alter's position. In order to construct an equilibrium between these two potentially opposing principles, an individual must reduce intellectual egocentrism in favor of a more mature social decentration. To construct this decentration, Piaget suggests three necessary conditions: (1) the shared possession of significant a priori knowledge and assumptions about the content and form of the interaction; (2) an a priori equality orientation to the interaction so that all discussants are respected as equals; (3) the acceptance of the ever-present possibility of bringing the typically implicit shared assumptions, knowledge, and values under explicit discussion.

Piaget contrasts this ideal interactional equilibrium with the more typical undisciplined or unstructured interaction, which he calls free exchange. The disciplined activity of these three ideal conditions is necessary to overcome the distortive inertness of intellectual limitations and egocentrism.

Piaget has also distinguished between the logic of an individual's personal thought and the logic of an interaction. Piagetian genetic epistemology demonstrates that the development of intellectual logic precedes the development of argumentative logic. The development of individual thinking shapes the logic of argumentation (Piaget, 1965b, p. 68). In other words, the general level of intelligence of the child precedes the formative interaction between individual thought and interpersonal action that generates the construction of the logic of argumentation.

Piaget's concept of interactional decentration is interesting, but it is largely limited to cooperation in the domain of logical and physical problems. For him, such cooperation means generating operations in common, such as the analysis of qualities or the construction of topographical schemes (cf. Forman & Kraker, 1985); that is, the coordination of partners' operations in an operational system. Each partner's coordinating actions are called integrative operations. The limits of Piaget's analysis are threefold. First, Piaget does not extensively study moral, political, social, or religious matters because he considers them to be by-products of real actions and to be in opposition to the real sciences. Second, Piaget has done very few actual analyses of child interactions. Third, even the little early work he did, resulting in his identification of parataxical and syncretic thought, did not produce a clear hierarchy of developmental structures. Piaget probably did not have a clear and complete conception of the nature of mature discussion. Whereas Berkowitz and Gibbs's (1983) theory of transactive discussion clearly analyzes the logic of interaction not simply in terms of the operational system of each partner but in terms of their integrative operations, their model of transactive discussion is based almost exclusively upon research with adolescents and young adults.

Others have attempted to study the development of sociomoral discussion. While a number of theorists have recently considered various aspects of sociomoral discussion (Bearison, 1985, in press; Bell, Grossen, & Perret-Clermont, 1985; Berkowitz & Gibbs, 1985; Berndt, 1984; Forman & Kraker, 1985; Leadbeater, 1986; Shantz & Shantz, 1985), only four empirical studies of the development of children's sociomoral disussion skills are available (Keller & Reuss, 1985; Lyman & Selman, 1985; Miller, 1981; Oser, 1981).

The first research concerning the development of sociomoral argumentation appeared in the late 1970s with a paper by Miller and Klein (1979) followed shortly by a more thorough treatment by Miller (1980, 1981). Miller has been concerned with the development of sociomoral argumentation in children and has focused upon the problem of moving toward a higher perspective in sociomoral argumentation by confronting opposing perspectives. His research has attempted to identify the means by which children transcend differences in sociomoral argumentation and move to dialectically more synthesizing positions. In investigating such discussion processes, Miller has studied young children (5 to 10 years of age) in discussion groups of four. Each discussion concerned Kohlberg's Heinz dilemma (see Colby, Kohlberg, Gibbs, & Liebeiman, 1983, pp. 77–78).

The stages he has tentatively identified are defined by problems of argumentation (coordination failures) that limit the adequacy of the sociomoral discussion at each stage. These problems are, in increasing developmental order, problems of:

Justification. The ability to provide an argument for one's position

Coherence. The ability to agree on the relative weights or places of accepted propositions in the argument

Circularity. The ability to differentiate between criteria for relevance in a given problem and criteria for validity of a proposition

Language. The ability to apply ethical theory to explicate the meaning of terms central to solving a moral argumentation

Even the 5-year-olds studied were able to solve the problem of justification. They were, however, unable to solve the problem of coherence. The 7- and 8-year-olds, while able to solve the problem of coherence, could not adequately solve the problem of circularity. Finally, the 10-year-olds were able to solve the problem of circularity, but were unable to solve the problem of language. Two shortcomings of this study that should be noted are: (1) the small sample size (only three groups of four children each), and (2) the limited range of ages (5 to 10 years; no children could solve the last problem and all could solve the first one). Nonetheless, Miller's work is an important pioneering investigation of the development of sociomoral argumentation.

Shortly after Miller first presented his case study, Oser published his large-scale investigation of the development of sociomoral argumentation, *Moralisches Urteil in Gruppen* (1981). He suggested that the traditional psychological perspectives on sociomoral argumentation ignore the interactional processes that govern their form and outcome. His goal therefore is to identify the developing capacity to solve sociomoral problems through discussion.

Oser studied the discussion of three sociomoral problems by 120 groups of 15-year-old adolescents. These discussions were found to vary along two relevant dimensions, the first of which was termed levels of interaction. They are summarized, in increasing developmental order, as follows:

Level 1: *Functional Perspective.* Solutions to the problem are proposed.

Level 2: *Analytic Perspective.* Proposed solutions are analyzed on the basis of relevant facts and conditions.

Level 3: *Normative Perspective.* Proposed solutions and their grounding facts and circumstances are evaluated on the basis of moral norms, rules, and principles.

Level 4: *Philosophical Perspective.* The moral evaluation of proposed solutions, facts, and norms is grounded in moral philosophy from a critical perspective.

Oser's second dimension is termed communication compactness. The three levels, again in increasing developmental order, are:

Level 1. Little or no coordination of perspectives

Level 2. Intermittent coordination of perspectives

Level 3. Coordination and clarification of units of communication

Oser's specific hypotheses concerned the differential impacts of three types of experimental–educational treatments on the sociomoral argumentations as assessed across the two dimensions. Supplying rules of justice to discussants increased their use of the normative perspective. Providing discussion strategy training affected communication compactness but not levels of interaction. There were also differences across the three dilemmas discussed.

Oser was thus able to describe the course of development, augmented by training, of sociomoral argumentation. However, his design was tailored more closely to identifying intervention effects than to identifying developmental trends. For example, he studied only one age group. He therefore was not able to observe all of his hypothesized stages of discussion behavior. While Miller's design allowed the study of only a limited age range, he was at least able to demonstrate a cross-sectional age trend. In fact, Miller has collected data from a much larger age range, although he only reports the results of a limited part of that sample. Subsequent analyses may lead to a refinement of his developmental scheme.

The third example of developmental sociomoral argumentation research is a study by Keller and Reuss (1985). They are interested in the development of forms of sociomoral discussion in children's responses to sociomoral dilemmas. Relying upon the traditional methods of cognitive–structural psychology (especially the work of Kohlberg and Selman), they begin with the sociomoral interview that such theorists use for assessment purposes, and redefine it as a sociomoral communication situation. Then, in charting the development of such communication, they turn to discourse ethics (and, most directly, to Habermas). They begin their analysis by describing the philosophical components of ideal sociomoral communication. Then they apply these principles to the developmental analysis of sociomoral argumentation. Finally, they apply such analyses to the problem of moral education. Keller and Reuss interviewed 7-, 9-, 12-, and 14-year-old children about friendship dilemmas (Selman, 1980). They derived three levels of (1) interpersonal-moral reasoning and (2) principles and strategies of justification from these interviews, as follows:

Level A (7- to 9- year olds). There is no consideration of a discourse principle; that is, a need to obtain the consent of all involved. Neither is there a recognition of the need to provide others with a justification for one's decisions. One's own needs and interests predominate and may serve as explanations that are not differentiated from justifications.

Level B (12-year-olds). One's own obligations are derived from strongly felt obligations to others with whom one feels a relationship. One must consult others in discourse before acting or deciding. Violations of this discourse principle lead to guilt from offending the relationship or the norm of truthfulness. Concrete self-interests are legitimate facts but not legitimate justifications. One cannot balance one's own claims with those of others because no procedure or rules to implement recognized need for reciprocity.

Level C (begins at 14 years). One can now balance mutually accepted relationship norms and the need for autonomous moral decision making. One understands discursive standards and recognizes legitimacy of situation-specific conditions for norm applicability. One recognizes that in conflicts one is obligated to enter discourse with goal of coming to a shared justified agreement.

These analyses represent an impressive step in conceptual study of the development of sociomoral discourse. They do not, however, focus directly on moral discussion. Rather they use interpersonal–moral reasoning abilities and hypothetical prescriptions about discussion to infer actual discourse skills. They need, therefore, to be applied to the actual discussion behaviors of children.

A fourth example of developmental study of sociomoral discussion is provided by Selman and his associates (Brion-Meisels & Selman, 1985; Selman, 1980; Selman & Demorest, 1984; Selman & Yeates, Chapter 3, this volume). In their theory and research, they have described a series of developmental steps in the acquisition of interpersonal negotiation strategies, both on cognitive and behavioral levels. Because Selman's work is explicated elsewhere in this volume, I will only briefly note its nature. The strategies children use in negotiating interpersonal conflicts are analyzed and placed into a developmental hierarchy of four stages:

Stage 0. Physical dominance or submission (3 to 6 years)
Stage 1. Verbal control hierarchy (5 to 9 years)
Stage 2. Reciprocally mediated exchange (7 to 12 years)
Stage 3. Collaboratively oriented coordination (10 to 15 years)

We can note that Selman and his colleagues have focused largely upon the clinical aspects of the scheme and have applied it largely to emotionally troubled subjects. Clearly, however, the applicability to "normal" children is not limited. It is also important to point out that Selman often works with real conflicts rather than solely the more common hypothetical dilemmas used in most other studies. As noted by Selman, this leads to somewhat different findings.

A final insight to the issue of development of moral discussion can be derived from the two studies of transactive discussion that included transaction among other measures of moral discussion (Damon & Killen, 1982; Powers, 1982). Other than the transacts noted earlier, Damon and Killen report the following interactional behaviors in the children from kindergarten to third grade whom they observed:

1. Direct agreement
2. Direct disagreement
3. Other contradictory statement
4. Ridicule
5. New solution not in agreement with previous statement
6. Misrepresentation or distortion of others' ideas

Unfortunately, no frequency of usage data are provided and no developmental analyses are suggested for the different age subjects. Nevertheless, these categories may be used to supplement further developmental analyses of young children's discussion skills.

Powers (1982) also offers nontransactive codes for sociomoral discussions, in her case of adolescents and their parents. They are as follows:

1. Intent for closure
2. Competitive opinion statement
3. Request for change
4. Simple disagreement
5. Distracting
6. Opinion statement
7. Simple agreement
8. Refusal to do request or task
9. Quit or devalue task
10. Distortion
11. Encouragement

12. Noncompetitive humor
13. Actively resist or threaten
14. Devaluation or hostility
15. Listening responses
16. Interrupted or incomplete statements

As can be observed from this list, Powers included many nonconstructive codes in her scheme. Again, no attempt was made to suggest a developmental hierarchy for these behaviors.

At this point, having sufficiently muddied the waters, we will return to the cross-cultural study we described earlier in our discussion of the development of transactive discussion. We have generated a preliminary stage scheme for the development of sociomoral discussion based upon the data from that study. The stages are not only based upon those data, but were generated in part a priori from the work of others, such as those just described in the preceding section.

Stage 0—Preargumentation

The discussant does not recognize a need for discourse. Justifications are only offered when requested and then they are idiosyncratic and irrelevant. The function of justifications is not understood because discussants have not developed the capacity for perspective taking. Actual conflicts are resolved by power manipulations, either physical or verbal, but without recourse to collaborative justified discourse. The strength of an argument rests upon:

1. One's desire to hold a specific position
2. Varied personal or idiosyncratic justifications, only when justification is demanded by alter
3. The degree of repetition, extension, or variation of the argument or of counterarguments to the discussion partner's position, but without justifications
4. The tendency to change the topic or specific argument abruptly
5. The tendency for justifications to be illogical
6. The tendency simply to agree, disagree, or repeat one's position without justification, but, for disagreements, with personal attacks

One "wins" an argument at this stage by sheer endurance, that is, by holding on to one's position longer than the other, or by "bullying" the other into submission by either physical or verbal attack.

The following excerpt from a discussion between two 7-year-old American boys, with an adult facilitator, about whether Paul's car accident was divine punishment for breaking a promise to God is an example of stage 0 argumentation.

A: Did this accident have anything to do with Paul not keeping his promise to God?

B: Come on . . . what is your answer?

A: Okay. Oh, boy . . . I don't know what to say.

B: I already have an answer.

A: Okay, then say it.

B: Um . . . I think . . . No, what was the question again? Oh, yeah, I think it does cause maybe he was out in a bar and maybe he was drinking champagne all night and then when he came home he got in an accident.

A: I think he had some whiskey.

B: Whiskey?

A: Yeah. Now do you think God punished Paul for not keeping his promise? Why or why not? I think "why" is an answer, Okay? Your turn.

B: I think he didn't.

A: I think he did.

B: I don't know why.

A: I think he did.
    (Adult: Why do you think God punished Paul?)

A: 'Cause he didn't keep his promise.

B: I don't think he punished him at all.

A: He had punished him. He ran into a semi.
    (Adult: No it doesn't say he ran into a semi; it says he was in a car accident. You said you think God punished Paul because he didn't keep his promise.)

A: Yeah, because he ran into that semi.
    (Adult: Peter, do you think God punished Paul?).

B: No.
    (Adult: Why not?)

B: I can't think of it.
    (Adult: Do you think God punishes people when we don't do what he wants?)

B: No, not all the time.

A: Not all the time. Sometimes because he probably cheated in driving school so he made him crash. Or they had a drunk teacher.
    (Adult: Okay, Peter, why do you think God doesn't punish us?)

B: I told you I can't think of it.

A: What's the television in here for?

Stage 1—Single-Reason Argumentation

The discussant's central position is characterized by isolated justifications, each repetitively bolstered by unconnected or loosely related arguments. This results in an apparently a priori endorsed solution that is only justified post hoc by a number of arguments. These arguments themselves are only used prag-matically to serve the maintenance of the chosen position. The strength of the argumentation depends upon three variables:

1. The a priori conviction that one's solution is correct
2. Isolated justifications that often are personal or idiosyncratic, such as the claim of personal experience with the dilemma, some part of the dilemma, or its solution
3. The degree of repetition, extension, or variation of the argument or of counterarguments to the discussion partner's position
4. The tendency to change the topic or specific argument abruptly
5. The lack of differentiation between descriptive and normative aspects of the argumentation

The argumentation must be "externally" powerful; that is, solutions and sup-portive arguments depend upon the ability to convince one's partner(s) by repetition, emphasis, and so on. One may recognize the need for alter to be "convinced" by a justification, but cannot generate effective justifications, due to an inability adequately to consider alter's perspective and a centration on one's own interests and point of view. Truth and rightness rely not on abstract rules or principles but on concrete probabilities, personal experience, capricious tastes, and to forth.

The following excerpt from a dialogue between two 8-year-old Swiss chil-dren about whether a father should steal a drug to save his son's (Roland's) life is an example of stage 1 argumentation:

A: Look, Roland doesn't want to die, he wants to stay alive, doesn't he?
B: Uh, yes! B-but otherwise the father would have to go into jail, and when nobody . . .
A: Not for so long!
B: No, 8 years of prison at least. If you only cause a car accident, you already get 10 years of prison.
A: Mmh, but me, look! But it would be great when you could . . .
B: But the kid, hey . . .
A: What, the kid? The boy?
B: Yeah.
A: He could stay alive and be at home.
B: Yes!!! But how could he stay alive?
A: Visit, visit.
B: But then all of a sudden a hoodlum comes, and everything is gone, and Roland is dead.
A: Yes, no—surely not. No, that's not certain. Well, no, a hoodlum certainly wouldn't come.

B: Anyhow. It isn't good!

A: Still, it is fairly good. After all . . .

B: No, indeed, it isn't.

A: Yes.

B: No [giggling].

A: But look, many do want to buy it [the medicine], too. It really is expensive!

B: He could have asked. He could have.

A: [reproachful] He did ask before!

B: He could have gone to other people, not only relatives. He will have lots of friends or something.

A: But look. He already asked everybody.

B: No, they are not related to him, these friends. . . . Friends are not relatives. It doesn't necessarily say, that friends are relatives.

A: Yeah, but [the story] doesn't say, they have to be relatives. He also asked friends.

B: But first it says, he asked friends, no, relatives. He could ask friends, additionally or something.

A: Yes, he has friends, too.

B: You see, he could have asked even more people: Please give me a tiny 100-francs-bill. Yes, actually he could go and ask.

A: Yes, he could, but. . . .

B: [screams] Then he would have!!!

A: [despairing] He did ask all of them, but he only had half of what he needed.

B: Yeah, then . . .

A: That's how it is!!

Stage 2 — *Maintaining Connections*

The discussants attempt to exchange multiple justifications with some logical coherency in an effort to (a) identify a central thesis and (b) enhance their mutual understanding by searching for a shared solution. The strength of one's contribution rests upon its value for a common enterprise. Stage 2 argumentation is characterized by:

1. The ability to produce second-order justifications for one's position; that is, the ability to create a hierarchy of arguments by producing a first-order justification for one's position, and then second-order justifications for the first-order justification

2. The tendency (and ability) to anticipate counterarguments by identifying weaknesses in one's position before one's partner does

3. The ability to identify similarities between one's own and one's partner's position (but without using these similarities to produce a shared solution)

4. The tendency and ability to avoid direct confrontation with one's partner
5. The introduction of personal affective responses to the dilemma problem
   (e.g., "If I were in this situation I would feel terrible")

At this stage, justice is not generalized and tends to be situationally determined. Truth and rightness are still not adequately differentiated. The goal or "bottom line" of stage 2 argumentation is not so much to win the discussion (as for stages 0 and 1) as to establish a common ground of opinion in problem solving.

The following excerpt from a dialogue between two 14-year-old Swiss girls about Kohlberg's Heinz dilemma (stealing an exorbitantly priced drug to save a wife's life) is an example of stage 2 argumentation:

B: I guess, if he gets caught by the police, first thing he'll have a criminal record, and sure as fate: He'll be in trouble for the rest of his life, and afterwards . . .

A: Yes, sure . . .

B: And then figure, there still hasn't been help for the wife and when she comes to know that her husband has stolen, she'll think: Christ! And then she'll be even sicker.

A: Certainly, that's how it is.

B: And I think, when he steals, the druggist won't give him anything all the more. As I see it.

A: I simply mean . . . Well, I feel he would get sort of mentally sick, he would . . . He'll always think: Had I broken in, had I stolen this, had I—well, then she wouldn't be dead, then she wouldn't have died, you know. And this is something depressing.

B: Yeah, maybe, but . . . I don't know . . . actually it only says the drug *might* help.
   [rereading the dilemma and subjects' initial answers]
                                    . . .

B: Of course I do also think the druggist is acting in a mean way.

A: Yes.

B: But if he, say, brings about a lot of the remedy. . . . here are so many people suffering from cancer, he could need more of it, he would become well-known.

A: Certainly he would. In any case it is . . . [incomprehensible], when they invent something.

B: Yeah.

A: And he can make such a lot of money.

B: Exactly, and that's why he should give this to the man. And, say, she would be saved, do you know what a reputation he would obtain! You must imagine this.

A: Yes and, well, then he could . . . still sell it for half the price, and later the man could pay it off.

B: Yeah.

A: I think it's simply . . . I deem it stupid what this druggist does.

B: Yes, me too, I really find it mean.

Stage 3—Counterevidence

This stage is characterized by the use of counterevidence, attempts at falsification, and defenses against such strategies when used by one's partner. A major new acquisition of this stage is the ability to identify logical contradictions both within an individual's position and between discussants' positions. Note the focus on "negative" strategies. The strength of one's position is determined by six characteristics:

1. The ability to survive a counterargument and maintain one's position through both truth analyses and normative or rightness analyses
2. The ability to identify the similarities and differences in the discussants' arguments, but with a tendency to focus on the latter
3. The ability to differentiate facts from normative "truths" (e.g., she does this but she ought to do that)
4. The ability to reason about another's reasoning (i.e., transactive discourse) and to use this capacity to differentiate the positions of the discussants, again limited by the focus on conflictual strategies such as producing counterevidence
5. The ability to dispense with weak or irrelevant arguments
6. The tendency to still think in terms of individual's positions and therefore to be concerned with the adversarial task of being right or correct.

This stage is marked by a bias toward conflictual modes of argumentation and a relative neglect of affirmational strategies. Affective assertions are often invoked as legitimate justifications. Much of stage 3 argument seems oriented to a conflict between *discussants* rather than a conflict between *positions*.

The following excerpt from a dialogue between two 16-year-old Swiss girls about the role of relationship in solving the Heinz dilemma is an example of stage 3 argumentation:

B: I only wouldn't do it [steal the remedy] in case of someone [sick person] who took another's life already.

A: So, a murderer?

B: If he cannot bear him.

A: So you don't act because of the deed he's done, not because of the man?

B: No, because I don't like him.

A: Ah, that's the way you see it.

B: But this . . . whether he deserves it . . .

A: No, I have a different point of view. If you fundamentally detest him, I don't know—I have no reason to detest anyone. I can imagine this may happen that you really don't like a person. Then I would act like the druggist—cold-blooded. What I find wrong with the druggist . . . I would act the same way, admittedly

B: Thus you would be a murderer too, indirectly?

A: Yes, but I wouldn't commit this because of profit, because of money, and surely I would regret it subsequently . . . I can well imagine I would do it in the heat of acting.

B: Then you do have a relationship to him?

A: Yes, I would have a relationship, but I would detest this guy. But let's get back to the issue of divorce. You would steal in any case?

B: When I compare human life and relationship, life is well in the fore.

A: It is in the fore for you. This is okay so far, but it's kind of paltry. No, then I wouldn't . . . I would be much more reasonable. Perhaps she'll die, perhaps she won't, you never can tell. It would be unreasonable for me to go straight away and steal the drug. For me, reason is . . .

B: But I stated a premise, however: *Only then* when there is no other way.

A: "Only then"— this is more reasonable than mine. You have this prerequisite: only when he would not give [the remedy]. And as to me, it was just— when he says no, the case is done and I go straight on and steal . . .

Stage 4—Shared Analysis

Stage 4 marks the onset of mutuality in discourse. The logic of shared analysis appears as if it almost could be generated "without" a partner because each argument is critically examined and understood to be subject to counterargumentation. Indeed this describes the individual mental process of reasoning about the argumentation. The goal of discourse is the identification of shared meaning, truth, and rightness. The strength of the shared position is determined by five characteristics:

1. The ability either to surrender a position or to maintain it only for the purpose of testing another's position (playing "devil's advocate")
2. The ability to generate supportive justifications for the partner's position
3. The ability to reason effectively about the partner's reasoning in order to generate a common position
4. The ability to differentiate accurately between normative and descriptive arguments
5. The ability to calculate the various possibilities and consequences in a situation and to test each with moral principles.

Furthermore, this stage is characterized by generalized rules. Either generalized rules are applied to the specific problem or solutions to the specific problem are subsequently generalized. In either case, the perspective is one of reflecting on solutions in the context of the principle of generalizability. Additionally premises and conclusions are now differentiated. Affective justifications are accepted as limited by metareflective recognition of their inadequacy unless justified by generalized normative rules. Often the general moral context of a problem is explicitly discussed.

The following two short excerpts from the same 20-year-old Swiss male dyad are examples of stage 4 argumentation. The first excerpt concerns the Heinz dilemma. The second excerpt concerns whether a nurse should keep a promise to God made before miraculously surviving a plane crash.

I.

B: Stealing is the easy thing to do. Surely there'll be problems in that, but the other way is more difficult—not to break in is more difficult. To make a lawful attempt is much more difficult.

A: But I thought you're one who's opposing exaggerated law-making, I'm sure you violated laws yourself, and I think you get to forget [neglect] the law if you can save somebody's life.

B: Sure you've got to forget the law. But somehow I think about the time following.

A: You are thinking, but you think of yourself, not of your wife.

B: Suppose the woman will die, then I'll stay here with the kids. When I broke in, I'll have my sentence to serve, as the case may be. I'm obliged to the children, too.

A: Okay, let's assume the man has children. The children do live on, but the wife doesn't. You can save her. You must not think from the perspective of her death, but you rather think while she is alive. You mustn't break in and say: When I get caught, then she'll die and the kids will stay alone. You must think: Now I'll break in to save my wife and it is finished.

II.

A: This is a critical situation, and I assume that she'll have a guilty conscience for the whole of her life if she does not keep her promise.

B: You talked of sin in the beginning [of the conversation], but now you express this old attitude: If she does not keep her promise, then, then, then her life won't be bright anymore—this is the ancient church.

A: I don't want to be misunderstood. I don't say she'd land in purgatory, when she doesn't go. She would have a bad conscience over and over again, but she wouldn't have this as a punishment for her. Whenever she'd hear something about the third world, she would say: I should be there and help now.

B: This should have come to her mind before the plane crash, in my view, I feel she must have had a bad conscience before, not only now.

A: I think that's true, my impression is that she couldn't have such an idea from one moment to the other.

Stage 5—Ideal Discourse

This stage describes ideal discourse and essentially follows the model of ideal discourse identified by Habermas (1984). Discussants recognize that everyone in a discussion must strive toward the most just or best solution to the problem under discussion. The strength of the ideal shared discourse is characterized by:

1. The testing of validity claims in rational argumentation
2. The maintenance of objectivity of perspective
3. The perspective of generalizability
4. The maintenance of consistency of arguments
5. The recognition of the potential fallability of each discussant's (including one's own) insights and arguments

STRUCTURE OF ARGUMENTATION AND MODE OF INTERPERSONAL ORIENTATION

The development of argumentative logic has been described by studying forms of peer conflictual discourse. We have shown that Berkowitz and Gibbs's (1983) model of transactive discussion represents a mature form of argumentative logic that develops with increasing age in American and Swiss children and adolescents. An attempt to identify less mature forms of argumentative competencies has led to the preliminary description of six stages of argumentative logic. Future research will help to refine these stage descriptions.

Nevertheless, the full complexity of sociomoral argumentation cannot be adequately captured simply in the logic of such discourse behavior. As a number of theorists and researchers have argued recently, the style of such interactions is also a significant variable in the nature of argumentation and its outcomes. For instance, Powers (1982) has demonstrated that a supportive style of family sociomoral argumentation is related to more positive sociomoral developmental outcomes. Noam (1985) has presented a tridimensional model of ego development that includes a dimension of style of interpersonal orientation. Much effort has been expended in recent years in attempts to explicate Gilligan's (1982) contention that there are two discrepant "voices" or styles in sociomoral reasoning. When we look more closely at these models, we can note that a common theme exists. Indeed this theme in some sense represents a traditional dichotomy in psychology. The styles may be characterized as either individuating or integrating. In early work on transactive discussion, Berkowitz and Gibbs (1979) referred to these dimensions as noncompetitive and competitive modes of transaction. Recently, Leadbeater (1986) has demonstrated that sociomoral discussions can be categorized in style as either alter-focused noncompetitive, competitive, or alter-focused mixed. Furthermore, in her small sample, the first group was composed only of females, the second only of males, and the third equally divided by gender.

TABLE 11.6.   Two Styles of Interpersonal Orientation

Style	Features	Stages
Autonomy–individuation	Point and counterpoint "Crossing the swords" Critique of arguments Competition	Single reason (stage 1) Counterevidence (stage 3)
Connection–Integration	Avoidance of "hard" argumentation Downplaying differences Emphasizing opportunities for mutual confirmation Cooperation	Maintaining connections (stage 2) Shared analysis (stage 4)

Precisely how such stylistic dimensions will interact with the structural model we have already proposed is still open for empirical investigation. At this point, we wish to offer two possible models of the interplay of structures of argumentation and modes of interpersonal orientation. We consider these models to be alternatives but do not preclude the possibility that they will turn out to be complementary or that some as yet unforeseen variation on one or both of them will be discovered. Both of these models are intended to account for the differences in discussion "styles" or dyadic climate that have been obvious to us in our research on sociomoral discussion.

Model 1—Oscillating Styles

Model 1 presumes that interpersonal orientation is a factor in defining the logic of argumentation. Changes in styles are directly related to changes in argumentation stages. Systematic changes in styles, in addition to growing complexity and differentiation of argumentative competencies, define the changing pragmatic character of problem-oriented sociomoral communication.

The two major styles resemble Selman's (Brion-Meisels & Selman, 1985), Kegan's (1982), and Noam's (1985) descriptions of orientations in social cognition and interpersonal negotiation. As noted earlier the focus is either on separation and autonomy or on integration and connection. Styles shift alternately as one moves through the stages of argumentative logic, with the first style (separation or individuation) being characteristic of stages 1 and 3 and the second style (integration) being characteristic of stages 2 and 4. Stage 0 is preargumentative and therefore cannot appropriately be characterized by these styles, and stage 5 represents an integration of the two styles in ideal discourse. Table 11.6 presents the two orientations in more detail.

Our data suggest that changes in styles may be necessary phases for experiencing the range of processes of understanding, confrontation, and negotiation. Furthermore, lower stages differ from higher stages in that they are primarily oriented to the relationship constituted by or involved in the discourse. At stages 0, 1 and 2, arguments serve interpersonal ends in the dyad itself (either ego's, alter's or the dyad's ends) or cannot be separated from the concerns of the particular dyad. At stages 3, 4, and 5, personal relations are subordinated to

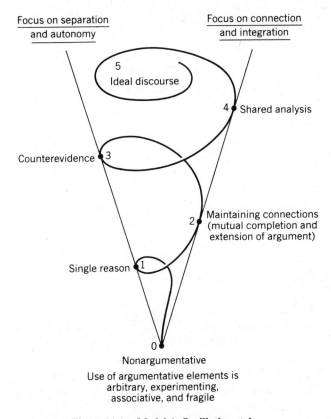

Focus on separation
and autonomy

Focus on connection
and integration

5
Ideal discourse

4 Shared analysis

Counterevidence 3

2 Maintaining connections
(mutual completion and
extension of argument)

Single reason 1

0
Nonargumentative
Use of argumentative elements is
arbitrary, experimenting,
associative, and fragile

Figure 11.1.   Model 1: Oscillating styles.

a focus on truth and truthfulness (i.e., a prior-to-personal-relationships perspective). Stage 3 is transitional in the sense of elaborating rational integrity in argumentation. Figure 11.1 represents the proposed form of Model 1.

Model 2—Alternate Styles

Model 2 rests on the assumption that the structure of argumentation and the style of interaction are fully independent dimensions. This would imply that at each of the stages of argumentation both types of interpersonal orientation would be found. This is analogous to Selman's descriptions of interpersonal negotiation strategies. Brion-Meisels and Selman (1985) describe stages of differing complexity of perspective coordinations, but suggest that at each stage one can adopt either of two different styles of resolving interpersonal conflicts, which they label self-transforming and other-transforming modes.

In Model 2, each level can be constructed and passed through using one of these orientations primarily. However, differences in style are relevant for structural change. Characteristics of the respective orientation may facilitate or complicate transitions. For example, the transition from stage 3 (counterevi-

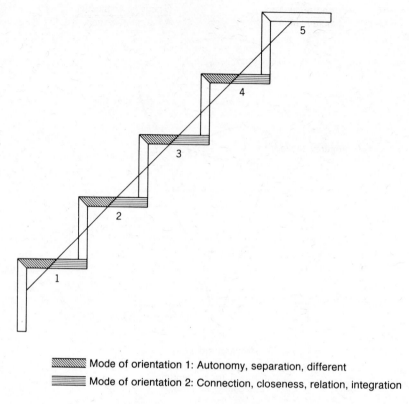

Mode of orientation 1: Autonomy, separation, different
Mode of orientation 2: Connection, closeness, relation, integration

Figure 11.2.   Model 2: Alternate styles.

dence) to stage 4 (shared analysis) will likely be easier for subjects with a marked mutuality or integration orientation. Figure 11.2 represents the likely form of Model 2.

CONCLUSIONS

Sociomoral discourse has attracted increased interest from psychologists, philosophers, and educators in the past decade. While its role as a developmental stimulant, educational technique, and philosophical construct has begun to be explored extensively, the path through which sociomoral discourse develops itself has received only limited attention. We have attempted here to raise some conceptual issues in the study of the development of sociomoral discourse and to review the sparse empirical literature on its development.

In first exploring the development of transactive discussion, we have seen that a comparative analysis of diverse studies and the data generated in the cross-sectional investigation introduced here support the increased usage of transaction with increased age. This has led us to raise the question of what forms of sociomoral discourse are modal at earlier ages if transaction is not. Our review of the few existing studies and the data from our cross-sectional study has led to a preliminary stage scheme.

Knowledge about interactional stages refers to knowing about psychological conditions of communicative possibilities at different developmental levels. Our results suggest that beyond the techniques of transactional dialogue there must evolve a substantial structure of propositional understanding. Differences in interpersonal orientations certainly are of significance for a person's ability to take the other into consideration—as a person with feelings, intentions, specific ways of understanding. Yet at this time we still do not know whether intraindividual (phaselike) differences or interindividual differences in style are of greater importance for flux and process in interactional development. Both images should be taken into account by further research.

Investigations of the validity and usefulness of the stage scheme are necessary. One step in this direction would be a longitudinal investigation of the development of sociomoral discourse. Another useful study would be a conceptual integration of the model with parallel models in other fields, for example, linguistics. If the stages are validated, then research into their developmentally stimulating characteristics, parallel to the transaction research, would be necessary as would attempts to train and facilitate their growth in applied settings such as the school or home.

We would like to suggest two lines of educational consequences. An educational aim should be to give teachers and parents information about developmental transformations in children's communicative competences. Further we should conduct or support interventional training for children controlling for structural growth. Observations of egocentric behavior in classrooms should be related to general structural competences of understanding in interaction. Lack of interactional decentration is not merely a matter of socialization effects but also an outcome of qualitative characteristics in the organization of children's interactional thinking.

Ultimately the developmental study of sociomoral discourse must be coupled with the other three perspectives on sociomoral discourse described by Berkowitz (1986), that is, growth facilitative, ethical, and instrumental. The study of the developmental stimulation potential at each stage responds to the first of these three perspectives, but analyses of the ethical bases of each stage and their instrumental value or potential need also be explored and integrated with the other perspectives for there to be a complete understanding of the phenomenon. Sociomoral discourse is central to the human enterprise in a variety of ways. It therefore behooves theorists and researchers to explore its nature. It is to be hoped that study of its development is one step in that direction.

REFERENCES

Arbuthnot, J.B., & Faust, D. (1981). *Teaching moral reasoning: Theory and practice.* San Francisco: Harper & Row.

Bearison, D.J. (1985). *Transactional cognition.* Paper presented to the International Society for the Study of Behavioral Development, Tours, France.

Bearison, D.J. (in press). Transactional cognition in context: New models of social understanding. In D.J. Bearison & H. Zimiles (Eds.), *Thinking and emotions: Developmental Perspectives.* Hillsdale, NJ: Erlbaum.

Bell, N., Grossen, M., & Perret-Clermont, A.-N. (1985). Sociocognitive conflict and intellectual growth. In M.W. Berkowitz (Ed.), *New directions for child development: Peer conflict and psychological growth.* San Francisco: Jossey-Bass.

Berkowitz, M.W. (1981). A critical appraisal of the educational and psychological perspectives on moral discussion. *Journal of Educational Thought, 15,* 20–33.

Berkowitz, M.W. (Ed.). (1985). *New directions for child development: Peer conflict and psychological growth.* San Francisco: Jossey-Bass.

Berkowitz, M.W. (1986). Four perspectives on moral argumentation. In C. Harding (Ed.), *Moral dilemmas: Philosophical and psychological reconsiderations of the development of moral reasoning.* Chicago: Precedent Press.

Berkowitz, M.W., & Gibbs, J.C. (1979). *A preliminary manual for coding transactive features of dyadic discussion.* Unpublished manuscript, Marquette University.

Berkowitz, M.W., & Gibbs, J.C. (1983). Measuring the developmental features of moral discussion. *Merrill-Palmer Quarterly, 29,* 399–410.

Berkowitz, M.W. & Gibbs, J.C. (1985). The process of moral conflict resolution and moral development. In M.W. Berkowitz (Ed.), *New directions for child development: Peer conflict and psychological growth* (pp. 71-84). San Francisco: Jossey-Bass.

Berndt, T.J. (1984). The influence of group discussions on children's moral decisions. In J.C. Masters & K. Yarkin-Levin (Eds.), *Boundary areas in social and developmental psychology* (pp. 195-219). NY: Academic Press.

Blatt, M. & Kohlberg, L. (1975). The effects of classroom moral discussion upon children's level of moral judgment. *Journal of Moral Education, 4,* 129-161.

Brion-Meisels, S. & Selman, R.L. (1985). The adolescent as interpersonal negotiator: Three portraits of social development. In M.W. Berkowitz & F. Oser (Eds.), *Moral education: Theory and application* (pp. 369-383). Hillsdale, NJ: L. Erlbaum.

Caldwell, J.A. & Berkowitz, M.W. (In press). Die Entwicklung religiosen und moralischen Denkens in einem Programm zum Religionsunterricht. [The development of religious and moral thinking in a religious education program.] In F. Oser (Ed.), *Wieviel Religion braucht der Mensch? Studien zur religiosen Autonomie.* Zurich: Benziger.

Colby, A., Kohlberg, L., Fenton, E., Speicher-Dubin, B., & Lieberman, M. (1977). Secondary school moral discussion programmes led by social studies teachers. *Journal of Moral Education, 6,* 90-111.

Colby, A., Kohlberg, L., Gibbs, J.C., Candee, D., Speicher-Dubin, B., Kaufman, K., Hewer, A., & Power, C. (In press). *Assessing moral judgment: A manual.* New York: Cambridge University Press.

Colby, A., Kohlberg, L., Gibbs, J.C., & Lieberman, M. (1983). A longitudinal study of moral judgment. *Monographs of the Society for Research in Child Development, 48,* (1-2 Serial No. 200), 1-96.

Damon, W., & Killen M. (1982). Peer interaction and the process of change in children's moral reasoning. *Merrill-Palmer Quarterly, 28,* 347–367.

Forman, E.A., & Kraker, M.J. (1985). The social origins of logic: The contributions of Piaget and Vygotsky. In M.W. Berkowitz (Ed.), *New directions for child development: Peer conflict and psychological growth.* San Francisco: Jossey-Bass.

Galbraith, R.E., & Jones, T.M. (1976). *Moral reasoning: A teaching handbook for adapting Kohlberg to the classroom.* St. Paul, MN: Greenhaven Press.

Gibbs, J.C., Schnell, S.V., Berkowitz, M.W., & Goldstein, D.S. (1983). *Relations between formal operations and logical conflict resolution.* Paper read at the meeting of the Society for Research in Child Development, Detroit.

Gilligan, C. (1982). *In a different voice: Psychological theory and women's development.* Cambridge: Harvard University Press.

Gomberg, S.H., Cameron, D.K,, Fenton, E., Furtek, J., & Hill, C.L. (1980). *Leading dilemma discussion: A workshop.* Unpublished manuscript, Carnegie-Mellon University, Pittsburgh, PA.

Habermas, J. (1984). *Theory of communicative action: Vol. 1. Reason and Rationality in Society* (T. McCarthy, Trans.). Boston: Beacon.

Kegan, R.G. (1982). *The evolving self: Problem and process in human development.* Cambridge: Harvard University Press.

Keller, M., & Reuss, S. (1985). The process of moral decision-making: Normative and empirical conditions of participation in moral discourse. In M.W. Berkowitz & F. Oser (Eds.), *Moral education: Theory and application.* Hillsdale, NJ: Erlbaum.

Kohlberg, L. (1984). *Essays on moral development: Vol. 2. The psychology of moral development.* San Francisco: Harper & Row.

Kruger, A.C., & Tomasello, M. (1986). Transactive discussions with peers and adults. *Developmental Psychology, 22,* 681–685.

Leadbeater, B. (1986). *Qualitative and developmental differences in the relational processes of adolescent and adult dialogues: The dialectic of intersubjectivity.* Unpublished dissertation, Columbia Teachers College, New York.

Lickona, T. (1983). *Raising good children: Helping your child through the stages of moral development.* New York: Bantam.

Lyman, D.R., & Selman, R.L. (1985). Peer conflict in pair therapy: Clinical and developmental analyses. In M.W. Berkowitz (Ed.), *New directions for child development: Peer conflict and psychological growth.* San Francisco: Jossey-Bass.

Miller, M. (1980). *Learning how to contradict and still pursue a common end—The ontogenesis of moral argumentation.* Unpublished manuscript, Max Planck Institute, Starnberg, Germany.

Miller, M. (1981). *Cognition and moral argumentation: Five developmental levels.* Paper presented to the Conference on Social Interaction and Social-Cognitive Development, Starnberg, West Germany.

Miller, M., & Klein, W. (1979). *Moral argumentations among children: A case study.* Paper presented at the Conference "Beyond Description in Child Language Research," Nijmegen, Netherlands.

Miller, S.A., & Brownell, C.A. (1975). Peers, persuasion, and Piaget: Dyadic interaction between conservers and non-conservers. *Child Development, 46,* 992–997.

Newport, E.L. (1977). The speech of mothers to young children. In N. Castellan, D.P. Pisoni, & G. Potts (Eds.), *Cognitive theory* (Vol. 2). Hillsdale, NJ: Erlbaum.

Noam, G. (1985). Developmental dynamics of the self in adolescence. In M.W. Berkowitz & F. Oser (Eds.), *Moral education: Theory and application.* Hillsdale, NJ: Erlbaum.

Oser, F. (1981). *Moralisches Urteil in Gruppen.* Frankfurt am Main: Suhrkamp.

Phillips, J. (1973). Syntax and vocabulary of mothers' speech to young children: Age and sex comparisons. *Child Development, 44,* 182–187.

Piaget, J. (1923). *Le langage et la pensee chez l'enfant.* Neuchatel, Switzerland: Delachauz & Niestle.

Piaget, J. (1965a). *The moral judgment of the child* (M. Gabain, Trans.). New York: Free Press. (Original work published 1932)

Piaget, J. (1965b). *Etudes sociologiques*. Geneva, Switzerland: Librairie Droz.

Piaget, J. (1972). Intellectual evolution from adolescence to adulthood. *Human Development, 15*, 1–12.

Powers, S.I. (1982). *Family interaction and parental moral development as a context for adolescent moral development*. Unpublished doctoral dissertation, Harvard University.

Reimer, J., Paolitto, D.P., & Hersh, R.H. (1983). *Promoting moral growth: From Piaget to Kohlberg*. New York: Longman.

Selman, R.L. (1980). *The growth of interpersonal understanding: Developmental and clinical analyses*. New York: Academic.

Selman, R.L., & Demorest, A.P. (1984). Observing troubled children's interpersonal negotiation strategies: Implications of and for a developmental model. *Child Development, 55*, 288–304.

Shantz, C.U., & Shantz, D.W. (1985). Conflict between children: Social-cognitive and sociometric correlates. In M.W. Berkowitz (Ed.), *New directions for child development: Peer conflict and psychological growth*. San Francisco: Jossey-Bass.

Taranto, M.A. (1984). *Microprocesses in moral conflict dialogues*. Paper presented at the Symposium of the Jean Piaget Society, Philadelphia.

Tobin, K.G., & Capie, W. (1981). The development and validation of a group test of logical thinking. *Educational & Psychological Measurement, 41*, 413–423.

Author Index

Subject Index